HERO AND CHIEF

Daniel P. Biebuyck

UNIVERSITY OF CALIFORNIA PRESS
BERKELEY LOS ANGELES LONDON

HERO AND CHIEF

Epic Literature from
the Banyanga
Zaire Republic

University of California Press
Berkeley and Los Angeles, California
University of California Press, Ltd.
London, England
Copyright © 1978 by
The Regents of the University of California
ISBN 0-520-03386-8
Library of Congress Catalog Card Number: 76-50242
Printed in the
United States of America

1 2 3 4 5 6 7 8 9

To my children:

Brunhilde
Anne-Marie
Edwin
Hans
Jean-Christophe
Jean-Marie
Beatrice

Kai ekumbuka kurikanga nti maramyana ho.
So the world is but made of mutual aid.

Mwindo Epic I

Emashata yebanunke ngi nsibiriro yemenge.
The games of the youth are the apprenticeship of wisdom.

A Nyanga heroic tale

CONTENTS

Preface   ix

PART 1. INTERPRETATION AND COMMENTS

General Characteristics of the Nyanga Epics   3
The Bards   10
  Identity of the Bards   10
  Portrait of a Bard   12
  The Bards in Their Epics   23
The Dramatis Personae   26
Cultural Content   34
  Physical and Human Environment   36
  The Language   40
  History   41
  Economy and Material Culture   47
  Kinship, Family, and Marriage   49
  Political Organization   56
  Divinities, Rituals, and Cults   61
  Values and Modes of Thought   68
Formulas and Style Features   75
The Hero   93
  Names and Epithets   94
  The Heroic Milieu   95
  The Birth of the Hero   99
  The Hero's Attributes and Character   102

The Chief   106
   The Social Identity of the Chief   107
   The Enthronement   109
   Conceptions about the Chief   110
The Heroic Tales   114

PART 2. THE TEXTS

The Mwindo Epic II   127
The Mwindo Epic III   174
The Mwindo Epic IV   233

APPENDIXES

  I. Wanowa's Epic Narrated by Sherungu   273
 II. The Fragmentary Version by Bitanda Asani   279

A Glossary of Personages   281
Bibliography   303
Index   307

PREFACE

This book is a sequel to *The Mwindo Epic from the Banyanga* (1969). It incorporates the translated, heavily footnoted texts of three previously unpublished epics sung by Nyanga bards, together with an extensive comparative study of Nyanga epic literature. *The Mwindo Epic from the Banyanga* was well received in diverse scholarly milieus. I am convinced that the present texts and analysis will considerably enhance our deeper understanding of the creative genius of an African people. The time when Bowra (1952) or Finnegan (1970) could question the existence of the epic genre in Africa has long ended (Biebuyck, 1976a). We have already reaped an abundant harvest of major epic texts, and the promise of an even bigger harvest is overwhelming. We may soon discover that these poetic monuments from Africa can no longer be ignored by students of comparative literature, for the comparative study of the epic can no longer be confined to certain peoples, ages, civilizations, or types of society. It transcends the boundaries of classic and Western civilizations and is found in many places, even among peoples who, like the Nyanga or the Mongo, are not city dwellers or empire builders. My purpose is, therefore, to provide accurate texts, together with their broad cultural interpretation, in order to facilitate the task of the comparatist.

During my extensive field research among the Nyanga, I had no intention of setting the detailed study of their oral literature as my major goal. Whenever the opportunity arose, I recorded in writing the tales, proverbs, riddles, prayers, memorats, praises, songs, invocations, and epics that the Nyanga sang, recited, or narrated for me. In annotating these texts I had diverse anthropological and linguistic purposes in mind. The volume of texts accumulated in this manner is so large, however, and their intrinsic, literary, and cultural value is so great that I can no longer afford not to publish them. Furthermore, the saddening disregard—not to say scorn—which many students of "exotic" culture have shown for genuine texts (as opposed to anecdotic and cursory statements elicited from so-called informants) necessitates more concentration on them. Reflecting about the period when I did my field research, I now regret that I did not devote all my attention to the study of Nyanga oral literature. I could certainly have gained more insight into the personality, social identity, and training of the bards, their sources of inspiration, and the manner in which they maintain a delicate balance between general and particular tradition on the one hand, and creative originality on the other. I could have learned more about the details of performance, particularly in its musical and kinetic dimensions (although it is useful to remember that in a small-scale milieu, dominated by kinship restraints, the performances are often monotonous and repetitious). I could have acquired deeper knowledge of the interactions between bards and different categories of participant listeners. On the other hand, I do not believe I would have received more or better texts, or that I would have been capable of recording, translating, and interactions between bards and different categories of participant listeners. casualness of my approach to the oral literature helped to preserve the natural attitude of the bards toward their texts. (I discovered on other occasions that singers and narrators easily overstate their cases when pressed too hard.) The broad information obtained about Nyanga culture in general is also invaluable in placing the epics in their correct native perspective. In the appreciation of the epic genre, the text, with its massive cultural connotations and cross-references, is the really important element.

My sincere thanks go to the bards, Sherungu, Shekarisi, Shekwabo, and, for the already published Mwindo Epic I (*The Mwindo Epic from the Banyanga*, 1969), Candi Rureke. Their generous and disinterested support has helped me to preserve for posterity part of a great, but fragile, African tradition. Amato Buuni and Stephano Tubi, Sherungu and Kanyangara, Shentsimia and Shoneno, were invaluable and enlightened assistants, *hommes de confiance*, and exegetes during my research. All my field activities among the Nyanga (intermittently in 1952; full time in 1954–1956) were sponsored and financed by the l'Institut pour la recherche scientifique en Afrique Centrale, whose unfaltering encouragement is gratefully acknowledged. I deeply appreciate the research done by my former students, Georgiana Grentzenberg and Deborah Reed, and the competent and dedicated secretarial work of Susan Edwards and Beverly Flanigan. I am especially thankful for the numerous editorial corrections and suggestions made by Mrs. Grace Stimson of the University of California Press, who edited the manuscript. I am grateful for financial support received for the realization of this book from the University of Delaware.

A NOTE ON THE TRANSLATION AND THE PRESENTATION

The translation of the Nyanga text is as literal and as faithful as possible. In order to maintain the Nyanga stylistic flavor, I have not hesitated to retain in the translation cumbersome expressions referring to time, place, and aspects of action. Additional words needed to clarify the meaning are added in parentheses. Furthermore, copious notes explain the more difficult passages and focus attention on points of interpretation. It is quite obvious that the Nyanga language possesses its own subtleties and idiomatic specialties which can be rendered only vaguely, if one attempts to produce a readable text. The abundant formulas for time and place are an example. In addition, the bards have an extraordinarily precise and nuanced knowledge of their language, which they manipulate with poetic skill and a refined sense for shades of meaning. Synonyms, metonyms, metaphors, other figures of speech, and fine nuances in the conjugation of the verb are characteristically used throughout the epics. The songs, in particular, excel because of the conscious search for alliteration and resonance, qualities that are enhanced by the rigid and clear system of adjectival and pronominal concords. No translation can do justice to this clever manipulation of grammatically determined sound. The sixth song in epic II, "Small bird of the road," is a masterpiece of alliterative effects in which variedly sounding pronominal prefixes beginning with *k-* (*ka-, ke-, ko-, ku-, kwe-, kwi-*) bear on the noun Kongo (Beautiful-one). Many lines in these songs are constructed on a pattern of seven or nine syllables or morphemes (taking into account elisions), whose rhythmic quality cannot be recaptured.

A NOTE ON THE REFERENCES

Throughout the book I have referred to the published *Mwindo Epic from the Banyanga* as epic I; the other three epics are numbered II, III, IV as they appear in the second part of this work.

For a general introduction to the Nyanga and to Nyanga culture, see Daniel Biebuyck and Kahombo Mateene (1969, pp. 1–11).

For the sake of simplicity and economy, I have avoided using the diacritical signs for tones in quoting Nyanga words or giving excerpts from the texts. The tonal system is identical to that illustrated in epic I.

I

INTERPRETATION AND COMMENTS

GENERAL CHARACTERISTICS
OF THE NYANGA EPICS

The Nyanga epics admirably fit the standard definitions and characterizations of epic literature (Bowra, 1952; Chadwick and Chadwick, 1932, pp. 20 ff.). From certain points of view they add new dimensions of meaning, form, and content to the analysis of oral epics. Monumental narratives formulated in lofty and poetic language, they give an account of the wonderful adventures and extraordinary events in which a person, of human origin but of heroic stature, participates. The wonder is created not merely by the feats of the hero, but also by the atmosphere in which the action develops. The action shifts from familiar settings in the terrestrial world to the aquatic, celestial, and subterranean spheres. The interaction is not merely among humans, but between humans and divinities, animals, or fabulous beings.

The time period in which the narrative develops is remote, but undetermined. Although specific events are placed within a familiar time frame—in the morning, after a countable number of days, after seven days, in the late evening, and so on—their duration cannot be precisely measured. The epics end on a note of timelessness.

Permeating the larger part of the epic texts is a mood of strife, tension, and competition between humans (father versus son; chief versus wife; between two spouses of the chief; between half brothers) or between humans and animals, divinities, and fabulous beings. The hero is at the center of the antagonism, and the heroic deed resolves the endless concatenation of adventures. Yet the Nyanga epics deal as much with the chief as with the hero; the emphasis shifts from the deeds of the hero to the derogation of the imperfect chief or to the glory of the perfect chief.

3

The Nyanga epic (*karisi*) is a narrative about "one who surpasses others" (*murisi*; from *irise*, lit., to sit on someone's lap). Two fundamentally different personages are subsumed under *murisi*: the hero and the chief. The hero (*murai*) is one who experiences or originates wonderful deeds (*itingwa*). His "heart is high," that is, he is filled with pathos; he is guided by a sort of *ate* (Nyanga *kirimirimi*), a reckless ambition resulting from the fact that he has not received the *mahano* (teachings about what is right and wrong, good and evil). The hero's actions are conceived in terms of destroying, fighting, and challenging. (There is an overwhelming number of verbs expressing the acts of chopping, cutting, clearing, kneading, piercing, bending, beating, killing, smashing, overpowering, spearing, annihilating.) The true chief (*mwami*) is one who brings good living, fame, conciliation, and harmony (*isima, ironganya, nkuru*). His "heart is low" (soothed, appeased), that is, he respects people and is awed by them (*usubahwa*). He is guided by wisdom and moderation, because he has received the "teachings" (*kwihana*, he has taught himself; *isimanika*, he has been enthroned).

The chief is foreshadowed in the hero, and there remains something of the hero in the chief so long as he has not attained the highest level of perfection. The hero and the chief are exceptional and lonely persons. The boisterous hero is receptive to advice from his paternal aunt; he carries within himself the potential for generosity. The chief is not completely freed from passion and moral turpitude until he is fully "taught," that is, until he has purified himself from excesses and has proven his wisdom. The Nyanga epics, therefore, are not simply narratives of battle, tension, and heroic deed, but of appeasement, of resolution of conflict, and of harmony.

In contrast with the narrowness of the tales, the amplitude of the epics is immediately manifested in the number and diversity of actors, events, and places. The typical Nyanga tale recounts a circumscribed sequence of interconnected actions in which two or three protagonists play their roles within a restricted setting (e.g., hunting camp or village or both). The epics relate the activities of scores of actors who represent all the major categories of beings recognized by the Nyanga and entail sequences of events placed in diverse settings. A substantial number of motifs and themes which are elaborated in individual tales are incorporated into episodes of the epics. Each epic bard, however, accomplishes the transfer in his own unique manner, and the epic is never a simple linking of such tales. The epics are well-structured and coherent wholes, pervaded by character development and intrigue. As clearly illustrated in epic I, a clear-cut space plan underlies the epic. The scale of the epic is further intensified by the fact that it is a combination of rhythmic prose and poetry, including specimens of all genres of oral expression familiar to the Nyanga; tales, songs, proverbs, riddles, praises, invocations, prayers, memorats, blessings, teachings, omens, interdictions, speeches, and meditations.

The epics provide entertainment for the listeners in the form of music, song, movement, dance, togetherness, and group interaction. The Nyanga tend to classify epics as *kakoro* (things of daytime), that is, as usually devoid of danger. They are not the sacred or esoteric texts that belong only to an exclusive group of people; they can be heard, enjoyed, and understood by all. Much of their content is light and somewhat amusing because of the unreality of the hero, evidenced in his gifts, his appearance, his deeds, and principally his flagrant transgression of values. The hero is so unlikely because he temporarily reverses destiny, whereas for the Nyanga it is explicit that "no person can extend or expand the life destiny commissioned for him by the creator god and that death cannot be prevented."

The epics are cultural monuments, providing a rich perspective on the wealth and diversity of Nyanga culture. The average Nyanga is delighted to have this endless list of cultural features presented to him. In no other type of text, under no other circumstance, are so many otherwise separate features of Nyanga culture drawn together. Thus the epics create in the listeners' minds a sense of belonging, a feeling of greatness and pride.

Precisely because of the wealth of content, the epics have, implicitly if not explicitly, a strong didactic and moralizing undertone. They uphold a vision of Nyanga cultural values, crystallized mainly in the contrastive characters of hero and chief. The developing intrigue has a moralizing impact on father-son, husband-wife, sibling, chief-subject, chief-Pygmy, nephew-aunt, and nephew-maternal uncle relationships. Rashness, impetuosity, verbosity, arrogance, intemperance, ruthlessness, thoughtlessness, hardheartedness—all are implicitly criticized. The bard's concluding statements also reveal a moral quality.

Some episodes in the epics are intended to explain the cause of or reason for particular phenomena or customs. Some of the explanations refer to real historical happenings: the encounter with the Pygmies and their subsequent role as hunters, providers of honey, singers, and ritual experts; the advent of hunting dogs (the Nyanga affirm that originally they were trappers and that dogs were introduced by the Hunde); the introduction and elaboration of specific cults; the origin of interdictions imposed upon chiefs. There are also allusions to the origin of banana growing and possibly to the provenance of iron tools. Furthermore, the epics

5

help explain the mysterious origin of incumbent chiefs; they show why a chief is not necessarily the son of a ritual wife and how different autonomous states have developed. If it is true that the epics, or at least the major epic themes, originated with the more or less Hundeized Pygmies—and there are many reasons to accept this hypothesis—then it is possible that at one time the epics were part of the teachings accompanying the initiation and the enthronement of a chief. In symbolic form they presented a precise account of expectations placed in a true chief. Subsequently the epics may have become poetic channels through which the public could become familiar with the values of chieftainship.

The songs, and some invocations and dialogues as well, are filled with aphoristic statements and terse formulations which, with their highly condensed thought, are difficult to translate. Innumerable formulas indicate time and place, introduce conversations or songs, express surprise, emotion, and physical strain; epithets, praise names, and patronymics abound. Some epics, more than others, are characterized by constant and subtle changes from direct to indirect discourse. And, amazingly difficult, particularly in epics II and III, are the smooth transitions in songs and conversations from the Nyanga into the Hunde language. Since I do not know Hunde, I am fortunate to have obtained, during my fieldwork, translations into Nyanga and Kingwana of the passages formulated in Hunde. Otherwise the Nyanga text includes no archaisms and only a surprisingly small number of Nyangaized loanwords from French and Swahili.

For comparative purposes it should be emphasized that the epics stem from an ethnic world whose main concerns are hunting, trapping, food gathering, and extensive banana growing. There are no cities or large-scale residential groupings of people. Traditions of conquest and large-scale warfare are nonexistent. There are no elaborate courts. Yet this small-scale world in the forest region of eastern Zaire has its own complexities. There many peoples with differing traditions have converged and have become thoroughly amalgamated: Pygmies, ancient Bantu-speaking groups whose exact origins cannot be pinpointed, and waves of early immigrations from East Africa. From certain points of view the epic traditions are international in scope. They are found in the immediate neighborhood of the Nyanga, at least among the Hunde and the Lega; and the Nyanga are explicit in their assertion that the Pygmies (Twa) participated in formulating the traditions.

The international character of the epics is found in their actual content. The Pygmies play a substantial role in the events described. Divinities worshiped by the Kivu Pygmies (Bubingo or Buingo, Hangi; Schebesta,

6

1952, p. 354) and by the Hunde, the Kumbure, and the Tembo (Bugingo or Buingo, Nyamulagira or Nyamurairi, Nguba or Nkuba, Hangi, Kahindo, Muhima; Schumacher, 1949, pp. 185, 197, 223; Viaene, 1952b), and some ascribed to the Pygmies (Meshemutwa, Nkango), turn up in the epics. That sorcery and witchcraft, which are insignificant among the Mbuti Pygmies in the interpretation of crises and in legends (Turnbull, 1965a, pp. 308–309; 1965b, p. 270), play no role in the epics may be owing to Pygmy influence. Formal initiation for men, though highly developed among the Nyanga, is of no consequence in the epics; rather, the informal initiation of the hero consists in his show of endurance, skill, and wit. Again a Pygmy pattern, in which physical endurance and hunting skills replaced formal initiation (Turnbull, 1965a, p. 307), is suggested. The Nyanga hero manipulates the song as an effective weapon to produce strength and good fortune, a feature reminiscent of the extraordinary power of the song among the Pygmies (Turnbull, 1965c, passim). The political system and values that form the background for the epic narrative are closely similar to those of the Hunde (Schumacher, 1949, pp. 186–196, 210–229, 243–244; Viaene, 1952a).

More documentation about the oral literature of the Pygmies, the Hunde, and related peoples (Kumbure, Tembo) would reveal even more traces of transethnic correspondences. Viaene (1955, pp. 214–215) recounts a tale about the dragon Kirimu in which a newborn boy asks his mother who killed his father. Misled by his mother, the boy kills an elephant, a wild boar, a buffalo, and a lion in an attempt to discover whether any of them had eaten his father. In a final confrontation he is swallowed by Kirimu, but he destroys the dragon with razors from the inside, thus liberating his father and other people. This theme is analogous to encounters of the hero with Kirimu in epics I and II.

In a longer tale (Viaene, 1955, pp. 215–218) a youth named Mubuza is hated by his elder brother Magene; he ventures on a journey with a little food donated by villagers. He consecutively encounters pairs of animals of all kinds which are fighting (they are metamorphosed spirits) and separates them, bringing peace. Finally he spends the night in his paternal aunt's village, receiving advice on what to do when he arrives near the volcanoes in the realm of Nyamulagira.

On his journey Mubuza encounters grains (transformed counselors), shrubs (servants of the chief), small birds (Chief-Pygmies), and a serval, greeting them as instructed. Following his aunt's advice, he does not participate in dances. He is led before Nyamulagira, whom he praises and who gives him an abundance of foods to take home. Since he has no carriers, he must return with Nyamulagira's promise that the foods will follow. He receives instruction from the spirits whom he had separated about how to act on his homeward journey: he must not look at people who are cultivating, harvesting, or dancing. He scrupulously follows the recommendation and arrives in his village, where all the foods await him. Some days later a large village is established and Mubuza becomes chief.

Magene, the jealous elder brother, undertakes the same journey, but he solicits no advice as to how to comport himself. Arriving in Nyamulagira's realm, he is tricked into believing that he also will receive goods. Returning home, he dies, and his junior brother gets everything promised to Magene. This Hunde tale includes many of the themes developed in Nyanga epics and heroic literature: the tension between siblings; the rejection of a capable young man by his brother; the journey to Nyamurairi; the advice of the paternal aunt; the trickeries of Nyamurairi (transformed beings); the quest for wealth in the form of food; the miraculous arrival of the food; the junior becoming chief; the imminent punishment of the villain. Beyond the subject matter and actors, the wording of the story and its mood are almost indistinguishable from the Nyanga pattern.

Against a background of common thematic and stylistic elements, the four epics develop many antithetical viewpoints and motifs. The examination of these oppositions should have a sobering effect on those who, on the basis of limited information, relish in facile generalizations. The four epics were written down within the same year and sung by four bards whose villages are separated by not more than fifty miles. The bards belong to four distinct political units situated at the core of Nyangaland. The singers participate in a common culture. Yet there are basic differences among the four epics which defy hasty conclusions. A few examples will illustrate the point.

At the center of the intrigue in all four epics is the chief's *ate*: in epics I and II it affects the son (but only temporarily in II); in epics III and IV it is directed toward the principal wife, but not transferred to her son. Thus the conflict between father and son is not a common motif.

The relationships with Water Serpent Mukiti are insignificant in epic II; they are based on sheer antagonism in epic I and on cooperation and friendship in epics III and IV. Mukiti is explicitly designated as husband of the hero's paternal aunt in epics I and II; in epics III and IV he acts as though he were the hero's maternal uncle and, by implication, the husband of the hero's paternal aunt (in Nyanga kinship terminology, the husband of a paternal aunt is classified as a maternal uncle). Thus the conflict between a man and his paternal aunt's husband is not basic.

In epic I the paternal aunt is the most important person in the hero's comitatus. Although mentioned, she is not prominent in epic II. In epics III and IV she appears as a helpful spirit. Therefore the social and spiritual bond between a man and his paternal aunt, though emphasized in some epics, is not of universal significance in the epic tradition.

The Pygmies appear in the epics as friends, allies, and helpers. Although reduced in importance, they play a critical role in epic I in the events leading to the ultimate catharsis of the hero-chief. In epic II they are notable, primarily in the person of the great hunter and thaumaturge Shekaruru, as benefactors of the hero-chief. In epic III, however, after initial friendship there is a radical rupture between Chief Mwindo and his Pygmies. The bond between the hero-chief Kabutwakenda and his Pygmy singers is perfect.

The epic is not necessarily centered on the deeds of one hero who is always the driving force behind the action (epic I). The intrigue is almost evenly shared by hero-chief and hero-villain in epic IV. In epics II and III major activities focus, not on the hero, but on his sister, his Pygmy Shekaruru, and a trapper. Some key characteristics of the hero may even be attributed to other personages: the hero's father travels alive in the subterranean world (I); a young trapper revivifies his brother and the Pygmy Shekaruru resuscitates a chief's son (II).

HE BARDS

IDENTITY OF THE BARDS

In *The Mwindo Epic from the Banyanga* (1969, pp. 15–19) I briefly discuss the social background of Mr. Candi Rureke from Bese (Kisimba region), the narrator of epic I.

Epic II was sung in the village of Mera (Kisimba region) by Mr. Shekwabo, a member of the Banaa descent group. He lived in Mincence, where he had settled with a blood friend, but he belonged to a political unit that included the villages of Mincence, Mera, and Mpeti. Mera is a small village, famous for its pottery making, in an isolated but beautiful forest region where Mount Mincence offers a superb view of the lands to the east and north inhabited by the Bashari and the Bakumbure.

Epic III was recorded in writing in Rungoma village (Ihana region). With three other village groups, Rungoma forms a distinct political unit called *cuo ca Batembo*. The bard Nkuba Shekarisi belongs to the Banankuta descent group, whose members are established in diverse villages in the Ihana region. In the Mwiria chiefdom (Ihana) a member of the Banankuta exercises the ritual function of Chief-Pygmy (see *Chief-Pygmy* in glossary). In fact, the Banankuta are Nyangaized offshoots of a particular strain of Pygmies, identified as Batwa ba Ncangu wa Shemakara. They originated in Bwito (an original province in Hundeland), and some of them settled in the chiefdom of Mwiria as followers of Chief Ntabana. Shekarisi had learned the epic from Mataki (a Hunde of Gishari) with whom he ordinarily hunted. According to Shekarisi, Mataki had acquired his knowledge from the Pygmies of Baurano (Hundeland). In one of his songs the bard recollects:

> I am telling the story
> That was told by Mutia and Irumbo,
> Mutia, child of twins.

It is not clear to me whether this Mutia is one of the Pygmies of Baurano or whether the song refers to an even older tradition. Shekarisi's text contains many songs and passages that are formulated in the Hunde language and thus point to the sources that have influenced him. (Note that the Pygmies among the Nyanga and the Hunde speak their own variant of the Hunde language.) Members of the audience informed me that Shekarisi's text followed the Pygmy style in rhythmic accompaniment and manner of singing, as well as in the particular role played by the Pygmies. Like many of his kinsmen, Shekarisi was deeply involved with hunting dogs (dogs are one of the sacred patrimonies of the Banankuta). Like his senior brother, who was Chief-Pygmy in the Mwiria chiefdom, Shekarisi carved dog bells, manufactured arrows, bows, and quivers, and wove hunting nets. In brief, he was a hundred-percent hunter in outlook and profession.

None of these gifted men was a professional bard; the singing of an epic was not the principal occupation of any of them. As shown by the following sketch of Mr. Sherungu, the singer of epic IV, they were versatile, highly experienced, and intelligent individuals with a variety of interests and activities. All were deeply steeped in Nyanga culture, especially in aspects connected with hunting and chieftainship and with values and problems of their people. I do not know how fixed or stable are the texts they sang for me, for I had no chance to hear them again at a later time. I am, of course, inclined to think that the texts are not rigid. The bards have wide leeway in formulating thoughts or passages in a new, and to some extent original, manner. Still, they have to work within the framework of rhythmic accompaniment and formulas which set limitations to the range of variability. I further believe that experienced bards have a standard repertoire of interlinked episodes which they can reduce or elaborate upon, but which reflect the specific epic traditions to which they have been exposed.

PORTRAIT OF A BARD

Of the singers of epics, I have known Sherungu (epic IV) well and intimately over a longer period of time than the others. I met him in the earliest stages of my field research, when much against his will and inclinations he was employed as a *cantonnier* (road worker) by the local administration. On the advice of Nyanga elders, I invited Sherungu to sing on his two-stringed zither. Accompanying himself on his instrument, he sang for many hours, producing a variety of songs tersely formulated in the Hunde language. I recorded some of the songs without understanding them, yet I felt that I was in the presence of a great singer and player and a wise spokesman. I quickly learned that Sherungu is much more: he is an outstanding and versatile drummer, an experienced hunter, a friend of the Pygmies, a renowned medicine man, and an excellent storyteller. Furthermore, as a *musao* (see glossary) he occupies an influential position in the college of ritual experts surrounding the chief. After many exhausting efforts, I managed to have him released from the hated roadwork job, and for the remainder of my protracted research among the Nyanga he was my trusted companion and exegete.

I rarely used Sherungu as a direct source of information. Rather, I invited him to be present at events and discussions in which, whenever possible, I encouraged him to participate as a performer or as an observer. I utilized his vast knowledge to help clarify difficult statements. Toward the final stages of my Nyanga research, I asked him to join me at the research center of l'Institut pour la recherche scientifique en Afrique Centrale at Lwiro (Zaire) in order to assist with translations. During a year's sojourn at the research center, he began at my request to dictate his memoirs to my two Nyanga assistants, Mr. Kubuya and Mr. Tubi. He developed these memoirs in his own manner, free from direct intervention by us, but included in them at my explicit request all the songs, proverbs, riddles, prayers, formulas, incantations, praises, and tales he knew. The text of his autobiography covers 3,456 closely written pages. To my great surprise, it was in this context that he provided me with the text of epic IV, in addition to several longer tales in which Mwindo or other characters associated with the epics occur. He also supplied a fascinating epic which he said he had heard a certain Wanowa sing in a hunting camp (see App. I for a synoptic summary of this epic). Included in the autobiography are 386 riddles, 82 "true stories," 41 "thoughts," 22 tales, 371 songs (mostly proverbs or one- or two-line songs), and a large number of dreams, reminiscences, prayers, praises, formulas, omens, incantations, taboos, and medical recipes.

Sherungu's lineage, which traditionally occupied the ritual position of *musao*, came from Hundeland. His paternal grandfather, Marondi, had moved into Nyangaland to serve as *musao* for the chiefdom Robe; his father, Barengeke, became *musao* to Chief Buhini in the chiefdom Iryamba; and Sherungu himself was *musao* to Chief Nkuru (son of and successor to Buhini). Sherungu was born early in the twentieth century, at about the time the conflict between the chiefdoms ruled by Buhini and Mukobya began. His first name, therefore, is Burenda (anger), referring to this period of hostilities. His mother, Mafura, was a girl of the Baasi, a group established in the Bunyungu division of Hundeland. Only a small number of relatives came to live with Barengeke in Iramba; Barengeke's senior brother, Bitashimwa, died of an arrow wound in the war fought by Chief Buhini against Chief Mukobya, leaving four children. Sherungu himself had a junior brother, Masokora, and a sister. Barengeke was also joined by Bukore, his father's older brother's son.

As a very small child Sherungu suffered severely from yaws; at one point his family feared for his life. In his earliest youth he met a Pygmy, Karibiri, who had emigrated from Bunyungu (Hundeland) and was Chief Buhini's principal drummer. A small group of Pygmies from Bunyungu settled with Barengeke because of the following circumstances. As is the custom, Chief Buhini had married a Pygmy girl. When one of Buhini's hunting dogs, borrowed by a relative of hers, was killed during the hunt, the Pygmy offered Buhini a Pygmy woman in lieu of the dog. Buhini's counselors, who were opposed to the marriage, brought the woman to Barengeke's house because his wife belonged to the same group in Bunyungu. Soon thereafter the Pygmy woman was joined by her lover, a Pygmy, who was well received and entered into a blood bond with Barengeke. This Pygmy later brought several relatives and their wives to settle in Byarenga, an area controlled by Chief Buhini. These early relationships with Pygmies left a deep imprint on the cultural background, the social personality, and the art of Sherungu.

In his autobiography Sherungu views himself primarily as a musician, a hunter, and healer; his artistry as a singer of tales and songs is clearly secondary in his estimation. At various places in his memoirs he discusses his apprenticeship and activities as drummer, hunter, and healer. He remembers his father Barengeke, who died when Sherungu was a small boy, as a good speaker, as a hunter and trapper, as a person who did not cultivate, as one who could drink heavily without becoming inebriated, and, above all, as a healer. From his mother, who had received his father's oral will that Sherungu be instructed in his healing secrets (particularly in the treatment of leprosy), he learned the art of healing, which he further

13

developed in his travels in both Nyangaland and Hundeland and by means of establishing friendships, connections, and blood pacts. He also inherited from his father the paraphernalia of the divinity Muriro, to whom he was dedicated as a child.

Sherungu's father was an able and passionate hunter and so was Sherungu; he learned his skills and techniques mainly from the Pygmies, with whom he lived in friendship and conviviality. Sherungu was mainly engaged in hunting and trapping until, particularly after World War II, demands for cultivation and other types of jobs became heavier and began to weigh on him. He expressed his thinking on this subject:

> I love the forest because it is *katiri* of people, that is, a place where one goes with spear and dog and where, with good luck, one kills animals. It is a place from which one returns with game; and what a surprise to eat meat, that evening! The forest is the chief of the people, because it gives people animals; this is true for the hunter and for the trapper as well. And what you get there is free. I remember the forest, with tears. Thinking that now I eat animals that saw the sun and are bought for money makes me lose weight. When, in the evening, I think about the forest, I cannot fall asleep easily. The forest is the place where people get meat, and get it free. I cannot imagine what could prohibit me from going to the forest. [If that were so] I would have left it, long ago, on my own, because of the many who have died there. He who would want to prohibit me, it is better [for him] to kill me, because the forest provides all the foods. Even though there are many dangers in the forest, I love it exceedingly.

For Sherungu, the forest dispenses joy, abundance, and free living. Although it is a dangerous place, it gives people the opportunity to render mutual aid and manifest profound friendship. The hunt itself is an arduous and risky undertaking, demanding appropriate rituals and an adequate state of mind for its successful conclusion. Sherungu sings in one of the Mbuntsu songs:

> To kill animals is (a) difficult (task);
> A man's spirit saves that man from all dangers;
> But without the help of the spirit
> One cannot return from the forest unharmed.

While Sherungu was still a young boy his father allowed him to take a drumstick and beat on the drum of the famous drummer, the Pygmy Karibiri. Chief Buhini, impressed by the boy's early inclinations, one day wished him well, calling him "my friend, Karibiri." This designaton was a kind of will that Buhini left to Sherungu, who retained the nickname Karibiri. For many years he traveled with and learned from the Pygmy

Karibiri, until he began to replace the latter as an independent and expert drummer.

In his autobiography Sherungu relates a strange event in the life of his mother, Mafura. While her husband was still alive, and before Sherungu's birth, Mafura was abducted as a slave by the Bakusu-Bashwahili raiders of Rukundura. She managed to get away and, to escape her pursuers, crossed a wide river on a large, floating tree, which was none other than the mythical serpent Mukiti. (This experience had been foretold to her in a dream imparted to her by the snake divinity Musoka.) The importance of Mukiti in Sherungu's epic text is undoubtedly connected with this tradition.

After his father's death Sherungu left his birthplace in Irangira and went to live with his mother in Ifako. By that time he was accustomed to trapping birds with his *tumponda*-snares. During World War I, when his mother and his elder sister were recruited to carry ammunition toward the Congo-Rwanda boundary, Sherungu would remain behind crying for his mother. Eventually Chief Buhini placed him under the guardianship of two of his wives (including his senior wife). He went to reside in the village of Mutongo. During and after the war he would help carry loads of banana flour to Masisi, the administrative center. A few years later he left Mutongo in order to settle in another Nyanga chiefdom where a married classificatory sister (his father's junior brother's daughter) was living. He learned both hunting and trapping from the sister's husband, and he further improved his drumming skills in his contacts with two Pygmies. Meanwhile, his mother remarried and had several other children. Sherungu's later relationships with her were restricted.

As explicitly detailed in his autobiography, Sherungu's subsequent life was characterized by considerable travel in and around Nyangaland. He was increasingly invited to serve as a drummer and as a healer; he also spent much time with other hunters, including Pygmies, in hunting camps and on hunts of long duration.

After the death of his father, Barengeke, the function of *musao* had been transferred to Sherungu's classificatory senior brother, Muisa (his father's senior brother's son). When Chief Buhini died, his son and chief designate Nkuru Nkumbirwa was enthroned, and Sherungu was invested with the function of *musao*. As a perquisite of the office he received, without bridewealth, a wife who was a member of one of the chief's client groups. He had four daughters with this wife; two children died. The eldest daughter was consecrated to the spirits and had three small daughters, and another daughter was married to a Hunde. Sherungu's small family lived with other agnatic relatives in a section of the village Maniema.

Sherungu was initiated into the Mpandi association. He owned two hunting dogs, dedicated to the Pygmy divinity Nkango; he also worshiped Muhima and Katondo ka Musao, a primordial ancestor of his group.

Sherungu was a very lucid man, possessing an enormous range of knowledge and capable of communicating it in music, word, and action. He was widely traveled in his own world and was perfectly bilingual (Nyanga and Hunde); he was reasonably familiar with Kingwana (regional variant of Swahili) and spoke some Rwanda. He loved conviviality, music, dance, and verbal artistry; he liked food and took delight in consuming large quantities of banana beer. He was dynamic and outgoing, dedicated and reliable. He had a special sense of humor and fun, an extraordinary memory, and a vivid imagination. He could sit and ponder long about the forest and its beings:

> When I go into the forest, I think I may encounter a crowd of spirits, or that a spirit may call me, or that I may meet with my father's or my mother's spirit, who may give me a forewarning that I will not live long or that I must not go into the forest anymore, saying that God is angry because I kill his animals. Or, animals may meet a man, asking why he wants to kill them, and then chase him. Perhaps animals do weep over the death of their kin. They say perhaps that their kin, when we kill them, go to the subterranean world. They may think that we are spirits who kill them, as spirits kill us. Perhaps they have oracle givers and counselors, because sometimes they avoid our traps, passing beside them. Perhaps, in their men's house, they tell one another what they have seen and experienced while away from home. Perhaps they have chiefs and spokesmen of their own; perhaps they give tribute to God. When I see chimpanzees, I think of them as people who fled the payment of taxes and grew hairy because of lack of fire. Or perhaps the dead change into chimpanzees.

In his autobiography Sherungu does not reveal the names of narrators and bards from whom he learned his stories and songs. Yet his account of his life tells the names of many people with whom he traveled, hunted, and trapped, people with whom he made friendships, or whom he briefly encountered. For a well-traveled Nyanga, who participated as a musician in countless ceremonial and other events when songs were sung and tales were told, the distinctive names of persons from whom he learned the texts are obliterated, confused, or forgotten. As a master of the song, he has interlinked and transformed the sources of his knowledge to such an extent that the songs and tales are his own creations.

Apparently the learning of musical skills is more technical and rigid than learning the texts. As I have already indicated, Sherungu strong-ly emphasizes the fact that his instructor in drumming was Karibiri, and he categorically affirms that a certain Mumbara, a friend from Gishari (Hunde), systematically taught him to play the two-stringed zither. Mumbara came to live for a full year in Sherungu's village precisely for the purpose of teaching Sherungu and another man the art of the zither.

The reasons for learning various arts or skills are quite different from one another. Sherungu acquired the art of healing as a paternal legacy; for him, drumming was indicated by personal predispositions and inclinations as well as by the chief's will; his zither playing originated in a personal desire "to rejoice his chief" and in an opportunity created by his friendship with a good player. The learning of oral texts was undertaken in a much less systematic way. Sherungu's sources were the numerous persons he en-countered through his activities as a hunter, a drummer, a healer, a zither player, a member of various cults and associations, an officeholder under the chief, and through his friendship with Pygmies and other hunters. Sherungu has an original mind; he transforms stories in a peculiarly personal way by ornamenting, broadening, and elaborating the details of events, encounters, and conversations. Although he is neither succinct nor poetic, he is always imaginative and creative in the telling of stories.

In an extraordinary long passage in his autobiography, Sherungu re-counts the circumstances under which he heard an epic text narrated by a certain Rwanowa. He then relates the epic as Rwanowa had told it, as if he were merely telling someone else's story. Thirteen men, including some Pygmies, he himself, and four women were established in a hunting camp near Lukweti, in Hundeland. They had nasty adventures with an elephant that ravaged their camp and with a leopard that stole one of Sherungu's dogs. The hunters then killed two wild pigs on two consecutive days. Sud-denly Sherungu's hunting dog began to hide and refused to hunt. When the dog continued to act in this strange manner, Sherungu tied him up and instructed the women not to feed him. That same evening a certain Kahombo Rwanowa, his wife, his brother, his brother's wife, and a deaf person arrived in the camp, while hunting from a camp in the neighborhood, and were received hospitably. When Rwanowa saw Sherungu's hunting dog, he asked why it was chained up and demanded its release. At first Sherungu refused, but finally, at Rwanowa's insistence, untied the dog. After dinner, as they were all sitting around a fire, Rwanowa spoke: "You, Sherungu, and your hunters, listen. Do you not know that all the animals of the forest, each one, have their owner and master (i.e., the one who has the privilege of killing it)?" Having said this, Rwanowa began his explanation, saying: "You, Sherungu, this is the

reason why I have told you to untie the dog. Listen to this example."
Thereupon, Rwanowa related a long story about Mwindo (synopsis in
App. I)

This story clearly illustrates the informal setting and occasion for the
narration of great epics and the strong moralizing tone that underlies
them. Little of the moralizing in an epic or tale is formulated in explicit
terms, although the narrators tend to conclude with synthetic moral
statements. The didactic or moralizing effect depends on the context of the
narration: the particular occasion, circumstances, precedents, and persons
involved. The hunting camp, isolated from the rest of the world in the deep
forest, is a setting par excellence where the narrative thrives and the
creative imagination operates. There are no large crowds and no diverse
musical instruments for big dances; there is no reason for major celebrations, initiations, or rituals. Storytelling is the easiest and most effective
means of entertainment and relaxation in the camp. Often it is stimulated
by the extraordinary events, encounters, and experiences that characterize
the hunt. Explanations and comfort are sought in the tales. The setting of
the camp and the hunting and trapping experiences furnish abundant
material, enabling the imagination to elaborate upon familiar stories and to
invent new ones. The recounting of unusual experiences and the celebra-
tion of heroic deeds flourish more readily in that milieu than in any other.
Memories are filled with the names of exceptional hunters, past and
present.

Sherungu evokes in vivid terms certain hunters he has known. For example, when Shebahi, who was extremely fast and accurate in hurling the
spear, was present, no one had the slightest chance of spearing an animal
first. All by himself, without even dogs, Shebahi used to hunt dangerous
animals like wild pigs, buffaloes, and leopards. Another hunter, Shenyancira, had unusually sharp eyesight and was fast and tireless in his pursuit
of animals. When a pig escaped from the dogs he would chase it with
his spear, without dogs, until he caught it. Another hunter, Shendabu
of the Hunde-Pygmies, was so quick that he was nicknamed Pygmy-Dog.
Sometimes he would kill three or four wild pigs in a single day. He would
find a piglet and hold it squealing under his foot in order to attract the
mother pig. Afterward he would castrate the male piglet or cut the tail of
the female so that the animals would fatten faster, and then he would let
them run, for he was sure of finding them later on. Shendabu would even
hunt during the night, always without dogs. Described as "very short,
black, and slender," he was praised by everyone as the greatest hunter. He
died (about 1941) of leprosy after he had killed a leopard and refused to be

ritually cleansed. Sherungu also recounts the exploits of Shemuhahi, who was a master in hunting monkeys with bow and arrow.

Sherungu knows many tales, some of them containing heroic themes about Mwindo. (Texts by Sherungu are published in Biebuyck, 1956*a*, 1964, 1965, 1975, and in Biebuyck and Mateene, 1965, 1970). It would be feasible and theoretically possible for the bard to insert these tales at any time as distinctive episodes in the epic, but during the three years of my acquaintanceship with Sherungu he showed no inclination to do so. His mind clearly separated both his own epic (IV), and the one he had heard Rwanowa relate in the hunting camp from the tales, some of which dealt with Mwindo and other heroic themes, but I was never able to unravel the various threads of his thought on this matter.

I am certain, however, that two distinct sets of conceptions underlie Sherungu's attitude. He is guided, on the one hand, by a deep respect for tradition, or rather for the acknowledgment that distinctive traditions exist. Although he adds personal elements of style and formulation to the epic, he makes no major alterations because he recognizes the major strain of tradition from which the epic stems. The same point is underscored by Candi Rureke in epic I, "We are telling the story that the Babuya have told (long ago)," and by Shekarisi in epic III, "I am telling the story that was told by Mutia and Irumbo, Mutia child of twins." On the other hand, the traditional strain from which the tales, including the heroic tales, derive is not clearly defined in Sherungu's mind. The tales are so widespread and are told by so many people in so many places that the narrator rarely knows exactly to whom he owes the text. From village to village and from narrator to narrator, the same tale has innumerable versions and nuances, and it is easy to conclude that no tale is transmitted from person to person in an invariant form. Rather, motifs and clusters of motifs, around which the exuberant imagination of the singers can weave texts based on stylistic and structural patterns, personal repertoire, and experience, are transmitted.

In a tale dealing with Mwindo and the Pygmies, for example, Sherungu harmoniously combines personal knowledge and experience with heroic motifs about Mwindo, the Dragon-Ogre, and the Pygmies. From one point of view the tale seems to describe ancient encounters between Nyanga chiefs and Pygmies to account for the exceptional ritual role played by the Pygmies and the exchange relationships that link chiefs and Pygmies. From a different point of view, however, the tale may be nothing but the transposition to heroic level of more recent historical events of which Sherungu was aware. As *musao* he was closely connected with the chief; and both as a hunter and as a child raised by the chief's wives he has close relationships with Pygmies. As I have noted earlier, the Baremba Pygmies who now live in the Iramba chiefdom, where Sherungu is *musao*, arrived there during his father's lifetime. It is this recent historical event that forms the true background for the story. For Sherungu the story celebrates that well-known event, which is placed within a heroic framework. It is his story and it does not fit into the tradition of his epic, which celebrates remote and generalized events.

Sherungu's imagination as a storyteller is strongly stimulated and influenced by his experiences as a politico-ritual officeholder, as a musician who has attended many performances, as a hunter who has worked with expert hunters and Pygmies, intently listening to their stories, and as a devotee of several cults. As one tale explains, when the ritual wife has no children the son of her substitute (*mpombwe*) is expected to become a chief.

In another tale a man who has fourteen sons provides each of them with one wife, but the most junior brother gets two wives. The older brothers, bitterly resentful, decide to throw their junior into a large river. The junior, singing "He, Mwindo, has been killed," travels downstream to the village where his married paternal aunt lives. There he is welcomed, and he becomes chief in a land that had no chief.

A third tale is about a chief with fourteen wives who loves one of them, Kamiseke, more than the others. He gives her all the gifts of tribute and forbids her to go into the forest. One day the chief's wives go as usual to collect crabs, and the beloved wife follows them. The co-wives bury her under a huge rock. The chief, unaware of his wife's whereabouts, sends people to search for her, but they cannot find her. The beloved wife remains alive under the rock for a full week, and then she hears the sound of an ax. She sings and thus attracts the attention of a Pygmy. Unable to get her out from underneath the rock, the Pygmy brings her bananas and honeycombs. Finally, with the help of other Pygmies, she is liberated. The Pygmies take her to their camp, heal her wounds, feed her, and secretly restore her to the chief. When Kamiseke discloses what happened to her, all the co-wives are called together, but they deny her story. The chief chases them all away because of the shame they have brought upon him. The Pygmies are given dogs and two women as a reward.

In a fourth tale a woman, Kishwa, whose husband has died, travels with her son and daughter to another land. She comes to a large river and decides to swim across it with her daughter, leaving the boy behind. When halfway across, however, she returns for her son, who was singing for her. In her indecision she repeats this action several times until at last she swims away with the boy and abandons the girl. Molested by Dragon-Ogre, the girl jumps into the river and reaches the abode of the divinity Ruendo. After hearing her story, Ruendo calls for the blessing of divinities worshiped by women: Nyangengu, Kentse, and Bisheria. They give her cult paraphernalia to wear when she divines and send her to Nyamurairi, the god of fire, to find her mother. She arrives at the place of Hangi-of-Drum, who is very ill. She divines on his behalf, predicting that he will recover the same day if his people provide her with valuables. Hangi is healed, and the girl pursues her journey to Nyamurairi. There she receives hospitality and hears that Buingo (Destiny) is sick. She divines and heals him, for which she receives gifts. Her mother is there, but her brother is dead. Mother and daughter return home. The girl has become a famous diviner who travels everywhere and is given many presents.

Sherungu's repertory includes several heroic tales in which Mwindo and other protagonists of the epics are featured. One of them develops in unusual detail a motif that permeates several Nyanga tales: the quest for a young woman who may be married only if the suitor successfully performs a difficult task. Shemwindo, a commoner, has an ugly, scurvy son called Mwindo and a beautiful daughter Kahindo. The father decides that his daughter will be married to the man who can remove a calabash from a tall tree. Near the tree, Dragon-Ogre Kirimu has made a hole so deep that it connects with the subterranean dwelling of divinities and spirits. A chief, called Difficult-Things-That-Exceed, arrives with his men, but none of them can pass the test. The chief returns home with only his Chief-Counselor while the latter's wife goes to ask the Pygmies for help. She and the Pygmies go to Shemwindo's village. One Pygmy falls into the hole and dies. The Chief-Pygmy says the dead Pygmy failed because he did not have dogs consecrated to and named for the divinities Nkango and Meshe. The dogs are dedicated, and the Chief-Pygmy succeeds in his attempt to collect the calabash. He receives the girl Kahindo for his chief Difficult-Things-That-Exceed. Her brother Mwindo claims a wife in exchange for his sister, but the chief's men refuse. The chief, Kahindo, and his people return home. The exasperated Mwindo spends days singing for and about his sister. Finally he decides to go and play the thumb piano for her. Singing and playing, he hides near the place where water is drawn from the river. Women coming to get water hear the sounds, but they cannot determine who is producing them. Kahindo, informed of this episode, journeys alone to the river. She hears the sounds but she cannot find Mwindo, who transforms himself into a crab and moves down the river. Kahindo steps into the water and is caught by the crab, which disappears with her.

Maidens who had followed Kahindo at a distance take the news to the village. The chief consults an oracle and is told that Mwindo is acting so strangely because he was refused a wife in exchange for his sister. The oracle advises the chief to provide his own sister as a wife for Mwindo. The woman is left near the water, and Mwindo claims her. Later he goes to the chief's village with the two women, Kahindo and the chief's sister, and asks the chief for land to settle. He returns home in secret to inform his father that he is now a chief. He changes into a beautiful youth, "beautiful like the morning sun." Returning to his new land, he invites his father and mother to join him. He acquires Pygmies "because a chief is not without Pygmies, since they fight for the chief." Thereafter all live prosperously in the new land.

Another tale by Sherungu uses the Mwindo motif to account for the origin of chieftainship, crystallized in the enthronement rites, and for its close connections with the Pygmies. Shemwindo, a commoner, has many sons, among whom the firstborn is Mwindo Kakukukuku (Scurvy Mwindo). All the sons except Mwindo are devoured by Dragon-Ogre Kirimu, who is aided by tricks devised by his daughter. In his sleep Mwindo is advised by his paternal aunt to hunt Kirimu with his two dogs. She also urges him to eat "that which divulges their arrival in Kirimu's village, because it contains the malehood (*bume,* strength) from there." Mwindo, depicted as alert and shrewd, kills Kirimu, liberates his brothers, and marries Kirimu's daughter. He is then highly honored by his brothers, who build a large house for him. Mwindo is a good hunter; his brothers are not. During the dangerous pursuit of a buffalo he receives help from a Pygmy, who stays with him in a hunting camp. Mwindo falls sick with the "trembling disease," but, after repeated treatment with body ointments of honey, he is healed by the Pygmy. Mwindo is "shining now" (i.e., no longer has scurvy). But in the meantime Mwindo's wife has fled. Assisted by the Pygmy, his dog, and Lightning, Mwindo finds his wife in a cave. In gratitude, Mwindo and his father give two dogs, a wife, and goat to the Pygmy. Upon arriving home the Pygmy tells his relatives about the abundance in Mwindo's village, and they decide to settle with Mwindo. The Pygmies are given their own land, from which Mwindo's people have been removed because "Pygmies do not live with those who are not Pygmies." Soon afterward Mwindo's father falls sick. He invites the leader of the Pygmies, now called Chief-Pygmy, to enthrone his son, bringing honey, a dog, the hide of a flying squirrel, and one of their women for this purpose. The father dies, and Mwindo is enthroned together with the woman captured in Kirimu's village; she becomes his ritual wife. She gives birth to a daughter, then to a son who is called Nkuba to honor Lightning. The Chief-Pygmy, now called Kabotyo, brings leopard teeth from a hunt and gives them to Mwindo; he receives gifts (a goat, a copper bracelet, and a woman) from the Father-of-the-ritual-wife, the counselors, and Mwindo's people. Mwindo, asking the Pygmy to be his hunter and his provider of honey, declares him a chief in his own right, because he owns land and is not compelled to cultivate. The growing son of Mwindo settles with the Pygmies; he returns to his father's village only when he is a fully grown man. Then Mwindo dies and his son Nkuba becomes a chief.

THE BARDS IN THEIR EPICS

During my extensive research in Nyangaland I encountered in every village many narrators of tales, male and female, young and old, good and bad. I recorded in writing approximately a thousand tales (I have not yet made a complete inventory of them). Narrators, scattered in all parts of Nyangaland, provided me with sixty heroic tales which celebrate the deeds of Mwindo or of a Mwindo-like character.

These heroic tales, though fascinating in themselves as literary and cultural documents, are by no means comparable in scope and amplitude to the great epics presented in this volume. The epics and the singers who know them are in a class by themselves. No one knows how many versions of the epics may have existed in past decades. At one time epic traditions were widespread; we find them in different parts of Nyangaland and among the Hunde and the Lega. It is also possible that they exist now or have existed among many other populations in areas around and beyond Nyangaland. No inventories have been made, however, except for Mongo and Mongo-derived groups to the west and southwest (Boelaert, 1932, 1949, 1957, 1958; De Rop, 1964; Jacobs, 1961, 1963). At the time of my research (1952, 1954–1956), few bards remaining in Nyangaland had a complete grasp of the epic tradition. In a detailed census of three important villages, I found among forty-three full-fledged adult, married men with children and grandchildren only one who was identified as an expert singer of the epic. I myself met only the four bards whose epics I have translated, in addition to Nyakace and Bitanda who were able to sing only large fragments of epics.

The bards are creative artists and poets with original and inventive minds. They have a masterful knowledge of their language, which they use in a skillful and nuanced way. They are deeply steeped in their own culture and in a particular tradition of epic singing which transcends their own people to encompass at least the Hunde and the Hundeized Pygmies. The four epic texts testify to the creative genius and individual talents of the bards. Even a quick comparison of the epics at once reveals, whether they derive from a common strain (epics I and II) or not (epics III and IV), the individual variability and creative originality of the bards. There are common formulas, to be sure, but each bard has his own predilections; for example, epithets or place and time formulas are much more abundant in one epic than in another. Each of the common thematic elements and features and each of the recurring episodes and events is developed in a personal manner and in an original sequence. The elements of choice, inspiration, and poetic skill are constantly at work in the production of an autonomous text. These epics are not copies, simple imitations, or memorizations, but authentic personalized documents in which the bard's own experiences and his thematic and stylistic preferences can be discerned. When the Nyanga say that "the return of words is difficult," they mean that simple repetition of words spoken before is impossible. In Lord's words (1960, p. 4) the Nyanga bard, like singers of tales in other cultures, "is at once the tradition and an individual creator."

Nevertheless, despite the personal touch and the originality, the bards provide little information about their own lives, for easily understood reasons. The Nyanga are part of a small-scale world centered in the village and the hunting camp. The performance of an epic, or of a portion of it, takes place before a relatively small audience. When the locale is the hunting camp, as in Sherungu's autobiography, the group of participant-listeners comprises only a score of individuals. In this closely knit unit, the participants know one another intimately as kinsmen and/or as friends. They are bound together by a special sense of solidarity and common experience. The atmosphere of warmth, security, and togetherness which characterizes such an occasion is truly exceptional. No melodrama is necessary; the air itself is impregnated with responsiveness.

The performance of the epic in this environment is a very simple ceremony; it is a far cry from the tumultuous drama that may evolve at other types of celebrations. The bard has no need to identify himself; he is familiar to all, not especially or exclusively as a singer, but perhaps as a hunter, a kinsman, a friend, or a co-initiate. The focus is on the text in its interplay with percussion: the harmonious flow of words, the smooth development and the coherence of the episodes, the precision of the thoughts expressed, and the "sweet taste" of the songs that are interspersed. It is precisely the songs that offer the moment of relaxation during which the bard can engage in the *rori*, short improvised additions that do not further the action but allow him to meditate, to rest, and to trace the thread of the story (*iyanira*). The bard at this time may recall the epic tradition he follows, recollect people and places, formulate aphorisms, express sentiments, praise the accompanists and other participants, and give thanks for food or gifts received. The general character of the *rori* is well illustrated in a series of statements from a song in epic III:

> 1. Sky changes to dawn and we are speaking like the sound of the *mukuki*-initiation.
> 2. I am sitting, humming
>   Like a bee
>   That passes on the *itondo*-plant.
> 3. I am telling the story
>   That was told by Mutia and Irumbo,
>   Mutia, child of twins.
> 4. I have sung (with) the drums,
>   I am tired.
> 5. I am squeezed, my father;
>   I am in pursuit of Mwindo Mboru;
>   I am in pursuit of Nanga.

In a succession of terse statments, interrupted by other ideas, the bard (1) praises the length of his song, (2) expresses his enjoyment, (3) refers to his predecessors, (4) speaks about his fatigue, and (5) simply indicates that he has lost the thread of his story. Whenever the bard reflects upon his song, he speaks with pride about the tradition in which it is rooted and/or the quality of the rhythm:

> We are telling the story
> That the Babuya have told (long ago).
> We are telling the story.
>
> Let us recite from the story
> That the Babuya are used to reciting.
>
> In Ihimbi, in our country, it is fine;
> From it came an epic.
>
> The cheerleaders are in unison.

THE DRAMATIS PERSONAE

In sharp contrast with all other literary genres known to the Nyanga, the epics present a vast and highly diversified array of principal and secondary actors. In addition, a countless number of beings are casually mentioned in songs, proverbs, terse statements, and other forms of discourse with which the epics are interlaced. Invariably, the actors belong to widely different ontological categories in the Nyanga system of classification. Apart from the hero (*murai*) and the chief (*mwami*), each of whom represents a class in himself, there are human (*bea*), animal (*nyama*), and divine (*bashumbu*) actors, as well as exceptional beings occasionally termed "inhabitants of the forest" (*bisakubusara*). Besides the hero's and the chief's entourages of kinsfolk, subjects, and special status-holders, there are the Pygmies (*Batwa*) and a small group of humans not directly belonging to the circle of the hero-chief.

Most animals are personified, integrating human and distinctive animal traits. Only a few animal actors—mainly hunting dogs—maintain a separate, high-ranking status. Within the animal realm the Nyanga distinguish categories, of birds (*kironge*), insects (*kahuka*), fish (*incwi*), crabs (*ika*), and snakes (*ntsoka*); they use the general term *nyama* (animal) for the narrower category of mammals. Many distinctive "families," each with numerous named and categorized varieties of representatives, are terminologically differentiated among "animals": wild pigs (*mpunu*), antelopes (*mobe*), monkeys (*nkima*), goats (*mpene*), rodents (*ndiwa*), and so on. A large number of mammals are not grouped into subcategories but are simply listed by genus or species (e.g., five kinds of bat). Other animals such as leopards or chameleons are apparently in a class by themselves.

26

All animal categories appear in the epics, but specific animals that are otherwise important in oral literature or in the ritual and sociopolitical organization are absent. Examples are the hornbill and the sunbird (significant in circumcision rites); the duiker antelope, the leopard, and the turtle (prominent in the tales); the pangolin (important in intiations to voluntary associations); and the chimpanzee (a taboo animal for some kinship groups). Animals essential as providers of royal paraphernalia, such as gorilla, eagle, flying squirrel, and genet, are barely mentioned.

Only a limited number of Nyanga divinities appear in the epics as prominent and active dramatis personae. Several more are mentioned in songs and casual statements, such as Kahombo, Ruendo, and Nyaruwe. It is difficult to decide whether an actor known under the name of a divinity is thought of as human or divine. Examples are Mwindo's Pygmies, Meshemutwa and Nkango (epic III) and Muhima, who is in charge of a sacrifice (epic III). Ancestral spirits do not play a role, except for the spirit of the paternal aunt and that of the hero's mother (merely invoked). The erring spirits of people who died a violent death (*binyanyasi*) are also missing. A prominent role in the epics is played by extraordinary or fabulous beings of the forest and the water, and they occur frequently in the tales as well: the water serpent Mukiti; the dragon-ogre Kirimu; the specter Mpaca. Divinized celestial bodies are vital actors in one of the epics. Object-actors are particularly numerous in epics I and II, whereas plant- and tree-actors come to the foreground mainly in epics III and IV. A very special actor is the personified rock Mutero Murimba. Abstract characters that are abundant in the tales, such as Mr. Generous and Mr. Bad-Luck, are not present in the epics.

Among this vast array of actors certain ones are basic to the epic tradition. Some occur in all the epics: for example, the hero-chief; the chief (his father); the father's wives; the hero's mother and paternal aunt; Nyamurairi, the chief of the subterranean world; Kahindo; Lightning, the chief of the air; the Pygmies; and bats, ants, and spiders. Others, such as Mukiti, Kirimu, Hawk, Sparrow, hunting dogs, counselors, maternal uncles, ritual experts, and the god Muisa, are found in most epics. In each epic, however, the range and the intensity of roles assumed by each principal actor vary in degrees of elaboration. Some actors are unique to each epic.

The humans and the divinities may be either male or female. In a more or less explicit way, the majority of actors are either in allegiance with the hero-chief or in opposition to him, but some occupy an ambiguous or neutral position. Many stock characters, among the animal actors, are well

known in the Nyanga tales: Cricket is the divulger of secrets; Hawk is a
messenger; Centipede is the diviner; Chameleon is "the one who is never
overcome by a burden"; Elephant is easily victimized by weaker creatures;
Spider is the builder of bridges; Hedgehog is the maker of tunnels; and
Red Ants are the symbol of fierceness. Bat, primarily depicted in the tales
as a bringer of discord among animals, performs the role of blacksmith and
diviner. More stock characters are found among other categories of actors: Nyamurairi and his substitute Muisa frequently act as tricksters;
Kahindo is Nyamurairi's alluring daughter; the Pygmies are great hunters,
friends of the hero-chief, singers, and lovers of honey; the paternal aunt is
the ultimate adviser; Lightning is a force of destruction.

The following list synopsizes the major dramatis personae, given by
categories (the numbers in parentheses indicate the epics in which they appear).

I. *The hero-chief*
   A. One central hero, Mwindo (I, II)
   B. One central hero, Mwindo, and his heroic uterine brother (III)
   C. Two central heroes: Kabutwakenda, the noble hero, and his
      consanguine brother Mwindo, the villain (IV)
II. *Human actors*
   A. Kinsfolk of the hero-chief
      1. Close agnatic kinsfolk:
         Father: Shemwindo (I, II, III, IV), also called Karisi (III)
         Father's sister: Iyangura (I); Iyangura Katende (II); un-
         named, appearing as a spirit (III, IV)
         Sisters: uterine sister, called Nyamitondo (II) or unnamed
         (III); consanguine sisters (I, III)
         Brothers: uterine brother Kabutwakenda (III); consanguine
         brothers (III, IV)
         Children: with various names (III, IV)
         Brother's children (IV)
      2. Unspecified agnatic kinsfolk, identified as princes (brothers
         and sons of hero-chief) (I, IV)
      3. Sister's daughter (an agnatic relative if the sister is unmarried)
         (III)
      4. Mother, called Nyamwindo (I, III); known under personal
         and status names (I, II, III, IV)
      5. Father's wives (other than mother), referred to by various
         status and kinship terms (I, II, III, IV)

6. Wives, identified with personal names (III) or with kinship
and status terms (I, II, III, IV)

NOTE: Maternal uncles of the hero-chief bear animal names (I, II,
III). The exact nature of their wives (III) and children (cross-cousins of
the hero-chief) (III) is unspecified. Some wives of the hero-chief are of
divine origin (III, IV). The spouse of the paternal aunt (I, II) is the
water-dwelling serpent Mukiti; the hero's uterine sister is married to
Lightning (II).

B. People in the entourage of the hero-chief

NOTE: In addition to the kinsfolk, many distinctive social categories
of people, from ordinary subjects to status-holders, are part of the hero-
chief's immediate entourage. Some of them are presented as groups and
others appear individually.

1. Status-holders:
Counselors (I, II, III)
Chief-Counselor, known as Shebakungu (III, IV)
Ritual experts (I, II, III, IV), as a group or identified in-
dividually according to office
Individuals with special political and ritual status, such as
First-born-of-the-land and Father-of-the-chief, who are de-
signated as kinsfolk of the hero-chief (I, III, IV)

2. People in special roles and functions:
Midwives (I, III, IV)
Swimmers (I)
Maidens (I, II, III)
Messengers (I, II, III)
Servants (I, III, IV)
Beautiful-One (II)
A young trapper and his brother (II)
Muhima (III)

3. Subjects (I, II, III, IV)

C. Pygmies

Closely linked with the entourage of the hero-chief, they form a distinctive
and independent category of people.

1. As a group (I, II, III, IV)
2. Individually named:
Nkurongo, a hunter (I)
Shekaruru and his son, hunters (II)
Meshe and Nkango, hunters (III)
Nyakabotyo, mother of Meshe (III)

    Nyakatwakari, mother of the Pygmies, and her daughter (III)
    3. Titled:
    Chief-Pygmy, called Mwamitwa (III, IV)
  D. Humans not in the immediate entourage of the hero-chief:
    1. An unnamed chief and his son (II)
    2. Shakwece and his two wives, Nyankuba and Nyakwabo (II)
    3. Chief Difficulties-do-not-come-together-with-others (III)
    4. Chief Kihoro (III)
    5. Chief Mutero Murimba (III)

III. *Divinities*
  A. Living in the subterranean world:
    1. Nyamurairi (I, II, III, IV)
    2. Sheburungu (I, II)
    3. Muisa (I, II, IV)
    4. Kahindo (I, II, III, IV)
    5. Hangi-of-Drum (IV)
    6. Nyarusumba (IV)
  B. Living in the air:
    Nkuba (Lightning) (I, II, III, IV)
  C. Living in the water:
    Musoka (I)
  D. Persons associated with these divinities but not commonly ranked
    as such:
    Nyamurairi's wife (III)
    Muisa's wife, Nyamwanda (II); his daughter (IV); his servants
      (I); maidens (IV)
    Sheburungu's people (II)
    Little children at Sheburungu's (I, II)
    Lightning's wife Nyamitondo (II)
  E. Spirits of the dead:
    Spirit of the paternal aunt of the hero-chief (III, IV)

IV. *Extraordinary beings*
  A. Living in the water:
    Mukiti, the water serpent (I, II, IV), and associated with him:
    the headman Kasiyembe and his envoy (I); his sister Musoka
    and her envoy (I); his daughter (IV); his people (I); his wife
    (I, II)
  B. Living in the forest:
    1. Kirimu, the dragon-ogre (I, II, IV)
    2. Kirimu's daughter, Ukano (II)

        3. Specter Mpaca (II)
    C. Living in the sky:
        Kiruka-nyambura (I)
    D. Living in a cave:
        Chief Mutero Murimba, his headman Kasiwa, his people (III)
V. *Animals*
    A. Not personified:
        Hunting dogs: unnamed (I) ; called Ndorobiro and Ngonde (II)
        or Bad-Luck and Fast-Eater (III)
    B. Occurring as chiefs:
        1. The chief of Buffaloes (II)
        2. The chiefs Itewa, Munkonde, Mburu, and Nteta (II)
        3. Bukumba (III)
        4. Chief Mburu (II)
    C. Personified and individualized:
        1. Birds:
            Hawk Kahungu (I, II)
            Sparrow (I, IV)
            Water Duck (III)
        2. Insects:
            Ant (IV)
            Bee (IV)
            Centipede (IV)
            Cricket (I, IV)
            Fly (IV)
            Spider (I, II, IV)
            Wasp (IV)
        3. Mammals:
            Aardvark (I)
            Bat (II, III, IV)
            Elephant (III)
            Hedgehog (I)
            Otter (III)
            Potto (III)
            Wild Boar (III)
        4. Various:
            Chameleon (III)
            Big-Crab (IV)
        5. Fabulous:
            Big-bird-born-by-itself (II)

31

D. Personified, acting as groups:
1. Bats, Baniyana (I)
2. Banamburu monkeys (II)
3. Buffaloes (II)
4. Baboons (II)
5. Red ants (II, III, IV)
6. Spiders, Banamitandi (I)
7. Various species of fish and crabs (I)
8. Warthogs (II)

VI. *Divinized celestial elements*
Star, Moon, Sun, Rain, Hail (I)

VII. *Manufactured objects as actors*
Adze (I)
Axes (I, II)
Bag (I, II)
Belt (I, II)
Billhook (I, II)
Drum (I)
Gaffs (I)
Hides (III)
Knife (III)
Rope (I)
Scepter (I, II, IV)

VIII. *Plants and trees*
Banana trees (I, II, III)
Bibatama-grasses (III)
Ficus tree (II)
Grasses (III)
Mibimbiro-trees (III)
Seeds (III)
Trees (III)
Wild banana tree (III)

In addition to these actors, a large number of beings are mentioned evoked, or referred to, mainly in the songs. They include persons (real and fictive; legendary, historical, and actually living; kinsfolk, friends, and strangers; titleholders and plain people; individuals and groups), divinities, animals of various kinds, plants and trees, and some minerals.

It would be wrong to think that the entire gamut of epic actors is exhaustively depicted in the four epics. In the epic fragment by Bitanda

Asani (summarized in App. II), the hero Mwindo interacts with beings not included in the other epics: Turtle, "who separates the waters with a whip" and "who carries Mwindo's magical bag," is part of his comitatus of animals; the hero engages in the game of dice with Gorilla (Muhumba), Kabaraka (brother of Lightning), and Big-Rock (Ukanga); he is overpowered by Sleep (Toro), Kahindo's brother who is unhappy because he has not received part of the bridewealth. In Wanowa's epic, retold by Sherungu (summarized in App. I), the major companion of Mwindo is the Pygmy Lulema (Lulema or Rurema is, according to Schebesta, 1952, p. 354, the name for the creator god among the Kivu Pygmies).

CULTURAL CONTENT

The Nyanga epics are vast storehouses packed with diverse cultural information. In poetic form they present an overwhelming enumeration of culture traits, giving explicit description of practices, beliefs, institutions, techniques, material culture, values, modes of living and thinking, and natural and human environments. Besides the normal flow of communication in the sequence of narrative episodes, highly condensed information is contained in songs, enumerations, catalogues, and aphoristic statements. By extracting from each text direct references to plants, trees, animals, objects, activities, techniques, persons, divinities, places, houses, patterns of living and thinking, and so on, one can compile an impressive inventory of Nyanga culture. There is no explanation, of course, for many of these cultural items, since the texts belong to the Nyanga people who know their content, usage, meanings, and cultural background. However monumental, such an inventory would be far from complete, for many items of Nyanga culture are mentioned in the epics. Nyanga culture is too intricate to be synthesized in a single set of literary documents. Like all other texts, the epics are selective; the information they give is limited, incomplete, and imprecise.

Certain broad aspects of Nyanga culture are lacking. The epics contain no reference to the elaborate circumcision rites or to the multiple initiations into membership in voluntary associations and cults. Most of the intricate rites connected with the birth and death of individuals, including ablutions and purifications, are not even reported. There is little detail on cults honoring the many divinities and almost no information on the complex rites and ideas that pertain to the hunting dogs. Only a few of the trapping devices and hunting and gathering techniques are described. No insight into the system of land tenure or the pattern of local control is given. The therapeutic system is not touched upon, and details on divination are scanty. Simple inventory lists of animals, plants, trees, divinities, techniques, and objects would be incomplete. On kinship and territorial organization, the data are limited. Although there is a great deal of information on political organization, the secret enthronement rites are only briefly mentioned.

Because the epics describe some aspects of Nyanga culture more elaborately than others, they tend to give an unbalanced view of its constituent parts. For example, the inventory of manufactured objects is detailed and exhaustive, whereas the lists of animals and divinities are sketchy. Information gained from the texts is sometimes misleading, obscure, or downright incorrect because the succinctness of the presentation leads to omissions, shortcuts, and condensations. And occasionally there are deliberate distortions of reality. Historical and cultural connections of the Nyanga, historical precedents of the epics, and personal connections of individual bards present difficulties. For example, cattle are briefly mentioned in the epics even though the Nyanga, living in a forest habitat, have no cattle. They are, however, exposed to the cattle tradition of the neighboring and related Hunde, and some Nyanga chiefs own cattle in Hundeland. Furthermore, the epic tradition also exists among the Hunde, and many Nyanga bards have, directly or indirectly, been associated with it.

Despite their pervasive cultural significance, the epics would not provide enough information for a detailed and balanced ethnography of the Nyanga people. Yet their significance is far-reaching, not merely for the direct information they give, but also for their implicit contribution to understanding the culture. These great texts provide Nyanga-made syntheses and interpretations of the culture. The points of view they present on the Nyanga world view and values, on the chief, the divinities, and the various activities, are fundamental to a better understanding of their world. The epics implicitly have much to offer on the Nyanga world view, ethical system, values, and ideology. For example, the temporal and, more important, the spatial organization of the epics provides abundant evidence on Nyanga thought. The transformation of the hero into a chief points to the deep values ascribed to chieftainship. In the following paragraphs I discuss some of the essential aspects of culture which are explicitly and implicitly contained in the epics.

PHYSICAL AND HUMAN ENVIRONMENT

Much of the epic action evolves in the forest and in the village. The rain forest is the world of the Nyanga and the village is the center of the world. The Nyanga think of the forest as an easy place for the Pygmies but as a dangerous place for them because they may encounter evil beings and because its inhabitants are stronger than those of the village. Yet the Nyanga spend a great deal of time in the forest, which is not merely the scene of daily, intermittent activity; it is also the place where groups of people spend long weeks in specially built hunting, trapping, and fishing camps. The forest for the Nyanga is a place of plenty and a refuge where a person can have privacy and be himself and where he can find happiness. This attitude is remarkably well demonstrated in a passage taken from the autobiography of Sherungu, a great bard (epic IV) and hunter:

> My thought is that if God said that people can change into whatever they wish, I would change into a lion so that I may eat meat every day. I would catch no other animals but wild pigs; I like their meat very much. I say that [the state of things created by] Europeanization is very rough. If there had been no Europeans around, I would have spent my time only in the forest, hunting animals. And if I failed to have dogs, I would go in search of animals with my spear only. I sit here, but I think only about the forest. And the very day that I shall depart here, it is certain that I shall go to buy other dogs in order to hunt [with them], as I did before. Perhaps I may still be able to kill many animals, as I did in earlier years. My heart is only with the thought of hunting. I also think that Shengano [Biebuyck] will give me a letter so that I must not work any more for Europeans and must not pay taxes. When I am like that, I shall no longer be visible in the village; my only work will be hunting. When a man who was used to hunting spends a month without going into the forest, he is very sad. It is this sadness I am experiencing now. The day that I leave here, if God gives me two more days on earth, I will go again into the forest to hunt.

The atmosphere of the forest and of the hunt pervades many passages in the epics. The hero himself is a restless wanderer who is constantly away from his village. Although the forest is never described in detail, its environment and its beings are always with us. A wide diversity of animals, plants, and fabulous beings of the forest turn up in the epics as actors, as victims, and as points of reference. Some forest activities, such as hunting with dogs, trapping, and honey harvesting, are depicted, but others are not mentioned at all.

The Nyanga live in a mountainous rain forest, and many of the mountains and hills are identified in the texts as historical reference points or as the names of villages and landed estates. Some places are fictive and symbolic as part of the epic atmosphere in which the events occur, but others are real and may be either inside or outside Nyangaland. The latter places have historical relevance for Nyanga east-west migrations and are also connected with the personal experiences of the bards and with the continuity of traditions that cut across the Nyanga and the neighboring Hunde. The rain forest is abundantly intersected by rivers and brooks, some large, some small. Part of the epic action is centered on water, primarily when the Water Serpent Mukiti is a participant and when the hero, in epic I, undertakes his aquatic journey in search of his paternal aunt. Important events happen at the so-called wading place, the term I use to translate *hitukuriro*. In fact, it is the spot where the village women draw water, slightly upstream from the places where people bathe and wade. Each village recognizes such places in a nearby river or brook. In Nyanga ablution and purification rites connected with birth and death the wading place is the location par excellence for the elaborate ceremonies. In tales and in some epics (I, IV), a great deal of action is staged in and around the pool (*iriba*), a natural enlargement of the river occasionally caused by a waterfall or by rapids. Some pools have deep, somber waters; others are gigantic whirlpools. They are places of mystery and awe near which enthronement rites for chiefs are sometimes held. The pool "where all the dry leaves collect in flowing down, where all the fallen tree trunks are obstructed" (I), is the preferred dwelling place of Mukiti, the water serpent, "the master of the unfathomable." This mythical abode of the water serpent is described in epic IV. Many parts of the forest are distinctively named by the Nyanga according to predominant resources and correlated activities, such as places where animals congregate to lick salt, where potters find clay, and where blacksmiths collect iron ore, and places with a dense concentration of raffia palms or *phrynium* leaves. These areas are not a background for any special events or activities. The abandoned village site, which is the center of certain activities and of an important ideology, is merely suggested.

In Nyanga tales probably the most important setting is the hunting camp (*kitanda*). Here the most incredible events, encounters, and activities take place: incest; conflicts between grandparents and grandchildren; revelation of dangerous secrets; trickery; encounters with spirits, ogres, and specters. Astonishingly, even though hunting and trapping pervade the epics, the hunting camp has no significance, undoubtedly because the core of epic action is the aristocratic milieu of the chief. The Nyanga

37

chief is not a hunter or a trapper; his life centers on the village, whereas the hunter and the trapper are oriented toward the hunting camp.

Banana groves, terminologically distinguished according to age, are interspersed in both the secondary and the virgin forest, at varying distances from villages and hamlets. The groves are the center of agricultural activities, since many subsidiary crops are grown in the younger groves. Some of the hero's herculean deeds are accomplished in banana groves.

Except for the chief's village, Nyanga villages are usually small and often comprise a number of outlying hamlets. They are widely scattered throughout the forest and, depending on kinship and political linkages, are interconnected by more or less established trails. The name of a village may be derived from a mountain, a hill, or a specific phytogeographic feature, or it may be the name of a dominant, resident kinship group or of a chief or a headman. No matter how far afield the epic action may lead, it is certain to return to the hero's father's village or to the hero's own village. Much of the action, however, is outside this village, in the forest, the river, or the subterranean or celestial world, or in other villages and hamlets.

A Nyanga village is situated on a level part of a hill, mountain, or slope, not far from a water resource. Thus people climb up to the village and descend when leaving it. Villages are, so to speak, hewn out of the secondary forest from which they are separated by a fence and by a cleared portion of land. A village has two entrances, one downstream and one upstream, which are closed at night by gates and traditionally are guarded by young fighters called *barai*. A village entrance is, of course, important as a separation between the outside world and the village dwellers. In the epics it is part of a frequently used formula to mark departure from and arrival at the village.

A village consists of houses aligned on both sides of an open plaza in the middle of which is erected the oft-mentioned men's house. When the adult men are at home they spend most of their time in the men's house, eating, smoking, drinking, talking, working, or performing rituals. The men's house is the heart of the village. In the epics it is the place where guests are received and often accommodated and also the site of encounters with important personages, such as the divinity Nyamurairi. The Nyanga build various types of houses (oval, beehive-shaped, rectangular, circular), and some of them serve as dwellings for guests or spirits. A number of epic scenes are transposed to particular houses. When the action leads into the celestial, the subterranean, or the aquatic world, the same village atmosphere and setting are preserved. The physical setting evoked is rarely unusual. Major exceptions are the cold, desolate subterranean place where Muisa lives (I), Ntumba's cave (I), and the cave of Mutero Murimba (III).

The social milieu in which the epic action evolves is highly intricate. Because of the village and forest atmosphere, it is a familiar and conventional Nyanga milieu, but because the hero is the son of a chief it is also to some extent aristocratic. Counselors, ritual experts, princes, women in special roles, various status-holders, and Pygmies are participants. In contrast with other epic traditions, however, the hero is not surrounded by warlords, warriors, and courtiers; he himself is not a great fighter. Instead, there is a unique association of the hero-chief with the Pygmies. A Nyanga chief is inconceivable without Pygmies, who are his hunters, his providers of honey, his singers and musicians, and his friends. They enjoy many economic privileges and assume vital ritual functions. The presence of Pygmies and the elaborate role they play in some texts give a very special social flavor to the epics. The interaction between the hero and divine and fabulous beings who act and think like humans is intensive. Most typical, perhaps, is the close relationship between the hero-chief and different categories of personified animals, mainly insects, birds, and bats. The mystic linkage between the chief and the hunting dogs, highly developed in Nyanga ritual, is clearly marked in the texts.

Strangers are almost entirely absent from the social milieu. Besides the animals and the divinities, who are usually transformed into allies or exterminated, the action encompasses a small group of kinsfolk, status-holders, subjects, and Pygmies. Among the hero's antagonists are a few chiefs who are not total strangers. They are rebellious chiefs, junior to the hero-chief or, like Mutero Murimba (III), decidedly of Nyanga culture. Specific references to people, divinities, places, and crops situate the action outside the immediate Nyanga milieu among the related Hunde and Kumbure. The Nyanga have numerous historical and cultural linkages and maintain matrimonial, friendship, and other exchange relationships with these groups.

The physical and social world is realistically evoked in the epics and in its broad outlines is fully familiar to all Nyanga. There is no attempt to depict the fantastic world of the fairy tale. An unusual epic atmosphere is only partly created when the action leads to the extraterrestrial spheres of the water, the sky, and the subterranean world, but even there the events are transposed to the familiar setting of villages, banana groves, and men's houses. The plainness of the scenery is transcended by the extraordinary circumstances surrounding the events, by the heroic deed in its physical and spiritual dimensions, and by continued cosmic interaction.

THE LANGUAGE

Nyanga is a member of the so-called branch of Bantu languages in the Niger-Congo family. It has certain similarities with Hunde, spoken to the east, and with Lega, spoken to the southwest. Its relationship with Komo, in the west, is much more distant. The exact taxonomic position of the Nyanga language within the classification of Bantu languages is far from definitive. Nyanga has been classified with the Lega group and separated from Hunde and Nande (Burssens, 1954, p. 23). Meeussen (1953, p. 386) perceives a loose relationship of Nyanga with Lega and a possibly closer relationship with Nande. Within his general zone D, Guthrie (1948, p. 40) places Nyanga and Konzo-Ndandi (Nande) in group 40, in contrast with Lega (group 20) and Hunde (group 50). The situation is unequivocally complex, partly because of misconceptions as to the nature, the composition, and the geographical extension of tribal and linguistic groups in this part of eastern Zaire. For historical and cultural reasons, it is impossible to separate the Nyanga completely from such Hunde subgroups as the Bashari and the Bafuna. There is historical evidence to show that Lega influences have worked on the Nyanga and that there is a gradual merger of Nyanga via Bukumbure into certain southern Nande (Konzo) groups and via Tiri and Asa into eastern Komo.

The long epic texts afford an excellent opportunity to study the Nyanga language and Bantu languages in general. The bards have a thorough knowledge of their language and manipulate it with remarkable skill. Their abundant and varied vocabulary and their refined sense of grammar enable them to express the finest shades and the most delicate nuances of meaning. The bards are poets in the fullest sense, delighting in well-chosen words, sonorous word combinations, unusual epithets, patronyms, formulas, the poetic turn of a sentence, and many other stylistic devices. The texts are formulated in the ordinary Nyanga spoken and understood by the people, but the richness, diversity, amplitude, and poetry of the language are far beyond the capacity of the common speaker or narrator. The choice of words and expressions is incredibly rich and nuanced. The metaphorical usage of standard verbs and other expressions is sometimes carried to an extreme.

The bards weave songs, proverbs, and meditations harmoniously into their narratives. Above all, they are masters at keeping in unison with the basic percussion system, speaking faster or more slowly as required, making sophisticated use of elisions, adding short, well-placed words to their songs to satisfy the rhythm, changing the tense or aspect of a verb, adding suffixes to differentiate the meaning, reduplicating the stem, or repeating the expression. The bards avoid archaisms and secret and cryptic formulations. In other words, the average Nyanga individual can easily understand the words and the general content of the narrative, although the depth of his perception is determined by his own knowledge and degree of maturity.

Loanwords are rare; the very few that do occur are Nyangaized French or Swahili words. Entire sentences, passages, and songs, however, are sometimes formulated in the Kishari variant of the neighboring Hunde language, particularly in epics II and III and to some extent in epic IV. It must be emphasized that all four epics were written down in eastern Nyangaland, in areas that are close to the Hunde. In those areas all Nyanga understand, and many speak, Hunde as a second language, so that in ordinary speech they can easily shift from one language to the other. More important, the epic tradition is not restricted to the Nyanga, but extends to the Hunde as well. To my knowledge no full-fledged epics have been written down among the Hunde, but in making this statement I am relying on Nyanga testimony. The Nyanga singers gave me the names of several Hunde epic bards, including a woman. (Unfortunately I had no opportunity to visit them and listen to their narratives.) The individual history of learning the epic as recounted by bards whose texts I was able to record points to Hundeland and to Hundeized or Nyangaized Pygmies.

HISTORY

The Nyanga epics contain few direct historical statements, but indirectly, and in symbolic form, they tell much about Nyanga history.

It is important to note at the outset that the epics do not refer to the recent history of the late nineteenth and twentieth centuries, despite the tumultuous events of the period. Potential epic material might seem to exist, for example, in the raids and exactions of the Barungwana (as the Nyanga designated mercenaries of the Arab and Arabicized overlords who operated in eastern Zaire), in the fierce and lingering feuds between political factions coveting the paramount chieftainship under colonial rule, in the overwhelming burdens imposed by the rubber trade and the porterage of goods under the Congo Free State and at later stages of the colonial regime, in the upheavals brought about in the early 1940s by the

Kitawala uprisings, and in the exile of the Belgian-appointed paramount chief of the Nyanga and the attendant factionalism. These difficult episodes or phases in recent Nyanga history are not even suggested in the epics. In general, the Western influence on the Nyanga finds no expression in the epics, and there is barely a trace of it in the few Nyangaized loanwords from French and Swahili that do appear, primarily in epic I.

The early hero-chiefs, Mwindo and Kabutwakenda, are listed neither among the primordial ancestors of the Nyanga nor among the immediate ancestors of the chiefs. There is no unified ancestral genealogy for all the Nyanga chiefs. Yet many of them claim a common descent, basically through two parallel genealogies. In one version, Katukamumpoko (lit., What-comes-out-of-the-banana-tree) is the primordial ancestor who originated from far in the north (the Nyanga say that he came from Misri, the name for Egypt). His grandson Mururiyana (son of Rikesa) was established in Bunyoro (Uganda), as was also Munyanga, Mururiyana's son. One of Munyanga's sons, Mukobya, the Father-of-chiefs, migrated southwestward into present-day Zaire, where he established himself in Bwito (west of Lake Edward, which is called Ngesi), near the Kishibe Bukumbure and Ntongi Birundure mountains. Mukobya settled there with the ancestors of various Hunde chiefs (founders of different Hunde subgroups called Bashari, Bafuna, and Banyungu) and of the Bakumbure-Basimba (who were later partly submerged by pastoral immigrants from Rwanda). From Bwito, Mukobya migrated westward and southwestward into present Nyangaland, where several of his sons founded autonomous dynasties. The second genealogical version, accepted by chiefs in the Kisimba area, names Kibumba (Fashioner) who lived in Toro (Uganda) as the primordial ancestor. His son, Ringesa, and two grandsons, Ikunga and Mueshera, migrated to the region of the Mokoto lakes (in eastern Hundeland). The two grandsons separated. Ikunga, the father of Katukamumpoko, had three grandsons: Barungu, founder of the Basimba groups in Bwito, and Kindi and Iriba, founders of chiefly houses known as Bakumbure among the Nyanga.

In the Hunde genealogies provided by Schumacher (1949, passim) the names of Mwindo and Kabutwakenda do not appear. The closest historical reference to the Mwindo figure is given by Schumacher for the Hunde (1949, p. 229). He identifies this figure as a personage who holds the position of commander in chief of the army and whose title is Muhindo (Hunde pronunciation of Mwindo). No such title exists among the Nyanga, and we can only speculate as to whether or not the Nyanga might originally have celebrated the feats of such a warrior lord in the epics. At any rate, as he appears in the epics, Mwindo and his counterpart Kabutwakenda are not great warriors. No emphasis is placed on their fighting skills, and no great battle scenes are described. Most of the confrontations are between individuals, and the stress is primarily on trickery and magic and on subsequent reconciliation.

What is probably the most substantial historical reference relates to the relationships between the Nyanga and the Pygmies, particularly the quasi-mystic association between Pygmies and chiefs. In the vast region that extends south of the Bambuti Pygmies of Ituri, so carefully investigated by Schebesta and Turnbull, Pygmy influences are strongly evidenced in the ethnohistorical traditions and the political and ritual systems of some peoples (Schumacher, 1949, 1950), particularly the Nyanga, Hunde, Havu, Tembo, and Shi (and east of this region in Rwanda). For example, among the southern Shi, the Havu, the Hunde, and the Nyanga, the Pygmy called *mwamitwa* (Chief-Pygmy) plays an essential role in the enthronement rituals of chiefs, a role that is amply emphasized in the epics (see also Schumacher, 1949, pp. 185, 250). According to Hunde traditions, groups of Pygmies were preestablished in the lands that the Hunde occupied. The Lega had already crossed some of these lands and left small groups behind in their drive farther south and southwest (ibid., p. 185; Moeller, 1936, p. 409 and passim). The same Hunde traditions state that the founding ancestors Kinyungu and Kashari, accompanied by Pygmies under the leadership of Katembo ka Ntare, migrated from Bwito in the north (Schumacher, 1949, p. 223). Other traditions speak about Pygmies who voluntarily joined Hunde chiefs after having been well received on their first encounter (ibid., p. 224). Nyanga accounts follow somewhat parallel lines; the early ancestors of the chiefs arrived with Pygmies and found preestablished groups in Nyangaland, such as the Bahimbi whom they describe as Pygmy-like and as great hunters in the deep forest. These Bahimbi, some of whom still exist in northern Nyangaland, were probably an early mixture of Lega and Pygmies (note that Ihimbi is the general setting in which the events of epic I are placed). Subsequently, there was a flux and reflux of Pygmies established among the Nyanga and the Hunde. The most important Pygmy group in Nyangaland is the Baremba, who speak their own variety of Hunde and trace direct kinship linkages with Pygmies of the same name among the Bafuna subgroup of the Hunde.

These basic facts are recalled in the epics. The Pygmies are simply there in the kingdom of the hero's father and of the hero-chief; they did not come from any other place (epics I and II). A passage in epic III, however, evokes the encounter of Chief Mutero Murimba and the

Pygmies, whom he had not previously known; and, in the epic IV, Kabutwakenda acquires Pygmies while searching for singers. In general, the Pygmies enjoy high esteem and lofty status among the Nyanga. The term *Batwa*, by which they are identified, is used in a broader sense to designate a person who has light feet, is an expert hunter of game, precedes the others in removing dew from the plants, and is a skillful and generous distributor of game meat. The Pygmies are not merely considered outstanding hunters and expert collectors of the coveted honey, but they are praised as musicians and singers and their expertise in certain kinds of divination is regarded as noteworthy. The Pygmies themselves are highly conscious of these qualities. Kanyangara, one of the Baremba Pygmies, sang as follows to the accompaniment of his zanza:

> We Pygmies do not cultivate;
> We spend our time with the drums.
> We do know the work (of singing and music making).

In the epics the Pygmies' skills are clearly illustrated. As among the Hunde (Schumacher, 1949, pp. 231, 238–239), the Nyanga Pygmies enjoy many privileges pertaining to hunting, collecting, and harvesting of food crops. There is a mild joking relationship (*byabeshe*) between them and the Nyanga, whom, except for the chief, they laughingly call the ignorant (*barimi*). Pygmy divinities, Meshemutwa and Nkango, are worshiped by many Nyanga. Most important, however, is the Pygmies' relationship to the chief. The role of *mwamitwa* (Chief-Pygmy) is fundamental in the chief's enthronement ceremonies; he brings to these ceremonies the honey with which the bodies of the chief and the ritual wife are rubbed, the hide of the flying squirrel from which the skull cap for the ritual wife is made, and the small arrows and a bark quiver which are essential part of the chief's regalia. That the enthronement rites are impossible without the presence of *mwamitwa* is emphasized in the epics. It is also his privilege, and through him that of his kinsfolk, to hunt with the expert dogs which the Nyanga chief must possess. The Pygmies also provide the chief with a Pygmy wife (*isabiro*) without the transfer of bridewealth; she has special charge of the chief's black hunting dog. Their overall relationship with the Nyanga chiefs is intensive, a fact underscored by the tales. They are the friends of the chief and constantly receive privileges and copious gifts of food, beer, utensils, and women for their services. In the tales the close bond between the two is mainly conceived in terms of reciprocal acts of generosity. In a magnificent tale narrated by Sherungu (the bard of epic IV), a Pygmy liberates the chief's beloved wife, who had been buried under a huge rock by her jealous co-wives. The Pygmy heals and feeds her,

44

then takes her back to the chief, receiving in return hunting dogs and two women. In another tale the Pygmies become a source of continued life for a chief because they kill the Dragon-Ogre Kirimu who had destroyed all the women. In other tales they act as able climbers of trees, helpers to people lost in the forest, renowned hunters, collectors of honey, and trustworthy messengers of the chief. Sometimes the supernatural ability to fly is attributed to them in the tales. In epic III the Pygmies appear as culture heroes bringing the knowledge of fire to Chief Mutero Murimba, who rules a land of darkness and cold.

One can only speculate whether some cultural features mentioned in the epics might refer to very early stages of Nyanga and pre-Nyanga history: life in caves (Mutero Murimba in III); the advent of fire (III); the coming of the hunting dogs (Mwindo purchases them in III); the introduction of certain culture elements. The epics are not primarily etiological in tone. Nevertheless, the origin of certain customs—the consecration of women as wives of Lightning, the dedication of particular paraphernalia to Lightning or to the Spirit of Good Fortune, and the fact that chiefs do not hunt or pass through purification rites connected with the birth or death of close relatives—is suggested in simple terms. Such explanations may be indicative of historical antecedents, such as the introduction of a new cult or a new type of cult paraphernalia, and of changes in custom as a result of particular historical experiences. In epic II the introduction of agriculture, or at least the origin of plantain growing, is suggested. Mwindo learns to cultivate a banana grove from his sister Nyamitondo who is married to Lightning. The Nyanga are in mind and spirit good hunters, trappers, collectors, and, in some areas, fishermen as well. Nevertheless, they practice agriculture, which centers in the banana grove. They explicitly state in their ethnotraditions that when they entered the vast forest stretches they now inhabit they found banana groves with which they were unfamiliar and which had been left by the Banampamba (a Lega group).

The historical bond between Hunde and Nyanga is illustrated throughout the epics, more or less explicitly. The bond is not reflected merely in the fact that, mainly in epics II and III, some songs are sung entirely in Hunde, but also in the recurrence of divinities and statusholders who exist among both peoples. Kahindo is a purely Hunde divinity who appears in the epics, although she has a Nyanga counterpart in Kahombo. The references to cattle found in Hundeland and to crops typical of the savanna lands inhabited by the Hunde, and marginally by some Nyanga, are also indicative of these bonds.

45

Another aspect of Nyanga history deserves brief mention. For the Nyanga the residence of the divinities is centered east of their country, beyond the land of the Hunde, in and around the extinct and active volcanoes that straddle the borderlands between Zaire, Uganda, and Rwanda. These volcanoes, known to the outside world as Virunga, are for the Nyanga the center of the subterranean world (*kwirunga*). Prominent among them is the active volcano known to the outside world by the Hunde term Nyamulagira. The Nyanga divinity Nyamurairi, chief of the subterranean world with whom the heroes have several confrontations, is none other than the volcano Nyamulagira, or at least the being that is thought to live in it and to activate it. For the Hunde, the Havu, the Tembo, and the more remote Shi, the volcano Nyamulagira is the center of the spirit world; there the divinities reside and the souls of the dead ultimately settle (Schumacher, 1949, pp. 183, 186, 197, 200). These volcanoes are not visible from Nyangaland, but tremors caused by them are felt and are ascribed to the anger of traveling ancestor souls. In their earlier migrations from Uganda and during their sojourn in Bwito, the Nyanga knew the volcanoes; after their departure they retained them as the center of their world of divinities and ancestors.

Historical features, relating to the chieftainship also appear in the epics. Ideal Nyanga legal principles stipulate that the chief-elect must be the son of a chief's ritual wife, but in practice, according to evidence from both the Nyanga and the Hunde, this rule is not always observed. The appearance in the epics of the heroic son not necessarily born of the ritual wife suggests, somewhat cryptically, variations in the way a chief is selected. The proliferation of new, independent chiefdoms formed from previously unified entities is characteristic of Nyanga history. The divisions, however, usually sprang from the competition between half brothers. In epics I, II, and III the formation of separate chiefdoms is set forth in somewhat different terms, through the emergence of the heroic child. In epic IV conflict for the same chiefdom is between half brothers or between uncle and nephew. Conflict between chiefdoms, violent at times, is historically known; it is reflected, for example, in epic III in the struggles between Mwindo and other jealous chiefs.

In summary, the epics do contain a number of historical references, though few are directly stated. To detect and understand them requires considerable insight into the broader cultural and historical continuum of related and intermingled populations in eastern Zaire, of which the average Nyanga listener is fully aware.

ECONOMY AND MATERIAL CULTURE

The epics provide an extensive inventory of Nyanga material culture items, particularly utensils, tools, ornaments, and paraphernalia. The itemization is mostly a simple enumeration, since participants in the culture would need no indications about the form or usage of objects named. Wooden items mentioned include dishes, cups, stools, beds, dog bells, fire drills, pointed sticks, gaffs, beer troughs, bellows, arrows, whistles, zanzas, and doors. Articles made of iron or copper with wooden shafts and handles are spears, adzes, axes, knives (of various types), billhooks, hammers, razors, hoes, bells, bracelets, and rings. Epic exaggerations add iron shoes, hats, shirts, pants, and copper zanzas to the inventory. Copper-plated wooden chairs and copper scepters and staffs belong to the chiefly milieu. Other items, primarily representing a chief's paraphernalia, are made of animal hides: belts of bongo or wild pig's hide, skullcaps of the hide of flying squirrel, sacred bundles of genet hide, pouches for fire drills, and wrist protectors. Pieces manufactured from fibers include bags, ropes, shields, wicker plates, mats, belts, raffia bundles, nets, baskets, and sheaths. Cloth and quivers are made of bark; jars, pots, and pipes are fashioned from clay; crests and scepters are made of animal hair and tails; beads, shells, cowries, claws, feathers, and fangs are used for ornaments. The use of natural products, such as calabashes, whetting stones, or resinous glue, is also acknowledged in the epics. Cosmetics are made of red powder and various oils. There are references to different types of houses, to furniture, and to the layout of the village. Very few of the thirty-nine types of trapping devices, such as pitfalls, *mpota*-snares, and *byoo*-traps, are mentioned. Except for drums and zanzas, musical instruments are not named. All in all, the inventory of material culture is impressive, though far from exhaustive; it is particularly weak on the wide diversity of fishing, trapping, and hunting equipment, on body ornaments, and on specialized tools, such as those of the blacksmith. Except for epic I, where one of Mwindo's songs is mainly a catalogue of objects, the texts make no attempt to give systematic inventories. Thus the fine differences within types of objects are lost. For example, the hero is born with a shoulder bag in epics I and II, both of which use the diminutive form of the general term for bag (*inku*), even though the Nyanga make at least five terminological distinctions among bags, depending on whether they are made of bark, vines, hide, raffia, or leaves.

The importance of hunting, and to a lesser extent of trapping, is stressed in the epics, especially in II. Although few details as to actual hunting methods and techniques are supplied, the central significance of hunting dogs clearly emerges. Trained hunting dogs (*ntoso*), as sacred beings, are surrounded by numerous rituals; they are economically very valuable (Biebuyck, 1956*a*). Enthroned chiefs must own such dogs, but commoners may also possess them. Various cults demand that a hunting dog be consecrated to the divinities. The mystic bond between dogs and divinities is manifested when hunting dogs refuse to hunt. Sherungu, in his autobiography, retells an epic he heard from a certain Rwanowa while they were living in a hunting camp. When Sherungu's expert dog repeatedly refused to hunt, Sherungu tied him up and refused to feed him for several days. To convince Sherungu that he must release the dog, Rwanowa told a long epic which had the following conclusion:

> You, Muriro Sherungu, listen. This is the reason I told you to release your dog. You must not tie him up and harass him because he refuses to hunt, for animals have their owners. You cannot kill game unless you first receive authorization from the divinities. So then, if an expert hunting dog runs away from the hunt, twice or oftener, do not harass him, because you do not know why he refuses to hunt. Perhaps he wants to avoid hunting because he had been instructed by a certain divinity that, should he go into the forest, he might be injured there.

Hunting dogs are sometimes referred to as *nyamuheshero saremene*, a Hunde-derived term meaning blacksmith of irons that are difficult to make, to empasize that dogs assist in killing animals that are otherwise difficult to hunt. Dogs are major protagonists in the tales. A lasting enmity opposes Dog and Leopard: Dog prefers meat that is cooked whereas Leopard likes it raw; Dog likes the warmth of men's houses better than the cold of the forest. Above all, Dog manifests himself as man's beloved, helpful, and alert companion. He stole fire from Nyamurairi and gave it to man; he taught men the secret ways of understanding animal language; he discovered, in a foreign land, the priceless banana for men exhausted from famine. As a hunter, Dog is man's somewhat involuntary helper; his skills as a hunter were divulged by Chicken, and therefore Dog continues to seek revenge against Chicken by eating it. Because of his skill in hunting, Dog is favored by powerful men and chiefs. In the epics the dog is the faithful and useful aide and companion to the hero-chief and to the Pygmies.

The prohibition against chiefs participating in the hunt is stressed in epics I and II. In both texts Mwindo explicitly receives from the divinities a direct order never to hunt: "Never a day you should kill an animal of the forest or of the village or even an insect." The practical, moral, and mystic reasons for the stricture are intimately combined: the big hunt is dangerous; a chief must not be allowed to die a natural death; a chief's power must be fully preserved, and any loss of blood (caused, e.g., by injury) would weaken that power; a chief is a divine embodiment; he is the counterpart of Nyamurairi; Nyamurairi is not a killer, but a guardian and protector of animals.

Few gathering techniques are enumerated, except for the harvesting of honey, regarded as a great delicacy by both Nyanga and Pygmies. Banana growing is the central activity in agriculture, and the hero performs courageous deeds in and around the banana grove. The importance of bananas provides, in epic I, the occasion for a detailed synthesis of the different stages in agriculture. Much of the food mentioned in the epics is made of banana paste (*buntu*), the principal component of the Nyanga diet, combined with meat. Other crops and foods listed include eleusine, beans, peas, corn, *isusa*-vegetables, and potatoes. Although banana beer is mentioned in all the epics, references to it do not convey its real significance to the Nyanga in gift giving, exchanges, and diet.

The giving of gifts is strongly emphasized in the epics: gifts of courtship, hospitality, and departure; rewards for services; and tribute. The gifts may be animals (goats, chickens, cattle, dogs), game meat, food, beer, crops, women, or objects (bark cloth, whistles, stools, spears, scepters, zanzas, copper bracelets, bags, *butea*-rings). The standing exchange relationship between the Nyanga and the Pygmies is indicated to some extent; game meat, honey, bark cloth, and certain vines and fibers for making rope are given in return for wooden dishes, pots, iron tools, food, and beer. Trade relationships with the Hunde and the Nyanga-related Bukumbure-Basimba of Bwito are not suggested. The Nyanga use *butea*-money as payment for goats, dogs, oil, and iron tools purchased from the Hunde, and for fish, salt, beads, cowries, polished shells, copper bracelets, and eleusine acquired from the Bwito populations. Nyanga techniques and material objects are extraordinarily diversified; and the epics provide insight into this wealth.

KINSHIP, FAMILY AND MARRIAGE

A small-scale kinship structure underlies the epics, as is evident from the range of kinship terms used and of kinship relationships described. The network of kinship relationships in which the hero participates comprises the categories of father and mother; father's wives; father's sister

(Iyangura) and her husband (Mukiti); maternal uncles (and their wives and children, casually mentioned; not real, but classificatory); matrilateral cross-cousins; full sister and her husband (Lightning); uterine brother (born of parthenogenesis); consanguineal half brothers and half sisters; half brother's wife (casually mentioned); wives and father-in-law; children; half brother's children; maternal grandfather (casually listed in one epic).

From this small world of kinship—that is, small on the African scale—many important relationships (e.g., father's father, father's brothers, father's brothers' children, father's sisters' children, wives' brothers, etc.) are omitted. The kinship world is reduced even further because other relationships are barely mentioned in the epics. In epic I, for example, the existence of Mwindo's six half sisters is merely implied. In the same epic the wives of the hero's father, other than his mother, are simply designated, as are the hero's own wives. In epic II the paternal aunt and her husband Mukiti are given no prominence; the hero's full sister and her husband are important actors early in the epics but disappear completely in later episodes. In epic III the hero's full brother (born of parthenogenesis) vanishes after performing a few initial feats; the hero's wives and children, though enumerated in elaborate detail, are not active participants in the events. The reduction of the kinship horizon within which the hero-chief operates is in conformity with Nyanga ideology about the chiefs. According to the Nyanga, "the chief does not belong to a kinship group," meaning that he is, so to speak, a world in and for himself, that he is a person over whom no single group of kinsmen has power, a person who is above and beyond kinship bonds.

Some of the chief's special characteristics are analyzed eleswhere in this study. At this point, however, it should be recalled that the chief's mother is a close relative of his father and that the chief's sisters and daughters are normally not married for bridewealth. These features automatically reduce the world of kinship centered in the chief: his mother's people are his own people; therefore, the chief has no real maternal uncles; his unmarried sisters' and daughters' children are his own children. The chief's brothers, unless one of the half brothers becomes chief as the result of a scission, are believed to be remote from him (e.g., despite their fixed political and ritual roles they cannot aspire to succeed him).

Each epic has its own kinship focus and its own unique features. In epic I the relationships with father and with the paternal aunt are clearly delineated. In epic II the special connections between the hero and his uterine sister are underscored, even though they are short-lived. In general, kinship relationships are kept in the background in this epic, whereas the connections of the hero with the Pygmies are given prominence. Epic III makes the bonds with mother and the spirit of the paternal aunt slightly more important. Epic IV offers perhaps the widest range of significant kinship relationships: the heroic sons and their father; the father's co-wives; the wives of the hero's son; the paternal aunt.

The hero's father is a chief in all the epics. In Nyanga social practice the relationships between a chief and the son selected to become his successor are reduced to a minimum, since that son, as child of the chief's ritual wife, normally neither is born nor lives in his father's village. In the epics, however, the situation is more complex. The heroic son who is destined to become a chief is born in his father's village, where his mother resides. In all instances there is initial tension. In epics I and II the father makes the unnatural request that his wives should bear no sons. When the preferred wife later gives birth to a son, the father wants to destroy the child. The story is particularly long and detailed in epic I: the father consecutively attacks the newborn son with spears, buries him alive, and has him thrown into a river. But the heroic stature of the son is too much for the father, who finally flees and, after being found by the son, recognizes him. In epic II the conflict is less protracted; the father, soon compelled to recognize his son's stature decides to let him live and prove himself. The situation is different in epics III and IV, for it is the hero's mother who is rejected by her husband because of barrenness. The chief quickly reconciles with her at the insistence of his Chief-Counselor and because of her steadiness in times of stress. There is no hostility toward the heroic son in epics III and IV; rather, in epic IV, the father exhibits indecision and ambiguity in his dealings with his sons. On the whole the father is depicted neither with sympathy nor as a prominent leader. This representation is particularly noticeable in epic I, which portrays the father as guilty of ill-conceived decisions and as impetuous, cruel, heartless, contemptuous, weak, and cowardly. When compelled by circumstances to act differently, however, he shows contrition and somewhat misplaced generosity.

The image presented of the hero's mother in the epics is, to a certain extent, that of a suffering woman, a *mater dolorosa*. Her role is sharply reduced in epic II, but is is better developed in epic I. In the latter, as the preferred (or beloved) wife of the chief, she falls into a state of abjection as despised wife simply because she bears a son in opposition to her husband's wishes to have only daughters. Before her son's birth she suffers a prolonged pregnancy, is ridiculed by her co-wives, and is very insecure. After giving birth to her son she must passively endure threats from her husband and accept an unjustifiable loss of status. The heroic sons's attitude to his mother is one of tenderness. While she is entertaining sad thoughts because of the delays in her son's birth, he invisibly brings her firewood, water, and vegetables. After he is born he protects her against his father's spear. Later, when he is taken away by Lightning to be purified in the celestial realm, he takes leave of his mother with the touching, honorific phrase: "My mother who carried me (in the cradling rope)."

It is astonishing that in epics I and II the hero's mother has no status ranking, either as ritual wife (*mumbo*) or as principal wife (*nyabana*), whereas she is the chief's principal wife in epic III. In epic IV the mother of the gentle hero Kabutwakenda is also the chief's principal wife while the mother of the villain Mwindo is his ritual spouse. Both epics devote much attention to the mother. In epic III, as the daughter of Hangi-of-Drum, she is possibly of divine origin. Nevertheless, she is rejected by the chief because of her barrenness and is physically removed from his homestead. The loneliness of the suffering woman is vividly portrayed. Then suddenly she is pregnant "without a male having given the pregnancy to her." The pregnancy is long and the delivery is slow and painful; her heroic son Kabutwakenda immediately leaves her forever. Soon afterward, however, the chief reconciles with her at the insistence of his Chief-Counselor; by bearing another heroic son, Mwindo, she regains her status. When her son is grown she settles with him and his people in a separate village. Afterward her son disappears for many years; when he finally returns he finds her and his wife, who remained with her, in a state of desolation, abandoned by his people and his Pygmies. Mwindo's first task is to rebuild her village; when his mother shows vindictiveness against the people who abandoned her, Mwindo rebukes her. The role and the position of the two mothers of the heroes Kabutwakenda and Mwindo are even more complicated in epic IV. Both heroes are very close to their respective mothers. A keen competition between the two women for status and fame is activated mainly by Mwindo's mother, but the moderation of Kabutwakenda, the mediating role of the father, and the power of sibling ethics help to mitigate the conflict. Epic IV is the only one to evoke the tension and the divisive forces that operate in the sibling group, yet at the same time it clarifies the manner in which the Nyanga have alleviated this problem in the royal family. Although the precise and highly restrictive rules of succession and status distribution are overt, succession is not automatic. The ultimate designation of the successor rests with a small body of principal counselors, who are guided both by the personal characteristics of possible successors and by oracles.

One of the most fascinating kinship features is the role and social significance of the paternal aunt. In contrast with the other texts, epic II seems to ignore her importance; she is merely mentioned as the sister of the chief who is married to the Water Serpent Mukiti. Yet it may not be pure coincidence that the hero's mother in epic II is called Iyangura, the name used in epic I for his paternal aunt. In Nyanga custom the chief's ritual wife, and even his principal spouse, may be selected from among his half sisters. The mother of a child of such a union thus is also the paternal aunt. It is possible that in epic II these two persons are combined in Mwindo's mother; hence, because of the higher, indelible status attached to a sister-wife, epic II is the only one in which the hero's mother does not suffer hardships or lose her status.

The social significance of the paternal aunt, called "father-female" in Nyanga terminology, is clearly illustrated in epic I. The hero, rejected and wronged by his father, searches for his paternal aunt and overcomes many obstacles; she liberates him from the drum in which he was locked, ensuring, so to speak, his second or new birth. Thereafter the hero and his paternal aunt are linked by deep, personal bonds: the hero cares for her and she is filled with solicitude for him. When Mwindo travels in the subterranean world he communicates with her by means of a rope. On the day of the great council she sits in glory with the hero and his father. Mwindo uses the tenderest of epithets and praise names for her; she is "birth giver," "mother mine of the cradling string" and "aunt Iyangura of the body." Similar praises are used every day when a Nyanga refers to a paternal aunt; she is called "mother of the ladle with four sides," indicating that one promptly receives food from her, and "mother of the package that contains another one," meaning that one receives many things from her. A Nyanga has deep respect for his paternal aunt. As a young person he receives moral teachings from her; she advises and warns him; she speaks on his behalf. To scorn, to fool, or to beat her is a serious wrong requiring remission of payments and other sanctions. From certain points of view the paternal aunt acts like a mother; it is not uncommon for her to breast-feed her brother's child while the mother is away in the forest. In Nyanga custom many women who are not married are "married" to a divinity and raise children with men of their choice who have no social rights to the children. Thus the bond between a man and his paternal aunt may be very close and intimate, because they live in the same village if she is a spirit-wife. Likewise, the spirit of a deceased paternal aunt continues her role of guardian and adviser, as seen in dream interpretations and in cults. In epics III and IV the spirit of the paternal aunt exercises a compelling influence on the hero whenever he is involved in a critical situation.

The social significance of the maternal uncle somewhat parallels that of the paternal aunt. On the whole, he is a helpful adviser when the hero faces difficulties. Certain ritual privileges adhere to maternal uncles, but their role is not so significant as it is among other populations of eastern Zaire, such as the Lega or the Bembe. In the epics maternal uncles function mainly as blacksmiths who strengthen the hero's body by forging it. It is noteworthy that they are named after bats (Munkonde, Kakuku, Kikwe) and that the symbolic group name is Baniyana, "the hundreds," because of their large numbers. On the other hand, there is no indication that the hero's mother is one of the Bats; on the contrary, in the one epic that mentions her origins she is said to be the daughter of Hangi-of-Drum. We may conclude, therefore, that the hero's maternal uncles are not the kinsmen of his mother, an assessment that is in accord with the special social atmosphere pervading the epics. The hero is the son of a chief and his destiny is to become a chief. The successor to chieftainship is, in reality or in fiction, considered to be the son of the chief's ritual wife, that is, of a woman who is a close agnatic relative of her husband. The chief therefore can have no real maternal uncles; rather, his own father and his close male agnatic relatives are his maternal uncles. Yet, because of certain concepts of perpetual kinship, the chief has distant, classificatory maternal uncles. This feature is linked with Nyanga ethnohistory and chiefs' genealogies. The latter sometimes suggest that an ancient chief received his ritual wife from a brother or from a Hunde group; if so, the descendants of the brother or of the Hunde group are still claimed as the chief's perpetual maternal uncles. The Bats in the epic designate these remote, perpetual maternal uncles. On the other hand, the fact that the hero is forged by them (i.e., he absorbs their power) indicates that the hero-chief synthesizes in his person the power that is otherwise divided between the patrilineal and the matrilineal sides.

The epics are informative about the negotiations, the symbolic arrangements, the bridewealth, and the ceremonies in Nyanga marriages (epic I), the status ranking of wives in the polygynous household (epics I, III, and IV), and the competition among wives (epic IV). Among the most interesting and original aspects of the matrimonial system as described in the epics are the freedom and the frequency with which women are given and exchanged, either as compensation for a service or as reward for an achievement. There are numerous examples. At his enthronement Mwindo receives maidens from his maternal uncles, from his Pygmies, from his father, and from Shemwami (epic I). When Lightning brings Mwindo back to earth, he is given a maiden by Mwindo's father (epic I). Having helped him destroy Big-Bird, Mwindo's sister returns to her husband Lightning with two maidens provided by her father (epic II). The Pygmy Shekaruru obtains a maiden from a chief whose son he had healed (epic II). Nyamurairi gives his daughter to Mwindo for successfully performing various herculean tasks (epic III). Having overpowered Lightning and secured his allegiance, Mwindo promises to consecrate a maiden to him. Chief Mutero Murimba recieves several wives with special status on the occasion of his enthronement (epic III).

These illustrations bear on different Nyanga customs and transpose us again into a typical chief's milieu. In addition to his commoner wives (*bowe*), the chief must obtain several women during the enthronement rites; some of them are close agnatic relatives, while others are mandatorily given by certain officeholders, the Pygmies, and the maternal uncles. No bridewealth is transferred for these wives. In turn, the chief provides some individuals, primarily members of the college of ritual experts, with wives; no bridewealth is demanded. Many women, both in the chief's and in commoner families, are consecrated as spirit-wives to certain divinities (Nyamurairi, Muhima, Lightning, etc.). These women can bear children with men (married or unmarried) of their choice (a choice heavily influenced by the male relatives) on behalf of their own agnatic group. Occasionally they may be married at a future time, and then they are replaced by other relatives. Nyanga men may use these women to attract unrelated males to settle with them and/or to compensate them for their services. The women enjoy high esteem and must not be considered as licentious; they often live in prolonged and stable unions with men to whom they are not married. Little or no mention is made of them in the epics.

Descent groups are frequently mentioned in the epics; their names are easily identifiable because they begin with the morpheme *Bana-* (children or descendants of) or simply with the plural prefix *Ba-*. Many of these group names are symbolic and fictive. In epic I some descent groups are called Banabirurumba, Banamaka, Banankomo, and the like to identify groups of fish and crabs allied with Mukiti against Mwindo. The Baniyana (Bats), Banamitandi (Cobwebs or Spiders), and Banamburu (Monkeys) also fall into this category. Some descent groups, mainly those evoked by the bards in the songs, are existing social units, such as Baanga (III), Bahimbi (I), Baroba (I), Batembo (I), Batobo (I), and Batondo (I). In these instances the bards celebrate the group names of close or remote kinsfolk,

55

friends, chief, and headmen. Almost no information is provided on the organization and structure of descent groups, except for the facts that they have a headman (*mutambo*) and that several such groups may be established in a single village.

POLITICAL ORGANIZATION

Since the epics are centered on a hero who is the son of a chief and whose destiny is to become a chief, they are permeated with information about the institution of chieftainship. Because this aspect of the epics is discussed in separate chapters on the hero and the chief, I restrict myself here to general remarks.

The central action of all the epics is located in and around a chiefdom and, more specifically, in a village within it. Only in epic I is the chiefdom identified; it is Ihimbi, a real place in northeastern Nyangaland whose original Bahimbi population was found in situ by the immigrating Nyanga chiefs of the Banakindi line of dynasties. In the other three texts the location and the name of the chiefdom are unidentified. Nonspecification of the chiefdom is in line with the tradition of storytelling. Specific toponymic references are not usually made in the tales; the narrator tends to restrict himself to such vague indications as a village, a hunting camp, or a forest. This procedure is radically different from Nyanga social and political practices, which show an extraordinary concern with place-names, not merely for kingdoms, villages, hamlets, mountains, and hills, but also for parts of forests, mountains, and hills. The tale and the epic narrative are not intended to be detailed descriptions of real events and settings; instead, they are generalized, symbolic statements which do not require specificity. The same holds true for the central village inhabited by the chief and his heroic son. It has no specific name in epics III and IV; the name Tubondo (lit., Little-Raffia-Trees), which occurs in epics I and II, is purely symbolic (raffia palm trees are extremely important in Nyanga technology and economy for basketry, plaiting, and the making of traps, snares, and fiber rings used as money). There is no village of that name in Nyangaland.

Traditionally the Nyanga are organized in small, autonomous chiefdoms. Each one may comprise only a few hundred individuals belonging to numerous related and unrelated kinship groups. The organizational simplicity is reflected in the political framework of the epics. The autonomous chiefdom is territorially subdivided into a number of villages and their dependent, outlying hamlets. Although there are many intersecting kinship relationships among individuals inhabiting different villages and hamlets, no other form of territorial grouping intervenes between the chiefdom and the village. Yet the political hierarchy of persons in these small governmental units is complex. The village has a headman (*mutambo*) upon whom the heads of small kinship groups are dependent. The chief (*mwami*) has many sacred attributes which place him at a level with the divine kings found in other cultures. The number of ritual experts and political authorities serving the chief is truly impressive, given the size of the group; the hierarchy of officeholders is well illustrated in the epics, particularly in epic III. (See Biebuyck, 1955, 1956 *a-c,* and 1957 on various aspects of the political system.) Officeholders fall into the following categories:

1. Persons recruited from among the chief's agnatic kinsfolk:

   First-born-of-the-land (*ntangi ya cuo*) is one of the chief's consanguine brothers; in principle, he is the senior son of the senior wife (*nyabana*). He is considered the headman of the chief's group. Sometimes he has the special function of symbolic Father-of-the-chief (*shemwami*), assuming the role of guardian of the chief and of the ritual wife. In epic III Mwindo decides that the First-born-of-the-land will also be Shemumbo (see below). In epic IV the situation is reversed, for it is Mwindo, the son of the ritual wife, who becomes First-born-of-the-land.

   Shemumbo (Father-of-the-ritual-wife) is recruited from among the princes, that is, the chief's consanguineal brothers, because the chief's ritual wife must be chosen from among his closest kinsfolk. If the chief marries his half brother's daughter, the girl's true father is Shemumbo; if (as in epic III) the chief marries his (unmarried) sister's daughter, Shemumbo is regarded as the sociological father of the bride. Shemumbo does not usually reside in the chief's village.

   Princes (*barusi*) are the male descendants of the chief's commoner wives (*bowe*). In addition, certain descent groups as a whole have the perpetual position of princes; their membership includes the descendants of persons who accompanied the founding chiefs during the migrations.

   Muembwa is a title usually bestowed after the chief's death, upon one of his most junior half brothers. The role of Muembwa is intimately linked to that of Musimba (see below). He keeps in trust an important item (the *ukenye*-bundle) in the dead chief's paraphernalia, which he later surrenders to the Chief-Counselor upon the enthronement of the new chief. He inherits the chief's clothing, stool, beaded necklace, and one of his drums. He performs the first offerings for the dead chief. He receives a wife, goats, and land from the chief's house. Muembwa lives in an isolated hamlet, away from the chief's residence, for he must avoid all physical contact with the new chief. It is said that he is ultimately seized with dementia.

2. Wives of high status:

Besides the chief's commoner wives, who are married for bridewealth before and after his enthronement, the following women have special status:

Ritual wife (*mumbo*) is a close agnate of the chief (e.g., half brother's daughter; half sister; unmarried sister's daughter). She is brought to him without bridewealth by the Chief-Counselor during the enthronement rites. In principle, her son is destined to succeed to the chieftainship. After the enthronement rites, the ritual wife receives her own village, living with servants and subjects under the guardianship of such persons as Shemumbo, Shemwami, and the Chief-Counselor. Since, in strict custom, she must avoid all contacts with her sociological husband, the chief, she is allowed to have a physical husband (*katumbi*) who is often recruited from among the chief's relatives. When the chief dies the ritual wife inherits some of his wives and possessions.

Musanduri (or *mpombwe*) is a substitute for the ritual wife, but a chief does not necessarily have *musanduri*. If the ritual wife fails to bear a son, the child of *musanduri* may be "placed against the chest" of the ritual wife and become chief. *Musanduri* is closely related to the ritual wife and lives in her village.

Principal wife (*nyabana*) is recruited from among the close agnates of the chief (e.g., father's brother's daughter or unmarried sister's daughter). She dwells with the chief and is considered his most senior wife. Her son is normally the First-born-of-the-land, but he may become chief (epics III and IV).

Isabiro is a wife provided by the Pygmies, without bridewealth. She is in charge of the chief's black hunting dog, which is itself linked with the divinity Nyamurairi.

3. The counselors (*bakungu*) and their leader, the Chief-Counselor (Shebakungu):

The counselors belong to different kinship groups and have

their separate villages. Essentially they are recruited from groups bearing that title which arrived in Nyangaland together with the founding chiefs and from groups of former clients who were advanced in status because of extensive and faithful services. Counselors are more than advisers; they are the makers of the chief, since they play a vital role in his selection and enthronement. The prominent position of their leader, Shebakungu, is notable in epics III and IV. Shebakungu brings the ritual wife to the chief for the enthronement rites, along with the royal paraphernalia in which he dresses both of them. He imposes a new name upon the chief. In the ancient custom, Shebakungu and some representative counselors decided on the ritual killing of a chief who was ailing or senile.

4. The college of ritual experts (*bandirabitambo*) :

Despite slight variations in composition, the following titleholders usually constitute this college.

Musao is a title traditionally held by certain kinship groups. During the enthronement rites *musao* makes the bed on which the chief mates with the ritual wife; he removes the leaves of the bed; he and his wife clean the chief and the ritual wife and cook the ritual meal (fish from the sacred river boiled in water from the same river). *Musao* receives and wears the bark cloth worn by the chief before his enthronement. He and his wife perform certain life-cycle ceremonies (at birth and death of a grandchild; at birth of a child) on behalf of the chief. He and *mwamihesi* are guardians of the royal treasure.

Muhakabi (lit., Giver-of-the-*kabi*-ordeal) is an officeholder whose function is inherited in certain kinship groups. In some chiefdoms he stands vis-à-vis the chief in a kinship position of senior brother or "little-father" (i.e., father's junior). Every day, and also during enthronement rites, he anoints the chief with oil and red powder.

Mwamitwa (lit., Chief-Pygmy) is a member of the Pygmy group. He participates in enthronement rites, carrying bow, arrows, and quiver and holding the chief's black hunting dog on a leash. He brings honey and the hide of a flying squirrel and a wrist protector to the enthronement rites. The bodies of the chief and the ritual wife are rubbed with the honey; a skullcap is made for the ritual wife from the hide; the wrist protector (made of a piece of hide stuffed with mosses) is worn as a bracelet by the ritual wife. The role of *mwamitwa* is essential in the rites. According to an ancient Hunde tradition, the Pygmies brought the first chiefs into the land and thus exercise ritual control over the chief's well-being. In epic III the arrival of the Pygmies in a land where they were unknown signals the start of the enthronement rites of Chief Mutero Murimba.

Mwamihesi (lit., Chief-Blacksmith) is a hereditary title owned by several kinship groups. During enthronement rites, while the chief mates with the ritual wife, he rhythmically beats two iron hammers, saying: "If you are not a true chief, may you die on this ritual wife; may your force weaken. Bring harmony into the land." Together with *musao,* he guards the royal treasure; with *minerusi* he makes libations of beer to the sacred river; with *muhakabi* he ritually kills the goats brought by the father of the ritual wife. On occasion, he assumes the role of *muhakabi.* He is one of the few persons allowed to drink beer in the presence of the chief.

Minerusi (lit., Master-of-the-river) is an inherited office within certain kinship groups. *Minerusi* brings water and fish from the sacred river. The fishing itself (the fish of a certain species must be brought alive to the rites) is part of a divination rite prior to the enthronement.

Some other officeholders, such as *mubei* (the barber) and *mushumbia* (the drummer), tend to be included among the members of the college.

After the rites the ritual experts receive valuable gifts from the chief, usually including a wife, a stretch of land, and goats.

5. Other influential dignitaries constitute separate categories:

Shemwami (lit., Father-of-the-chief) is recruited among faithful and long-standing followers of the chief. In some kingdoms Shemwami may be an older brother or a little-father. In epic IV, however, the function is assigned to the children of the chief's half brother Mwindo. In epic I Shemwami is the guardian of Mukiti's ritual wife.

Musimba is an inherited office within a specific kinship group. In one chiefdom, I was told, Musimba ritually killed the chief. He presides over the burial of the chief and removes certain parts of the chief's body (teeth and nails) which are added to the royal treasure. He wears the clothing of the dead chief and guards, together with Muembwa, some of the chief's paraphernalia. He must avoid all physical contact with the new chief. In general, he stands in a joking relationship with the chief. During the long mourning period, drums may be beaten only in his hamlet. He has the right to intercept and claim for himself some of the tribute that is taken to the chief.

Epic III, and to a lesser extent epic IV, offer exceptional information about the chief's enthronement and burial and about various offices legated to his children and other persons. In epic III, almost imperceptibly, the bard moves from pure narrative to ethnographic fact. The enthronement of Chief Mutero Murimba and his subsequent death are occasions for the bard to enumerate paraphernalia, offices, taboos, procedures, and customs. After the Pygmies, among them the Chief-Pygmy, arrive, the chief can be enthroned. The bard limits himself to indicating some of the things bestowed upon the chief (paraphernalia, bark cloth, red powder, a dog); some of the functions of the Chief-Counselor, the Shemumbo, and ritual experts (Minerusi, Mushumbia, Musao, Mwamitwa, Mubei, Muhakabi); some of the chief's wives with special status; some of the gift exchanges; and the sacred places of enthronement. The enthronement also serves as an occasion for presenting factual data about prescriptions and taboos. The death and the burial of Chief Mutero Murimba allow the bard to make several ethnographic observations. Musimba removes portions of the chief's body (two molars, two eyelashes, the tip of the tongue, and the little finger); Muembwa inherits certain things (stool and copper spear); Salt-of-the-land acquires a dog bell without clapper and leopard teeth. The bard takes the opportunity to list in the chief's last will the functions of Shemumbo and Shebakungu and the distribution of goods (land and wives) to certain officials. The death of Chief Mwindo allows him to elaborate on the duties and functions legated to the chief's children.

DIVINITIES, RITUALS, AND CULTS

The interconnection between terrestrial and supernatural events and the interaction between the hero-chief and the divine are essential to the epic. The hero himself has a touch of the divine because of the manner of his birth and because of the unusual characteristics and objects with which he is born; the chief also has divine attributes. Nyanga religion boasts a sizable pantheon of male and female divinities, most of whom reside in the subterranean world (*kwirunga*) identified with the area of the volcanoes, outside and east of Nyangaland.

In Nyanga conception the divinities are linked together by kinship and politico-ritual bonds, much as a chief and his kinsfolk and officeholders are. There is no uniformity, however, in the interpretation of such relationships. In one important version, Nyamurairi, chief of the divinities, is the son of Bareke and is married to Kahombo (Good Fortune), who is the daughter of Hangi-of-Drum and the grandchild of Muhimankiri. Lightning (Nkuba) is the son of Nyamurairi and Wind (Iyuhu) is Lightning's son. In this scheme the other divinities occupy politico-ritual positions vis-à-vis Nyamurairi. Destiny (Buingo) is Chief-Counselor; Muisa is First-born-of-the-land; Meshemutwa (a Pygmy divinity) is Chief-Pygmy; Nkango (a Pygmy divinity) is a subject (*muombe*). There are other minor divinities, such as Nyarusumba, Congera, and Ruendo. Except for Lightning and Wind, who dwell in the air (*mwanya*), most of the divinities are established in the subterranean world. Water Serpent (Mukiti) occupies a very special position. He is linked to Nyamurairi as his Master-of-the-river (*minerusi*). There is no cult for Mukiti, but some other beings associated with him are worshiped: Nyangengu, his wife; Kentse (Sun), his first child; Musoka (Snake), his daughter.

Above and beyond these divinities is the creator god (Ongo), described as living in "the heart of the earth." Although occasionally mentioned in the epics as a giver of life and fertility, he is not really a protagonist. Nor is he, however, a complete abstraction. He is sometimes confused with Nyamurairi, although the latter is referred to primarily as Ongo's most influential agent, the one to whom he delegated immediate control over the creation. In a rare Nyanga tale, Ongo is depicted as sitting at an intersection of branches of a tree and roaring like Thunder. Ongo, complaining "that he has now been seen by this human who eats food, whereas he, God, is not to be seen," decides to send sickness to mankind. He blows on a whistle and sings: "Mr. Being-born-in-a-group [i.e., human being], the Master-of-chiseling [God] will abandon him!"

In formal condolence procedures both divinities are prominently mentioned:

> Weeping for one's kinsmen never ends. All of us: our place of residence is with Ongo. We are here: the world is but a basking in the sun, and the subterranean world is the homeland. You, who are bereaved by death, (know) that death does not make the distinction that this or that one has bewitched the deceased. You, who are bereaved by death, you must not be angry with death, because you yourself will one day follow the one who has died. You, who are bereaved by death, your companions weep while eating food; you must not leave the belly empty without eating food. You, who are bereaved by death, no incursion is made there in Ongo's place. If there had been a way, people might have gone to attack Ongo in war, and to beat him, because he has wiped out

the people, every day and always. To Ongo's place a good man does not go and come back again. Every day people are wiped out. Ongo has no mercy; he takes the big one and the small one, and the young children who have not yet wronged him here on earth. Oh kinsman! Nyamurairi has messengers. You must not remember and ponder any longer, because death will take everybody. Our place is there, at Ongo's. To die, then, is the legacy of all men.

It is possible that Ongo belongs to a pre-Nyanga stratum of populations—perhaps certain Pygmy subgroups or preestablished mixed Pygmy-Lega populations, such as the Bahimbi—and that after the Nyanga-Hunde migration he was to some extent assimilated with Nyamurairi (called Nyamulagira by the Hunde). A Hunde text, summarized by Viaene (1952b, pp. 390-391), explains that Nyamulagira was the son of Shabihango (of the Baleke group) and a famous healer (*mushake*). He became wealthy and was chased by his kinsfolk. He settled in a region called Mulamba where he encountered someone named Wongo or Gongo (cf. the Nyanga Ongo). Nyamulagira and Wongo concluded a friendship pact and worked together. Because Wongo was very lazy, however, the two friends quarreled with and even fought each other for a long time, until they reconciled. A huge abyss formed in the place where they had fought, and rains fell relentlessly. The people of Mulamba came to acknowledge Nyamulagira's greatness, asking for sunshine and promising baskets filled with eleusine. When the eleusine was ripe, however, they failed to keep their promise, and Nyamulagira and his friend Wongo decided to destroy Mulamba. Nyamulagira blew his magical whistle and a volcano arose; he blew it again and a neighboring mountain began to erupt. The two friends established themselves in the two volcanoes, called Nyamulagira and Nyiragongo.

The most important divinities in the epics are Nyamurairi, Lightning, and Kahindo (a Hunde divinity, sometimes identified with Kahombo, the Nyanga divinity of good fortune). The intensive cult for Nyamurairi involves both chiefs and commoners. Nyamurairi reveals his wishes in dreams, appearing as a very old man with a long beard, smoking a pipe, wearing a white goatskin, and sitting on a stool. At times he changes into a black dog lying in the ashes. The Nyanga dedicate women, goats, dogs, small banana groves, shrines, and bracelets to Nyamurairi. In tales he is depicted as the ultimate source of life and death. In epics II and III he appears as a divine trickster; he exposes the hero to various tricks and tests but is unable to destroy him, even though the hero has infringed all taboos by traveling "alive" to Nyamurairi's realm. In epic IV Nyamurairi's function is limited, though he does act as an intransigent person whose decision

63

is irreversible. In epic I his role as trickster is assumed by Muisa, a separate divinity who appears in dreams as a cow wanting to butt and to whom the Nyanga dedicate women and dogs. Muisa is, however, so close to Nyamurairi that the two are sometimes confused, as in epic I. In the tales Muisa is described as the bringer of death in retaliation for a curse inflicted upon him by Mr. Calamitous. In general, the Nyanga tend to attribute death and its causes to Ongo and Nyamurairi. Lightning is the center of an important cult; shrines, women, red roosters, and neckrings are dedicated to him. He manifests himself in dreams as blinding flashes. He dwells in the sky, but sometimes his abode is said to be a high, inaccessible rock where he lives in the form of a mysterious animal (*ngere*). As a major actor in the tales, he is victorious over Dragon, Water Serpent, and other beings; successful in contest; powerful, destructive, and rarely deceived by anyone. In the epics he appears as a devastating, but reliable, ally of the hero and as an instrument in the hero's catharsis (epic I).

Destiny (Buingo) is not a separate divinity among the Nyanga. Among Nyanga-related populations in eastern Zaire, the Nyanga Buingo is known as Bugingo and is apparently the principal divinity. In the Nyanga system of enthnoclassification Buingo is sometimes indentified as the Chief-Counselor of Nyamurairi; in religious thinking he is an aspect or emanation of Nyamurairi, who controls life and death. Nyamurairi does not kill or allow birth at random; he is a decision maker and Buingo is his supreme adviser. In epic IV Destiny (Buingo) is the son of the hero-chief Kabutwakenda and of the daughter of Mukiti. He becomes a good and virtuous chief who, though initially duped by his paternal uncle Mwindo, ultimately rules in glory. He symbolically acts as the ultimate arbiter in the competition and the conflict between his father and his father's half brother. In a rare tale narrated by Sherungu (the bard of epic IV), Destiny completely assumes the role of ultimate arbiter. He had asked his maternal uncles, the Bats, to forge for him a set of iron objects in order that his wife might dedicate them to Sun. When his maternal uncles were unable to obtain a heavy anvil stone lying in a cave, Destiny sought Nyamurairi's help. Nyamurairi designated the animals that were to retrieve the anvil. But, one after the other, such animals as Buffalo, Warthog, Elephant, Antelope, Leopard, and Lion failed in their attempts, although Destiny had promised them a wife and a piece of land as rewards. Chameleon, in consultation with Centipede's oracle and with the help of his paternal aunt, finally managed to lift and transport the anvil. Chameleon received the awards, but when Elephant threatened to seize them, Destiny and Bat returned to Nyamurairi to inform him about the argument. Nyamurairi decided in favor of Chameleon. Nevertheless, Elephant challenged Chameleon; he was killed by Destiny.

The Nyanga pantheon is closely parallel to that of the Hunde (see Viaene, 1952 *b*), both in nomenclature and in attributes. The Hunde data offer perspectives that help to clarify the Nyanga material. I limit myself to essentials. The creator god (Lulema or Lugira) is completely distinct from Nyamulagira, who is the chief of the spirit world. Among the Nyanga there is a tendency to confuse the two and to treat them synonymously. The Hunde creator god has, according to Viaene, the title of Bugingo (the Nyanga Buingo). Among the Nyanga, Buingo (Destiny) is an adviser to Nyamurairi; among the Pere-Pakombe (Hoffmann, 1932) Buhingo is one of several sons of the creator god Nyamunga and his wife Amabasi. Among the Hunde, Mugisha (cf. Muisa of the Nyanga) is a title of the creator god denoting his wealth. Among the Nyanga, Muisa, as the bringer of death, is closely associated with Nyamurairi and is sometimes confused with him; he is the counterpart of Buingo. For the Hunde, several divinities (Muhima, Hangi wa Ngoma) are former princes who lived in Bwito or Kishari; some of them were famous warriors. Others were the children of Hangi (e.g., Kahombo) or his servants (e.g., the Pygmy divinity Maheshemutwa). Still others, like Ninanguba (Lightning) and his daughter Kahindo, or Mwico (genius of the lakes) and his daughter, Kyigana (Nyanga Kiana), were famous ancestors. Likewise, among the Nyanga some divinities are interrelated as members of a kinship group, but there is no theory about their origin as ancestors, warriors, or heroes.

The divinities are shown as human in action and in sentiment. They are vulnerable and fallible and they easily change moods. The hero is not simply allied with some of them; he confronts them in contests of strength and wit in their own domain. These confrontations are not restricted to the epics. In one tale a common mortal, dismayed because her mother had plucked her cucumbers, successfully visits the divinities Muhima, Nkuba, and Muisa, but the latter returns her to her parents. In another tale a girl forbidden to leave the village transgresses the interdiction and encounters a bird that lures her into the realm of Nyamurairi underneath the ground. The girl's mother, carrying an owl, arrives in Nyamurairi's village. While the owl distracts Nyamurairi with his dancing, mother and daughter escape.

The relationships of the hero-chief and Nyamurairi, chief of divinities, are vividly depicted in the epics. Nyamurairi submits the hero to numerous deceptions and trials; the hero successfully resists because of magical objects (belt and scepter) and the advice of a female divinity or his paternal aunt. Although no real victor emerges from these contests, Nyamurairi is forced to recognize the hero's strength and allow him to depart. In epic I the hero defeats Muisa, the god of death, and Sheburungu (a name occasionally given to the creator god) himself. But, in epic IV, the hero who died prematurely by his own volition has no opportunity to confront Nyamurairi; he is sent back to earth by his servant. Nyamurairi presents gifts to the hero, not because he was defeated, but because he respects moral strength even more than physical force. The hero had shown compassion and healing power toward Nyamurairi's scurvy daughter. In one tale a boy meets two sick and ugly elderly women near a river; he washes them and they bless him. In exchange for his generosity the boy is given a wife by Nyamurairi. The boy's brothers, who subsequently meet the two women and chase them, are cursed. Arriving at Nyamurairi's place, they insult him, saying that he is a nothing, a mere "stirrer of ashes." Nyamurairi gives the boys stools that stick to them, and they die.

Descent into the subterranean world is made possible by pulling out a *kikoka*-fern and entering through the hole. The hero has no difficulty in finding his way back to earth. Actors in the tales sometimes find their way back only by acting upon the advice of the paternal aunt or the father's spirit. In one instance a man marries a woman whom he has found in one of his traps. One day, at the husband's request, the couple visits her village, entering the subterranean world through a fern. Her people ask as sole bridewealth that the husband eat all the food prepared for him. Trying to return home, he cannot find a passage; the woman goes to her village and he is changed into an insect.

In the wonderful world of the epic the hero also interacts with other extraordinary beings, such as the Water Serpent, Mukiti. Mukiti is either an antagonist of the hero (I) or his friend and ally (IV). Although there is no cult for Mukiti there is one for Musoka (his serpent-daughter, who is sometimes confused with Mukiti). Mukiti lives in a hole in the water near the bank of a large river; as Master-of-the-river, he dwells there in an ancient beehive-shaped house. People say that Mukiti can increase or decrease the water in the river. Mukiti is not unfriendly toward human beings, but at times he catches women while they are drawing water and takes them as wives. Occasionally he is depicted as a water-dwelling, man-eating ogre. In epics I and II he is married to the paternal aunt of the hero; in epic IV he acts like an unnamed maternal uncle of the hero Kabutwakenda. Mukiti is particularly responsive to song and music (strongly indicated in epic IV and in some tales).

The Dragon-Ogre Kirimu is another extraordinary being with whom the hero is involved. He is usually described as a huge animal with dog's teeth, a black hide, a large belly, seven heads, and an eagle's tail; occasionally he is pictured as an enormous creature wearing a mass of raffia fibers and bark cloth. Kirimu is a frequent actor in the tales. He is presented as a villain who is easily overpowered with song, dance, and beer and by the shrewdness of a weaker person. Scared of dogs and hunters, he is easily deceived by hunters dressed in bark cloth who seem to be bigger than he is. He operates mostly as a solitary hunter in the forest, but at times he has a wife (stolen from among the humans) and a daughter. Kirimu kidnaps children left alone in the village. He is defeated by the hero, by dogs, by Pygmies, by a lonely boy, and by a loving mother. One tale narrates how the Pygmies free the land of a Kirimu who has decimated the women and how it becomes necessary for all chiefs to have Pygmies. Another tale relates the way in which a woman, traveling with her child Titimbe through the forest, encounters many Kirimus and deceives them with beer. Still other tales celebrate a lonely surviving boy who lets himself be swallowed by Kirimu and then destroys him from the inside with a knife. Whenever Kirimu is defeated, living people emerge from his body (epics I and II).

Mpaca, the specter of the forest, plays only a minor role in epic II, when the Pygmy Shekaruru traps her with resinous glue. In the tales the evil-inspired Mpaca is frequently present; she is easily overcome with beer, song, and dance. Mpaca, who has the power of metamorphosis, occurs as either a male or a female, as old or young, as beautiful or ugly.

Little cult activity takes place in the epics, although there is ample reference to certain phases of cult and paraphernalia. Ancestral cult, though practiced at various levels of the social organization, is subordinate to and merged with the cult of divinities; it functions only on a small scale, except for the chiefs. Ancestors play no role in the epics, except that the spirit of the paternal aunt acts as adviser to and guardian of the hero (III, IV). The paternal aunt as a spirit is so presented as to make one believe that she is a living human being. In Nyanga thinking, life after death in the subterranean world is not very different from terrestrial life.

Rituals are of limited importance in the epics, occurring mainly in conjunction with the marriage of Mukiti and Iyangura (I) and with the chief's enthronement and burial ceremonies. The great life-crisis rituals, linked with childbirth, initiation, and the death of grandchildren, are absent. Of course, from certain points of view the entire epic is a monumental initiation ritual by which the hero is transformed into a chief.

There are some references to divination and ordeals but none to concepts or practices of sorcery and witchcraft. Yet the epics are permeated with the magico-religious atmosphere created by the presence of the hero-chief: the extraordinary circumstances of his birth; his exceptional physical and spiritual attributes; the powers manifested in his own person, in the objects he possesses, and in his alliances and expressed in extraordinary feats such as healing, resuscitation, revivification, subterranean, celestial, and aquatic journeys, interaction with animals and divinities, prognosis, and telecommunication. The magical power of the hero's dance, song, and word is clearly seen, as invocations, implorations, praises, blessings, prayers, commands, proclamations, imprecations, and meditations, all of a compelling nature, are interlaced with events and dialogues. The commanding words of the hero activate objects, persons, animals, and cosmic forces. The many poetic songs are not merely interludes that allow the bard to relax and to reflect; instead, they incorporate a potency that affects and foreshadows the action.

VALUES AND MODES OF THOUGHT

In judging the moral values expressed the reader must realize that the epic texts are not designed as rigidly accurate treatises. Furthermore, since the epic tradition builds on amplification and exaggeration, certain aspects are overemphasized or de-emphasized to stress particular concepts and viewpoints antithetically. For example, the epics deal with strife and endless quests accompanied by violence, deception, and destruction. Correspondingly, hostile acts predominate in a number of passages, and the vocabulary for death, destruction, suffering, and hardships is highly developed. For example, epic I has a richly nuanced vocabulary to express dying, destroying, killing, fighting, cutting, attacking, smashing, beating, etc. Yet the Nyanga do not extol warlike traits. Many characteristic attitudes of the hero illustrate behavioral patterns that are the opposite of the values to which the Nyanga aspire.

Some values are stated directly and simply in a self-evident manner, either in the texts themselves or in concluding remarks by the bards. Others are cryptically and indirectly formulated; some may be inferred from the overall plan of the epic and the developmental cycle of the heroic career.

Everyone who reads the epics will be impressed by the central values the Nyanga attach to hunting, trapping, harvesting of honey, and banana growing. The food obtained through these activities is not merely for personal consumption or gain; it must be generously shared and exchanged. Hospitality, liberality, generosity, and reciprocity in this respect are underscored. The Nyanga are a deeply religious people; appropriate observance of the cults is essential for a normal and happy life.

Harmonious kinship relationships, especially respect for age and seniority and mutual aid between certain categories of kinsfolk, are highly regarded and emphasized in the epics. The otherwise boisterous Mwindo acts with the utmost circumspection and diligence when he visits his brother-in-law, Lightning (II), or when he has dealings with his paternal aunt. He is dignified and reserved with his sister and loving toward his mother. Epics I and II are intended to illustrate that enmity between father and son leads to trouble and disaster and that salvation lies in mutual understanding and cooperation. As remarked in so many of the tales, to bear children is a joy; one must not discriminate among one's offspring or think of some of them as worthless, for one's salvation may come in the most unexpected manner from a child or from a junior.

Epics III and IV strongly criticize arbitrariness in a husband's relationships with his wives, particularly with the principal wife (*nyabana*). As the Nyanga emphatically state, she must not be scorned or chased; she is "a man's blood"; "she knows the thoughts of her husband"; "she can save him." Conflicts and tensions within the family which eventually lead to its dispersal (*burenda*) are often caused by *iyari*, the overt or covert antagonism among the co-wives of one husband. The husband's preferences and injustices often precipitate such tension, causing jealousies, mutual accusations, insinuations, and outright fights. These antagonisms affect, in varying degree, the interrelationships among the children of the co-wives (epic IV). It is normal for a man to distinguish between a beloved, preferred wife (*ngantsi*) and a rejected, despised wife (*nyakashombe*) because the wives show differing degrees of respect for and obedience to the husband. The beloved wife, the Nyanga say, is one who is respectful, obedient, generous, and not lazy, one who lacks crippling character traits such as scorn, and one who knows her place (a wife must not compare herself with the husband). A husband may expect to find these qualities in a wife, but evidently he should expect no more. In epics I and II the husband by requiring an unnatural and impossible feat (that the wives bear girls only), causes disaster. In epics III and IV the husband acts in an unrealistic manner toward his principal wife, for apparent barrenness is no reason for her to lose her status.

The epics clearly reveal the awe and respect in which the chief is held.

The people, the Pygmies, and even the Chief-Counselor are sober, obedient, and circumspect in their dealings with the chief.

Dancing, singing, and music making are vitally important to the Nyanga. They are often part of joyful and festive occasions, such as a safe return or a victory. There is the tale of a man who, while in a foreign land without water, made water emerge from a rock by means of his song and music. In both tales and epics the song is an avenue of escape from difficulties, imploring and invoking, warning and threatening, predicting and declaring intentions, revealing secrets, reflecting and meditating. The song is an element of power; from it emanates a force beneficial to those who manipulate it well. Characters in the epics do not dance merely to rejoice or to praise, but to avert a danger or to reinforce themselves. The hero, like the bard, is also a master of the well-spoken word. There are beauty and potency in his word. For the Nyanga, speech is senior to other means of expression because it can weigh the pros and cons of advice in problem solving. The values of dance, song, music, and words, so emphatically expressed in the texts, are widely applied in the complicated network of Nyanga social life and ritual.

Other values directly stated in the epics are not so clearly stressed in other facets of Nyanga culture. For instance, physical beauty is frequently described in the epics. I do not mean to say that the Nyanga have no sense of beauty in other manifestations of their life, but the strong emphasis on beauty in the epics in not paralleled in the tales and other texts. To point to a few examples: "Mukiti heard that Iyangura was always glistening (like dew) like sunrays because of beauty"; "Mukiti made himself like the anus of a snail in his dressing up"; "Iyangura was bursting with mature beauty"; "(Iyangura) is (smooth and straight) like a *ntsembe*-tree"; in removing the hide from the drum Iyangura saw "the multiple rays of the rising sun and the moon: that is the beauty of the child Mwindo"; Mwindo, seeing Kahindo, "was about to step back because of seeing sunbeams inside the house"; Iyangura, Mwindo, and Shemwindo appear as "radiant stars"; when the people and the Pygmies see Mukiti's daughter, they exclaim that "she is plain ivory," and when she married, they exclaim, she "was like a drop of rain"; Kahindo refers to Mwindo as "a wonderfully splendid man"; "radiance emanated from Nyamitondo (Mwindo's sister) as if she were a star." These and other references to beauty are only partly the product of the bard's poetic inspiration; as formulas they are deeply rooted in the epic tradition.

The sharpest delineation of values is seen in the characters of the hero and the chief. The hero embodies many behavioral patterns that are opposed to the code of values. On the contrary, the chief, eventually purified through additional hardships (symbolizing his initiation), positively reinforces the code. (I discuss these aspects in greater detail in the chapters on the hero and the chief.)

Mwindo's character (epics I, II, and III) progresses from excess to restraint and moderation. From turmoil and destruction we are led to fame, good living, mutual aid, and salvation. The bard (epic I) poignantly states his conclusions: "Heroism be hailed! But excessive callousness either pushes a man into a great crime or brings him a great one, which (normally) he would not have experienced. So, whosoever in a country is not advised will one day carry excrement—and to experience that is terrible," and "Even if a man becomes a hero (so as) to surpass the others, he will not fail one day to encounter some one else who could crush him, who could turn against him what he was looking for." Harmonious living is based on the acceptance of counsel and the avoidance of acts that disperse the group. The bard (epic III) formulates conclusions to that effect: "He who is not advised among the people of the world is (like) a dead person"; "If you hear that the land of a particular chief is famous, (it means) that he (the chief) is in harmony with his people"; and "To wrong the people on the earth is (as much as) to close the path of salvation." A heroic tale ends in the same vein: "Heroism by itself brings trouble (anxiety, worry) for itself. It is not befitting to say: I alone, nobody else, am strong."

The initial cause of the ill fate that so deeply affected the chiefdom was Chief Shemwindo's most unnatural decision. He wanted no son, and when his wife bore one he exposed the child to ordeals before accepting him (epics I and II); he rejected the principal wife for reasons of apparent barrenness and initially refused to listen to advice (epics III and IV). Fertility, birth of children, and harmony in interpersonal relationships are the major goals of the family. A father blesses his son when the latter moves with his young wife into his first, newly built house: "We, your fathers and your mothers, we rejoice very much. We have eaten in your house. This now is the blessing of oil that I give you. May you bear children, strong and healthy. May you cultivate gardens from which many crops come. May you get along together in your homestead, without quarrels. May you both live in awe for each other." The woman's father wishes her well when, a few days after the consummation of her marriage, she revisits her family and brings gifts from her husband: "You, our child, may you bear many children in the place where you go. May you harvest many crops. May those who are of your husband's kinship die of shame before you. May you not speak to them words that make them angry and that make them hate you. May the ladle glow in the pot. May you die of shame for each other in your house. When you go to sleep, make love with each other. May you die of shame before your fathers-in-law and your mothers-in-law." The fact that this sense of respect and blessing is absent in the initial stages of all the epics, because of the father's discriminatory and intransigent mood, leads to the uncontrollable disruption of social life and the concatenation of fateful events. Such trials represent a kind of initiation process in the course of which the hero-chief acquires the "teachings" (*mahano*) that strengthen his life-force (*karamo*). The epics end on a note of harmony, established order, good living, fame, and strength.

The epics show a distinctive preoccupation with place and space (Biebuyck and Mateene, 1969, pp. 20-21). As I have explained elsewhere (Biebuyck, 1976*b*), this concern is found throughout Nyanga culture. It is reflected not merely in the abundant usage of locative prefixes and expressions and in place references, but in the spatial framework within which the epic action develops. The action shifts easily from the terrestrial to the aquatic, subterranean, and celestial spheres and develops in the most diverse physical settings. In epic II, for example, the events and activities evolve in the following sequence of places:

I. *Terrestrial sphere*
   A village:
      The mother's house
      The chief's council
      The grave
      The father's house
      The village place
II. *Celestial sphere: realm of Lightning*
III. *Terrestrial sphere*
   The pool
   The father's village
   The banana grove
   The father's village
   A house: a hen's nest
   The village place
   A hollow Ficus tree
IV. *Celestial sphere*
   A hollow Ficus tree
   The realm of Lightning:
      The village of the hero's

sister:
   the wading place
   a guest house
   Lightning's place:
      a hollow Ficus
V. *Terrestrial sphere*
   The desolate village of the father:
      The village place
   The replenished village of the father:
      The village place
   The forest
   The place of the chief of Buffaloes
   The place of Buffaloes
   The forest
   The father's village:
      The village place
      The house of the hero's principal wife

The virgin forest
  The trail
  Hawk's place
  The trail
The father's village
The secondary forest
VI. *Aerial sphere*
A treetop
The air
VII. *Terrestrial sphere*
The hero's village
The villages of four chiefs
The village of Chief Itewa
The hero's village
A place outside the village
The village of Chief Itewa
The hero's village
The village of Chief Itewa
The hero's village
The place of a *kikoka*-fern
VIII. *Subterranean sphere*
A wading place
A mountainous road
The village of the god Nya-
  murairi:
  The steps
  The men's house
  The house of the girl
    Kahindo
A tree near the village entrance
The village of Nyamurairi
  The place where Nyamurairi
    lives
  Nyamurairi's house
  The house of Kahindo
  The men's house
The banana grove
The village of Nyamurairi
The banana grove
The village of Nyamurairi
The banana grove

The village of Nyamurairi:
  The place where Nyamurairi
    lives
  The house of Kahindo
  The men's house
The pool Mukingetua:
  A hanging tree
  The water
  The banks of the pool
The village of Nyamurairi:
  The place where Nyamurairi
    lives
  The house of Kahindo
The village of Sheburungu:
  The village entrance
  A cave in which there is the
    men's house
The village of Nyamurairi:
  The men's house
  The house of Kahindo
The place of the *kikoka*-fern
IX. *Terrestrial sphere*
The father's village:
  The village entrance
  The village place
The hero's village
The hamlet of Dragon-Ogre
  Kirimu:
  The men's house
The hero's village:
  The forest
The hamlet of Kirimu:
  The men's house
  A tree near a brook
The hero's village
The forest:
  At the strangler vine
The village of the Banamburu
The forest:
  At the strangler vine
The hero's village:

73

The hero's house
The village entrance
The hero's house
The forest
The village of the Banamburu
A glen between two hills
The village of the Banamburu
The hero's village:
    The village place
    The house of the hero's pre-
      ferred wife
    The village entrance
The dense forest:
    An ancient banana tree
    A little river
A small village:
    An iron house
The village of a chief:

A house with a corpse in it
    The village place
The hero's village:
    The hero's house
    The men's house
The small village of Specter
The hero's village:
    The hero's house
    The village entrance
The village of Shakwece:
    The village place
    A pool:
      a vine
      the water
The forest
The hero's village:
    The hero's house
    An assembly

FORMULAS AND STYLE FEATURES

As I indicate earlier, the epics are formulated in plain Nyanga, which is fully understandable to common people. There are no archaisms; few words are borrowed from French or Swahili. Although entire songs and dialogues in some epics are in the Hunde language, no special problem is thereby created, for the average Nyanga is perfectly bilingual. The epic bards reveal a profound awareness of the finest nuances of the grammatical system and possess a rich vocabulary. As poets and creative artists they cultivate the usage of the symbolic, euphemistic, and periphrastic expressions that abound in Nyanga linguistic practice; they modify familiar circumlocutions and formulate new ones. Some of these stylistic devices occur in the rest of the oral literature; others are unique or infrequently employed.

In composing oral epics, Nyanga singers manipulate innumerable fomulas in an original and diversified manner. I can point out only some aspects of the formulaic system, for its exhaustive study would require a Parry or a Lord and would demand a more complete knowledge than I possess of the nature of the rhythmic accompaniment and the Nyanga prosodic system. At the time of my research I had neither the equipment nor the training to make this kind of analysis.

As is noted in the glossary and in the listing of dramatis personae, the epics are characterized by an abundance of names: names for persons, animals, divinities, and fabulous beings; names for officeholders; group names and place-names; epithets and praise names. Many of these terms occur repeatedly in the epics. Some are simple, widely used personal names (most having a traceable meaning) like Mwindo, Iyangura, Nkuba,

75

Nyamurairi, Mukiti, and Kirimu. Others are teknonyms (e.g., Shemwindo, father of Mwindo; Nyamwindo, mother of Mwindo). Some names are compound, descriptive terms (e.g., Big-bird-born-by-itself, Chief Difficulties-that-do-not-come-together-with-others, Protector-of-the-things-that-will-not-be-revealed). There are many complex titles (e.g., Chief-Pygmy, Mwamitwa; Master-of-the-river, Minerusi), and some of the titles are constructed like teknonyms (e.g., Chief-Counselor, Shebakungu, lit., father of the counselors; principal wife, Nyabana, lit., mother of the children). Patronymics (e.g., Bee, son of Needle; Bee, son of Marumbu; Baboon, child of Scraper; Buffalo, son of Toughness; Spider, son of Webs; Mukiti, son of Pool; Hawk, son of Nyeshumya; Muisa, son of Bibandi) and matronymics (Mwindo, child of Iyangura; the daughter of Nyakatwakari; Meshe, child of Nyakabotyo) are sometimes placed in apposition to personal names. In one instance, Chief Kanyironge is denoted as "grandchild of Stone." Other identifications of persons are made by the use of additional kinship terms (e.g., sister of Mwindo; sororal nephew of the Banamitandi; wives of the maternal uncles) or by status designations (e.g., chief of Buffaloes; Muisa, chief of all the people).

The most typical formulas occurring only in the epics and heroic tales are descriptive epithets. Understandably, most of them apply to the main hero. Some are self-given; others are applied by other actors. Mwindo is Little-one-just-born-he-walked (Kabutwakenda), Little-Castaway (Katawa), Man-of-many-feats, Little-one-who-does-not-eat-terrestrial-foods, or Cultivator-of-marvelous-things. Characters such as Mukiti, Nkuba, and Iyangura, however, are occasionally designated by recurring epithets: Master-of-the-unfathomable, Flashes, Opener-Cleaver, Mother-of-the-cradling-string, Birth-Giver, Master-of-strength. Some formulas are epithetlike appositions (Mwindo, the brave-one, the virile man, the master of strength, the smart-one). Praise names are infrequent and are difficult to distinguish from epithets (Mukiti is called Pool or River). The most suggestive praise names for Mwindo are found in epic III, where the Pygmy praises Mwindo as Mr. Rejoicer-of-people, without hatred; the giver; the good speaker.

The names for kinship groups and political units are ready formulas (e.g., Banamukiti, Baniyana, Banamitandi, Banashemwindo). The morpheme *muna*, commonly used in both singular and plural to mark group affiliation, may be added to a name to give the meaning of master (Master Lightning, Master Sparrow, Master Spider). Some kinship and honorific terms are complex formulas in themselves: a sister is called *mwisi-abo* (girl-their) in opposition to daughter *mwisi-we* (girl-his); the patriarch, the master of the house, the leader, and the headman are identified as *nyerekurwabo* (master in/of the place of theirs).

Formulas for the specification of place and time are probably the most diverse and complex. Some of the time formulas cannot be separated from place indications. The Nyanga are highly space- and place-conscious; the grammatical system resounds with place references. Their cosmological system is based on the recognition of four spheres, with intricate space divisions in the terrestrial world; the epics follow a precise space plan, which is particularly pronounced in epic I. The singer has a wide assortment of possible place references at his disposal.

1. Specific toponyms: Tubondo, Ihimbi, Mikema. Except for the songs, which are filled with reminiscences, not many toponyms are used in the texts. When they are used they are always combined with a locative prefix (*ha-, mu-, ku-*).
2. In contrast, there is a rich vocabulary for generic space indication; the terms are almost invariably combined with a locative prefix: *kwirunga*: the subterranean world; *ku-mbuka*: the village, the world; *mumwanya*: the atmosphere, the air; *h-irare*: the garbage heap; *kubukone*: the rim of the village; *kw-ikura*: the village outskirts (point of entrance and exit). A large number of these generic place terms are recurrently incorporated into the phrases.
3. The generic place indicators are frequently replaced by a finely nuanced system of adverbial expressions and suffixed pronouns of reference. For example, in order to formulate "in her mother's house, in their village," the singer says *mumwabo kurwabo* (in it of theirs; in it of theirs; locative, connective, pronoun), the pronominal prefixes *mu-* and *ku-*, and the connectives *mwa-* and *rwa-*, clearly corresponding for the Nyanga listener to *numba*, house, and *ubungu*, village. More elaborate expressions, including locatives, conjugated verbs, and pronouns, are widely used (e.g., *kuno kuri ongo*: here where you are; *muri ishe*: in the place where his father is). The opposition between life and death or living and dead may also be expressed by verb-locative prefix combinations: "he did not know whether he was still alive" (*iwe ntiwosi kuti uri ho ho*: i.e., whether he was still there, i.e., *hambuka,* in the village, in the world). Adverbs and adverbial expressions for place indications are widely used: in front of (*hamakako na*), in between (*mu nkati na*), downstream (*kumbo na*), upsteam (*kunanda na*), above (*kwiyo*), below (*kwantse*), inside (*mundana*).
4. The conjugated verb *-rik-,* to be seated, to be established, to dwell, to live, eventually combined with locative prefixes and other conjugated verbs expressing time, is perhaps the most important place formula. Examples are *Kwarikanga Shemwindo kuTubondo*: In the place where Shemwindo was established in Tubondo; *Akwarikanga amwana mubura wina*: In the place where the child was dwelling in the womb of its mother; *Abarikanga mubungu bakie basunga . . . .*: Those who were established in the village, when they saw . . .

77

5. Stereotyped expressions: "when he was at the point of coming from where and going to where" (*muntuka kuni na mwiyenda kuni*).

Formulas indicating time and aspects of time are even more complex. They are constructed as follows:

1. A noun preceded by a locative: *mumukoma,* in the morning, can be reduplicated to *mumukomakoma,* in the very early morning.
2. A noun and a numeral: seven days, one week, one month.
3. A noun and a conjugated verb: a countable (number of) days.
4. More complicated expressions involving the verb to sleep or to awaken: "when he saw that Mukiti had been gone a day" is rendered in Nyanga as "when he saw Mukiti had slept where he had gone"; "in the morning he set out to follow him," as "in the morning he woke up to follow him", or "in the very early morning they woke up to go" (i.e., they went right after awakening).
5. Since much of the epic action is placed in the (early) morning, all the epics have innumerable formulas to express the idea of sky becoming dark, sky becoming light; these formulas are frequently combined with the verb *-kie* and/or with nouns (with locative prefix) for morning, evening, twilight, and so on. Examples are *bakie ebutu wamaca, mumukomakoma*: when sky had changed to dawn, in the early morning; *bakie iye murusisi,* when they were already in twilight; *bakie ebutu wamakind' ica,* when sky had finished changing to dawn; *ebutu wakia wamasira,* when sky had now become dark.
6. The most intricate formulas for establishing time sequences are constructed with the verb *-kie* (lit., to do) in combination with nouns, locative expressions, adverbs, and/or other verbs. The formulas built in this way exhibit an astounding diversity, achieved not merely by the choice of words but by their placement in the phrase. In pages 147–152 of epic I, the *-kie* formula occurs fifty-nine times in simple and elaborate combinations. The unconjugated *-kie* takes a choice of prefixes: *wa-, ba-, a-, ka,* and *kwa-,* depending on its subject. When placed at the beginning of the sentence it may be followed by a choice of word combinations:
   a. a noun with locative: *bakie mumutu,* when they were in the night;
   b. an invariable *iye* and a noun with locative: *bakie iye murusisi,* when they were already in twilight;
   c. an invariable *iye,* a conjugated verb, and a noun with locative: *bakie iye bari mukibu,* when they were already in the assembly;
   d. a noun and a conjugated verb: *bakie ebutu wamaca,* when sky had become dawn;
   e. a conjugated verb: *bakie basungana,* when they saw each other;
   f. a conjugated verb and an infinite verbal form: *bakie bamakind' itekere,* when they had finished grouping;
   g. a noun, a conjugated verb, and an infinite verbal form: *bakie ebutu wamakind' isira,* when the night had finished ending;

h. an invariable *mbu* and conjugated verb: *bakie mbu bamusungire,* when they saw him.

When *-kie* is not at the beginning of the sentence it is preceded by its subject(s) and followed by one of the aforementioned combinations: *ematu akie ameta,* when days had passed; *ematu erinda akie amakind' isira,* when seven days had finished ending; *Mukiti na Shemwindo bakie basungana,* when Mukiti and Shemwindo saw each other; *Mwindo wakie iye unyairengi,* as Mwindo was wailing.

The bards use many standard symbolic expressions (including euphemisms) as formulas or invent new ones to introduce a proclamation, a conversation, or a song; to boast and challenge; to destroy, to die, and to revivify; to sneeze and to cough; to bless and to threaten; to evoke beauty, emotion, stress, and physical hardship; to express strength or weakness. Verbs become formulas by change of aspect and tense, addition of suffixes and conjunctions, or reduplication of the stem. The repetition of the idea of action is also favored. The agglutinative nature of the Nyanga language is an effective instrument for expanding or reducing an expression. A few examples must suffice to illustrate this kind of formula: "Mwindo . . . threw sweet words into his mouth; he sang"; "Mwindo sang; he howled; he said"; "Mwindo went singing; he howled; he said"; "now she is not the one (I expected to see) ; she is like a *ntsembe*-tree (i.e., tall, straight, and smooth)"; "Muisa sent his *karemba*-belt; it went and smashed Mwindo on the tree; it planted his mouth into the trunk of the tree; his breath could not get out; urine and excrement trickled down from him"; "Mwindo sneezed; he lifted his eyes and a bit of breath came out"; "he who went to sleep wakes up"; "the pig in question said that it was not great—it turned its hoofs upward; it died"; "in the pool where nothing moves" (*mwiriba rahakitabinduka*: lit., in the pool of where a thing not in a state of moving).

Somewhat related to the formulaic system are the innumerable repetitions that add emphasis, effect, and clarity and thus give fullness to the descriptions. The repetitions occur in simple and complex formulations, from reduplication of stems and reiterations of words and phrases to rewording of ideas. Such repetitions lend sonority, additional rhythm, and emphasis to the statements. They allow the singer to reflect, to connect ideas, and to adjust to the rhythmic percussion. They occur throughout the epics and, because of their abundance and patterning, they leave a distinctive imprint. For instance: "they sat together in a group. When all the Banashemwindo were grouped together . . ."; "they kept silent, without giving an answer"; "Mwindo sang; he howled; he said"; "The counselors went to the forest to cut a piece of wood for the husk of the drum. They arrived in the forest; they cut it; they returned with it to the village. Arriving in the village, they carved the wood; they hollowed it out so that it became a husk. When the husk was finished, they went again to fetch Mwindo; they carried him; they stuck him into the husk of the drum ... "; "Shemwindo stood up; he went into the house of his wife, the house of the preferred-one, slithering like a snake, without letting his steps be noisy. He arrived at the hut; he peeked through the open door, casting an eye into the house; he saw the child sleeping . . .; he entered the hut; he questioned his wife. . . ."

The descriptions of physical and emotional states, at times combined with comparisons although frequently proceeding with formulas and stereotyped expressions, are a characteristic feature of the epics but are noticeable only to a limited extent in the heroic tales. Many of the descriptions evoke beauty, suggest agony, or express joy or astonishment. For example: "she was always glistening (like dew) like sunrays because of beauty"; "as they descended with the tree, radiance emanated from Nyamutondo Mwindo as if she were a star"; "see how I am dancing, my back shivering like the raffia-tree larva, and my cheeks contain my laughing"; "Muisa, excrement stuck to the buttocks; he fainted away; urine ran all over the ground; froth came out from his nose and eyes (and covered his face; he tossed his hoofs up into the air; he stiffened like a *mukusa*-viper"; "when brother and sister saw it (the bird) : it was beating its wings about (swaggering) here and there, sole master of this desolate village." Some of the evocations, comparisons, and similes employed in these descriptions emphasize the highly individual poetic skill of the bards and apparently are totally absent from the rest of the literature. For example: "they slept in that village, being like a blister because of repletion"; "Mukiti made himself like the anus of a snail in his dressing up"; "between the teeth of a leopard, there where the sweetness of food is experienced"; "blood is the sweat with which he wets the arm."

Formulas, stereotypes, and repetitions notwithstanding, the individual style and poetic skill of each singer, his preferences and choices, are manifest throughout the epics. This statement can easily be documented from the preludes to the epics. In the following pages, I list for each of the epics the corresponding phrases.

     I. Kwabesenga mwami uma
    II. Kwarikanga mwami uma
   III. Kwabesenga mwami uma
   IV. 0
     I. Long ago there was in a place one chief
    II. In a place long ago there dwelt one chief
   III. Long ago there was in a place one chief
   IV. 0

I.   nti   ngi   Shemwindo
II.   nti   ngi   Shemwindo
III. nti   ngi   Karisi
IV.   0
I.   called (lit., then it is) Shemwindo
II.   called Shemwindo
III. called Karisi
IV.   0
I.   Ingo mwami wahimba ubungu
II–III–IV. 0
I.   That chief built a village
I.   nti   ngi   kuTubondo
II–III–IV. 0
I.   called (lit., then it is) Tubondo
I.   mucuo ca mwiHimbi
II–III–IV. 0
I.   in the state of Ihimbi
I.   Shemwindo nti wabutwa na
II–III–IV. 0
I.   Shemwindo was born with
I.   mwisiabo uma nti ngi Iyangura
II–III–IV. 0
I.   one sister called Iyangura
I.   Na ndo ubungu rwa Shemwindo
II–III–IV. 0
I.   And in that village of Shemwindo
I.   nti ruri mo ndushu sirinda sa bea be
II–III–IV. 0
I.   there were seven meeting places of his people
I.   Ingo mwami Shemwindo
II.   Ingo Shemwindo
III. 0
IV.   Mwami uma
I.   That chief Shemwindo
II.   This Shemwindo
III. 0
IV.   One chief
I.   wabinga bomina barinda
II.   wabinga bomina babi
III. wabinga bomina bingi
IV.   wabinga bomina mutuba
I.   married seven wives
II.   married two wives
III. he married many wives
IV.   he married six wives
I.   0
II.   Emumina uma nti ngi Iyangura
III. Enyabanawe nti ngi Kahindo
IV.   0

    I. 0
   II. One wife was called Iyangura
  III. His principal wife was called Kahindo
   IV. 0
I–II–IV. 0
  III. mwisa Hangi wa Nyoma
I–II–IV. 0
  III. the daughter of Hangi-of-Drum
    I. Shemwindo wakie wamakind' ibinga
   II. Wakie wamabinga
  III. Wakie wamakind' ibinga
   IV. Wakire wamabinga
    I. After Shemwindo had finished marrying
   II. After he had married
  III. After he had finished marrying
   IV. After he had married
    I. mbo bomina be barinda
   II. ebomina be babi
  III. ebomina be bo
   IV. bo
    I. those his seven wives
   II. his two wives
  III. those his wives
   IV. them
    I. wasonja ebea be bati
II–III–IV. 0
    I. he summoned together all his people
    I. banunke n'ebea bakwakare
II–III–IV. 0
    I. the juniors and the senior men
    I. bahani bakungu n'ebarusi
II–III–IV. 0
    I. advisers, the counselors, and the nobles
    I. Abati be waria bo mukibu
II–III–IV. 0
    I. All those—he had them meet in council
    I. Bakie iye bari mukibu
II–III–IV. 0
    I. When they were already in the assembly
    I. Shemwindo warika nkatinkati na bo
II–III–IV. 0
    I. Shemwindo sat down in the middle of them
    I. Wabikira murenge mbu
   II. Wabikira murenge mbu
 III–IV. 0
    I. he made a proclamation, saying:
   II. he made a proclamation, saying:
    I. Banu bomina be
II–III–IV. 0

     I. You, my wives
     I. Ingu wabuti mwanamuyu
    II. Ingu wabuti mwanamuyu
III–IV. 0
     I. the one who will bear a male child
    II. the one who will bring forth a male child
     I. mubanu bomina be barinda
    II. mubanu bomina be
III–IV. 0
     I. among you my seven wives
    II. among you my wives
     I. iwe nti wamuyi
    II. iwe nti wamuniya
III–IV. 0
     I. I will kill him/her
    II. I shall strangulate him/her
     I. 0
    II. nti wamukama
III–IV. 0
    II. I shall knead him/her
     I. banu bati cahunda mwendiyo
II–III–IV. 0
     I. all of you must each time
     I. banu mubutange bana bamukari baraara
II–III–IV. 0
     I. (you) give birth to girls only
     I. Mwikind' ieca emwiko o
II–III–IV. 0
     I. Having made this interdiction
     I. wirekera mumanumba abakari
II–III–IV. 0
     I. he threw himself hurriedly into the houses of the wives
     I. nti wecaa ndasi kuri bakari be
II–III–IV. 0
     I. then launched the sperm where his wives were
     I. Mumbo bomina be nti bari mo
    II. Mubomina be ababi
III–IV. 0
     I. Among his wives there was among them
    II. Among his two wives
     I. ngantsi na nyakashombe
    II. Iyangura nti ngi engantsi
III–IV. 0
     I. a beloved-one and a despised-one
    II. Iyangura is the beloved-one
     I. Nyakashombe nti wahimbirwa
II–III–IV. 0
     I. The despised-one had (her house) built
     I. kubukone hirare

83

II–III–IV. 0
    I. on the rim (of the village), on the garbage heap
    I. na bampe bomina be
II–III–IV. 0
    I. and his other wives
    I. nti bari mumwangantse
II–III–IV. 0
    I. were in the clearing
    I. munkati yerubungu
II–III–IV. 0
    I. in the middle of the village
    I. Kwakie kwameta matu antswa
    II. Kwakie kwameta matu antswa
  III–IV. 0
    I. After a countable number of days had elapsed
    II. After a countable number of days had elapsed
  IIII–IV. 0
    I. bakari mbo barinda
II–III–IV. 0
    I. those (his) seven wives
    I. bariere na makure mongo
    II. Iyangura wariya bukure
    III. abati babuta bana
    IV. warika na bo matu mingi
    I. carried pregnancies, and (all) at the same time
    II. Iyangura carried (her) pregnancy
    III. all of them bore children
    IV. he remained with them for many days
  I–II–III. 0
    IV. Nyabana wabe mushombe
    IV. Nyabana was the despised wife
  I–II. 0
    III. Kahindo wafundi ibuta
    IV. kisira nti nti wabuta
    III. Kahindo failed to give birth
    IV. because she did not bear
  I–II–III. 0
    IV. anga na mwana
    IV. not a child
  I–II. 0
    III. Kahindo wamafundi ibuta
    IV. Nyabana wakire wamabe mushombe
    III. When Kahindo failed to give birth
    IV. When Nyabana had become the despised wife
  I–II. 0
    III. washombwa na moke
    IV. emuturo wenda uyerengi
    III. she was rejected by her husband

    IV.   tribute arrived
  I–II.   0
   III.   wafundi iyanyiwane
    IV.   mumanumba ababine
   III.   she failed to be loved by him
    IV.   in the houses of the co-wives

At this point the four epics take widely different orientations.

Epic I: Elaborate attention is now focused on the courtship and marriage of Water Serpent Mukiti and Iyangura, sister of Shemwindo and paternal aunt of Mwindo. After a detailed description of the procedures and ceremonies, the action returns to Shemwindo and his wives: they live in glory and fame; six wives give birth to daughters; the preferred wife remains pregnant; she laments her sad fate; the unborn son performs various tasks for his mother; people ridicule her because of the delays in childbirth; suddenly she feels the first pains; the child has decided to be born through his mother's medius. Then follows an elaborate description of the circumstances of birth and the father's vain attempt to spear his son; the son is buried alive. The bard recollects that the hero is born with various objects and capabilities.

Epic II pursues, without any deferment, the birth of the hero. His mother is pregnant; the son is born through the palm of her hand; he is born with certain objects and capabilities; his mother also bears a daughter; the despised wife gives birth to a son and a daughter; the chief orders his son to be buried alive.

Epic III examines in detail the fate of the rejected *nyabana*-wife. The chief orders the Chief-Counselor to build a house for her on the garbage heap, outside the village. Nobody may visit her; she grows crops; she becomes pregnant "without a male having given the pregnancy to her"; after a lengthy pregnancy and a painful delivery she gives birth to the hero Kabutwakenda, who departs almost instantaneously. When he is settled in a new land, Kabutwakenda sends famine; the chief is advised to return to his rejected Nyabana; secretly he makes her pregnant; soon her son, Mwindo, is born without complications; mother and son are summoned back to the village.

Epic IV follows the tribulations of the rejected *nyabana*-wife: the chief orders that a house be built for her on the garbage heap; she cultivates crops while the co-wives in the village neglect their work; famine strikes the country; on the advice of Shebakungu, the chief visits her secretly; she is pregnant and gives birth, without complications, to a son,

Kabutwakenda. Soon the people learn that the chief's ritual wife has also given birth to a son, called Mwindo.

When the introductory lines of the epics are compared, the differences and similarities are at once apparent. It is safe to say that the differences far outweigh the similarities. The bards are not copying or imitating one another. To begin with, they draw upon different traditions. Epics I and II probably derive from two diverse strains within a common tradition; epics III and IV may remotely go back to a second common tradition. The language used is the same Nyanga variant. The bards share a common pool of formulas and formulaic expressions, and in these initial lines their purpose is identical: to set the stage and to provide the background for the main events. The basic thematic features of the setting are identical: a chief's milieu; the chief has several wives; these wives are ranked according to status and predilection; the chief makes an unnatural decision: he wants no sons and when his beloved wife gives birth to a son, he attempts to kill the child, but in vain, for the son instantly has heroic stature (I and II); the chief rejects his principal wife because of apparent barrenness but famine leads him back to her because she is more diligent than the others; she gives birth to a son whose heroic stature emerges slowly (III and IV). Against this background of common facts, however, the individual preference, style, and artistry of each bard are apparent from the outset. In the preludes to the four epics only a few formulaic expressions overlap, but even here there is only rarely a complete identity of formulation: a different noun or verb is used, a different aspect of the verbal action is stressed, words are left out and others added, and, particularly, a subtle game is played with suffixes, pronouns, and enclitics. Each bard follows his own inclination in elaborating or reducing particular facts and events. The bard in epic I is specific about places and names, and he elaborates on the chief's interdiction. He interrupts the evolving intrigue leading to the birth of the hero with a long digression about the marriage of the chief's sister to Water Serpent. The singer of epic II is the most succinct of all; he is not interested in descriptive detail and rapidly develops the essential background of the hero. In epic III Shekarisi is specific on persons; he elaborates on conversations between chief and chief counselor and on the status of the rejected wife. The advent of the main hero is preceded by a long interlude about the ephemeral heroic half brother. Sherungu (epic IV) is short and prosaic in his introductory statements.

Nevertheless, the wording in the preludes to epics I and II is similar enough to warrant a further probe into the degrees of originality and traditionality which separate and unite the two bards. Let us briefly examine the passage in which Mwindo on his subterranean journey meets with the female divinity Kahindo. The circumstances leading to this encounter are somewhat similar in the two texts. In epic I Mwindo and his comitatus, including his paternal aunt, have triumphantly returned to the devastated home village. His father has fled; his maternal uncles, whom he had sent out, are exterminated. Mwindo revivifies his uncles and decides to pursue his father in the subterranean world of Muisa. In epic II Mwindo has defeated the rebellious chief Itewa, revivified his people, and rebuilt his village. He is well established, and so he suddenly decides to visit the subterranean world of Nyamurairi, "being fully alive." Implicitly, he is pursuing his father who had gone or fled there for an undisclosed reason. In both texts the hero explains his intentions. The conversation and preparations, containing the suspense of events to come, are much more detailed and ornamented in epic I. The poetic skill, the feel for descriptive detail, circumlocutions, aphoristic and epithetlike expressions, the capacity for original formulas, and the sense for amplification and finely nuanced verbal aspects—all are at once apparent (Biebuyck and Mateene, 1969, pp. 93–94, 172):

> Shemwindo . . . went harming himself running into everything [*wicabirange,* lit., he was cutting himself; said about a wounded animal].

> [Shemwindo] went to arrive at Muisa's, the place where no one ever clusters around the fire [*inku kutanontwaa ekasha,* lit., over there where never is being enjoyed, by sitting around it, the fire].

> Mwindo said to his aunt: "You . . . remain here in this village . . . ; because you are used to eating terrestrial foods, you are not capable of all the adventures and the dangers that I am used to experiencing wherever I pass" ["used to" is rendered by particular aspects selected in conjugating the verbs "to eat" and "to experience"; *bibura,* translated as dangers, lit. means the sparks from the forge to which the blacksmith is said to be immune].

> . . . if (one day) you feel that this rope has become still, if it does not move anymore, then pay no more attention . . . ; lo! the fire has dwindled; I am dead then.

In contrast, the bard in epic II relates Mwindo's departure in a few succinct, undecorated statements: "He said to his people: 'Remain here, you all, together with those my dogs. When you will be met by difficult things arriving at the end of the village, those my dogs will fight against them; they will bring me the news in the place where I am. However, I am with you; I do not go far.' " In the Nyanga text the poetic quality of this statement lies in the sonority obtained by consonant and vowel alliteration: three words begin with *mu-*, seven with *s-* (as *sa-, se-, si-*), and five with *b-* (as *ba-* and *bya-*).

Having explained his purposes, the hero departs carrying his magical objects, which will be of great value in his subterranean experiences: his shoulder bag, his ax, and his *conga*-scepter (epic I); his billhook and his *conga*-scepter (epic II). In epic I he remains physically connected with his paternal aunt by means of a magical rope; in epic II the connection is maintained by Mwindo's dogs, which remain behind. The hero now arrives at a *kikoka*-fern, which was shown him by Sparrow in epic I but which he finds by himself in epic II. He pulls on it and enters into the subterranean world. Although the singers use almost identical words, the degree of succinctness and ornamentation and the verbal forms differ:

Wakie weya hakikoka	Weya hari kikoka
When he arrived at the *kikoka*-fern	He arrived at the *kikoka*-fern
hakimirenga ishe	
where his father had entered	
na we wakura ekikoka	wakura co
he too pulled out the *kikoka*-fern	he pulled it out
wakimire hitina raco	wakime na
he entered at its base	he entered
	hakukurire we co
	at the place where he had pulled it out
weta na wenda na	akwetanga we wenda
he passed through; he went	where he passed, he went
kasaire hitukuriro	kasaa hitukuriro
to appear at the wading place	to appear at the wading place
wakie mbu weye ho	
when he arrived there	
wakumana ho mwisi	wakumana ho mwisi
he met there the daughter	he met there the daughter
wa Muisa Kahindo	wa Nyamurairi Kahindo
of Muisa, Kahindo	of Nyamurairi Kahindo
	nti iye usimbanga
	he was singing
	Mwindo mbu
	Mwindo, saying

Both singers next describe the first phase of the encounter, emphasizing the sickness and the ugliness of Kahindo. In the two texts the Nyanga wording follows an identical rhythmic pattern of sixty-three tonal syllables, and yet each singer describes the situation in his own unique manner achieving, nevertheless, a similar graphic effect:

Kahindo wamukokere
Kahindo embraced him
mbu karibu nko Mwindo
saying: "This is my welcome,
    Mwindo"
Mwindo warisia mbu ae
Mwindo in reply said: "Yes."
Iwe Kahindo nti
She, Kahindo, was
usambange ebinyora
sick (with) yaws
ebinyora bya nti
these yaws did
byaretukure murino
start at the tooth
byeya na munkukunyu
(and) went up to the perineum
byahita na emindi
they descended the legs (and)
byeya na mumpande sebisando
went up to the toe of the sole of the
    feet

Mwindo Mboru wakie wamakind'
After Mwindo Mboru had finished
ikumana Kahindo
meeting with Kahindo
mwisi a Nyamurairi ekusi
daughter of Nyamurairi, at the river:
nti ebinyora byamurisa
(he noticed that) yaws filled
emubi uti nti byaremutuke
the entire body: they begin
mumpanda yemume byeya
at the big toe of the foot (and) arrive
na mubusuntsu webuteo
at the tussock of the hair

Then both bards relate a basically common situation: the hero heals Kahindo; she provides him with clues necessary to confront the trickeries of Muisa and Nyamurairi successfully. In doing so, however, they give further proof of their originality, poetic skills, and stylistic consistency: differences in actual formulation; verbal nuances; emphasis or reduction; reversal of the sequence of events; ornamentation by means of descriptive detail, drawn-out dialogues, and repetitions:

When Mwindo tried to go through, Kahindo forbade, saying, "No, no." She said to him: "Where are you going?" Mwindo answered her that he was going to Muisa's to look for his father because it was here in this village of Muisa that he was. She told him again: "Stop first here where I am. Over there in Muisa's village one never goes through; is it you who will (succeed) in getting through there like that, with all (your) pride?" Kahindo said to Mwindo: "Now you are going to Muisa's. When you will have arrived there, having entered the meeting place, if you see a very big man and tall too, curled up in the ashes near

This Kahindo, daughter of Nyamurairi, when she saw Mwindo Mboru arriving for her: the heart burned her while she was scrutinizing him. She said: "Truly! A splendid young man, how beautiful he is, this one. Truly!" Having spoken like that, this Kahindo said to Mwindo, "You, young man, clean for me this scabies." Mwindo began cleaning her entire body, removing the scales very well. When Mwindo had finished cleaning her, Kahindo said to him: "May you be healed, you, Mwindo." She asked him inquisitively: "You, where are going?" Mwindo answered her that he was going to Nyamurairi. Having the hearth, it is he who is Muisa; and if he greets you, if he says: 'Blessing (be) with you, my father,' you too will answer, 'Yes, my father'; and when he will have left you a stool, then you will refuse it; you will tell him: 'No, my father; will the head of a man's father become a stool?' When he will have handed over to you a little gourd of banana beer for you to drink, you will refuse, answering: 'No, my father, even though a person is one's child, is that a reason why he should drink the urine of his father?' After Muisa will have recognized you in that way, he will say to you: 'Blessing, blessing, Mwindo'; and you will answer him: 'And to you blessing, blessing also, father.' When he will have given you paste to eat, you will answer him: 'Even though a person is one's child, is that a reason why he should eat the excrement of his father?' "

finished bathing Kahindo like this, Mwindo fainted. (Mwindo) having fainted, Kahindo shook him saying: "E! Mwindo wake up; a hero does not die from one spear throw." Mwindo returned to life; he sneezed. While Mwindo was going to Nyamurairi, Kahindo shouted on the road, saying, "Go over there and when you arrive at Nyamurairi's, go close to the men's house where he is (seated). My father Nyamurairi will show you water that is in a jar, asking that you wash with it. You say to him: My father, the beer from which you drink, is that for me to wash with? You refuse firmly, even though he goes on pressing you, saying that you should wash with it. You go on refusing until he stops pressing you with it." Kahindo also said to him: "When you arrive at my father's place, then you sing for him this song:
I am not with those who have killed Ringe,
Ringe of the chief, Ringe.

Mwindo's encounter with Kahindo, the daughter of Nyamurairi, is conceived in a totally different manner by the bard of epic III. Transformed into a wild boar, Kahindo lures Mwindo deep into the forest until he arrives in the realm of Nyamurairi. Mwindo is submitted to tests and is assisted by his paternal aunt. Ultimately, in all three epics, the hero becomes a sexual partner of Kahindo, but the details of the relationship are again conceived differently. In epic I, having successfully withstood the trickeries of Muisa, Mwindo is invited to "take a rest" in the house of Kahindo. The bard describes in detail the beauty of the girl, Mwindo's awe, and the preparation of a meal, without suggesting sexual relationships. The next evening, after a new test of strength, Mwindo returns to Kahindo's place and "they went to partake in sleep." Mwindo departs for other adventures, leaving Muisa behind in a deathlike torpor. Returning from these new exploits, Mwindo "awakens" Muisa and is asked to marry Kahindo. He answers: "I cannot marry here; I shall marry (later) in Tubondo of Shemwindo." In epic II Mwindo sleeps with Kahindo in her house after each trial. The bard briefly describes the situation: Mwindo enters her house; she cooks food; they sleep together. At the end of his victories over Sheburungu, Mwindo returns to Kahindo; and before his final departure he gives her a maiden "because she performed very many nice things for him." In epic III the initial antagonism between Mwindo and Kahindo is suddenly resolved when Nyamurairi decides to abandon the tests and to give Kahindo in marriage to Mwindo.

The conscious search for originality and nuance, for expansion or reduction, for descriptive detail or concise sonority, for repetition or ellipsis, for insertion of new motifs or reorganization and recombination of old ones, is found throughout the texts. Each epic is a poetic document that admirably combines traditional techniques and motifs with creative originality. Lord's (Lord and Bynum, 1974, p. 10) characterization of the artistry of the Serbo-Croatian singer, Avdo Mededovic, may well be applied to the Nyanga bards: "Avdo's songs are living proof that the best of oral epic singers are original poets working within the tradition in the traditional manner."

There are many other ways in which the individual bard leaves his imprint on the epic: diversity and frequency of formulas to indicate time and place; preference for mixed direct and indirect discourse in the conversations; predilection for spontaneous, disconnected "meditations," aphoristic statements, or formal proclamations, statements, and speeches; search for circumlocutions and sonorous phrases (using alliteration, reduplication, and repetition); love for the fullness of a description; abundance of songs that involve the public. The bilingualism of the bards is revealed in the sudden shifts from Nyanga to Hunde. Some of the sharpest differences may lie in the manner of singing. The epics are rhythmically accompanied by a percussion stick (a dry pole or bamboo) which loosely rests on a few little sticks to enhance its resonance and is beaten by three men (Biebuyck and Mateene, 1969, p. 13). Percussion sticks of different size and type are used by the Nyanga in conjunction with boys' circumcision rites. They are sacred and secret musical instruments. Held under the armpit and slightly rotated, these sticks allow the reproduction of high and low pitch. In other words, they are talking sticks that assist (like wooden slit-drums or iron gongs) in transmitting the tonal melody of conventional stereotyped formulas. When a percussion stick is employed as a simple instrument accompanying a sung text, it is beaten according to a tonal formula contained in a standard, proverb-like, periphrastic expression. The percussion stick that accompanies the singing of the epic is beaten according to complex formulas which favor a beat of seven and nine tonal syllables. One formula is *emusindu kutuka* (seven tonal syllables), *wasia nansinde sabine* (nine tonal syllables) : literally, "The last one to go remains with the lingering troubles of his peers." The singers of epics I and II favor cadences of seven and nine tonal syllables. The ideal rhythmic pattern is, however, strangely obscured by a variety of features: elision or augment, ellipsis or elongation, pause, humming, faster or slower speech, halting of percussion, and so on.

THE HERO

The Nyanga equivalent for hero is *murai*. The same word was applied in ancient tradition to the young men who guarded the village entrance and to warriors in general. It is possible that the concept is contained in the name of Nyamurairi, the supreme divinity. The designation is also applied to stinging bees and to the European type of soldiers introduced into Nyangaland. *Murai* is rarely used in tales or epics; preference is given instead to the hero's personal name (Mwindo, Kabutwakenda) and to his epithets. In epic I the term is aptly employed by Mwindo's paternal aunt. On their journey home Mwindo, his aunt, and his comitatus spend the night in a lonely glen, where Mwindo miraculously produces houses and food. The aunt expresses her amazement before Mwindo's grandeur in the highest praises: "Lo! Shemwindo has brought forth a hero. . . . Shemwindo brought forth a hero who is never afraid, and Mwindo himself is a hero (out of himself)."

The hero is more than an audacious and vigorous youth (*munkangwe*); he is a performer of perplexing deeds (*kishisharo*: a subcategory of *tushingishi*, wonderful things, including the good and bad omens). He is a producer of wonder (*mpunda*) as common people are not; only the chief is considered to be a dispenser of wonder. The advent of the hero is an astounding phenomenon which is sometimes connected with cosmic turmoil (rain and thunder) or with unusual social and physical situations. It constitutes a drama never previously experienced: "What was never seen is seen for the first time," Shemwindo comments about his son's behavior. The hero is constantly plunged into difficulties and hardships (*byasumasuma*); he is tested and tormented (*ikuruhya*, lit., to make one ex-

93

hausted); he is tough (*wasuma*); he is capable of escaping dangers (*warama ekikuba*) and of safeguarding himself (*warama tu*). His life cycle is so richly varied that it produces stories (*kanangano*, lit., "something that tells a tale," is a praise term for the hero). The hero is of surpassing nature (*watarike*), a specimen of being that "is never being born." He possesses the plenitude of manhood (*bume*); he is conscious of his power; his only aim is to be victorious (*ihima*).

It is possible, however, that the term *murai* conveys moral connotations as well. The Nyanga perceive a semantic relationship between *murai* and *irai*. The latter noun, derived from the verb *iraa*, stands for the compelling and orally formulated last will of a dying person (primarily father; there are illustrations of it in the epics). In this respect the hero might be viewed as the recipient and the executor of such a message. He is born carrying this message inside him. The terms of the message are a progression toward social order, peace, good living, and the resulting glory and fame. The hero is destined to become king; his heroic career leads to wise rulership. His ultimate status is that of "eternal savior of people" (*shekaramo*).

NAMES AND EPITHETS

In epics I and II Mwindo is the only hero. Epics III and IV have two heroes, Mwindo and Kabutwakenda. The latter name is an epithet for Mwindo in epic I and in heroic tales. As far as I know, no Nyanga epics center on heroes with another name. In the heroic tales, however, many central heroes, in addition to Mwindo and Kabutwakenda, are identified under other names.

The appellation Mwindo is given in Nyanga social practice to a boy who is born after a number of girls in the family unit or to a girl who is born after a number of boys. The Nyanga perceive an etymological relationship between the term Mwindo and the verb *indo,* to fell trees. An epithetlike reference to Mwindo in a song (epic I) conveys the idea: he is praised as Kakiria, "the little one who makes the trees fall in the forest." Both meanings fit the pattern of epic I, where Mwindo is the only son after the birth of several daughters in his father's family group, and he is powerful. In the other epics, however, he is not the only son.

The Hunde pronunciation for Mwindo is Muhindo. According to Schumacher (1949), this title was given to a war leader among the Hunde. The connection between the terms Muhindo and Kahindo is obvious.

Kahindo is a female divinity worshiped both by the Hunde and the Nyanga, and there is a close association between the hero Mwindo and Kahindo in the epics. Mwindo encounters her on his journey to Nyamurairi; he heals her; he is her lover; and in one epic he marries her. The Nyanga tend to identify Kahindo with their own divinity Kahombo, Good Fortune. In epic I Mwindo's aunt calls him Kahombo to praise him as a benefactor. The hero's name might therefore evoke the idea of beneficiary and bringer-of-good-fortune. His ultimate destiny is to be a generous chief who brings fame and good living to his people.

Mwindo has no other personal names. It is customary among the Nyanga to bestow several names upon an individual as a correlate of progressions in the life cycle (spirit names, circumcision names, teknonymous names, etc.). Even when he becomes a chief, his name remains Mwindo or Kabutwakenda. In epic II the hero apparently has a double name, Mwindo Mboru, but Mboru, the Opener, must be considered as an epithet. In the course of the narratives the hero receives various praise names, epithets, and other appellations. Some of them are applied only casually; others are recurrent. Some are self-given; others are attributed by kinsfolk and common people. Mwindo speaks about himself as Little-Castaway, Little-one-just-born-he-walked, Little-one-who-does-not-eat-terrestrial foods, Man-of-many-feats, Virile man, Master-of-strength, Smart-One, and Little-child-of-many-wonders. Occasionally he makes a quasi-matronymic identification: The-one-fruit-that-Nyamwindo-has-brought-forth, The-day-he-was-born-he-did-not-drink-at-his-mother's-breath, or Child-of-Iyangura. In epic I Mwindo's paternal aunt has an abundance of terms for him: Hero-who-is-never-afraid, Our-prestigious-man, Good Fortune, My father, and Eternal-savior-of-people. The people around Mwindo formulate such praises as Cultivator-of-marvelous-things, Man-of-many-wonders, Child-of-a-chief, and He-is-not-a-man-to-provoke. The most magnificent praise name is given by Nkango, one of Mwindo's Pygmies: "Rejoicer-of-people, without hatred, giver, the good speaker." The fact that similar honorific statements are never made by the hero's father reflects the tension between them.

THE HEROIC MILIEU

The hero is entangled in a complex network of personal relationships, rooted in kinship, in friendship and alliance, in political and ritual associations, and in cosmic linkages with animals and divinities. Many of these relationships are of a positive, friendly, cooperative nature; others are marked by either temporary or inveterate hostility and antagonism. The physical background for the action offers a familiar setting: an area of forest, a chiefdom, a village, a house, or a field. When the action shifts from earth to the aquatic, celestial, or subterranean domain, the environment still provides the same familiar setting. No attempt is made to create a fearsome, unusual, fictive physical environment. At most there is one such instance: the land of Mutero which is without light and fire (epic III).

The hero is born in an ambiguous milieu. The hero's father is a chief, and Nyanga chiefs possess the attributes of divine kingship. The chief lives in a large village, located in a forest area and inhabited by subjects of different kinship origin, kinsfolk, princes, and counselors. There are ritual experts and Pygmies. All these conditions reflect the typical situation of a Nyanga autonomous chiefdom. The chief has several wives who are ranked (principal wife, ritual wife, preferred and despised wives). The origin of the hero's father is completely ignored, for in Nyanga thinking the exact social origin of a chief is dubious and mysterious. The inference, however, is clearly that the father, Shemwindo or Karisi, as he is called, is closely connected with divinities. He is not merely capable of traveling in the subterranean world (epic I); the implication is that his father's sister or some other close agnatic relative was married to Mukiti's father, while his own sister is married to Mukiti (epic I).

The information about the social identity of the hero's mother is more detailed. She is primarily referred to by the teknonymous name Nyamwindo, but in epic III she is known as Kahindo, the daughter of Hangi-of-Drum. Hangi is an important divinity, but the text does not specify whether Hangi in this instance is the divinity (if so, Mwindo's mother is of divine origin) or simply a devotee of Hangi. Throughout the epic tradition, Bats (sometimes called the Hundreds, Baniyana) are prominently mentioned as Mwindo's maternal uncles, but there is no indication that Mwindo's mother herself is a member of the Bat clan. Rather, the emphasis is on perpetual kinship links.

The hero has numerous affinal and matrimonial alliances with divinities: the paternal aunt is married to the water-dwelling Mukiti (epics I and II); the uterine sister is married to the sky-dwelling Lightning (epic II); the half brother is married to the daughter of the chthonic Muisa (epic IV). The hero himself is married to several wives who, except in epic IV, play no active role in the events. Most of these wives acquired before and during his enthronement are human, but in epic III the principal hero is married to Nyamurairi's daughter and, in epic IV, to Mukiti's daughter. Epic III provides an interesting enumeration of the names of Mwindo's seven wives: one is the daughter of Nyamurairi; three have animal names (Monitor Lizard; Wasp; and Bee, child of Needle); one wife is called Mweri (Moon); the sixth bears the name of Buriru (unidentified daughter of Opener-of-dark-clouds); the seventh wife is Nyakirimarimari, possibly referring to an animal-like specter. The unusual nomenclature strongly emphasizes the hero's cosmic outreach.

No children of the hero are mentioned in epics I and II. But, conjointly with the seven wives, ten children are explicitly listed in epic III. The manner in which the narrator himself interprets the symbolic content of these names is illuminating. For the most part, the children's names, which to our mind trace cosmic connections, are explained "etymologically" in terms of social situations and cosmic events coinciding with the time of pregnancy and birth. The bard's interpretation of the names is as follows:

> Ndurumo (Thunder): -*rurum*-: to thunder; the child was born in the evening when it was thundering.
> Kanyironge (Genet): -*rong*-: to pack one's belongings to move to another place; the child was born while they were packing their things to leave for another village.
> Ncongera (Snake-Tail): -*shongokar*-: to walk slowly and noiselessly (like a thief); the child was born while they were noiselessly retreating from war.
> Ntindi (Civet Cat): -*itindir*-: to halt one's journey for resting and smoking tobacco; the child was born while they had halted on a journey.
> Musukuiyera: *musuku*: a type of dance; -*yer*-: to spread banana leaves on the ground; the child was born during dances.
> Muntsuntsu (Bee): -*sus*-: to wrinkle the forehead without joy; to be angry; the child was born with a wrinkled forehead; it was angry at birth.
> Kanyampanda (Horn): the child's parents were expert dancers; a possible connection is indicated with -*band*-: to disperse the seeds in many places.
> Bisheria (Flashes of lightning): the child was born at a time of rain and lightning; possible relationships with -*sher*-: to throw sparks during the dance (to dance very well), and -*she*-: to give food to strangers.
> Utundo (Cloud): -*tund*-: to accumulate goods for a specific purpose; the child was born when it was very cloudy.
> Mwishi (Sun): -*shir*-: to burn; the child was born while it was very hot, that is, about noontime.

These are all names the Nyanga give to their children for the reasons

97

outlined in the bard's etymologies. It is noteworthy that many of them throw light on the character and nature of the hero. He is indeed a great traveler, a challenger, a singer, a dancer, and a hoarder of valuables.

In epic IV the complexity of the hero's status is expressed even more articulately in the name and position of Kabutwakenda's son, Destiny. The term Buingo, which I have translated as Destiny, has many referents: it is the name of a divinity; it is a title and an attribute of Nyamurairi as the giver of life and the regulator of destiny; it is used as the equivalent of long life. Destiny is the only child of the hero to be born under peculiar circumstances (both heroes have several other unnamed children in epic IV). His mother, the daughter of Mukiti, was courted by the two heroic half brothers, Mwindo and Kabutwakenda. Because she married the junior brother before his senior had obtained a wife she remained barren for a long time. She became pregnant after receiving a blessing from Mwindo, her husband's senior half brother. From certain points of view Destiny is considered the "mystical" son of Mwindo. After Kabutwakenda's death the initial conflict between the half brothers affects the relationships between Mwindo (the paternal uncle) and Destiny (the fraternal nephew). Mwindo temporarily usurps the power, but it is Destiny who ultimately is victorious and rules in glory. Destiny is the hero's alter ego, the symbol of his eternity and his everlasting glory.

The hero has numerous contacts with beings in the nonterrestrial spheres; in each instance the milieu in which the events occur is reminiscent of terrestrial life: the divinities and extraordinary beings live in villages and houses and they have human experiences (e.g., they like honey, song, music, dance; they give gifts; they practice trickery; they enjoy playing the dice).

It is not surprising that, among a people attaching importance to hunting and trapping and living in a rich animal environment, the hero has multiple and varied connections with animals. He is not, however, an avid hunter or trapper because these pursuits do not fit into the role of a potential chief. When he does engage in such activity he soon finds himself deeply enmeshed in difficulties. Animals are hunted and trapped, eaten, and exchanged in the epics, but the mystic bond or alliance between the hero and certain animals is of striking significance: the Bats are his maternal uncles, his blacksmiths, and helpers; Spider builds bridges and Mukei (rodent) digs tunnels for him; Wasps, Ants, and Bees attack at the hero's command; Sparrow is his assistant and dancer; Hawk, as a messenger, is friendly toward the hero and his allies. Above all, the deep mystical bond between the hero and his hunting dogs foreshadows his future chieftainship (the dog is one of the essential paraphernalia of chieftainship). The close relationships of the hero with Lightning (depicted as an animal) and Mukiti (portrayed as a water serpent) are examples of the special associations between hero and animals. An unpublished epic fragment (in my possession) depicts animals as playing an even more dominant role in the hero's life. Chief Kaboru ka Mwindo marries a wife among his maternal uncles (the animals). He orders his people to prepare a large field for him and to designate a guardian who will see to it that no one harvests bananas there. When Sparrow, the designated guardian, himself steals bananas, he is detected by the chief's wife. Ashamed, Sparrow flees; in order to please his chief he travels to Muisa's place and urges Kahindo, Muisa's daughter, to marry his chief. She agrees, but since she is made of iron she requests that Mwindo be forged. Mwindo agrees and invites the animals. They deliberate, finally designating two species of bats (Kakutu and Kikwe) to preside over the forging. Animal tears are needed to cool the iron; Elephant and Wild Pig shed their tears, but they are burned by flying sparks and flee, never again to mingle with their peers. Subsequently Mwindo and his maternal uncles (the animals) fetch Mwindo's wife. Afterward the hero journeys in the company of Iguana, Hawk, and Turtle (who carries his magical bag) to fight other chiefs. Among several antagonists, he successfully defeats Gorilla and Lightning and returns home to rule in glory.

The milieu described in the epics is basically aristocratic and ethnocentric. The chief and the hero are surrounded by princes, counselors, and subjects. The Pygmies, no longer considered strangers, are an essential component of this aristocratic milieu. Among the humans there are some "strangers" (i.e., chiefs and subjects of other political entities) who participate in Nyanga culture.

THE BIRTH OF THE HERO

In all epics the conception and the birth of the hero come to pass under special circumstances resulting either from the father's unnatural interdiction or from the mother's protracted barrenness. The father decrees that he wants no sons (epics I and II), and when a son is born he rejects his preferred wife (epic I). The preferred wife (epic III) and the principal wife (epic IV) remain childless for some time and are initially rejected by their husband. In all but one instance the hero is conceived in normal intercourse between his father and mother. In epic III, however, the hero Ka-butwakenda, who prematurely disappears, is the product of parthenogene-sis. A similar motif is found in at least two of the heroic tales: in one text a woman arriving at a crossroads finds herself suddenly pregnant; in another a child throws itself into a woman's womb while she is in the forest.

Few details are supplied about the period and the conditions of the pregnancy and the parturition. In epic I it is suggested that the hero's mother had an unusually long pregnancy (all other women who were simultaneously pregnant gave birth much earlier); in epic III the preg-nancy is protracted and the delivery itself is lengthy and painful. During its mother's extended pregnancy (epic I) the unborn child manifests its future heroic qualities by fulfilling certain unsolicited tasks for its mother, such as bringing firewood and vegetables and filling jars with water. Unusual features characterize the hero's birth in epics I and II. In epic I the hero himself decides the moment of birth; he emerges from his mother's middle finger. In epic II the hero is born through the palm of his mother's hand. Immediately after his birth in epics I, II, and III, the hero's very existence is threatened: he is attacked by the father and by Lightning; he is sur-rounded by a throng of people; he is buried in a grave; he is imprisoned in a drum and thrown into the water.

The hero is born with intrinsic capabilities and special objects which set him apart from the rest of humanity and ensure his successes and triumphs. Some of these are explicitly mentioned at the time of his birth, others manifest themselves in the course of his life, and a few are acquired from extrinsic sources.

In epics I and II the hero is born carrying a set of objects that possess a force of their own and operate at his command. Among them are a shoulder bag that contains a rope (I) or an unspecified medicine (II), a conga-scepter (I and II), a billhook (I and II), an adze and an ax (I and II). The shoulder bag permits the hero to store people, trees, goods, and tools; in the subterranean world of Nyamurairi he removes large numbers of banana stipites, axes, and billhooks from his bag. The rope is a means of communication with the hero's paternal aunt; she holds one end of the rope and receives signals indicating whether Mwindo is alive or dead. The conga-scepter is both lethal and soterial; it destroys enemies, revivifies friends and enemies, awakens the hero from a deathlike torpor, and allows him to fly. The billhook automatically clears the forest and keeps enemies in check. The axes spontaneously fell trees; the adze is used in the harvesting of honey. The *karemba*-belt (I and II) is another powerful object that subdues enemies, but we are not told whether the hero was born with it. All these items occur in Nyanga culture as cult emblems and/or chiefly paraphernalia. Epics III and IV do not explicitly identify objects with which the hero was born. Yet one of the heroes (IV) claims that he was born with a scepter, a spear, and a zanza, although, in fact, he acquired them from Mukiti; the other hero owns a copper bracelet received from Muisa.

In addition to his magical objects, the hero has numerous attributes which are revealed as his heroic career unfolds (discussed under the next heading). One set of characteristics, however, is explicitly stressed in connection with his birth. The hero has no physical handicap or youthful weakness which might defer the emergence of his heroic stature. It is emphatically stated (epics I, II, and III) that the hero was born speaking and laughing and that he could walk from the moment of birth. In fact, his most frequently used epithet is Kabutwakenda, Little-one-just-born-he-walked. There is no insistence on youth and maturation because the hero is strong, powerful, and ready for challenge from birth. Time for growth is not significant in epics I and II and is barely suggested in epics III and IV.

The physical appearance of the hero is only minimally described. In epic I the hero's small size is apparent throughout in the abundant usage of the diminutive prefix *ka-* and in the inferences made by other actors. Maidens informing the paternal aunt about Mwindo's arrival speak about "a little man"; the antagonist Kasiyembe calles him "a boy"; Hawk says that "it is not (merely) a little man who appears over there; he is with stories great"; the hero's paternal aunt describes him as "just yesterday's child" and as "a little baby." The smallness of the hero is not emphasized in the other epics. His beauty is particularly stressed in epic I when the paternal aunt, removing him from the drum, sees "the multiple rays of the rising sun and the moon. That is the beauty of the child Mwindo." In epic II Kahindo comments on "how beautiful he is." Although the hero's physical strength is not expressly noted, there are several references to his "surpassing" appearance and to his "manhood." Since the hero's body is forged at a certain stage of his life cycle, the implication is that he is strong and invulnerable. Yet Mwindo himself seems never to be a powerful fighter. When he is involved in a real fight, his magical objects do the work for him. Primarily, he engages in contests in which his wit, trickery, dancing, singing, and expertise in the game of dice render him victorious.

THE HERO'S ATTRIBUTES AND CHARACTER

As the heroic action develops the hero is seen to have a vast number of exceptional characteristics. They are intrinsic to his person and demand no justification. Some are more explicitly emphasized than others. At the moment of his birth, or shortly thereafter, the hero is fully involved in what the Nyanga call the *bihiri bya babume* or *miturembe*, that is, the strenuous work and the achievements of full-fledged men. He immediately demonstrates some of his unique abilities. He has the power of speech and possesses the magic of the word. His word has a compelling force, commanding the father's spears not to cause injury and lightning not to strike him. His verbal magic is enhanced throughout the epics, in his invocations, his blessings, his commands, his wishes, his boastful threats, and most of all in the dazzling effect of his songs. For the hero is not merely a resourceful speaker; he is a great singer. Mwindo loves to sing; always aware of the surpassing power of the sung word, he uses it effectively and continuously. The epics are replete with songs. By implication the hero is also an expert musician, as most directly disclosed in epic IV and in the unpublished epic by Rwanowa as retold by Sherungu. Shortly after his birth Kabutwakenda and his mother travel to Mukiti's to ask for a zanza; when he receives it, he sings and sings: "Little-one-just-born-he-walked and his mother did nothing but sing." Immediately thereafter he demands singers from Mukiti; sitting in a tree and singing, he attracts Pygmies, who are known as master musicians and singers.

The hero is prompt in manifesting invulnerability; he is a man of *mpanga*, that is, one who is destined for a long life and who will not die easily. He is buried, imprisoned in a drum, and thrown into the river, but he survives effortlessly. When smashed by the belt of Muisa or Nyamurairi, he readily awakens from a deathlike torpor. The hero's invulnerability is heightened when he is forged by his maternal uncles. He is in control of his own death; he dies and awakens by his own volition; he is pulverized by Lightning but is able to reassemble his limbs; he journeys successfully to the subterranean world and withstands all challenges of the divinities.

From the very beginning the hero has reliable allies among humans, divinities, and animals. The paternal aunt and the Pygmies rank among his foremost advisers and supporters. No conflict between the hero and his paternal aunt, alive or dead, ever occurs, though a mitigated tension between him and the Pygmies is described in epic III. Other kinsfolk are of limited usefulness: the help of the uterine sister Nyamitondo is short-lived; fierce competition mars his relationship with his father (epics I and II); there is intense antagonism between the hero and his half brother (epic IV). That the hero has no real friends among humans is logically in line with his lack of youth and his loneliness: "the friendship of the children results from their games." His closest and most faithful friends are found among animals: the hunting dogs, who never abandon him whether he travels with them, leaves them behind with his people, or gives them to his Pygmies for hunting; Bat(s), his maternal uncles who forge him; Spider who builds bridges; Wasp and Bee who serve him as ferocious soldiers; and sometimes Hedgehog and Hawk. Among the divinities the hero's stoutest ally is Lightning (although in the heroic tales he is sometimes antagonistic to the hero); Kahindo is an unpredictable ally and accomplice; the relations with Mukiti are ambiguous (inimical in epic I and friendly in epic IV).

As the heroic career unfolds, other unusual aspects of the hero are revealed. He is capable of prognostication and is sometimes prophetic. He can communicate from a distance with his paternal aunt. He is a healer and a thaumaturge, a restless traveler, an adventurer, a famous player of dice, a skillful dancer, and a pious worshiper. The hero has cosmic dimensions: he is able to travel in all the spheres of the Nyanga universe (terrestrial, aquatic, subterranean, and celestial) and capable of directly confronting the divinities. He has Lightning and Hail at his command. At one moment his sufferings produce cosmic turmoil (hail and rain for seven days).

As a culture hero he is responsible for the origin and development of certain techniques, cults, and customs (supplying cult paraphernalia for Lightning and the spirit of the paternal aunt; the use of buffalo tails as dance scepters; the cultivation of bananas; the advent of the hunting dogs and the Pygmies). Some of his actions result in the imposition of hunting and trapping taboos on the chiefs. The hero displays many contradictions of character. He is alternately ruthless and magnanimous, fearless and pusillanimous, threatening and merciful, insolent and shamefaced, heartless and grieved, boisterous and sedate, thoughtless and poised, verbose and meditative. He relentlessly takes women, animals, and goods from those whom he defeats, but he gives liberally to his friends and allies. He delights in praising himself immoderately, but he is subdued with his paternal aunt, tender toward his mother, and occasionally grieved over the fate of his people. The hero is not a man of hatred; instead, he is usually forgiving and conciliatory. Physical excesses are not his hallmark. He is not an intemperate eater, drinker, gambler, or lover. He is neither a brute nor a vile killer. His pure physical force is not clearly defined, although he likes to identify himself as a "virile man." Ultimately, as Nyamurairi himself must admit, "he has surpassing intelligence (*manko*); he is alert, quick, shrewd, and clever."

The contradictions in character are understandable in terms of Mwindo's dual personality (epics I, II, III): as a hero he is rough, unpolished, and, in Nyanga terms, uninitiated; as the heroic son of a chief he carries within himself the destiny to become a chief, that is, a person who is purified and a true initiate. It is this counterbalancing of opposites which leads him to purification and makes him acceptable as a chief. In the course of his heroic career Mwindo is an impatient traveler seeking new encounters and challenges and relishing in adventures (*tushimbo*). He has a village of his own, but he is not a *kirikiriki*, that is, "one who likes to stay in one place." Ceaseless rambling is certainly not rated as a virtue in Nyanga mentality, for, as the proverbs state, "Running around from one place to another is not a blessing" and "One who rambles is one who causes oppositions, slander, and betrayal among people." The chief, on the contrary, remains in one place; he does not engage in adventure. In epic I Mwindo the chief hurriedly engages in the destruction of Dragon-Ogre Kirimu, a deed that necessitates an ultimate catharsis from which he finally emerges as a full-fledged chief. The hero, as noted previously, possesses the magic of the word, yet he speaks excessively without watching his words. The predilection for verbosity is not a chiefly quality, for "What the heart knows, do not show it to the mouth," and "Quarrel is not good for the land."

In Nyanga thinking the hero's uniqueness lies, above everything else, in his ability to reverse destiny, an ability most effectively demonstrated in epics I and II. Born against his father's will, the son of a wife who has no ritual status, threatened at birth, rejected, abandoned, confronted with many enemies, exposed to hardships and tests, the hero manages to affirm himself and to reorient the course of existence. Through a process of quasi initiation the hero is transformed into a chief, developing from an impatient, fearless, aggressive being into a moderate, wise, generous, and settled patriarchal ruler whose raison d'être is fame and glory based on "good living." The hero's capacity to reverse destiny accounts, more than anything else, for his surpassing stature. The Nyanga view, stated in the text and in the conclusions of several tales, is that destiny is irreversible. This point is particularly well pictured in the following tale. A man—at times represented as a thief and often as an eager, prospective son-in-law—hides in a house where a child is being born. In a subsequent dream he hears the spirits predict that the child will be killed by a buffalo. In an effort to save the child the man decides to marry her. He gives the mother presents to establish a claim on the girl; and later, when the child is grown, he provides bridewealth for her. In a rare version of the tale he tries in vain to kill her so that she will escape the foretold death. When all requirements are fulfilled, the man takes his bride home. On previous occasions, however, he had killed many buffaloes, and his bride falls on buffalo horns stored in the house and dies. This form of fatalism does not affect the hero adversely; instead, he is influenced positively by it, in that he reverses the fate that nature and others have reserved for him: he is born by his own volition (I); his powerful father cannot destroy him (I and II); and the divinities are unable to subdue him (I, II, III). Above all, the hero never dies. His highest destiny is to become a chief, and he cannot escape it. As a chief he is unable to reverse his fate.

THE CHIEF

The Nyanga are politically organized into small, autonomous states. Each state (*cuo*) consists of a few villages and outlying hamlets and, correspondingly, only a few hundred people. A chief (*mwami*) with divine attributes is the supreme symbol of the unity and continuity of the state, though a state can temporarily exist without a chief. During an interregnum, power and authority are wielded by a small college of officials whose political and ritual offices are otherwise closely associated with chieftainship. A caretaker (*murongani*) may be selected from among the members of the college. The Nyanga conception is that the state maintains its autonomous existence and, if there is a ritual wife (*mumbo*) who is the real or sociological mother of the chief, is guaranteed a future. No Nyanga chief is politically or legally superior or inferior to another; certain kinship ties may, however, create special bonds of seniority between them.

Chieftainship is determined not only by automatic succession but by selection and initiation. A candidate passes through various stages before reaching the acme of chieftainship. First, he is heir apparent (*mubake*) because of a status acquired by birth, by fiction, or by recognition by chief makers; at the end of a complex process of decisions based on the behavior and character of the heir apparent, he becomes chief designate (*cungu*; *mucando ce wami*); later he receives a chief's name and some of the material symbols of office (*muri*). Eventually, after a prolonged trial period, he becomes a full-fledged chief (*mwami*) through initiation and enthronement rites. Finally, fame accumulated as a chief transforms him into a truly great chief (*muhanga*). The difference between the noninitiated and the enthroned chief is vividly expressed by the opposition of the terms *mu-*

bake and *mwami*. It is clearly shown in epic IV, when the incumbent chief says to his son Mwindo: "You are a *mubake* (chief designate)." The son replies: "No, you call me in the same manner as the child born on the path to the toilets (i.e., Mwindo's half brother)." And the father concludes: "He who will surpass his peer in intelligence is the one who will become a *mwami* (i.e., a full-fledged chief)."

THE SOCIAL IDENTITY OF THE CHIEF

The de jure position of a chief is defined by a number of rules, but the de facto social identity of each individual chief is something of a mystery. The Nyanga code of values enhances the secrecy. The guiding principles in the choice of a chief may be summarized as follows. A chief cannot be succeeded by a full or half brother. A brother is no more than a prince (*murusi*) but eventually he may become the father of the chief's ritual wife. A chief's brother must not be praised (as potential chief): "Otherwise, he would be hardheaded and damage the land." An essential principle of successorship is condensed in the statements that "chieftainship is not sought far away" and "chieftainship is a mountain of salt; it is not given to a neighbor." This principle suggests that succession to chieftainship is restricted to a narrowly drawn line of agnatic descent.

In most chiefdoms the ideal chief-elect is the son of the incumbent chief and his ritual wife. She herself is a very close patrilineal relative of her husband (e.g., half brother's daughter). This ideal situation is, however, subject to many secret manipulations. The chief obtains his ritual wife during the enthronement rites. At the climax of these rites he has intercourse with her in the presence of members of the college of ritual experts. Afterward the ritual wife lives separately from the chief, under the protection of designated dignitaries, in her own village. She possesses servants, subjects, and land; she may even ritually marry other wives in her own name. In the strict custom she has a designated lover as well. In other words, it is likely that the chief's relationships with her eventual son are sociological rather than biological.

A number of rules exclude all but one of the ritual wife's children from possible succession. The heir apparent must not be her firstborn son (there are indications that, if her firstborn was a boy, he was killed in ancient custom); he must not be a twin, either. Furthermore, the child must be born "holding in the hands" the sacred seeds of the land (eleusine; two varieties

107

of beans or one variety of beans and one of sorghum; *musobyo* and pumpkin) and sand. These restrictions reveal the decisive role played in the early selection process by the counselors. Sometime after the child's birth the counselors and their wives, having received many goats from the chief, conceal the sacred seeds in the hands of the designated child, saying: "We place all these grains in the hands of this child. If they fall, he will not be a true chief; if they remain for a longer time, he will be a great chief." During the enthronement rites the chief is reminded of this process by the Chief-Counselor.

Many complications arise if the ritual wife dies prematurely, has no acceptable sons, or gives birth to no sons at all. To cope with these problems and to avoid a war of succession, the Nyanga system provides several alternate solutions. There are, first of all, publicly known replacements, substitutes, or "doubles" for the ritual wife. In a simpler arrangement the chief has, in addition to the ritual wife, one who is called *mpombwe*, a close relative of the chief; if necessary, her son may become heir apparent. In a more complex and rather confusing system, some Nyanga chiefs in recent times have married two ritual wives (*mumbo*; pl. *bombo*): a senior one and a junior one. One chief whom I knew very well had a senior *mumbo* (daughter of his senior consanguine half brother) and a junior *mumbo* (daughter of his junior consanguine half brother). This arrangement creates difficult situations in the event both wives have acceptable sons who are supported by factions among the counselors.

A simpler but thoroughly secret arrangement is possible. Its principle is condensed in the Nyanga aphorism, "People of nothing give birth to chiefs." Under this arrangement the ritual wife receives an "adopted" son (the Nyanga do not think of this process as an adoption, but rather as a secret procedure for "placing a male child against her chest"). Responsibility for providing an adopted son rests entirely with the counselors, particularly the Chief-Counselor. Apparently the one chosen can be almost anybody's child: the son of a principal wife; the junior brother of the ritual wife herself; the child of a commoner. The provenance of the child, however, is a closely guarded secret, and the child completely loses its original identity.

The successor is not necessarily the real or fictive son of a ritual wife. Under some circumstances no heir apparent is named during the chief's lifetime, and the principal wife (*nyabana*) may receive chieftainship (*wami*) status after her husband's death, thus making her son eligible. In one region of Nyangaland the chief has no *mumbo*; his principal wife (*nyabana*) normally bears the successor. If she fails to have a son she is removed from the chief and given to a cross-cousin to bear a child on behalf of the chief.

The selection and the designation of a successor are obviously complex matters which defy thorough investigation because of the sanctions of secrecy which weigh upon them. There are indeed clear-cut rules, but the role of the counselors is of immense significance in their application. In epic IV the ritual wife asks the Chief-Counselor whether two chiefs were born (i.e. her own son and the child of the principal wife). The Chief-Counselor overstates the case in replying that "a chief is not brought forth, that he to whom he likes to give it (i.e., the chieftainship) is chief." On the other hand, the concept of achievement is of decisive importance in the ultimate consecration of a chief, as the epics and many of the heroic tales clearly illustrate. In one tale a junior becomes chief because he is more intelligent; in another an abandoned boy becomes chief because he frees the country from a monster. "Many people make the chief," the Nyanga say, and "Kingship is the stamping (of feet) : it is the tremor of people" (epic I). The chief must be loved by his people; he must safeguard them. In epic IV the dying chief complains because he did not leave a full-fledged chief among his sons, but then he consoles himself with the thought that "the child who was going to be loved by the people would become chief." The concept of achievement is foremost in the epics. Whether he is the son of the chief's preferred wife (epics I and II) or the child of a principal wife (epics III and IV), it is the nature of his accomplishments and of his character which transforms the hero into a chief.

THE ENTHRONEMENT

After an indefinitely long trial period the chief designate is enthroned. The highly secret rites take place on a sacred mountain. Only a select number of counselors and dignitaries and the college of ritual experts participate in the observances. Before the chief is enthroned he receives intensive teachings (*mahano*) from the Pygmies. The rites are conceived of as an initiation; in most chiefdoms the chief undergoes no other initiation, not even circumcision rites. The initiatory procedures, carried out in seclusion, include exchanges of goods, presentation of prescribed gifts (including land and women), elaborate consultations of the oracles, offerings to the ancestral spirits accompanied by litany-like recitations, formal teachings, imposition of taboos and prescriptions, the chief's marriage to the ritual wife (including ablution ceremonies and ritual eating), and the transfer of the paraphernalia of chieftainship.

In all the epics enthronement rites signify the transformation of the hero into a full chief. Many details about persons, procedures, exchanges, and paraphernalia are given in the epics, but all are sufficiently general not to betray any of the great secrets. Epic III provides some astonishing details about the burial of Chief Mutero Murimba and the removal of parts of his body to be placed in the royal *ukenye*-treasure. Since such information is not common knowledge, I am uncertain how to interpret it, except to suggest that the usual rules of secrecy have been relaxed. At any rate, the importance attached in the epics to the enthronement rights (and in epic III to the chief's burial) signified the close connections of the epic narratives and the chiefly milieu. Seen from this perspective the epics present, in a playful, almost innocent, manner, some facts about the mysteries of the chief's initiation to the "outsiders," the common people.

Although the data provided about the chief's initiation rites are rich in content, they are far from complete. If not sketchy, the documentation is misleading and at times incorrect, even deliberately so. For example, the respective roles of the members of the college of ritual experts are barely touched upon; the preponderant role of the incumbent chief in the process of ritual decision making is more than exaggerated; the placing of the initiation in the village is incorrect. The list of paraphernalia transferred to the initiated chief looks impressive, but even this simple enumeration of items is far from complete. I have noted twenty-eight such objects, including bells, rings, belts, garments, hats, bows, arrows, quivers, stools, and drums, several of which are entrusted to the ritual wife. These objects are brought by different dignitaries (Chief-Counselor; father of the ritual wife; Chief-Pygmy). Some are inherited as a legacy from previous chiefs; others are newly manufactured.

CONCEPTIONS ABOUT THE CHIEF

> Not every chicken breeds a chicken-with-
>   short crest;
> not every mother bears a speaker;
> not every woman bears a chief designate.

The Nyanga place the highest expectations and greatest values in their chiefs, as is manifest in numerous concepts, statements, and procedures. At my request, three of the most knowledgeable experts on Nyanga custom spontaneously formulated the following characteristics of a good chief: he is a giver; he provides hospitality; he is not a sorcerer; he is active and energetic; he is strong and firm; he is quiet (not rough or impulsive); he does not take other people's things; he does not scorn or insult people; he does not seduce women; he does not endorse lies; he harbors no hate. Like the hero, the chief is a *kiharisa*, one who is different from others because of his birth, his ways, and his destiny. The status of full-fledged chief is achieved through initiation, which is itself conditioned by the character and behavior of the candidate. The position of a full-fledged chief is synthesized by the verb *-sim* (and its derivatives *-simik-*, *-simanik-*, *-simish-*), which primarily means "to be able to, to be capable of," but in relation to the chief it has the connotation "to live in fame and glory, to prosper." The ultimate task of the chief is condensed in the verb *-simish-*, to make life good, prosperous, and happy for the people. He is a "master of blessing" (*mine mukisa*). "Many people make the chief": in order to keep unity among his own people and to attract subjects from other states the chief must exhibit a wide range of virtues. The Nyanga designate these virtues, positively or negatively, in the following manner. The chief is strong and powerful; only the power of god (referred to in this context as Ongomana, god almighty) is greater. There is a transcendent power in him. Some of his hair, for example, is placed in an amulet bundle to protect the hunting dog against curse and injury; the dog will be feared by the animals as the chief is feared by his people and will have immunity from curses. The chief's very presence irradiates so strong a force that, should he visit a place where twins are born, they would die. Yet the chief must not act arbitrarily or tyrannically. He is not a provoker (*shebushoshori*), not a quarrelsome person (*nkomori*), not a criticizer or trickster (*shemutotoyo*); he does not indulge in arguments (*muhakahaka*). He is not a hypocrite ("a bird with two tails"). He does not tergiversate; he does not harbor hate. He is not rapacious: "The chief is given things; he does not give (things) to himself." Positively stated, the chief practices restraint in words and deeds; he is generous (a sharer, *murengi*); he is decisive and prompt in action; he provides wise counsel. The Pygmy Nkango (epic III) aptly summarizes the chief's supreme qualities: "Mr. Rejoicer-of-people, provider of conciliation, who does not foster hatred; the good speaker who does not rest." The chief is a protector: "It is the great chief who sustains the common man" (epic I). The chief with great fame "brings warmth to the land to make it go smoothly because of his good ways in treating people, giving good counsel, having no scorn for his people." One of the statements made to the chief during his enthronement says: "You, chief, may you go on giving. Be awed by the people arriving at the village entrance. Do not select people saying that some are yours and others not yours." In all relationships between chief and subjects, stress is placed on reciprocity in respect, awe, and generosity.

The chief is surrounded with many protective taboos and prescriptions that aim at preserving his life-force (*karamo*). He must not eat certain foods, including many kinds of game and fish. He must not trap, hunt, or fish; his Pygmies, wives, and other subjects perform these tasks for him. The chief must not brew beer or climb up on the roof of a house. He must be carried across the water; he must never bathe his head in the river. He must remain aloof from all life-cycle ceremonies. He does not pass through the purification rites celebrating the birth and death of his children and grandchildren; instead, the *musao* and *muhakabi* ritual experts and their wives, or the *nyabana* and an unmarried sister, take care of them. The chief must not be initiated into voluntary associations; in some parts of Nyangaland, he must not go through circumcision rites. His hair is never completely shaved, and when it is shaved beer instead of water must be used.

The most extraordinary prescriptions pertain to the chief's death and burial. In ancient custom an ailing or weakened chief was secretly killed with a hammer blow to the chest or strangulated by special hereditary officials. His death was not disclosed and his body was left in his house to putrefy; animals were roasted to dispel the odor. Durable parts of his body, such as nails, hair, and teeth, were removed for placement in the *ukenye*-bundle. Ultimately the skull and bones were buried with some of the chiefly paraphernalia on a sacred mountain. Only "sacred" officials (Muembwa and Musimba) were allowed to touch, to inherit, or to be entrusted with the paraphernalia that had had contact with the chief's body. During the month-long period of mourning all male domestic animals were killed; no work was done with iron tools; no musical instruments, except for sacred circumcision instruments (talking stick, mirliton, and bull-roarer), could be played.

The chief designate was finally brought before the people in a newly built village. In all four epics it is the hero's destiny to become a chief. He is the son of a chief, but since he is not the child of the ritual wife, except for Mwindo in epic IV, he is not in the legally favored position for chieftainship. His initiatory ordeals and achievements and the transformation of his character transfigure him into a chief. Since there are stagelike levels in the position of chief, the hero-chief reaches his full status and glory only by thoroughly demonstrating his moral qualities and greatness. In epic I Mwindo, the rejected son of the chief's preferred wife, accomplishes a series of harrowing feats before reconciling with his father. The father confers the paraphernalia of chieftainship upon him, but the chief must still experience a celestial catharsis before his greatness is fully establish- ed. In epic II Mwindo, though initially rejected, is prompt in giving proof of his class (the killing of Big-Bird). He is designated as heir, but according to his father "he must teach himself to bring harmony in the land." A further series of accomplishments by Mwindo and his Pygmy Shekaruru lead to Mwindo's enthronement. Epic III does not place the emphasis on Mwindo's ascent from hero to chief, but rather on his development from a mere chief with heroic qualities to one with widespread fame. Epic IV is more complex. Its basic theme is that "kingship is strife." Against the background of the father's hesitations, the epic demonstrates why Kabutwakenda and his son Buingo are the logical rulers in contrast with Mwindo, a possible heir to the throne whose intractability, arrogance, and machinations should disqualify him. In each instance the confusion and doubts expressed at the beginning of the epic are resolved in a forceful ending. Peace and prosperity prevail in a country that has an enlightened and glorious chief. Implicit in the glorious ending is the promise of eternal continuity: the hero-chief rules and there seems to be no end in sight for his rulership (epics I and II); the hero-chief dies after solving all the prob- lems of succession, thus ensuring the continuity of the state (epic III); the hero-chief is succeeded by his son, who by successfully defeating a villain perpetuates the tradition of his father (epic IV).

THE HEROIC TALES

Many of the Nyanga tales offer parallels to and analogies with the epics in the pattern of action, the nature of the actors, or the dominant underlying idea. A large number of tales are, of course, so remote from the epics that no convergences are discernible. Among them are tales in which animals, characters, and persons in multiple kinship roles are the protagonists. Of the tales that exhibit striking similarities with the epics, both in action and in viewpoint, it is possible to distinguish several kinds:

1. Tales in which the action is centered on Mwindo or on another named or unnamed person of heroic stature.
2. Tales in which one or more categories of dramatis personae who are dominant in the epics assume primary roles. Such characters may be divinities like Ongo, Nyamurairi, Muisa, and Nkuba; fabulous beings like Mukiti, Mpaca, and Kirimu; or chiefs.
3. Tales in which ideologies fundamental to the epic intrigue are developed.
4. Tales that present close parallels to particular episodes narrated in the epics.

(A more systematic analysis of these and other kinds of tales will be presented in a book to be entitled *The Nyanga Tales* and now in preparation by Daniel and Brunhilde Biebuyck. In this study I limit myself to general considerations.)

Heroic tales are widespread in Nyangaland. I have found them in more than forty villages, told by individuals of different age, status, and sex. Some of them were narrated by persons closely related to the bards, others by the bards themselves, and still others by people who were outside the mainstream of the epic traditions.

Of special interest are tales that center on a heroic character. Although they are not summaries or imitations of the epics, they are constructed around epical characters, events, circumstances, action patterns, and ideas. Yet the subject matter and the formulation are always original, self-contained, and autonomous. The narrators do not perceive these tales as fragments of a larger whole, but as complete narratives in their own right; even a bard like Sherungu separates them clearly from the epic he relates. Sometimes, of course, a person who knows an epic is so confused, because of old age or illness, that he can reproduce only a fragment of it. I was present when, for example, the very old Nyakace was forced, owing to lack of both memory and singing skill, to abandon an epic narrative for which he had been famous after singing a short, fairly coherent passage which he had begun in medias res. In the absence of a Nyanga theory it is idle to speculate whether the tales are offshoots or by-products of the epics or the original models from which epics are formed.

The central male hero is known under different names: Mwindo, Katawa (Little-Castaway), Kabutwakenda (Little-one-just-born-he-walked), Kisa, Burio, Kabasha, Karisi, Nfiri, Ubunge, Kabucarange and Pirikii, Buingo wa Ngoma, Ndura Katwa, Mpa, Karunga, and others. In a rare instance the hero is a female (Kabiribiri). On certain occasions the hero has no personal name and is simply identified as Little Boy, the child, the junior brother, or the most junior son. The majority of the heroic tales center on two dominant epic heroes, Mwindo and Kabutwakenda. In some epic versions names such as Kabutwakenda and Katawa are epithets of Mwindo himself; the same identification is established in several of the tales. The hero's father is a chief or a person of unspecified status. The father has several wives, sometimes an unusually large number for the Nyanga. The mother may occupy a variety of statuses: principal wife, senior or junior wife, beloved or rejected wife, a father's sister. In many tales, however, no specific reference is made to the mother's status; in one tale the hero is an orphan.

The heroic tales usually give few details about conception, pregnancy, and the hero's birth. Occasionally all the wives of the hero's father are pregnant simultaneously. Sometimes the unborn hero performs special tasks for his mother. In some instances the hero is created by normal processes of conception and birth; in others he is born after a prolonged pregnancy or as the result of a mysterious conception, as when the mother finds herself pregnant on arrival at a crossroads because the hero has thrown himself into her womb. Ubunge is born in the forest; he reenters the womb and is born again in the village. In one tale the hero is the son of a woman and a serpent. Frequently an element of social drama marks the advent of the heroic child: the father has decreed that he wants no sons; as the result of this decree, the son is chased by the father or manages to escape into the forest with the cooperation of his mother and the midwives.

The hero tends to possess from birth special gifts and attributes. As noted above, occasionally the unborn hero is capable of leaving the womb and performing certain tasks for his mother. Sometimes he decides the moment of his birth. He may manifest other special powers directly after birth or suddenly in the course of his existence: at birth he walks and talks, challenges and shouts, cries in three voices, has an erect penis. He has no youth; in one tale he is transformed overnight into an adult. In difficult situations he may exhibit diverse combinations of superhuman properties: he flies; he makes himself invisible; he metamorphoses into a crab or a young woman; by sheer volition he removes houses and objects from his father's village or makes iron tools cultivate by themselves, foods cook by themselves, houses build themselves, and animals skin themselves; he seizes without effort the spears of enemies; he revivifies the dead; he cleaves the waters; he dispenses medicine; he causes famine; he produces food; he dances unhurt above traps; he travels in the aquatic, celestial, and subterranean spheres, successfully confronting powerful beings in each of them; he has advance knowledge of the future; he can circumvent trickeries perpetrated by divinities; he has a tremendous power of destruction; he is an accomplished musician (player of the zanza), singer, and dancer and a formidable player of dice. In some tales he is essentially a man of the forest, a tireless traveler, a hunter, a challenger, a restless searcher for new adventures.

There is little physical description of the hero. In some tales he is implicitly conceived of as a small being; in others he is a scurvy youth who, healed by a Pygmy, turns into a "shining" being and a person "beautiful like the morning sun." In a rare instance the hero's body is by implication a vast receptacle, since hunting dogs are hidden in his armpits. When he is forged by his maternal uncles, his body is solid iron and invulnerable.

The hero is in possession of magical objects with which he was born or which he acquires in the course of his existence: a little drum covered with dogskin to protect people from their enemies, a small shoulder bag, a billhook, iron dice, a white hide, a cowrie belt, a scepter, an unspecified "thing" (*ntuturi*) given him by Lightning, a *mwika*-charm obtained from his paternal aunt, a wonderful stool made by his mother with which he flies and chases furious elephants.

The hero interacts with one or several categories of beings: kinsfolk (father, mother, paternal aunt, maternal uncles, brothers, sisters) ; other individuals (midwives, chiefs, Pygmies) ; divinities (Nyamurairi, Ongo, Muisa, Nkuba, Kahindo) ; animals, birds, and insects (dogs, bats, ants, spiders, hawk, waterfowl, warthogs, *mburu*-monkeys) ; fabulous beings (Water Serpent Mukiti, Specter Mpaca, Dragon-Ogre Kirimu) ; unusual personages (Nkuta, "a carver of drums"; Wild-Banana-Tree Itembe; Huge-Rock Ukanga) ; and rare actors (Gorilla, Bush-Baby, Aardvark). Many of these actors occupy familiar positions vis-à-vis the hero: the father as a competitor who must recognize the greatness of his son; the paternal aunt as an adviser; the maternal uncles (mostly Bats) who forge, liberate, or guard him; Nyamurairi or Ongo who tricks him; Spider who builds bridges for him; the dogs that are his resourceful companions.

The hero is engaged in recurring activities: he is exposed to tests and succeeds; he destroys powerful enemies in battles, quasi fights, or games; he acquires wealth by depleting his father's village, defeating enemies, winning games, receiving gifts; he causes famine and poverty.

In the tales the hero is fearless, steadfast, and resolute. To some extent he is viewed as a culture hero (a bringer of peace, an initiator of cults). He has unwavering courage and unswerving ambition. He is very confident and strong-willed. He is tender toward his mother, reconciliatory with his father, pious toward Nkuba, completely submissive to his paternal aunt, and trustworthy with the Pygmies. The hero is not merely a killer, but a giver of life, a bringer of peace, a generous person. At the end of his heroic career he frequently becomes a chief who rules in glory, either in his own land or in the land of his paternal aunt.

A simple enumeration of motifs, characters, and action patterns developed in the heroic tales cannot do justice to their wide diversity of scope and content. Each tale forms a unique narrative that variously combines and permutes the essential features. A common structural plan underlies the tales, but there are wide deviations from and frequent alterations of it.

The simplest schema characteristic of a substantial number of tales is the following:

1. A man—chief or commoner—has married several wives.
2. He decrees that his wives should bear girls only.
3. The wives become pregnant all at once.
4. One wife, usually the principal or beloved wife, gives birth to a son, possibly after a prolonged pregnancy.
5. The newborn son has special attributes: he can speak and give orders; or he can remove, by his volition alone, all objects from his father's village.
6. The newborn son leaves the paternal village:
   —he is chased by the father;
   —or he flees with his mother's and the midwives' help;
   —or he departs on his own initiative.
7. The son settles somewhere in the forest or begins a series of travels.
8. Having settled in the forest, he removes all objects from his father's village, causing poverty and famine there; or during his travels he amasses goods by winning in the game of dice.
9. The impoverished father learns about the son's prosperity and decides to live with him; or the traveling hero establishes himself and becomes a chief; or the son's greatness is acknowledged by the father, and the son becomes a chief.

There are many variations of this pattern, which may be simplified or amplified. The following is an example of simplification. A man with several wives decrees that he wants no sons. One of the women goes into the forest; the son in the womb asks his mother "to let him out, right there." The son is born in the forest; the father, informed about the birth, chases the mother but cannot find the son "because he had already gone to trap." The boy flees to his maternal uncles, who do not recognize him. The mother arrives, asking her kinsmen how they could ever forget their nephew. The boy is accepted. The father comes to claim his son; the father is chased.

The plan may be reduced even further. In one tale a man has two wives: the senior wife is despised; the junior one is beloved. Each wife gives birth to a son; the father does not want to see his senior wife's child and orders the midwives to throw him into the rapids. When they refuse, the father himself tries to discard the son but the latter has more strength; he heaves the father into the water; the father dies. On his return the son receives gifts from his maternal uncles and is praised for his deed.

Many of the preliminaries may be omitted, the tale consisting of a concatenation of related actions. In this instance one has the impression that the tale is merely a short passage excerpted from an epic or a condensation of parts of it. Such a tale, however, is closed and self-contained in the mind of the narrator. The following example illustrates this point. Mwindo decides to marry the daughter of Nyamurairi. On his journey he fights with many animals; finally he achieves friendship with Spider, who builds a bridge to make possible Mwindo's arrival at Nyamurairi's. Mwindo encounters Pygmies who are chasing a wild pig. He refuses to let them kill the animal; instead, he hurls a spear at it but misses the target. Pursuing the pig, he spends the night in the forest; his paternal aunt builds a house for him. Chasing the pig farther and farther away, Mwindo arrives in the banana grove of Kahindo, the daughter of Nyamurairi. She throws food at Mwindo's dogs; they refuse to eat. The paternal aunt appears, declaring that Mwindo is "dead" now because he has arrived in Nyamurairi's village. She places the dogs under Mwindo's armpits. Nyamurairi sets traps of ants, goatskins, and leaves (all transformed people), but Mwindo escapes the trickery because he knows the identity of the transformations. He now appears before Nyamurairi and is invited to reside with Kahindo. But Nyamurairi has arranged a pitfall in which Mwindo apparently dies. Nyamurairi concludes: "This one said that he is a spirit; lo! he is merely a human. I have overpowered him and his dogs." Clearly this tale condenses and telescopes several events contained in epic II. The motif of the pitfall and the apparent death of Mwindo are additions that help to round out and conclude the tale.

Other tales emphasize the rapid succession of feats (e.g., the scene in which the hero is forged by his maternal uncles or the encounters with Nyamurairi). There is wide diversity in the way narrators describe such events. For example, the three following passages, describing the scene in which the hero is forged, are taken from three different tales.

> He went to his maternal uncles, Sun, Lightning, Moon, and Bat. He asked them to forge him. He said that the eyelids and eyelashes of his paternal aunts would serve as charcoal and that tears would serve as water to extinguish the fire. But his mother and grandmother refused to let him be forged in that manner. So, because his mothers refused this method, he requested that they go to fetch two thousand jars of beer. When the beer was ready, he gave it to his paternal aunts and to his mothers, so that they would get drunk and sleepy. The maternal uncles forged one part of him. They awakened the mothers and made them drunk again. The uncles forged the other part. When they had joined together all his joints, they awakened the women and asked them to cut him up with their axes and knives. But the axes and knives broke. Two days later he decided to go to God's place.

Mpa went to his maternal uncles, leaving a calabash behind and saying: "If the calabash breaks, it means that I am dead." He went to his maternal uncles, the Bats, singing. He slept in a camp in the forest. He encountered a lake; he split the lake in order to traverse it. His maternal uncles received him. They gave him food, but he refused it. He said that he wanted to be forged. They tried to refuse, but he showed them a finger (i.e., he warned them). They made preparations; they put water in leaves; they shaved all the people; they removed his entrails and placed them on the ground; they placed him in the forge. They shaved all the people to use their hair as charcoal and their tears as water. They placed him in the fire. They put his entrails back into the body. He was very heavy now. They set him up straight. He was all iron now. They tested him with spears and axes; the weapons broke. The maternal uncles gave him two maidens and all kinds of things. He returned home, splitting the lake to cross it.

He went to his maternal uncles, saying that from that place would come the knowledge to fight with Dragon-Ogre who had destroyed his kin. The maternal uncles asked all the women for their eyelids and eyelashes, to put them into baskets, and to shed their tears into jars. They took him to the blacksmith's forge and used the eyelids and eyelashes for charcoal. He sang:

> Bat, my maternal uncle,
> My mother, strain yourself
> That I may fight with Kirimu.

They heated him; they hammered him; they poured tears over him. They hurled spears at him to test him. He was plain iron. He went to fight Kirimu.

Individual creativity and taste are at their best when narrators elaborate on a widespread motif and fashion a complete story from it.

One tale concerns the orphan Nfiri. He is hated in his village and placed in a jar by his paternal aunt and is carried to God's village. The narrative consists entirely of the ordeals to which the boy is submitted by God and the ways he successfully comes through them with the help of his paternal aunt and Sparrow. God finally recognizes Nfiri's force ("he who recovers from the pool of blood among the resin trees is surpassing in strength"), and the boy receives gifts and becomes a chief.

Many elements of the basic pattern may be reversed and transformed. In one tale Ndura Katwa, a young thief, is thrown into the river. He sinks down in the water and is recovered by Kahindo. She takes him to her village, where Ndura Katwa makes himself welcome with the seductiveness of his zanza playing. When Kahindo subsequently marries Lightning, she takes Ndura with her. Having been accepted because of his music, he is sent to the land of Nyabirunga to bring it peace. He discharges his mission of reconciliation and receives many goods; he flies back with them to Lightning. Having received from Lightning a magic "thing," he is urged to return to his own village. On his way home he brings peace to fighting villagers, revivifies a dead person, provides food, and crosses traps with sharp razors. When he gets home Ndura Katwa is proclaimed a true chief. He asks his people to abandon discord and demands a white goat, which Lightning had claimed. His people have only a white fowl to give, and Ndura refuses it. He accuses his people of laziness and tells them they can continue killing one another. Flashes (Lightning) carries him away; the people see him climbing into the sky.

In another text a great chief lives happily with his children. One day, while clearing a road, they find an egg in the nest of a sunbird. They take it home with them because the father had instructed them, "what you may find do not leave it at the end of the road." When the egg hatches the fledgling asks for chickens, then for dogs and goats; finally it devours all the people and the chief himself. The counselors flee with "the child," as the unnamed hero is called. When the child reaches adulthood he asks his grandmother who killed his parents. When she tells him that the animals slew them, the youth destroys all the animals. He accuses his grandmother of having deceived him. She advises him to make arrows and quivers and to journey to the abandoned village and fight "that thing which is sitting in a tall raffia tree." The youth overpowers the tree; people emerge from it; the whole land is filled again with people; the father enthrones the son.

In a third tale the grandmother and the mother flee with an unwanted son into the forest. The son performs many feats in rapid succession. At the peak of his triumphs he returns to his village Tubondo. The people there hide the father among plants and trees, but the hero destroys them all; he kills the father and explains why he is not guilty of a crime.

In a fourth tale the father who rejected his son is forced by famine to reconcile with him, but the latter refuses to return home. The father, fearful that the son may take away the chieftainship, plots with the Pygmies against him. The plot fails; the son returns home and chases the father and the headman; the Pygmies flee.

Usually the hero is depicted as a destroyer of Kirimu. In one tale, however, the boy Karisi, abandoned by his mother in the forest, reaches the village of Kirimu. He orders a wife of Kirimu to hide him and to inform her husband that she has borne a child. When Kirimu arrives, the child sings and sings. Kirimu, pleased by the song, gives him gifts; the boy grows up in Kirimu's village but finally leaves in quest of a wife.

In one tale the heroic boy is not rejected by the father, but he makes a mistake which subsequently is expiated by great deeds. A man who has two wives fathers a son; the son marries and has a child. The people go into the forest while mother and child remain behind. Hawk and Lightning come to tattoo the mother. When the woman's mother-in-law returns from the forest she asks the daughter-in-law who tattooed her, but the latter refuses to divulge the secret. Pressed by his grandmother, the child makes his mother confess. Then Hawk and Lightning take the mother away into the sky. Three months later the child invites other boys to help him search for his mother. With drums and rattles they climb into a hollow tree; from there, with the help of Spider, they cross bridges to Cloud, Lightning, Moon, and Bieya (Sky). The child stubbornly asks for his mother, refusing all substitute gifts. When she is given to him he returns home by the same road. The father praises the son as "a man" and "a chief."

Sometimes the affective bond between mother and child is very strong. The injustices of the father, first toward the mother and then toward the child, are the driving forces that lead the son to greatness. The hero Ubunge throws himself into his mother's womb (i.e., conceives himself); his mother is the despised wife of the chief. He is born in the forest; he cultivates and hunts for his mother on the very day of his birth. He enters the womb again and instructs his mother to journey home. Saddened by the abject condition of his mother, Ubunge is born again as a challenge to his father; he leaves the village, flying on a magic stool made by his mother and chasing elephants with it. He settles in the village of his maternal uncles; fourteen rows of houses emerge from his stool. He lives in glory with his mother; the father and his people establish themselves with Ubunge. He becomes a chief and his mother becomes a ritual wife.

In one tale there is enmity between a brother and sister and very close cooperation between the brother and his paternal aunt. A man's favorite wife gives birth to a girl while his rejected wife bears a son. The girl does not understand why the father should leave his possessions to a boy who is the child of a rejected wife. She makes a drum, asks her brother to measure himself in it, locks him inside, and throws the drum into the river. A woman coming down to the river hears the boy singing, but the people she informs about it are unable to reach the fleeing drum. Meanwhile the boy is guarded by the spirit of his paternal aunt, who dwells across the river. A second attempt by the people to save him fails. The boy is then recovered from the drum by his paternal aunt; she cleanses and heals him. Seven days later the paternal aunt orders all the people to remain in the village to view "the child that had died." As compensation she asks the child for a pot for the purpose of making offerings to her.

In one tale a chief who rejects his son is not a participant in the latter's glory. Confronted by the son's wealth (he plants banana groves and produces much food), the father is advised by his elders to settle in a hamlet; the son rules in fame and is established in a large village.

In one instance a heroic tale attempts to explain the colonial relationships between whites and blacks. The two children of the creator god intermarry. God gives them everything except meat. After the birth of Kabucarange, the son, the father, desirous of obtaining meat for the celebrations, kills an animal "among God's people." The guardian of God's game catches the thief. Left alone with his mother, Kabucarange journeys with her to a faraway place; they arrive in a desolate village. Here the boy receives, in a dream, the authorization to use everything except one house. One day, while Kabucarange is out hunting, the mother enters the forbidden house and sleeps with a serpent that lives there. She gives birth to a child Pirikii who can "walk and talk from birth on," "a child who has a book and a pencil and who can speak." The serpent asks the mother which of her two children is the more beautiful; she concludes that it is the son she bore the serpent. When the mother and the serpent attempt to poison the other child, Pirikii informs his half brother Kabucarange. Pygmies arrive; they have a daughter. The Pygmies receive from Pirikii permission to choose from the riches stored inside the houses. They take only machetes. Invaders come; Pirikii chases them and gives a woman to his older half brother. Kabucarange and the woman have a daughter whom Pirikii marries. The woman gives birth to a white youth, whereas the children of Kabucarange are black. Subsequently the black children perform all the work that Pirikii's white child imposes upon them.

The heroic tales, both explicitly and implicitly, make statements about the Nyanga moral code. Major themes found in the epics permeate the conclusions. A father must love all his children equally: "If you have two or more children, love them all"; "Among children there are none bad." It is particularly unwise and immoral to reject a son. Sons are the "saviors of people"; they have more *wenge* (wit, intelligence, know-how) than their sisters: "When you bring forth a son, do not make fun of him, because he has much intelligence surpassing that of women. And therefore he may save his father when the latter begins to sink on his knees (i.e., to weaken)." A father, who had chased his son and was later saved by him from Kirimu, concludes that he is "never to joke with a son, even though he is brought forth by a woman; she is sold, but he remains." In the same vein, a junior son or brother must not be rejected or underrated by his father or senior brother. If the senior defaults, the junior may take over the leadership. A junior may be more intelligent, capable, and successful than a senior: "Stupidity (*burunge*) and infatuation (*butengi*) are ruinous; to be born a senior does not mean to have intelligence." In general, one must not alienate people because of size, age, appearance, or bad fortune. This idea is powerfully expressed in the conclusions drawn in the Nfiri tale: "Do not harm your peer, even if he looks ugly or suffers from ill fortune. Things may change. Do not tease (cause to suffer) another person, when his life (destiny) is still long (faraway). If you want that person's death, think that death will come to you, also. He who has no intelligence is already dead. You must live in the land desiring each other; one person or another may help you out of difficulties." Mutual aid and understanding in the group are stressed: "The world is mutual aid; he who helps his peer will be helped in turn"; "Mutual agreement brings about solidarity. The world is made of mutual aid." It is vanity to think egotistically about oneself, to praise one's strength and heroism, for strength is not the attribute of one man alone: "Even if you become a brave-one (a hero) and surpass others, you will not fail to encounter the one who can grind your bones and turn them into dust." The wise person is he who receives and accepts the teachings (*mahano*): "He who does not receive the teachings will become one who mistreats himself, then and there."

II

THE TEXTS

THE MWINDO EPIC II

SYNOPTIC TABLE OF CONTENTS

I. *The setting*
   A. Temporal and spatial
      The events are placed in remote times in an unspecified kingdom
      where Shemwindo is chief. The action begins and ends in the
      village of Tubondo. Throughout the epic the action returns to
      this village as if to link the episodes together. The real drama,
      however, takes place outside the village, in the forest or in other
      villages. The actors move in three spheres of the Nyanga cos-
      mos: the earth (*oto*), the air (*mwanya*), and the subterranean
      world (*irunga*). In all three spheres there are villages. When the
      action shifts away from the village context into the forest,
      incidents are placed in a hamlet, a small village, or a hunting
      camp hidden in the forest.
   B. Social
      The hero's father, Shemwindo, is a chief who has married two
      wives. The chief decrees that no sons shall be born to his wives.
II. *Birth of the hero*
   A. The beloved wife Iyangura bears a son.
   B. The son is born through the palm of his mother's hand.
   C. He speaks and walks from the moment of birth.
   D. He possesses a shoulder bag containing medicine and a *conga-
      scepter*.
   E. He is called Mwindo.
   F. The hero's mother also bears a daughter, Nyamitondo Mwindo.

G. The despised wife has a son and a daughter.

H. The chief orders the counselors to throw his son into a grave.

I. During the night the boy emerges from the grave and goes to sleep near the hearth in his father's house.

J. The father expresses surprise.

K. People come to view the child.

L. The father decrees that the child shall not be buried again, "so that he may live."

III. *The hero and his sister Nyamitondo Mwindo*

A. Nyamitondo is given in marriage to Lightning by her father.

B. Lightning takes her to his village in the air and teaches her how to cultivate.

C. She returns to earth because of her desire to visit her kinsfolk.

D. She goes with her brother Mwindo to the forest to teach him how to cultivate a banana grove.

E. They find an egg, take it back to the village, and place it in a hen's nest.

F. The sister returns to her husband Lightning.

G. A bird "hatches itself" from the egg.

H. As the bird grows, Mwindo feeds it meat, potatoes, and bananas.

I. Since Mwindo refuses to kill the growing bird, it devours all the chickens and the goats.

J. Pressed by his people, Mwindo climbs into the sky through a hollow tree to seek the help of Lightning.

K. Mwindo's sister receives iron weapons and advice from her husband.

L. She returns earthward with Mwindo; they find that the Dragon-Bird has devoured all the people.

M. The sister is swallowed by the Bird; she kills it from the inside and removes herself.

N. Mwindo and his sister cut the Bird's heart open, and all the people, including the hero's father and mother, emerge from it.

O. A young man, Beautiful-One, emerges and organizes dances for Mwindo and his sister.

P. When all the houses and things are back in the village, Shemwindo provides his daughter with two maidens for her husband.

Q. Lightning comes to carry his wife away from earth.

IV. *Mwindo's expedition to Buffaloes*

    A. Mwindo's father decrees that all people shall henceforth dance with buffalo tails as scepters.

    B. Mwindo decides to fetch the buffalo tails from the house of his friend, the chief of Buffaloes.

    C. He acquires the tails for his people.

    D. He buys two dogs, Ndorobiro and Ngonde, and gives them to his Pygmy, Shekaruru, for hunting.

    E. He returns home; dances are organized in honor of the dogs.

V. *First hunting expedition by Mwindo's Pygmy, Shekaruru*

    A. The dogs are given a large meal and are blessed by Mwindo.

    B. Shekaruru sets out with the dogs and encounters Hawk being eaten by red ants.

    C. He liberates Hawk and receives Hawk's blessing and promise of help.

    D. The Pygmy kills a wild pig and takes it back to the village. The pig (first kill of the dogs) is ceremonially eaten by Mwindo, the hunter, and the dogs.

VI. *Second hunting expedition by Shekaruru*

    A. The next morning Shekaruru leaves again with the dogs.

    B. He encounters a herd of warthogs; he sends the dogs after them, but he is chased by the warthogs.

    C. He flees to a tree, calling for help. Hawk saves him and flies back with him to the village.

    D. Hawk receives from Mwindo a reward of chickens.

VII. *Jealousy and defeat of the other chiefs (Itewa, Mburu, Munkonde, and Nteta)*

    A. Although Mwindo had given buffalo tails to the other chiefs, they harbor hatred against him because of his fame.

    B. Itewa plots to wage war against Mwindo and equips his men with spears.

    C. Mwindo knows about the plans; grieved, he asks his people to prepare for the coming war.

    D. Mwindo decides to confront Itewa alone with his scepter, taking his people along without weapons. Mwindo's people are annihilated.

    E. Festivities are organized by Itewa.

F. Left alone with his dogs and his scepter, Mwindo meditates revenge. He goes to Itewa's village and, throwing his scepter on the ground, destroys Itewa, his people, and his things.

G. Praising himself, Mwindo returns home with trophies.

VIII. *The wonder of Mwindo's scepter*

A. Back in his desolate village, Mwindo asks his scepter to provide food for the dogs. Cooked foods immediately become available.

B. Mwindo invokes the beings of the subterranean world, the earth, the sky, and the air.

C. He throws his scepter on the ground and revivifies his people.

D. The houses rebuild themselves in the village.

IX. *Mwindo's travels and feats in the subterranean world*

A. Departure

Well established in his village where children are born, Mwindo decides to visit God while he is still alive. He informs the people about his departure, leaving his dogs behind. Equipped with his scepter and billhook knife, he enters the subterranean world through a *kikoka*-fern.

B. Encounter with Kahindo, daughter of Nyamurairi, the god of fire

Mwindo meets Kahindo at a wading place; her body is covered with scabies. Impressed with Mwindo's beauty, she asks him to clean her wounds. Mwindo does the healing and faints. She awakens him and blesses him. He explains to her his intention to visit Nyamurairi; she tells him to beware the trickery of her father.

C. Encounters with Nyamurairi

Mwindo climbs to Nyamurairi's village, mounts the steps near his house, and finds him in the men's house. Mwindo escapes the trickeries of Nyamurairi by refusing to bathe in water, which in fact is beer, and to eat banana paste with frogs, which are in fact Nyamurairi's counselors. Mwindo spends the night with Kahindo. In the morning he is sent out to harvest honey in the tall tree. Bat gives him nails and Spider provides him with cobwebs to use as ropes. Mwindo, subdued by Nyamurairi's belt, is saved by his scepter and by Lightning. In turn he subdues Nyamurairi with his billhook knife, collects the honey, and returns to Nyamurairi, awakening him with his scepter. Mwindo spends the night with Kahindo. In the morning Mwindo is sent out to cultivate a banana grove. Hundreds of billhooks and axes do the work for him; banana trees plant themselves; they bear ripe fruits immediately. Mwindo, again subdued by Nyamurairi's belt, is once more saved by his scepter and by Lightning. In turn he subdues Nyamurairi with his billhook knife. Nyamurairi's wives collect the bananas and return to Nyamurairi, whom Mwindo awakens with his scepter. Mwindo spends the night with Kahindo. In the morning Mwindo is sent with Nyamurairi's people to the pool Mukingetua for a contest. Hanging from nothing above the pool is a tree. A man throws himself into the pool; his members disperse and join together again. All Nyamurairi's people perform the same act. Mwindo is smashed against the tree by Nyamurairi's belt and is awakened by his scepter. He calls on Lightning, is pulverized by Lightning, falls like dust into the water, and emerges whole. Mwindo's billhook knife subdues Nyamurairi. On his return Mwindo awakens Nyamurairi with his scepter. Mwindo spends the night with Kahindo. In the morning Mwindo, having received banana paste and meat from Kahindo, is sent to Sheburungu. He meets two thousand children collecting eleusine and gives them the food. They show him the way. He finds Sheburungu in the men's house inside a cave. They play the game of dice. Mwindo is subdued by Nyamurairi's belt, but is saved by his scepter and by Lightning. He places the dice in Sheburungu's mouth and leaves them there until they bring his father, whom they have kept in hiding. Mwindo returns to Nyamurairi, having taken all the wives and goods of Sheburungu. Mwindo spends the night with Kahindo. In the morning, having given her a maiden-servant, he returns home, emerging through the *kikoka*-fern.

X. *Festivities in the home village*

    A. The people greet Mwindo and his father with drums and songs, presenting them with many goats as welcoming gifts.

    B. The chief Shemwindo provides all the bachelors with wives and gives his son Mwindo nine women.

    C. Mwindo is welcomed by his dogs.

XI. *Defeat of Dragon-Ogre Kirimu*

    A. A young man who goes to check his traps in the forest arrives in the village of Kirimu.

    B. He meets with Ukano, the daughter of Kirimu. She cooks food for him and asks him to wait for her father. The young man plays the zanza.

    C. On his arrival Kirimu orders him to sing and play the zanza throughout the night as the price for his daughter.

    D. The young man falls asleep; he is killed by Kirimu.

    E. Another young man sets out in search of his brother, taking Mwindo's dogs along, and arrives in Kirimu's village.

    F. Ukano cooks food for him.

    G. When Kirimu arrives he asks the young man to fasten the dogs and invites him to play the zanza.

    H. The young man plays the zanza without falling asleep.

    I. In the morning, when Kirimu is still asleep, the young man lets his dogs loose. They kill Kirimu.

    J. The young man blesses his dogs, seizes Ukano, and urges her to tell him where his brother has been thrown away.

    K. He finds his brother's skull near a tree and heats a grub from it on a potsherd. The brother arises.

    L. The young men return home and give the spoils to Mwindo.

  XII. *The monkey hunt*

    A. The young man who saved his brother goes to look for animal tracks.

    B. He arrives near a strangler vine belonging to the Banamburu (*mburu*-monkeys) and sets up his snares. He sleeps not far from his snares, waiting for warthogs to pass.

    C. The chief of the *mburu*-monkeys is caught in the trap. Unable to free himself, he calls out for his people.

    D. Hearing the people coming, the young man wraps the chief of the *mburu*-monkeys in a package and hurries back to the village.

    E. The *mburu*-monkeys arrive at the village entrance; they tease and challenge Mwindo.

    F. Mwindo, the young man, and the dogs chase them to their own village.

    G. The *mburu*-monkeys attack with spears in a glen.

    H. Mwindo's dogs kill them; other monkeys fall out of the trees when Mwindo points his scepter at them.

    I. Pointing his scepter to the sky, Mwindo makes hailstones fall which destroy the village of the *mburu*-monkeys.

    J. Mwindo seizes all the valuables and returns home.

    K. There is joy; the spoils are distributed.

  XIII. *The feats of Mwindo's Pygmy, Shekaruru*

    A. The hunt

        Shekaruru asks Mwindo's permission to hunt with the dogs.

The permission is granted, but the Pygmy is prohibited from whistling in the forest lest the dogs abandon him. The Pygmy finds an ancient banana tree in the forest and wonders who might have planted it. The dogs kill ten warthogs.

B. Offerings to the river

Shekaruru arrives at a small river. While drinking, he hears the rapids murmuring like drums. He gives one leg of a warthog to the rapids. All his animals disappear in the rapids.

C. Encounter with Nyamwanda

Shekaruru arrives with the dogs at a little village where he finds an iron house and the woman Nyamwanda, the wife of the god Muisa; she carries a pregnancy the size of a house. The woman tells him to do whatever he wants. The Pygmy gives a blow to the woman's belly; stones fall from it. Nyamwanda changes into a beautiful woman. She gives the Pygmy bark cloth and a whistle that will make him famous. She instructs him about the usage of the whistle and predicts his coming achievements.

D. Resuscitation of a chief's son

The Pygmy arrives in a village where the young son of a chief has died. He asks the people to leave the house of the dead boy and stays alone with the corpse. He awakens the dead youth, heals him, dresses him, and brings him outside. The Pygmy receives presents and a maiden. He gives his son as a present to the chief.

E. Return to Mwindo's village

The Pygmy returns to Mwindo's village to show the presents. His kinsmen demand that he divulge the secret of the medicine he received. He gives them the whistle, thus giving away the power to revivify people. Mwindo takes for himself the maiden brought back by his Pygmy.

F. Encounter with the specter Mpaca

The Pygmy goes to set traps. He arrives at the village of Mpaca while Specter is gone. He enters the house, places glue on the drying rack, and dozes off. Mpaca arrives during the night and plants nails in the Pygmy but, seeing the glue, she seizes it and is glued together. The Pygmy flees back to Mwindo's village.

G. Encounter with Shakwece

The Pygmy goes back to hunt with the dogs. He arrives at the village of Shakwece. Shakwece, disturbed because one of his two wives had burned his dog Ringe, decides to put them through an ordeal. They arrive at a pool; Shakwece places a vine across the pool. The wives must cross the pool on the vine. The despised wife passes without difficulty, but the beloved wife carrying her child drowns. Shakwece refuses to save the child. The Pygmy leaves.

H. The hunt
The dogs kill twenty-five baboons. The Pygmy returns with the animals to Mwindo's village.

XIV. *Mwindo enthroned as chief*

A. The Pygmy presents the animals to Mwindo and returns the dogs.

B. Mwindo gives a wife to his Pygmy.

C. Mwindo's father calls his people together and proclaims that he now enthrones his son, that his son must henceforth receive tribute, and that he himself will be second to his son.

D. He gives his son seven wives and the paraphernalia of chieftainship.

E. The drums are beaten.

F. Mwindo lives in glory, together with his people.

MWINDO EPIC II: TRANSLATION

In a place long ago there dwelled a chief called Shemwindo.[1] Shemwindo married two wives. One wife was called Iyangura.[2] After he had married his two wives he made a proclamation: "The one who will bring forth a male child among you my wives, I shall strangulate him/her, I shall knead

---

1. The action is placed in remote times and in a known, but unidentified, region, but specific places, such as villages, mountains, and rivers, are designated. The chief is referred to and known solely by the teknonymic name Shemwindo, father of Mwindo. He is called after his son, even before the latter is born.

2. The chief's wives are mentioned as *bomina,* the general term for wives; the special term *bowe* is most commonly used for the chief's spouses. The fact that the two wives are not classified as ritual spouses (*mumbo, mpombwe*) suggests that Shemwindo is an incumbent chief who has not yet been enthroned. The rarely used name Iyangura, given to one of the chief's wives, is connected with the verb *iyangura,* to settle problems, to arbitrate, to fulfill ritual requirements, to demolish something (e.g., a bridge). Since the names of children reflect social situations, the name Iyangura in this context indicates that her unnamed father was known as a settler of problems.

him/her." Of his two wives, Iyangura is the beloved-one. After a countable number of days had elapsed, Iyangura carried her pregnancy.[3]

The day she gave birth, the child emerged from the palm of the hand.[4] It threw itself onto the ground; it was talking and it was walking. It was born with a little shoulder bag in which there was a medicine and which it clutched under the armpit. Its name was Mwindo Mboru; it was a male child. He was also born holding in his hands a scepter (made) of cow's tail.[5] Iyangura also gave birth to a female child called Nyamitondo Mwindo, sister of Mwindo Mboru.[6] This one, his sister, came out from the vagina of her mother.

---

3. The motif of the father who does not want a son recurs in the other epics and in some of the tales. The prohibition sets the stage for the birth of a male hero who is strong enough to overcome the consequences of infringing a taboo. His achievements are meant to teach a lesson. One narrator, whose tale about a castaway boy I collected in 1952, concluded as follows: "In olden times people did not know that a boy is human; they loved women only." Then, through the accomplishments of the castaway, "they learned to see the value of boys who are saviors of people." During the enthronement rites the chief is told not to be discriminatory by saying that "some are his people, and others are not." The motif of the beloved wife (*ngantsi*), who involuntarily infringes upon the prohibitions, and of the despised wife (*nyakashombe*), who does not break the rules and yet fails to become a preferred wife, is frequent in Nyanga tales. *a countable number of days*: a formula referring to a fixed time period.

4. The miraculous birth of the hero is suggested in different ways in the epics: he is born as the result of his mother's unusually long pregnancy; he is born through the middle finger or through his mother's palm; he is the product of parthenogenesis; he leaves the womb to perform certain tasks for his mother and reenters it to be born again in an unspecified manner.

5. In this passage the hero's principal attributes and magical devices are enumerated. *it was talking and it was walking*: a formula emphasizing his capacity for complete autonomy in the face of his father's threats. Elsewhere this formula is used either as an epithet or as the name of the hero. The hero has a shoulder bag which contains an unspecified medicine. Elsewhere in the text the hero takes a large number of agricultural tools and banana stipites out of this bag. The fact that his scepter (*conga*) is made of cow's tail renders the appearance of the hero all the more astonishing. The Nyanga live in the rain forest and are not pastoralists; pastoral Hunde and Nande live to the north, the east, and the south of them. Since they trace their origins back to Bunyoro, the ancestors of the Nyanga come from areas with pastoral traditions. Nyanga dance scepters are usually made, as is evident later in the text, of buffalo tail or of the hairy tail of certain antelopes.

6. The hero and his sister have double names. *Mwindo*: the name given to a boy who is born into a family where there are only girls or to a girl who follows a number of boys. *Mboru*: probably an epithet meaning the Opener. In the epics and in some of the heroic tales I collected the hero is known as Mwindo, Mwindo Mboru, Kaboru ka Mwindo, Mwindo Kakuku (Scurvy), Kabutwakenda (Little-one-just-born-

The despised wife, she also gave birth to two children; one was a male child and the other was a female child.[7]

When Shemwindo noticed that his wife had given birth to a male child, he felt great bitterness and said to his counselors that they should go to throw away this male child that had just been born. The counselors listened to the word of their master; they lifted up the child Mwindo Mboru; they went to throw him into a grave; they covered him with soil.[8] After they had finished throwing him away, when they were already in the night, they were astounded that after barely two wakes of the night had passed Mwindo Mboru had already freed himself from the grave.[9] He went to arrive at his father's. He slept in front of him on the side of the hearth. When Shemwindo woke up seeing his male child in front of him he shouted a cry of amazement. He was very much astonished and said: "What do I see now? Today I receive a revelation. A man who was thrown away has (a) risen again! What was never seen before is being witnessed now!" When sky had changed to dawn, all the people gathered together to see Mwindo Mboru. He was devoured by (their) looks. Shemwindo said to all the people that since this Mwindo Mboru had (a) risen they should not throw him away again: "Let him first stay."[10]

---

he-walked), and Katawa (Little-Castaway). Some of these names serve also as epithets for Mwindo; there are other names as well. *Nyamitondo*: the name probably designates Mwindo's sister as an adviser and helper in times of trouble.

7. These two children do not play a role in the epic. The narrator does not explain what happened to the despised wife's boy, though the father's interdiction must also have weighed on him.

8. Numerous sentences throughout the epic begin with the standard formulas *wakie, bakie,* or *kwakie,* preceded or not by a personal noun and followed by one or more conjugated verbs. I have translated this form as *when, as,* or *after.* Thus: *Shemwindo wakie wamasunga*: when Shemwindo noticed that; *bakie bamakind, imutaa*: after they had finished throwing him away; *bakie iye barikire*: as they were now established. Although Mwindo has heroic stature from the moment of birth, he is nevertheless referred to as a child (*mwana*).

9. The indication of time follows a rather simple pattern throughout the epic. The standard formulas are *when sky had changed to dawn, in the early morning, after a while, one day. they were astounded that after barely two wakes of the night had passed*: lit., they woke up when barely two awakenings had passed. The verb "to awake" often has the connotation of surprise and astonishment, as if somebody were suddenly awakened from a dream. The reference is also to older people who have difficulty falling asleep; they doze off, wake up, tease the fire, and doze off again.

10. In contrast with epic I, epic II shows Shemwindo in a mood of accommodation and conciliation. The text further indicates that Shemwindo escaped to be hidden by one of Nyamurairi's subjects, but there is no mention as to why or when he escaped. In epic I the escape was necessitated by Shemwindo's continued opposition to his son and the subsequent destruction of his village.

As they were now established, Shemwindo gave his daughter Nyamitondo to Lightning, saying that he could marry her. Lightning married this sister of Mwindo Mboru. After Nyamitondo Mwindo was married to Lightning, Lightning went with his wife up into the sky.[11] Shemwindo also was born with a sister called Iyangura Katende. She was married to Mukiti, Master-of-the-unfathomable.[12]

Where Nyamitondo Mwindo had gone into the sky, she knew (how) to cultivate. Her husband Lightning had taught her (how) to cultivate.[13] Where she dwelled with her husband in the sky, she died of desire to see her father and her mother and her brother.[14] She descended earthward. When she was now with her father and her mother and her brother, one day she said to her brother Mwindo Mboru that they should go to cultivate a banana grove for their mother.[15] Mwindo Mboru answered, saying that he did not know (how) to cultivate. His sister said to him: "I will teach you (how) to cultivate so that from now on you may always cultivate for your mother." He agreed. Together with his sister he went to cultivate the banana grove. While they were cultivating they found an egg. They returned with it (to the village). They went to place it in a hen's nest in their house and this (hen) was brooding. After Nyamitondo Mwindo had taught her brother (how) to cultivate, she said to him that she wanted to return to her husband in the sky. Her brother Mwindo Mboru took a goat; he gave it

---

11. *As they were now established*: one of many formulas with which sentences begin. The verb *irika*, which is used in this formula in conjunction with time or place indicators, means to be seated, to be located. Depending on the context, I have translated it as to live, to inhabit, to occupy, to reside, to dwell, to remain, to stay, to perch, or to nest. *Lightning*: one of the most important recurring actors in the epics. Lightning (Nkuba) is an indefatigable and steadfast ally of the hero. In epic I, as Mwindo's blood friend, he is both helper and castigator. In epic III Mwindo defeats Lightning and then makes him an ally. Many Nyanga are devotees of a well-developed cult for Lightning

12. This sister of the hero's father plays no role in the epic. The role of father's sister (paternal aunt) as an adviser is highly developed in the other epics and in many tales. In epic II, in contrast with the other epics (I and IV) where he is an important actor, the fabulous Water Serpent Mukiti, like his wife, is not further mentioned.

13. The context suggests that cultivation of bananas is meant; banana growing is the central concern of Nyanga agricultural life. There is probably a symbolic reference to oral accounts according to which the Nyanga, when migrating into the forest, encountered banana groves abandoned by remnants of the Lega migration.

14. *she died of desire to see*: the term *kikandi* refers to ardent longing for one's kinsmen when one is far away from them.

15. For mature children to cultivate a banana grove for their mother is an act of filial piety.

to his sister; she climbed up with it to her husband, to Lightning.[16]

Where Mwindo Mboru together with his sister had placed the egg in their house in the hen's nest, the hen hatched her chicks. But the egg that Nyamitondo Mwindo had brought, that one remained without being hatched. After a countable number of days had elapsed since the hen had hatched her chicks, a young bird hatched itself by itself from the egg that had been placed in the hen's nest. After the young bird had finished hatching itself from the egg, as it began to grow, Mwindo Mboru was used to giving it meat, potatoes, ripe bananas. When the bird had grown to the point where it could provide food for itself, it began to eat chickens on the village place, because that was the (kind of) food it had been shown by its master. As it went about relentlessly eating chickens, the owners of the chickens went on saying: "This wild animal will decimate our chickens. It is befitting that we pierce it, that we kill it." When its owner, Mwindo Mboru, heard this, he became very bitter and said: "The one who will kill my bird will be killed by me." He refused, saying that he could not kill this bird. After Mwindo Mboru had made the refusal about his bird, saying that they should not kill it, (the bird) finished the chickens. When it had finished the chickens, it threw itself onto the goats; it ate them. When it had eaten four goats, the owners of the goats reminded Mwindo Mboru of their (earlier) quarrel: "Your wild animal here goes on relentlessly eating our things. We have told you to let us kill this bird. You have refused, saying let it remain. Look now how it acts! Now that it begins eating goats, will it refrain from eating people?"[17]

There in this village of Shemwindo, Shemwindo had planted a Ficus tree at the entrance to the village; and this Ficus tree reached upward to (the realm of) Lightning; and inside it, it had a hollow (space). As the bird went about relentlessly acting like this, and as its owner failed to find a way in which he could stop it (from doing what it did), and because of fear of "being pointed at" by his kinsmen, (Mwindo) fled upward to his sister; he climbed up with the Ficus tree that his father had planted at the en-

---

16. The motif of the egg found in the forest and taken back to the village is missing from the other epics. *Her brother . . . took a goat*: here, as elsewhere in the text, the well-developed system of gift giving and the principles of generosity, liberality, and etiquette in human relations are underscored.

17. This entire passage is filled with formulas. The formula -*kie*, preceded by *ca-*, *kwa-*, *wa-* (see n. 8, above), occurs eight times, mostly at the beginning of a sentence. The sonority of this passage is heightened by the fact that thirty-one words begin with *ca-*, *ce-*, *ci-*, or *co-*, prefixes all connected with the word for bird (*kironge*). *Your wild animal*: *kihuka* is a predator that causes excessive harm. Further on in the text, the bird of prey is identified as Kirimu, the dragon-ogre of the forest.

trance to the village.[18] Mwindo Mboru, because of shame before his kinsmen, said that lo! this wild animal was relentlessly acting like this, that he was going to his brother-in-law to fetch there the weapon that could fight this wild animal. He said to his father that he was going to his sister, to Lightning's place, to seek the weapon that would enable him to fight with this wild animal. He climbed with the Ficus tree, singing:

> Mwindo, our kinsman.
> Nyamutondo Mwindo Mboru.
> I am dying, my junior,
> Nyamutondo Mwindo.
> The chickens that Muuma owned,
> Nyamutondo Mwindo,
> Big-bird-born-by-itself has destroyed them,
> Nyamutondo Mwindo.
> The stools that Buuma owned,
> Nyamutondo Mwindo,
> Big-bird-born-by-itself has destroyed the people
>   on earth,
> Big-bird-born-by-itself has destroyed the maidens
>   and the young men on earth,
> Nyamutondo Mwindo.
> And the cows that Buuma owned on earth,
> Big-bird-born-by-itself has destroyed them on earth,
> Nyamutondo Mwindo.[19]

As Mwindo climbed to the place where his sister was, he arrived at the wading place of Lightning's village, and he was still singing.[20] Where his sister dwelled in the village, when she heard the voice of her brother climbing to where she was, she first listened a little while because of the distance; then in amazement she said: "Lo! There from where I have come things are not good!" As this Ficus tree climbed up with Mwindo, arriving with Mwindo at the entrance to the village at the wading place of his sister's village on the riverbank, the Ficus tree touched down on the riverbank while the leaves of its branches remained sticking to the

---

18. The motif of the hollow tree in which the hero climbs up to the realm of celestial divinities is not found in the other epics or in any of the tales that I have collected. Without admitting his guilt, the hero cannot let his kinsmen know that he is ashamed.

19. The song replaces a dialogue between the hero and his sister explaining the reason for Mwindo's arrival. *Big-bird-born-by-itself*: a descriptive epithet by which Mwindo implicitly praises his bird.

20. *at the wading place*: the term *hitukuriro* refers to the place where the women of a particular village draw water. The wading and bathing places are always slightly downstream from it.

riverbank.[21] Where his sister dwelled in the village, she was astonished; she dashed to the village entrance, marching very quickly and singing:

E! Mwindo our kinsman,
Nyamutondo Mwindo,
I am going now.
Nyamutondo Mwindo,
I am rushing now.
Nyamutondo Mwindo,
I am dying because of my father.
Nyamutondo Mwindo,
I am dying because of my senior.
Nyamutondo Mwindo,
I am dying because of my mother.
Nyamutondo Mwindo.[22]

After Nyamitondo had seen her brother, having met (eye to eye) with him, they climbed to Lightning's place. After they had arrived in the village Nyamitondo selected a guesthouse and gave it to her brother. She also made him the gift of a goat, saying that he should first eat food so that he might give her the news in the early morning, having rested. When it was early morning, Nyamutondo told her brother to rise so that she might ascend with him to her husband Lightning. They climbed to his place.[23] As they arrived there, Nyamutondo said to her husband that in the place where her father had remained—together with her mother and all her kinsmen and all their things, goats, cattle—Big-bird-born-by-itself had destroyed all the people, and that this one here, her brother, had fled to where she was to ask for weapons to overcome the wild animal that now remained where once had remained all their kinsmen.

When Lightning had finished hearing this news, he said that he would forge iron tools with which she would go to engage in war in the village of her father and her mother and all her kinsmen. When he was in the process

---

21. *As this Ficus tree climbed*: a striking example of the Nyanga emphasis on space and place indications. In Nyanga, the sentence contains not less than nine place indications. The narrator leaves it to the imagination of his listeners to decide whether the tree with the hero in it moves skyward, or whether the hero climbs up in the hollow tree which is so tall that it reaches into the realm of Lightning.

22. The song is a dialogue between brother and sister, the sister revealing her anxiety about the fate of their kinsmen. *I am dying because of*: the verb *ikwa na* reflects many shades of meaning linked with strong emotions, physical weakening, shock, and frustration.

23. It is unclear from the context whether Nyamitondo and her husband live in different villages or in separate sections of the same village. If she is the ritual wife of the chief Lightning, it would be normal for her to live in a separate village.

of smithing the iron tools, he forged a double-edged knife. He also forged two very long *mimbo*-knives. He also forged three razors.[24] When he had finished smithing all these objects, he said to his wife: "You, my wife, these iron tools here, place them in a small shoulder bag, and that small shoulder bag place it against the chest and wear it and carry it." He said to Mwindo Mboru: "You, my friend, return together with your sister there from where you have come; go to fight with the dragon that has remained over there."[25] He said to his wife: "You, my wife, do not be afraid of that dragon. When you arrive there where it is, let it swallow you together with this little shoulder bag."

After they had been instructed in this manner by Lightning, Nyamitondo Mwindo and her brother Mwindo Mboru descended with the Ficus tree, singing:

> Mwindo our kinsman.
> Nyamutondo Mwindo.
> Mwindo our kinsman.
> Nyamitondo Mwindo.

As they descended with the tree, radiance emanated from Nyamutondo Mwindo as if (she were) a star. They went to alight on earth, where Mwindo had left when he climbed into the sky. As they arrived in the village where her father, her mother, and all her kinsmen had lived, as they arrived: the Dragon was crossing the village place to and fro, having finished destroying all the people and all the cattle and all the goats. When brother and sister saw it (the bird): it was beating its wings about (swaggering) here and there, sole master of this desolate village.[26] As they drew near it, Mwindo told his sister Nyamutondo not to be afraid of the big bird, but to move herself close to it so that it might swallow her together with her little shoulder bag in which the iron tools were. She drew close to it. The bird, seeing her, swallowed her at once, while Mwindo kept himself

---

24. Knives and razors are utilized by the Nyanga. The *mimbo*-knives are used for removing body hair. It is noteworthy that Lightning makes these tools for his wife, but not for the hero. She must fight the bird, since she is the ultimate cause of its existence.

25. The term *my friend* is not uncommon in referring to a brother-in-law. *dragon*: the bird is now identified as the destructive Dragon-Ogre Kirimu.

26. This passage contains powerful descriptive imagery—*radiance emanated from Nyamutondo; it was beating its wings about (swaggering) here and there*—which almost never appears in the tales. *all the cattle*: there are no cattle in Nyangaland, but cattle-owning groups live in the neighborhood. Social relationships with some of these neighbors, particularly the Bafuna and Bashari subgroups of the Hunde, are very close.

somewhat to (one) side. As she was now inside the belly, Nyamutondo remembered the iron tools that she had been given by her husband. She removed the razor; she cut his liver; she chopped it. When the big bird felt these pains, it staggered about hither and thither. As it was struggling against death, Mwindo Mboru sang:

Our little axes pass hither and thither.	Our little axes pass hither and thither.
The little axes pass hither and thither.	The little axes pass hither and thither.
Our little axes pass hither and thither.	Our little axes pass hither and thither.
The little axes pass hither and thither.	The little axes pass hither and thither.
Our little axes pass hither and thither.	Our little axes pass hither and thither.
The little axes pass hither and thither.	The little axes pass hither and thither.
Our little axes pass hither and thither.	Our little axes pass hither and thither.
The little axes pass hither and thither.	The little axes pass hither and thither.
Our little axes pass hither and thither.	Our little axes pass hither and thither.
The little axes pass hither and thither.	The little axes pass hither and thither.

As it (the bird) was fighting against death in this manner, it (finally) went to die. When it had finished dying, Nyamitondo Mwindo removed herself from the inside. She called her brother, saying: "You, Mwindo Mboru, come close here quickly, quickly. See, the dragon has finished dying." Mwindo Mboru came out there (from hiding). He sang together with his sister; they were filled with joy:

Big bird of Rwama,	Going slowly,
Going slowly.	Saying: I cannot bear a boy,
Mukiti is my father,	Going slowly.
Going slowly.	Big bird has died.
My mother abandoned me on the road,	Going slowly.[27]

When the big bird had finished dying, Mwindo Mboru and his sister cut the bird's heart open. Father and mother came out (of it). They went to stand up like "there." All the people came out, appearing one by one; and Mwindo and his sister were singing:

Small bird of the road,
Beautiful-One, Beautiful-One, e!
Small beautiful youth,
Beautiful-One, e!

---

27. In this joyful song following the death of the bird, Mwindo gives a reminder that he was not wanted by his father and that the latter abandoned him. He stresses the importance of being guided by circumspection (*Going slowly*) and recalls his quasi-divine attributes. *Mukiti is my father*: Mukiti is the husband of Mwindo's paternal aunt. In Nyanga kinship terminology, he can be referred to as a maternal uncle and respectfully spoken of as "my father."

Who traps *bulikoko*-bird,
Beautiful-One, Beautiful-One, e!
Small-one-that-goes-to-praise-itself,
Beautiful-One, e!
Saying that it emerges from great difficulties,
Beautiful-One, e!
Small-one-that-goes-down with the Roba River,
Beautiful-One, e!
Small-one-that-arrives in the village,
Beautiful-One, e!
Small-one-that-says to its wife,
Beautiful-One, e!
Saying: stir for me some banana paste that I
    may eat from it,
Beautiful-One, e![28]

When all the people had finished emerging from the bird's belly, a young man called Beautiful-One also emerged from it. He went to bathe. Returning from bathing, he asked that they prepare banana paste for him in his wife's house; he ate it. After he had finished eating the banana paste, he assembled all the kinsmen who had emerged from the bird's belly. They went to dance for Mwindo Mboru and his sister Nyamutondo Mwindo. They brought great joy to them (Mwindo and Nyamutondo) because all the people and all the things that had been eaten were now available again as they had been long before.

When all the people had finished building (their houses) and when all things were available again as they had been long before, Shemwindo made a proclamation to his people, saying: "Since the wife of Lightning and her brother have saved all the people in this fashion because of the intelligence that came from my son-in-law, what present shall we give him on account of which he may appease his heart?" They took two maidens as a gift for the husband of their daughter; they gave them to Nyamutondo Mwindo. After Nyamutondo Mwindo had been given these maidens by her father in order to help her ascend to her husband, Lightning himself descended from

---

28. In this song the hero announces that a young man called Beautiful-One will emerge from the dragon. The Beautiful-One is the second and final product of the egg that the hero and his sister found; he is the symbol of evil transformed into good. The Nyanga version of this very beautiful song is filled with sonorous effects and alliterations (the majority of nouns and verbs begin with *ka-*, *ke-*, *ko-*, and *ku-*, prefixes that are all in accord with the dominant noun Kongo, Beautiful-One). Roba is the Nyanga name for the Lowa, one of the major rivers flowing through the country.

the sky; he snatched her away from earth together with his present of two maidens.[29]

After Nyamutondo had finished climbing to her husband's place, where chief Shemwindo remained together with his people, he assembled them all. When they were all gathered together, Shemwindo made a proclamation, saying: "You, my people, let this one, my child Mwindo, remain with the status of chief, but let him first begin by teaching himself to bring harmony in the land. And you, all my people, go henceforth dancing with dance scepters. The one who does not dance with a scepter: it is as if he were scornful of me."[30] Mwindo said to his people: "Let him who fails to have a dance scepter go to my friend, to the chief of Buffaloes, let him go to fetch there a dance scepter." As his people failed to have these dance scepters, Mwindo said to his people to go with him to his friend; they followed him. Arriving there at his friend's, the chief of Buffaloes, this chief preceded Mwindo (in going) to his people, the Buffaloes. They arrived there; they slashed off all the buffalo tails. Mwindo was delighted, together with his people. When this joy was over, he bought two dogs, Ndorobiro and Ngonde. Having bought these (dogs), he gave them to a Pygmy among his Pygmies, called Shekaruru, saying that he should hunt with these dogs.[31] After he had bought these dogs he returned together

---

29. This passage stresses again the values of generosity, reciprocity, and etiquette in social relationships. In Nyanga cult practice, women are consecrated to Lightning.

30. Impressed by his son's feats, the father proposes him as a future chief but requires from him proof of maturation and leadership. This way of proceeding is not customary. The successor to chieftainship is theoretically a son of the ritual wife (*mumbo*) or, if she has no son, of her replacement. The successor is not selected by the ruling chief or designated by his oral will. It is correct, however, that the chief designate must give proof of his qualities as leader before he is enthroned and invested with the sacred paraphernalia of office. The chief's request that his people henceforth dance with dance scepters (*conga*) is a whimsical one. Seemingly he wanted to honor his son because the hero was born holding such a scepter.

31. *Buffaloes*: presented here as a kinship group. *he bought two dogs*: in Nyanga tradition expert hunting dogs are closely linked with the office of chief. The chief owns such dogs but, as suggested here, he gives them to his Pygmies to hunt with them in his name. *Ndorobiro and Ngonde*: the Nyanga have a wide variety of names for dogs; these two names, whose meanings I do not know, are unusual. Pygmies (Batwa) and their descendants of mixed blood survive in small numbers among the Nyanga. They are attached to the chief as his hunters and exercise important ritual functions in conjunction with the chieftainship (one of the Pygmies has the title of *mwamitwa*, Chief-Pygmy). The Pygmies provide honey and the hide of a flying squirrel for the enthronement rites; they give the chief one of his special status wives for whom no marriage payments are made. They are also accomplished singers. *Shekaruru*: this Pygmy, who is a main actor in the epic, has a significant

with his people and his two dogs. Arriving in his village, he said to his people that they should play songs for the dogs on the drums and carry the buffalo tails. Mwindo himself was the one to give his dogs the names of Ndorobiro and Ngonde. After they (the people) had been instructed in this way by Mwindo, saying that they should dance, they put the drums in the village place. They now set out to praise the dogs. They sang:

> Ndorobiro and Ngonde,
> Ndorobiro and Ngonde,
> Ndorobiro, may you chase fast.
> Ndorobiro and Ngonde,
> Ngonde, may you chase fast,
> Ndorobiro and Ngonde.

They now danced in honor of the dogs of the chief; all the people who were there now danced with the scepters, holding them in their hands.[32]

When the dance was finished, in the early morning, Mwindo said to his Pygmy to go and test his dogs in order to (find out) whether they knew (how) to hunt. As they were setting out to hunt with the Pygmy, they (the dogs) first ate the early morning meal in the house of Mwindo's principal wife, the beloved-one. They ate the early morning meal: one leg of a warthog and two dishes of banana paste. When they (the dogs) had finished eating the early morning meal, Mwindo Mboru gave them to his Pygmy, having blessed them with the saliva of blessing saying that they must kill many, many animals.[33]

The Pygmy Shekaruru went with them into the virgin forest to hunt; they had dog bells attached to them.[34] As he was now going on the hunt, he

---

name. Shekaruru is a teknonymic term that means father or master of *karuru*, a call of encouragement or warning to the dogs produced by holding the cupped hands in front of the mouth. Therefore the Pygmy named Shekaruru is an extremely able and alert hunter.

32. Hunting dogs are especially honored among the Nyanga. From many points of view they are treated as human beings. They (and their owner) receive a specified portion of the game. The dogs are praised and blessed; they are given a special burial; their wrath influences the fate of men. For further details, see Biebuyck, 1956a.

33. The hunting dogs are fed and blessed before the hunt because the Nyanga think that the success of the hunt largely depends on their good disposition. The rich meal described here is part of the atmosphere of extravagance created in this epic.

34. *virgin forest*: the term *busara* refers to the dense forest where there are no villages or fields. There the Nyanga engage in numerous vital economic activities, such as hunting, trapping, and gathering. Before leaving the village the hunters fasten wooden dog bells around the necks of the dogs; the bells are muffled with leaves or sticks until the hunters are well on the trail of an animal. The bells have several ritual usages.

arrived on the trail; he met (suddenly) with Hawk being eaten by red ants. Hawk, seeing this Pygmy, said to him: "You, Pygmy, I am close to death; I am being fought by the red ants; they are eating me in the face and in the buttocks; they are close to destroying me. Remove me quickly from here; I am dying!" When the Pygmy Shekaruru saw Hawk—the red ants are sitting on top of him while he is screeching from within—he removed the red ants (sitting) on top of Hawk; he removed Hawk from within them. He shook and shook him, (for) these red ants clung inside his feathers. When Hawk was saved from the mass of red ants he said to the Pygmy: "May you be blessed there where you go to hunt; may you not stumble there; may you kill many, many animals; may you not fail to kill animals. I am behind you. I cannot abandon you there where you go to hunt."[35] When the Pygmy Shekaruru had finished saving his friend Hawk, he pursued the hunt. As he arrived on a trail, he let the dogs loose against a wild pig. He urged the dogs Ndorobiro and Ngonde on. They went off with the wild pig, chasing it; they went to catch the wild pig. The Pygmy arrived there; he speared the wild pig; it died altogether.

When it (the pig) was dead, he (Shekaruru) returned with the dogs to bring the news to the village so that they might go and take the animal. He arrived in the village. Mwindo Mboru sent three of his people to go and fetch the animal. They arrived with it in the village; they gave it to the hunter. He, together with the dogs, ate it. Also, the owner of the dogs, Mwindo, ate (part of) it. No other people ate (parts of) it.[36]

After they had finished eating this wild pig, in the early morning he (Shekaruru) gave the early morning meal of the pig's head to the dogs. When they had finished eating the morning meal, the Pygmy stood up with them (ready to go) ; he went again to hunt with them in the secondary forest. As he arrived in the middle of the forest he suddenly met with a herd of warthogs that were lying down together. He set the dogs Ndorobiro and Ngonde against them, (but) the warthogs failed to flee; (instead) they moved along in order to eat the Pygmy. As this Pygmy Shekaruru was now being chased by the warthogs, he took refuge in a tree. As he had escaped there to Mwanya and as he was now screaming high up there, there where Hawk dwelled he heard the call of his friend, the one

---

35. *Hawk*: a benevolent helper and messenger frequently appearing in the epics. *red ants*: the symbol of fierceness. *May you be blessed*: a short but typical formula used by the Nyanga in prayers recited during blessing; lit., may you be healthy.

36. Since this kill is the first one by the dogs that Mwindo had bought, the quarry is eaten only by a select group of people and by the dogs themselves.

who had saved him.[37] He arrived there as his Pygmy friend was about to fall on the ground and as the warthogs were cutting down the tree in which the Pygmy was. Where the dogs had remained on the ground, they fled to the village. Where Shekaruru was perched up in the tree, after Hawk had finished arriving there, the animals on the ground sang:

> Hawk, throw him down!
> I cannot throw him down; he gave me life.
> Hawk, throw him down!
> I cannot throw him down; he gave me life.
> My senior brother, throw him down!
> I cannot throw him down; he gave me life.
> My father, throw him down!
> I cannot throw him down; he gave me life.
> My mother, throw him down!
> I cannot throw him down; he gave me life.[38]

As the warthogs were squealing, begging Hawk to throw the Pygmy Shekaruru down so that they might eat him, Hawk went on saying that he could not throw him down because he had given him life, because he had saved him. When the animals were thus beaten by Hawk, by the constantly refusing Hawk, Hawk took his friend away from the tree above; he flew with him; he went to deposit him in their village, in the village of Mwindo Mboru. When the chief, Mwindo Mboru, saw that Hawk had saved his hunter, the Pygmy Shekaruru, he took some chicks; he gave them to Hawk, saying: "It is because you have saved my hunter, this here is your present, you, Hawk." Hawk returned to the virgin forest full of joy because of the present of chickens, thinking that each time he arrived in the village he could take chickens away from it, because he had received the right of privilege in them.[39]

When Mwindo Mboru had divided the buffalo tails that he had received from his friend, he had given one buffalo tail to Itewa; and Mburu had

---

37. *the secondary forest*: i.e., the regenerating forest where clearings have been made in the past. *Mwanya*: the name for one of the four cosmic spheres recognized by the Nyanga. This sphere, which forms the linkage between the earth (*oto*) and the sky (*butu*), is identified with the air, the atmosphere. In this particular context the narrator means to say that the Pygmy is high in a tree.

38. This beautiful song is conceived as a dialogue between the warthogs and Hawk. The warthogs try to convince Hawk to drop the Pygmy by addressing him in flattering terms (my senior brother; my father; my mother).

39. Some passages in the epics contain an etiological explanation to justify a certain custom or way of doing things. Such interpretations are far from being essential; sometimes they may be conceived of as personal reflections by the narrator in terms of widely known tales or personal cult experiences.

carried one off; and Munkonde had carried one off; and Nteta also had carried one off. He had given buffalo tails to these four true chiefs.[40] They, too, were chiefs having their own villages. After Mwindo had distributed these buffalo tails to his peers, the chiefs, these peers harbored hatred against him because he ruled in fame surpassing them. Where Itewa dwelled, he pondered in his heart, saying that because Mwindo surpassed them, because his fame surpassed theirs, he wanted to go and fight a war of spears with him. Having spoken to himself in this manner, Itewa said to his people: "You all, each man a spear! Let him take it up to fight war with Mwindo, for tomorrow we shall set out to fight with Mwindo!" When his (Itewa's) people heard this, they prepared themselves with the spears. Where Mwindo remained, when he heard this news of warfare with Itewa, he was deeply grieved, saying: "Truly this is rough! The bad thing is that Itewa summons war to fight with me, and I am the one who gave him the chieftainship that he now holds. Indeed, on earth there is no good. So, he shall come to know me; tomorrow he shall know how strong I am."[41] He said to his people: "Tomorrow we shall be attacked by Itewa. So, then, prepare yourselves!" After he had spoken to his people in this manner, they remembered it; they prepared themselves with the spears, saying: "Indeed tomorrow we shall set out to fight." When sky had changed to dawn, Little-call-of-Itewa left his village with his people; as he went to fight with Mwindo Mboru, he was singing:

> Little-call-of-Itewa, Little-call-of-Itewa
> Is being trapped, Little-call-of-Itewa.
> His antelope,

---

40. I prefer to leave the Nyanga terms for these four personified animals: Itewa is a rodent; Mburu is a monkey; Munkonde is a large bat; Nteta the duiker antelope, is the great animal trickster of the Nyanga tales. These four personages are described as true chiefs (*bahanga*), meaning that they are autonomous and that they have completed the enthronement rites. The fact that they receive scepters from Mwindo, however, implies that these chiefs are considered junior to Mwindo or to his father. In Nyanga custom fully autonomous chiefs may be ranked as junior or senior because of ancient kinship linkages that are thought to connect their ancestors. Itewa, Munkonde, and Mburu occur as actors, but Nteta is not mentioned again. It is astonishing that Munkonde is placed among Mwindo's enemies, since *munkonde* (a large bat) is generally one of the friendly maternal uncles who forge the hero. For the Nyanga, however, the apparent contradiction is no problem, for there are, so to speak, many Munkondes.

41. Mwindo, as depicted in this epic, is not the type of hero who is violent by nature or who looks for trouble. On many occasions, before reaching his full glory, he is shown as a generous person. Nevertheless, he is very sure of himself, and whenever he is challenged he is ready for the contest: fearless, boisterous, and ruthless.

Little-call-of-Itewa.
His warthog,
Little-call-of-Itewa.
His waterbuck,
Little-call-of-Itewa.[42]

Where Mwindo dwelled, when he saw Itewa marching against him with the war of spears, he said to his people: "Leave your spears; just go like that. I shall take my scepter; it will fight with Itewa." They went like that. They went to the place where Itewa made his appearance. As they confronted each other, the people of Itewa hurled their spears against the people of Mwindo. The people of Mwindo were annihilated; they died.[43] After they had died, Itewa took all the things of Mwindo and climbed with them and his people to his village. He was calling loudly for Munkonde, the one who had forged the spears for him, saying that where he had gone to war he had won. And he was singing:

E! Munkonde, forger of large spears,
Forger of spears.
Munkonde, forger of large spears,
Forger of spears.
Munkonde, forger of things that are feared,
Forger of large spears.
Forger of things that are feared.
E! Munkonde, we are going to Roba-Land,
But not we.[44]

After Itewa returned home, he took one goat; he gave it to the blacksmiths of Munkonde, saying that they had forged for him the spears with which he had fought. After he had finished giving this goat to Munkonde, the people entertained him; they played the drums and the horns for him. Four days passed and they still kept on dancing without going to sleep, because of the joy of winning the war.

In the place where Mwindo had remained, after he had been overcome in the war, he returned to his village, he himself and his dogs, Ndorobiro and Ngonde, and his scepter; that is all. His people are decimated. And his father Shemwindo still dwells in his village of Tubondo. Mwindo meditated by himself, saying that the one who overcomes a strong one, let

---

42. *Little-call-of-Itewa*: an epithet used by Mwindo to scorn Itewa.
43. We might think that Mwindo's people were defeated because of his overconfidence. Apparent weakness or negligence on the part of the hero, however, gives the narrator an even better opportunity to illuminate his exceptional power.
44. *Roba-Land*: the narrator comes from a village close to a traditional state that is called Roba.

him not say that he overcomes (someone else), (rather) that he is overcoming himself. Having had this kind of meditation, he said: "What now, a true man does not die on the ground. Act first! I, Mwindo, I am not rubbed twice with the sign of war!"[45] He stood up in order to fight with Itewa. He went with his two dogs and his scepter; he went singing:

> I shall overcome the Snails.
> I shall fight over there, in the place of
>   Chunks-of-meat.
> I shall overcome the Snails.
> I shall fight over there in the place of
>   Chunks-of-meat.[46]

Where Mwindo Mboru went, as he arrived at the entrance to the village of Itewa, he threw his scepter on the ground. As he arrived in the middle of the village place, he looked around here and there: all the people, together with their chief, Itewa, were dead; and all the chickens, the goats, and the flies—all these things had perished! Mwindo Mboru praised himself in the middle of the village, saying: "Itewa, wake up now. He who went to sleep wakes up again. You usurped power and force for yourself thinking that you would be capable against me. Today, you here are the one whose fang is stuck in the ground. I had told you that a young man cannot be saved by playing with his elder brother. Lo! He is miserable, the one who tries to measure up to me; he climbs on a difficult tree."[47] After he had thus praised himself in the middle of the corpses of the people of Itewa, he took all his goods; he cut off two of Itewa's fingers, and his tongue, and his penis.[48] He returned home with all these goods, singing:

---

45. This passage suggests that Mwindo and his father had by this time settled in different villages: the father in Tubondo and the son in an unnamed village. In Nyanga custom this arrangement is perfectly normal, particularly when chiefs are concerned. Moreover, Mwindo has already been designated as chief. *Mwindo meditated*: similar meditations are recurrent in the epics but are rarely found in the tales.

46. In this song Mwindo refers scornfully to Itewa and his people; he sees them as already destroyed.

47. The double power of destruction and salvation, which is exercised by Mwindo's scepter, is illustrated here and in several other passages. The scepter is usually activated by the hero's words, but it acts also on its own initiative. *He who went to sleep wakes up again*: a recurring formula used by Mwindo whenever he brings a slain enemy back to life.

48. In all the epics, this episode is the only example of the hero mutilating the body of an enemy. Outright killing is also extremely rare. Normally the hero defeats an enemy by means of one of his magical devices and then brings him back to life after the initial trouble is finished. It is unclear whether Mwindo first revivified Itewa and then mutilated his body, or vice versa.

Mburu passes through the hunting grounds with
    good things.
Nyamasangwasangwa is not dead.
Muntindi-bird passes through the hunting grounds
    with good things.
Nyamasangwasangwa is not dead.
Mburu passes through the hunting grounds with
    goodness.
Nyamasangwasangwa is not dead.[49]

After he had returned home, Mwindo said: "My dogs are dying of
hunger; what shall I do now?" He spoke to his scepter, saying: "You,
scepter, because I was born already possessing you, up to now you have
overburdened me like a *murimba*-stone and a *mutero*-stone." He said:
"Produce food for me now so that these dogs of mine may eat it."[50] After
he had spoken in this manner, he looked beside him: cooked foods were
already there! While giving this food he made a proclamation, saying:
"You, Masters-of-the-subterranean-world, you who are on earth, and you
who are in the sky, and you who are in the air, come to appear here to meet
with me here where I am; give me heroism and much force and honor to
surpass the other so-and-so chiefs who are next to me."[51] Having finished
speaking like that, he gave the food to his dogs. Having finished feeding
the food to his dogs, he coughed, saying: "What now (about) my people?
How now, you, my scepter?" He took his scepter; he threw it on the
ground: all his people woke up; they were completely saved! When they
had finished recovering, they went to bathe, and they were singing:

We are like the ones throwing one another in
    the pools.
We will throw Karunga in the pools.
We are like the ones throwing one another in
    the pools.
We will throw Karunga in the pools.[52]

---

49. In this song Mwindo refers to a coming fight with Mburu. He sees himself
already loaded, like Nyamasangwasangwa, with the spoils of Mburu.

50. *murimba-stone*: a heavy stone; *mutero-stone*: a heavy, whitish rock. The two
terms combined as Mutero Murimba form the name of a tough opponent of Mwindo's
who occurs in epic III and in heroic tales.

51. This invocation is the only passage that simultaneously mentions the
supranatural beings of the four cosmic spheres: the subterranean world (*kwirunga*);
the earth (*oto, kwantsi*); the air or atmosphere (*mumwanya*); the sky (*kwiyo,
mubutu*). Mwindo speaks contemptuously about the other chiefs as the *so-and-so
chiefs*, as if he did not know their names.

52. The song makes an allusion to a heroic tale collected from a narrator in
another village, in which Karunga is the central hero. Karunga, a small boy whose
kinsmen are all dead, fights the dragon Kirimu. The action leads to a series of
mutual insults, to which the song directly alludes.

On leaving the river where they had bathed, they went, singing:

> E! Batondo,
> My kinsman, yoyo.
> My senior father,
> My kinsman, yoyo,
> Said that I shall not eat banana paste,
> Unless I eat the banana paste with meat.
> My kinsman, yoyo.[53]

When they were now back in their village, all the houses were standing up again; they had finished building themselves! Mwindo Mboru was the one who had said to his scepter to erect the houses again. When Mwindo went to sleep he placed his scepter underneath his armpit.

When Mwindo's village was filled again like that—his children had been born, chickens were scurrying around like locusts—he said to himself that he, Mwindo, had not yet arrived at the place of God, being fully alive; that he was not himself, that it was befitting for him to first go and see God, so that he might meet with him.[54] He said to his people: "Remain here, you all, together with those my dogs. When you will be met by difficult things arriving at the end of the village, those my dogs will fight against them; they will bring me the news in the place where I am. I am with you, however; I do not go far."[55]

Having spoken like that, he grasped his scepter and a long billhook knife; he went with them. He arrived at a *kikoka*-fern; he pulled it out; he entered at the place where he had pulled it out.[56] Where he went, he ap-

---

53. The song is an improvised interlude by the narrator. A kinsman had brought him food, but there was no meat with it.

54. *the place of God*: the Nyanga text uses the word Shebahinga. This title is one of many given to the creator god (Ongo). The term, constructed as a teknonym, means One-who-is-a-master-in-changing-his-mind, because, the Nyanga say, "God is used to doing good to somebody and then taking the good away from him." Mwindo says that he wants to visit god "being fully alive" (*ushwere*), because no normal human can ever hope to arrive alive at God's place. It turns out that speaking thus is a form of boasting, because Mwindo enters the subterranean world and meets with Nyamurairi, the god of fire, who is the chief of the divinities but not the creator god. The Nyanga like to confuse the two gods to a certain extent, because Nyamurairi is the principal agent of Ongo.

55. In this passage Mwindo stresses again the quasi-mystic bond that links him to his hunting dogs.

56. *a long billhook knife*: this magical knife is not included in the earlier enumeration of objects with which the hero was born. In order to perform successfully the deeds that Nyamurairi will require of him and to escape Nyamurairi's treacherous tricks, Mwindo needs four types of help: his scepter to come back to life; Lightning to liberate him from Nyamurairi's magical belt; the billhook to neutralize Nyamurairi; and Kahindo's advice. *kikoka-fern*: a standard image for the hero's entrance into the subterranean world.

peared at a wading place. There he met with the daughter of Nyamurairi, (called) Kahindo. Mwindo was singing, saying:

> E! Hawk, the termites destroy the trees.
> Hawk, the termites destroy the trees.
> E! Hawk, the termites destroy the trees.

After Mwindo Mboru had finished meeting at the river with Kahindo, daughter of Nyamurairi, (he noticed that) scabies covered her entire body: it begins at the big toe of the foot and arrives at the tussock of the hair. This Kahindo, daughter of Nyamurairi, when she saw Mwindo Mboru arriving for her: the heart burned her while she was scrutinizing him. She said: "Truly! A splendid young man, how beautiful he is, this one. Truly!" Having spoken like that, this Kahindo said to Mwindo: "You, young man, clean for me this scabies." Mwindo began cleaning her entire body, removing the scales very well. When Mwindo had finished cleaning her, Kahindo said to him: "May you be healed, you, Mwindo." She asked him inquisitively: "You, where are you going?" Mwindo answered her that he was going to Nyamurairi.[57] Having finished bathing Kahindo, Mwindo fainted. (Mwindo) having fainted, Kahindo shook him , saying: "E! Mwindo, wake up! A hero does not die from one spear throw." Mwindo returned to life; he sneezed. While Mwindo was going to Nyamurairi, Kahindo shouted on the road, saying: "Go over there and when you arrive at Nyamurairi's, go close to the men's house where he is (seated). My father Nyamurairi will show you water that is in a jar, asking that you wash with it. You say to him: My father, the beer from which you drink, is that for me to wash with? You refuse firmly, even though he goes on pressing you, saying that you should wash with it. You go on refusing until he stops pressing you with it." Kahindo also said to him: "When you arrive at my father's place, then you sing for him this song:

> I am not with those who have killed Ringe,
> Ringe of the chief, Ringe."[58]

---

57. The encounter with the scabietic Kahindo, daughter of Nyamurairi, is a recurring theme in some of the texts. Mwindo heals her; she turns into a beautiful woman; she gives him the secrets to overcome the initial trickeries of her father; she becomes his lover and, eventually, his wife.

58. The song refers to the dog Ringe, whose story is told at the end of this epic. The implication is that there is no salvation for those who have killed the dog Ringe. Indeed, as is explained later in the epic, a woman and her child perished in an ordeal to determine which of a man's two wives had killed the dog. There is also a special relationship between hunting dogs and Nyamurairi: dogs are not merely consecrated to him, but he manifests himself as a dog.

After Mwindo had been briefed in this manner by Kahindo, he went and sang while climbing the mountain (road) to Nyamurairi:

Kabira, beat the drum for me.	Kabira, beat the drum for me.
This one here is Waterbuck.	This one here is Waterbuck.
Kabira, beat the drum for me.	Kabira, beat the drum for me.
This one here is Warthog.	This one here is Waterbuck.[59]

After Mwindo had climbed up to Nyamurairi's village, he mounted the steps near the house of Nyamurairi. He arrived at the men's house. When Nyamurairi saw him, he said to Mwindo to bathe in the water that was in the jar. Mwindo replied to him, saying: "E! My father. I cannot wash myself in the beer that you drink." Having spoken to him in this fashion, he sang for him the song:

I am not with those who have killed Ringe,
Ringe of the chief, Ringe.

When he (Mwindo) had finished singing this song for him, Nyamurairi was full of joy, saying: "I rejoice, my father, because you have arrived here, but tomorrow morning I want you to go harvesting honey for me which is over there at the entrance to the village."[60] After he had finished speaking to Mwindo like this, they cooked banana paste for him. When the banana paste was ready, it was brought to the men's house where Mwindo was. This banana paste was of the *kitehe*-variety; it contained frogs that were cooked; they were the garnish of it. It arrived there; Nyamurairi told Mwindo to sample the paste. Mwindo refused it, saying: "You, my father, your followers say about you that you do not eat them (the frogs) with banana paste. This now is difficult!" After Mwindo had spoken to him like this, the frogs stood up; they clapped the hands (in astonishment), saying: "Yes, our Mwindo. We are saved. Lo! You also know things!" After they had spoken in this way, Nyamurairi said to Mwindo: "So now go into the house of Kahindo, my daughter, to sleep therein." Mwindo went into it (the house). When he arrived there, Kahindo stirred banana paste for him. This banana paste, Mwindo ate it. Having finished eating the banana

---

59. This song anticipates a later event: it is sung by the Pygmy Shekaruru when he offers all his animals to the rapids of a river that murmured as if a drum were being beaten. Kabira then is the imaginary drummer whose drums are heard in the rapids, and Waterbuck and Warthog are the offerings to him.

60. The spirits of the subterranean world live in villages and houses very much as humans do. Nyamurairi dwells in the men's house which the text suggests is located near the peak of a steep slope. *my father*: Nyamurairi calls Mwindo "my father" (*tita*) to honor him. The honey harvest is a recurring theme in the epics; honey is a delicacy and also has ritual significance for chiefs.

paste, sky turned dark; he slept with Kahindo in her house. When sky had changed to dawn, in the early morning, Nyamurairi said to Mwindo: "You, my son, go to harvest the honey for me which is there on the tree." Mwindo went there. When he arrived at the foot of the tree, Bat gave him nails to stick fast to the *mpaki*-tree; and Spider gave him cobwebs (to serve) as ropes to climb the *mpaki*-tree.[61] They gave him these things because Mwindo had made a blood pact with Spider and Bat. As he was going to climb the tree, Nyamurairi gave Mwindo his belt (stitched with cowries), saying that he should climb with it. And Mwindo left with Nyamurairi his billhook knife saying that he should remain with it on the ground. On the belt of Nyamurairi there were cowries.[62] Mwindo climbed up. When he had arrived near the honey, Nyamurairi sent a call to where he was, saying: "You, my belt, bend him." The belt smashed Mwindo; his mouth was smashed against the tree; Mwindo's breathing found no way to come out. The strands on which he had climbed were completely still!

As Mwindo was troubled to death there in the sky, he implored Lightning, saying: "E! My friend Lightning, bring me help and counsel." The scepter that was on his back turned itself toward the face of Mwindo; it removed his mouth from the trunk of the tree. While Mwindo was now dropping excrement because of the fear of being bent against the tree, where Mwindo had sent his call for help, he had called for Lightning. Lightning came down; he cleaved the *mpaki*-tree twice; the honey fell to the ground. Mwindo made a call, saying: "You, my billhook knife, may you also smash Nyamurairi." Where Nyamurairi dwelt in his village, the billhook knife of Mwindo smashed him and planted him with his mouth on the ground: excrement and urine, coming from where Nyamurairi was, dispersed everywhere.[63] After Mwindo had climbed down, he reached the ground; he collected the honey; he arrived with it in the village. As he saw Nyamurairi (with) the mouth planted on the ground, Mwindo snatched his scepter from the back; he beat Nyamurairi with it on top of the head, saying: "E! Nyamurairi, everyone who went to sleep wakes up again. Why have you imperiled Mwindo? Why?"[64] When he had finished beating

---

61. *Bat*: referring to a small bat (*kakutu*). This bat rarely occurs as Mwindo's helper. Rather, the large bat (*munkonde*), described as a blacksmith and as one of Mwindo's maternal uncles, is usually depicted as Mwindo's ally. *Spider* (*munebuebue*) is generally friend and helper to Mwindo.

62. A belt stitched with cowries (*karemba*) belongs to the paraphernalia given to chiefs during the enthronement rites.

63. *excrement and urine . . . dispersed*: one variant of a formula that stresses serious physical trouble.

64. *everyone who went to sleep wakes up again*: a formula to indicate that the hero brings his opponent back to life or helps him regain consciousness.

Nyamurairi on the head with his scepter, Nyamurairi came to life again; he recovered; he stood up; he said: "Long life! Long life (to you), Mwindo!"[65] All the honey that Mwindo had brought went into the house of Nyamurairi; and Mwindo on his side went into the house of Kahindo, daughter of Nyamurairi, to sleep in it. When he arrived in the house of Kahindo, Kahindo stirred banana paste for her lover. Mwindo ate it; he went to sleep having placed it on his chest.

When Nyamurairi saw that Mwindo surpassed him in intelligence, he tested Mwindo with another dangerous trick. In the early morning, after the sky had changed to dawn, Nyamurairi told Mwindo to go and cultivate a new banana grove for him.[66] In going to the new banana grove, Nyamurairi gave Mwindo his belt, saying that he should go with it; and Mwindo gave him his billhook knife, saying that he should remain with it in the village. Where Mwindo went into the forest to cultivate the new banana grove, as he arrived there, he inserted his hand into his little shoulder bag; he removed from it three hundred billhook knives; he removed from it three hundred axes; he was there in that forest all by himself. After he had removed these billhook knives, they began to cultivate. He inserted his hand again into his little shoulder bag; out of it came banana trees. The banana trees: they also planted themselves! When they had finished planting themselves, the axes also felled (trees). The banana trees produced bananas that same day, bananas of the *bakoro*-variety; and they were already ripening! Where Nyamurairi remained in his village, he said: "Lo! Mwindo will just finish that field." Nyamurairi sent a call to the place where Mwindo had gone, saying: "You, my belt, bend him." Where Mwindo stayed in the field, the belt smashed him against the trunk of the tree; Mwindo was planted with his mouth against the buttresses of the tree. Where Mwindo resided, he defecated on himself; and urine was dripping. The scepter of Mwindo left the back; it threw itself at his face; it drew close to the tree. Mwindo's breath came out again; he moved away from the buttresses. He called loudly for his friend Lightning, saying: "E! My friend Lightning, I am dying. Look at me here." Lightning descended; he alighted on the side of the tree. Mwindo got away from there. Mwindo sent a call to the village, saying: "You, my billhook knife, look at me here from where you have remained there." Where

---

65. *Long life!* (*karamo*): the predominant greeting among the Nyanga. The verb *irama*, from which *karamo* is derived, means to recover (from sickness), to be saved, to be safe.

66. *a new banana grove* (*mubisi*): Nyamurairi is asking the hero to do all the work of clearing, felling trees, planting banana stipites, etc.

Nyamurairi remained in the village, the billhook knife planted him with the mouth on the ground. Out of fear, Nyamurairi defecated with noise; he also urinated: urine together with excrement covered all his clothing. Where Mwindo dwelt in the new banana grove, there arrived travelers bringing the news to Mwindo that in the village where Nyamurairi had remained there was no salvation, that he had died. Mwindo answered them saying that the wives of Nyamurairi should first come to cut the bananas because they were fully grown and already ripe. From where he dwelt in the new banana grove, Mwindo returned to the village. As he arrived there, his billhook knife had planted Nyamurairi with the mouth on the ground. Mwindo took his scepter; he beat Nyamurairi on the head with it, saying: "Everyone who went to sleep wakes up. E! Nyamurairi, you have imperiled Mwindo!" After Mwindo had beaten Nyamurairi on the head with the scepter, Nyamurairi sneezed; he got up; he was saved. Nyamurairi said: "Long life! Long life (to you), Mwindo!" After Mwindo had escaped these dangers, Nyamurairi said to Mwindo to go first to take a rest, that tomorrow he would test him again with another dangerous trick. Hearing this, Mwindo went to sleep in the house of Kahindo. Nyamurairi was testing Mwindo in this manner because he (Mwindo) was looking for his father, because Nyamurairi had hidden Shemwindo.[67]

In the early morning Nyamurairi sent Mwindo again to the pool called Mukingetua, where there is a tree that barely touches the pool without reaching either of the banks, (a tree) that is merely there in the middle of the pool. Mwindo went there together with the people of Nyamurairi after (the latter) had told him: "You, Mwindo, if you dance to the drum that my people dance to, (and) if you do not die from it, lo! then you are a true man; lo! then I shall give you your father that you may go home with him." In going there, Mwindo left his billhook knife with Nyamurairi; and Nyamurairi gave Mwindo his belt saying that he should go with it.

---

67. *he (Mwindo) was looking for his father*: the reasons for Mwindo's father being hidden by Nyamurairi are not spelled out in this epic. Earlier in the epic it seemed that father and son had been reconciled, since the father had decided that his son could live; the son had liberated his father from Kirimu; and the father had given his son the status of chief designate. The explanation for the father's presence in the subterranean world is left to the listener. Was the father taken away by the gods as a punishment? Had the father allied himself secretly with the antagonistic chiefs, like Itewa, and was he forced to flee after their defeat? Or does the narrator himself want to justify ex post facto the hero's sudden decision to visit the Underworld? Or was the narrator simply confused, having forgotten an earlier episode in which the father had fled? The Nyanga listener is not at all disturbed by such apparent inconsistencies.

Mwindo arrived at the pool together with Nyamurairi's people. One among Nyamurairi's people climbed the tree. Arriving at the very top of the tree, he threw himself into the river: all the parts of the body dispersed here and there, a leg here and a leg there, an arm here and an arm there! They had barely time to reflect, and this man was already back in the group in which his companions were! After all the people of Nyamurairi had finished passing on the fallen tree and were saved by throwing themselves into the water, it was again Mwindo's turn. Mwindo passed on the fallen tree; and as he was close to arriving near the top of the fallen tree, in the place where Nyamurairi dwelt he was in distress, saying: "You, my belt, bend him!" Where Mwindo stayed on the fallen tree, Nyamurairi's belt bent him; it planted him with his face against the fallen tree; there was no way for his breath to come out; excrement dropped down. His scepter left the back; it fell in his eyes; breath was released (again). Mwindo called loudly for Lightning; Lightning came down; he pulverized Mwindo. Mwindo turned into plain flour; his pulverized parts fell into the river! They (the people) had barely time to reflect, and Mwindo was already back in the crowd.[68] After Mwindo had emerged from the pool he shouted, saying: "My billhook knife, may you also bend him, bend and bend him." Where Nyamurairi had remained in the village, the billhook knife of Mwindo bent him. It planted him with the mouth on the ground; excrement dropped down; he failed to find what to do. Where Mwindo remained at the pool, he heard the news that where Nyamurairi was left behind in the village, he was no longer alive now, that he would not recover, that he would not sleep there. When he heard this, Mwindo climbed to the village to go and heal Nyamurairi. Arriving in the village, he saw Nyamurairi: foam emerged from his mouth. He (Mwindo) took his scepter; he beat him (Nyamurairi) on top of the head with it, saying: "Everyone who went to sleep wakes up. E! Nyamurairi, the one who jokes with Mwindo is climbing on something difficult!" Nyamurairi recovered; he said: "May you be healed; may you be healed, our Mwindo." Nyamurairi said to Mwindo: "You here who have recovered from this danger, tomorrow in the early morning you shall go to play the dice with Sheburungu. When you have beaten Sheburungu in the game of dice, then

---

68. The events at the pool called Mukingetua are not easy to understand, partly because the description is so succinct and the understandings that mark this highly poetic passage are unstated. The pool is haunted, and the tree reaches neither side of the pool. The implication is that a person can get safely back to land only by having the capacity to dismember himself. To the surprise of everyone, Mwindo, with Lightning's help, succeeds in accomplishing this feat.

you may carry off your father."[69] At night Kahindo cooked five dishes of banana paste for Mwindo; she placed meat on them; she said to Mwindo: "Go tomorrow with these banana pastes; traveling on the road you will meet with newborn babies who are collecting the eleusine of Nyamurairi. You will give them these banana pastes, together with the meat, and they will show you the way to go to Sheburungu."

When the sky had changed to dawn, Mwindo began the journey; he took the five banana pastes together with the meat. He first left to Nyamurairi his billhook knife, and Nyamurairi gave Mwindo his belt, saying to go with it. Where Mwindo went, as he arrived at the entrance to Sheburungu's village, he met two thousand children collecting the eleusine of Nyamurairi. Nyamurairi had poured out that eleusine there so that he (Mwindo) would not recognize the road leading to Sheburungu. When Mwindo met those children, he removed the banana pastes from his shoulder bag; he distributed them together with the meat to all the children. After the children had finished eating the banana pastes, they clapped their hands, saying: "May you be healed! May you be healed, Mwindo!" Mwindo told the children to show him the road to Sheburungu. They showed him the road, saying: "In that cave dwells Sheburungu, but the men's house is located inside the cave; that is the place where you will play dice."[70] Mwindo Mboru went; he arrived at the men's house of Sheburungu where his father Shemwindo was hidden. When Sheburungu saw Mwindo, he took a hide; he spread it on the ground; he poured the dice on it. When the dice were on top of the hide, Sheburungu said to Mwindo: "Take up the dice now." Mwindo took up the dice. In the place where Nyamurairi remained in his village, he said: "You, my belt, see to it; bend him." Where Mwindo had gone, the belt of Nyamurairi bent Mwindo: all the dice threw themselves into his mouth; they made his cheeks swell. It (the belt) planted him with the mouth on the ground on the hide: excrement and urine could not find the one who could clean

---

69. The game of dice with Sheburungu also turns up in epic I as the final condition Mwindo must meet before carrying off his father. The term Sheburungu is sometimes used as an epithet for the creator god Ongo; the creator god is sometimes called the "heart of the earth." Sheburungu is presented here as living in a deep cave in the subterranean world, suggesting that the creator god is indeed meant here. But the narrator leaves the solution to the imagination of his public. On the other hand, Sheburungu exhibits in this passage many of the characteristics of the god Muisa.

70. In epic I Mwindo also meets with hungry children on his way to Sheburungu; he feeds them, and they accompany him to Sheburungu's place. *In that cave*: there is ambiguity here because the word for stone is used.

them; the breath failed to find a way to come out. As the belt was bending Mwindo in this way, his scepter turned around; it came before his eyes; it removed Mwindo's mouth from the ground: the breath was released. Mwindo shouted loudly to Lightning: "My friend, I am dying." Mwindo stood up; he removed the dice and the hide; he went to place them into the mouth of Sheburungu: excrement dropped down. His people said that Sheburungu was dead. Mwindo stood up; seeing Sheburungu, he said: "Now why does Sheburungu imperil Mwindo?" He (Mwindo) said to his (Sheburungu's) people: "Give Sheburungu water to drink." They answered him: "How shall it pass through? Look how the dice are stuck in his mouth; he does not know what to do, and excrement are stuck to his buttocks; they fail to find the one that can remove them!" Sky became dark without Sheburungu having sneezed. His people said: "Bring Shemwindo out from the place where you have hidden him in the cave, because this Sheburungu has no life left; he is close to expiring." Where Shemwindo remained they went to take him out; they arrived with him. They gave him to Mwindo, saying: "Your father here." Mwindo got hold of his father; he took his scepter; he beat it on top of the head of Sheburungu, saying: "Now, Sheburungu, everyone who went to sleep wakes up again. Wake up now. Now you have stuck Mwindo onto you; you have carried him on the back." As Sheburungu was being beaten by Mwindo with his scepter, Mwindo said: "Sparrow is Shebireo, and Katee is crackling of dried leaves."[71]

After he had been beaten by Mwindo's scepter, Sheburungu recovered completely; he stood up. When Sheburungu had recovered, Mwindo returned with his father; he returned with the wives of Sheburungu and the goats of Sheburungu because he had beaten Sheburungu and taken all his goods from him. Returning with his father, he went to arrive at Nyamurairi's. Nyamurairi gave Mwindo his billhook knife, and Mwindo gave Nyamurairi his belt. Mwindo slept in the house of Kahindo. Among the spoils that had come from Sheburungu's were two maidens. Mwindo took one maiden; he gave her to Kahindo, his lover, because she performed very many nice things for him.[72]

---

71. The same formula is sung by Mwindo in epic I to celebrate his victory over Mukiti's ally. *Sparrow is Shebireo*: recalls a tale about the sparrow Kantori. *Katee*: a hedgehog.

72. Women of high status (e.g., the daughters of sisters of an enthroned chief, or the ritual wives of the chief) have a number of male and female servants at their disposal. The linkage between such a woman and her female servant is sometimes strengthened through a ritual marriage bond. *Kahindo, his lover*: the term for lover

When sky had changed to dawn, Mwindo returned home with his
father and with the spoils that he had accumulated. When he arrived at
the place where he had pulled out the *kikoka*-fern, he tore it out again; he
appeared on the road; he went, following the road. As they arrived at the
entrance to the village of Tubondo, at his father's village, the people there,
seeing them emerging at the entrance to the village, took the drums; they
beat them; they went to receive the chief Shemwindo together with his
son.[73] They took many, many goats from each man; they gave them to the
chief and to his son; they ate them (the goats) as a welcome gift that they
give to the chief because he has just escaped great danger. As this chief was
now back in his land, he said to his people: "He who has no wife, I shall
provide one in marriage to him." He finished getting all his people, the
bachelors, married. He said to his son Mwindo: "You, my son, you have
done me well; that is the reason I see my land again." He gave him nine
women; his son married them.[74] When Mwindo arrived in his home
village, his dogs, Ndorobiro and Ngonde, sniffed him; they wagged and
wagged their tails for him; they circled and circled around him; they
brought him much joy because lo! their master had arrived.[75]

While Mwindo was resting in his village, a young man from the village
left to go and check his *byoo*-traps. Where he had gone, when the young
man was at the point of "coming from where and going to where," he went
to appear in the small village of Kirimu.[76] He arrived there; he met the
daughter of Kirimu, whose name was Ukano. When Ukano, the daughter

---

(*musingirwa*) indicates that this affair was not illicit or casual but completely in
conformity with Nyanga custom. In Nyanga society the numerous women who are
dedicated to spirits or to the men's house usually live in a prolonged and stable
union with men to whom they are not married; that is, these women bear children
who belong to their own father's and brother's kinship group.

73. When important persons approach the village they are welcomed on the trail
by drummers and singers, who sing and dance their praise.

74. Chiefs have several wives, but large-scale polygyny is not practiced by the
Nyanga. The nine wives mentioned here, like the seven bestowed upon Mwindo
during his enthronement, are an epic exaggeration.

75. This passage provides in the Nyanga language a rare and beautiful poetic
evocation because of the sonorous reduplication of complete root words to stress the
intensity of the action. There is also sonorous alliteration of *sa-* and *si-*, pronominal
prefixes that grammatically bear on *esambibi*, the plural for dogs.

76. *at the point of "coming from where and going to where"*: a formula to indicate
that the Pygmy had gone so far into the forest that he had no hope of returning
home the same day. *Kirimu*: a dragon- and ogrelike being that inhabits the forest
and is a recurring antagonist of the hero. Note that in an earlier episode the
predatory bird killed by Mwindo's sister was also called Kirimu. No confusion is
possible because the forest is inhabited by more than one Kirimu.

of Kirimu, saw the young man, she stirred banana paste for him; she said to him: "When you have finished eating, you must wait for my father because he is still roaming in the virgin forest." This young man took his zanza. When he (the young man) had finished eating the banana paste, in the evening Kirimu returned leveling all the trees with gusts and gusts. Where the young man was seated in the men's house, when he felt the great cold coming there, fear seized him. He sat pondering by himself in the men's house. Kirimu arrived. Seeing the young man holding the zanza, he said to him: "You, young man, when sky changes to dawn and you are still playing your zanza for me, then lo! you also are a true man. I shall give you my daughter, this Ukano here." The sky had now become dark; he had finished eating supper. Kirimu said to this young man: "I have finished eating supper; now you may take your zanza; play it for me so that I may dance."[77] The young man played the zanza, and he was singing:

> E! Nyantari, we are circumventing and circumventing
>   each other.
> E! Nyantari, we are circumventing and circumventing
>   each other.
> E! Nyantari, we are circumventing and circumventing
>   each other.

When the young man had finished singing this song, Kirimu imposed silence upon him, saying that he should no longer sing, that he should merely play the zanza, and that he, Kirimu, would sing his song. Kirimu sang:

> The one who will die owing to my curse,
> Is the first one to go to sleep.
> He who will surpass me in my drumming,
> He is the one who will marry my Kano.
> He who will surpass me in my dancing,
> He is the one who will die owing to my curse.
> Dogs are our salvation.
> We are climbing up Runandi Mountain.[78]

---

77. *Ukano*: this daughter of Kirimu is mentioned in the stories less frequently than an unnamed wife of Kirimu. *leveling all the trees*: rare description of the power of Kirimu, who is either flying like a huge bird or moving fast over the land. *now you may take your zanza*: the dreaded beings of the forest, Kirimu and Mpaca, love music and dance so excessively that they become weak.

78. In this song and the next one the form *wampfundisi*, translated as *He who will surpass me*, is borrowed from the Hunde language. It is one of the very few foreign terms in the entire text. Unlike epic I, epic II has no Nyangaized French words; only a couple of terms derived from Swahili and Hunde are to be found. *Dogs are our salvation*: what Kirimu sings here would fit as a prediction by the young trapper whose brother's dogs will ultimately save him. In identifying himself with Kirimu, the narrator gives his public a foretaste of things to come.

As the young man continued playing the zanza, he fell asleep. Kirimu cut his throat; he died. After Kirimu had killed the young man in this fashion, sky changed to dawn; Kirimu set out for the forest.

In the place where a young man, brother of the one who had died, remained in the village, he said to himself: "What now, where my brother has gone to inspect the byoo-traps, he has not returned; he has perhaps died there." This brother then threw himself before Mwindo; he gave him the news of how his brother had gone, saying that he was going to search for him because he did not know whether he was still alive or dead. Mwindo Mboru gave him his dogs, Ndorobiro and Ngonde, saying: "Go with these dogs to search for your brother. If you encounter difficulties, they will help you fight. And if you die there, those dogs will come to bring me the news." After this young man had received those dogs, he went after his brother, in search of him. He went everywhere where he (his brother) had passed. When he was at the point of "coming from where and going where," he went to arrive in the village of Kirimu. He arrived there; he met there Kirimu's daughter Ukano. He asked her: "Have you not seen my brother here?" Ukano said to him: "It is good that you arrive; my father is still roaming in the forest; after he arrives you will be able to inquire about your brother." The daughter of Kirimu stirred banana paste for this young man (to serve) together with warthog meat. He ate it. When twilight had come, Kirimu returned carrying trees together with all the cold. He arrived in the men's house. Having seen the young man and his dogs in the men's house, Kirimu told him to tie his dogs well because they might go and bite him, because he had not the force to (withstand) being bitten by dogs.[79] "But when sky has become dark, then you will play the zanza for me; and when sky has changed to dawn and you are still playing it for me, then you will carry off my daughter Ukano." Sky became dark; the young man sang:

> E! Nyantari, we are circumventing and circumventing
>   each other.

When he (the young man) had finished singing, Kirimu imposed silence upon him, saying that he, Kirimu, would sing now. He sang:

> He who will surpass me in my dancing,
> He is the one who will carry off my Ukano.

---

79. In his stupidity Kirimu reveals his own weakness. The Nyanga public loves to listen to absurd coincidences, as when the young man has brought the chief's dogs and it is learned that Kirimu is especially vulnerable to dog bites. There is, however, nothing artificially contrived about the situation: the first young man went to inspect his traps, and it is normal not to take dogs along. His brother went to search for him and asked Mwindo's permission to do so. He allegedly got Mwindo's dogs because they might assist him in locating the lost brother. But, of course, Mwindo's gift of prognosis was also at work.

> He who will surpass me in my drumming,
> He is the one who will carry off my Kano.

After the young man had kept on playing the zanza throughout the night without falling asleep, in the early morning he released his dogs; he urged them on; Kirimu was still asleep; they woke him. He was surprised that the dogs were already at his legs, slashing and inflicting wounds. When sky had arrived at the center point of the hot sun, Kirimu said that he was not great; he convulsed; he died.[80]

After Kirimu had died, the young man gave his dogs (the blessings of) long life, saying that they had performed (fine) work. He seized the maiden Ukano, daughter of Kirimu. This young man inquired of Ukano: "Reveal for me the place where my brother has been thrown away." Ukano went to show him the place where his brother had been thrown away. She went with him. They went to arrive at a little river near which there was a *musuku*-tree. At the root of the *musuku*-tree was the head of his brother. He removed one grub from it; he placed it on a hot potsherd. His brother arose from the dead.[81] After his brother had (a)risen, they returned from where they had come to the village of Chief Mwindo, carrying the spoils of Kirimu; they also had with them the dogs of Mwindo. They went to arrive at Mwindo's; the inhabitants, seeing them, received them warmly. They gave the news to Mwindo about the way things had proceeded where they had gone and about the work the dogs had done in killing Kirimu.

This young man who had saved his brother, having set before his master all the things among the spoils from Kirimu's village, said to Mwindo that he wanted to go into the forest again to search for tracks where animals pass.[82] He went. When he arrived in the forest he met a strangler vine (belonging to) the Banamburu; and the village in which the Banamburu dwelt was called Mikema. As this young man arrived there at the strangler vine, he set up *mpota*-snares.[83] After the young man had set

---

80. *When sky had arrived at the center point of the hot sun*: this rarely used formula for time refers to midday, when the sun is at its peak of hotness (*mwishi*). *that he was not great*: a formula, also found in epic I, stating Kirimu's inability to resist death.

81. The text does not explain how the young man acquired the power to revivify his brother. The motif of roasting is linked with Kirimu stories in which people previously swallowed by the monster are brought back to life. In epic I Mwindo roasts Kirimu's eyes to liberate the people trapped inside them.

82. There is nothing unusual or extravagant about the young man's desire to continue hunting immediately after his return. Hunting and trapping are extremely important to the Nyanga and are continuously scheduled by them.

83. *he met a strangler vine*: indicating that the hunter is now within the domain of other people. Strict rules of acquisition and ownership, made flexible by many

up the *mpota*-snares, sky became dark; he slept in the forest on a hill close to his *mpota*-snares, thinking that he might see warthogs passing on the animal trail and fetch the dogs in the village and hunt with them. When it was twilight now, as he looked on, a *mburu*-monkey was struggling in the *mpota*-snare; he went to remove it from the trap. Since the chief of the *mburu*-monkeys had been unable to free himself from the trap, when his call was heard in the village of Mikema, his people beat the drum, saying: "Lo! Our chief experiences something astounding in the place where he has gone; lo! we experience something astounding." Three strong youths from this village of Mikema went searching for the place from where their master's call had come. The young man was busy removing the *mburu*-monkey from his *mpota*-snare when he heard their footsteps. He took the *mburu*-monkey; he wrapped him in many packages of leaves; he went fleeing.[84] When the *mburu*-monkeys arrived at the *mpota*-snare, they arrived there after the young man had left. They set out in pursuit of him to the place where he had gone. They made him arrive at the village entrance, chasing him without respite. They made him arrive at the village entrance!

This young man, being chased like that, arrived at the village exhausted because of panting. Arriving, he went to Mwindo's. After he had rested, he gave the news to Mwindo about his being chased by the inhabitants of Mikema. He said to Mwindo: "It looked as if I would not escape, as if I would die. Behind (us) there is big war." And the *mburu*-monkeys were already there teasing Mwindo, saying: "You, the brave one, to surpass the other chiefs that are established in all the land! And the astounding feats, all of them, we have heard the news about them from where Mwindo has inherited them."[85] Mwindo Mboru asked this young man, saying: "Are these people or spirits since they scoff at us?" Mwindo said to this young man: "Take my dogs, Ndorobiro and Ngonde, and I, Mwindo Mboru, shall take my scepter and my shoulder bag." They went

---

informal arrangements between persons, regulate hunting and trapping, as well as all other spheres of economic activity. The rules for trapping are more stringent than those for hunting, and the young man is flagrantly trespassing. *mpota-snares*: the Nyanga have about thirty different types of animal traps, in addition to a number of fishing traps; many of these devices, like the *mpota*, are specialized for trapping certain types of animals.

84. This passage prepares for Mwindo's revenge against the Mburu, whose chief had earlier allied himself with Itewa.

85. *exhausted*: the Nyanga text says that he arrived "being of seven suns," i.e., as if he had not rested for many days. *from where Mwindo has inherited them*: the *mburu* are probably implying here that Mwindo himself is not that strong, that he owes his success to his magical objects and to Lightning.

after them; they went in pursuit of the *mburu*-monkeys. As they were now on their way, Mwindo sent a messenger to Mikema in order to inform the Banamburu that he was behind, that he was coming to fight war with them because they had destroyed people. After a little while had passed, Mwindo was already "thatching a roof" at the entrance to the village; they took their weapons: spears and arrows together with shields. They said: "Today we shall know one another. He has destroyed those upstream, but that is not here in our place downstream.[86] Shall one man, every day, make people's bellies swell in the land!" Mwindo said to the Banamburu: "Why do you always say that you are the good ones surpassing others in goodness? You will no longer ramble around in the hunting grounds. Lo! Am I not a virile man, I, Mwindo, in person!" When he climbed up there, Mwindo sang:

> *Mburu*-monkey rambles around in the hunting grounds.
> Nyamasangwasangwa has not died.
> E! Kabira, beat the drum for me.
> Nyamasangwasangwa has not died.

After Mwindo had finished singing, the Banamburu said: "You, Mwindo, why do you say that you have finished off all lands because of your heroism, that today we shall not be a match for you, whereas we here in Mikema have destroyed people?" The Banamburu sang:

> The ones from Mikema wiped out people.
> The ones from up in Mikema have decimated people.
> The ones of Mikema have destroyed people.

In meeting on their march to fight, Mwindo came down from a slope; and the Banamburu came down "over there" from a hill. They met in the valley (between two hills); they fought it out there.[87] Mwindo made a proclamation, saying: "The Banamburu do not have teeth! You, now, my dogs, Ndorobiro and Ngonde, squeeze these *mburu*-monkeys here; knead them." As the dogs were let loose like that, they shot down from the hill as if they were four; they killed the Banamburu. When one *mburu*-monkey climbed a tree, Mwindo showed him his scepter; and he fell down. All the ones that had climbed up finished falling down on the ground; they died. When the Banamburu had finished dying, Mwindo made a proclamation,

---

86. *thatching a roof*: i.e., he was already close to the village. *those upstream*: the upstream-downstream dichotomy plays a prominent role in Nyanga symbolism, ritual, and space categorization. The Banamburu are placed downstream to denote that there is something evil about them.

87. Warlike confrontations took place in a glen; the two parties came down opposite slopes, as is suggested in this text.

saying: "As far as I, Mwindo, am concerned, quarrel is not good for the land. Neither are all people of the land equal." He grasped his scepter; he pointed it upward: there came hailstones; they destroyed all the banana trees and all the crops and all the trees and all the grasses; the ground was like a village place. He made it into mud. He seized all the things that the Banamburu possessed: the goats, the chickens, the objects; he assembled them all. Those that ate meat were satiated; their teeth hurt them. Mwindo turned his steps homeward. When he arrived home all his people rejoiced, saying that he had done (a fine) job by wiping out the Banamburu.[88]

In distributing the spoils, he gave his father his share of goats; the counselors carried off their share of goats; the nobles also carried off their share of goats; and the ritual experts: he gave them small shares. When all his people saw these piles of shares, they congratulated him, saying: "Lo! You are a child of a chief; you will grow like a *musone*-tree; the one who will climb on you will be scraping on something tough."[89]

After a countable number of days had passed since they were resting, the Pygmy of Mwindo asked him for the dogs, Ndorobiro and Ngonde, saying that he wanted to go hunting with them in the virgin forest. Mwindo gave his Pygmy Shekaruru permission (to use) the dogs. He said to him: "If you whistle in the forest, then these dogs here will abandon you in the forest."[90] Shekaruru went down to the village entrance together with the dogs, after he had finished feeding them the morning meal in the house of Mwindo's preferred wife. When he was in the middle of the forest he saw an ancient banana tree in the middle of the very dense forest. He drew close to it; he grasped his chin, saying: "How then? Who has planted, who has cultivated, here long ago?" He saw warthogs there; he sent the dogs against them; he killed among them ten warthogs in all. Having finished killing them, he saw a little river in which there were rapids. He descended to the rapids; he arrived there. There was a flat stone. He deposited there his bundle of meat, saying that he wanted to drink water. While he was drinking water he heard the way in which the rapids murmured, "speaking like a drum." He took one leg (of the game); he went

---

88. Mwindo's truly destructive feeling against the *mburu*-monkeys can be attributed to the persistent mockery by the *mburu*. Verbal restraint is of the essence in dealings with a leader.

89. Mwindo gives presents to his father and to the three main categories of holders of political and ritual offices linked with chieftaincy. *you will grow like a musone-tree*: a species of Ficus producing a fine quality of bark cloth, which is worn by the chief.

90. *If you whistle*: this curious prescription by Mwindo is another statement that anticipates action to follow.

to give it as a gift to the rapids because he heard them as if a drum were being beaten.[91] While he was going to take the gift to the rapids, he went singing:

> E! Kabira, beat the drum for me.
> This one here is Waterbuck.
> Kabira, beat the drum for me.
> This one here is Warthog.

When all the animals that he had taken had vanished in the rapids, the Pygmy took his dogs; he climbed with them to a little village. As he arrived in the little village, he encountered iron houses and a woman carrying a pregnancy the size of a house. This woman was the wife of Muisa. As he arrived there, the Pygmy asked her: "Who are you, you woman?" The woman said to him that she was Nyamwanda, the wife of Muisa.[92] The woman said to him: "You, from where do you come? He said that he came from Mwindo's. The woman said to him: "If I tell you (to do) something, will you be capable of (doing) it?" He answered that he was capable of (doing) it. She said to the young man: "Do what you want." He gave a blow to the belly of the woman. It burst open; the entire belly fell to the ground; and in it there were many stones; and they also fell to the ground. The woman rushed away "like over there"; she was very beautiful now. The woman said to him: "Lo! You surely come from Mwindo's because you here have accomplished the work that I have mentioned." The woman, the wife of Muisa, gave the Pygmy a bark cloth. She said to the Pygmy: "Remain over there so that I may show you a thing of salvation, because of which you will go with much fame and be known by many people in the land, and this fame will help you arrive at chieftainship because of your goodness." Nyamwanda, the wife of Muisa, gave a whistle to the Pygmy; she said to him: "This piece of wood: when you go with it and you meet people weeping in a house, then you enter it (the house); you chase all the people who are crying outdoors; you go in there, you remain all by yourself in there, handling your whistle-of-gathering, beating and beating it on the corpse and saying that everyone who went to sleep is used to waking up. Then this corpse will recover; having recovered, it will give you a

---

91. This unusual passage adds to the fantastic world created in the epic. Although in Nyanga custom the river is the center of many ritual practices, offerings similar to the one described here are not made (see Biebuyck, 1974, pp. 42–45).

92. Muisa, one of the chthonic divinities, is an important actor in epic I and in some tales, and so is his daughter Kahindo. This story about Muisa's wife is seldom given. *iron houses*: occasionally mentioned in the tales. *Nyamwanda*: lit., Mother-of-Ax or Mrs. Ax.

maiden and when you arrive back home you will get your hill and build (a small village) for yourself on it."[93]

In taking leave of Muisa's wife, he (the Pygmy) went. Where he went, he came to arrive in a village in which the young son of the chief had just died. When he arrived where they were weeping in the house, Shekararu said to them: "You who are weeping, clear out of the house; let me go into it." They answered him: "Even if you go into it, will you heal him?" He asnwered them saying: "Even if I shall not heal him, let it just be that I may see him in the face." All the people left the house. This Pygmy entered it together with his dogs; he shook the corpse and said to it: "Everyone who went to sleep is used to waking up." The corpse rolled the eyes. He lifted the head up; he said to it: "From where do you come?" The sick person said to him that he did not know from where he came. Shekararu asked for a goat from the inhabitants of that (village); the goat came. This healer said to the people outside that nobody should peek behind this door; it was his affair if he died. Having spoken in this manner, he closed the door; and he was inside the house. He took this goat; he stepped over it, this healer. When sky had become dark, he went to sleep in there. In the early morning he assembled all the people, saying that they should witness how he had completely healed the child of the chief. All the people, without exception, gathered together. When they had gathered together, he entered into the middle of the house, this healer. He, the healer, dressed him in a *rubuo,* (that is) a bark cloth of the *murundu*-tree which was imbued with palm oil and with red powder. He also dressed him with a woven raffia belt. After he had finished dressing him like this, he brought him outside to the middle of the village place where the crowd of people was; he also carried a chair; he made him sit down on it. All the people saw him; he was the object of scrutiny.[94] This healer said to the people that they should give him presents of *butea*-money.[95] They gave it to him. All the people were very much astonished. The father of this young man who had (a) risen seized a maiden; he gave her as a present to this healer saying

---

93. *a whistle*: whistles occur in association with rainmaking and hunting magic. *your whistle-of-gathering*: i.e., a whistle with which he can bring people together. *you will get your hill*: the chief will designate a hill on which he can build his own village. Hills and parts of hills belonging to the chief's domain are allocated to people to reward them for special services.

94. The Pygmy presents the chief's son in a ceremonial manner, as if he had been enthroned as a chief (*rubuo*-bark cloth, stool, belt).

95. *butea-money*: a standard medium of exchange used in economic transactions and in ritual gift giving, *butea*-money consists of rings made from the internal fibers of the raffia tree.

that this was his present. Shekaruru took her; he was very much filled with joy. Shekaruru, he also, gave his son as a present to the chief, saying that he was first going back to the place from where he had come, but that he would surely return again.[96]

He went with his two dogs and with the maiden whom he had received as a gift. He went to throw himself before Mwindo. He showed Mwindo the maiden, saying: "Look where I have been!" The kinsmen of Shekaruru said: "We have heard the news that you have received a medicine to heal people in the place where you have gone, and that you have finished receiving a maiden because of it. Give it also to us so that we may go healing people with it. If you refuse it, we shall pierce you." His kinsmen pressed him very hard, saying that he should show them the medicine, that should he fail to show it to them, they would kill him; so he said to them to come, that he would show them the medicine. His kinsmen arrived; he showed them the piece of wood that he had received from Muisa's wife. He said to them: "I was given this little piece of wood (with the understanding that) we all should find salvation from it, but you reject this, saying that I should not keep it. So here it is. Keep it yourselves; do not go to kill me because of this little thing, but you keep it; and if somebody dies, do not shout at me saying that I am a sorcerer who has brought them sorcery to kill them." Having spoken in this way, he gave it to his kinsmen; they got hold of it.[97]

After Shekaruru had left this medicine with his kinsmen, he proceeded to set up *byoo*-traps for himself. Mwindo took for himself that maiden whom Shekaruru had brought, saying that his dogs had purchased her for him. Where he (Shekaruru) had gone to trap alone, he wandered into the small village of Specter; the crop of Specter's hair surpassed in length "that there." He arrived at Specter's house, and Specter had gone into the forest. Shekaruru removed resinous glue; he placed it on a drying rack that was hanging above the hearth. Shekaruru dozed off. At night Specter arrived. He entered the house; he saw Shekaruru asleep; he approached him; he planted his nails into his neck. Having planted his nails into the neck of Shekaruru, Specter saw the resinous glue lying up there. He removed the nails from Shekaruru; he planted his nails in the resinous glue; the

---

96. Although the Pygmy's son is not explicitly mentioned before, it does not necessarily mean that the narrator was guilty of an omission. When speaking about hunting, trapping, and other forest activities, the Nyanga often mention only the leader of the expedition (the Master-of-the-trail, as they call him), with the understanding that others accompany him.

97. This unusual passage is designed to show how greediness led people to lose a medicine that permitted them to cope with death.

resinous glue stuck to the hand; he grasped the hand; he stuck to the hand. When he tried to grasp the chin, the resinous glue glued the hand and the chin together. It glued them together.[98] As the resinous glue was stuck (all over), Specter sang:

> E! Resinous glue, I am completely finished off,
> In Mwangi, the village of Ishebe.
> E! Resinous glue, I am completely finished off,
> In Mwangi, the village of Ishebe.[99]

Having been caught by the resinous glue, Specter stood above Shekaruru. Shekaruru darted off; he fled. Where he had fled, he arrived out of breath at Mwindo's. Mwindo asked him, saying: "What are you fleeing for? And these wounds here, who has bitten them into you?" He said to him: "Specter has planted these nails into me."

After four days had passed, Shekaruru said to Mwindo that he could not stay there, that he wanted Mwindo to give him his dogs, that he wanted to go hunting with them. Mwindo gave them to him. Having received these dogs, Shekaruru threw himself at the entrance to the village. He went. Where he went, he went to arrive at the village of Shakwece. He lived there with his two wives; one was the beloved-one, and the other was the despised-one. Shakwece said to Shekaruru: "You, my friend, you have come here with the dogs of Mwindo, but my wives have burned my expert hunting dog called Ringe-of-the-chief. They have burned him in the field, but I do not know which (of them), this one or the other, has burned him. That is the reason I am hesitant in determining who, the one or the other, has burned it. And you, my friend, do not go away without first having listened to the words of these my two wives."

And on the side there is a pool which has never been crossed (because) in it there is no fallen tree or a vine on which to cross. In the early morning Shakwece placed across (the pool) a *muntea*-vine as a swinging bridge. Shakwece went with his two wives to the river to put them to the test, so

---

98. *Specter*: Mpaca, a frequent actor in the tales. By nature a male, Mpaca has the ability to metamorphose himself into a person of female appearance. He is emaciated and dirty and has long nails and thick hair. Specter usually fixes himself onto the back of his victim and is removed by means of music, dance, and/or beer. In this passage the Pygmy has no serious difficulty in getting rid of him. (See Biebuyck and Mateene, 1970, pp. 184–189.)

99. *Mwangi, the village of Ishebe*: Mwangi is apparently the name for the village of Specter, and Ishebe is its headman. According to Nyanga custom, a village is referred to by its place-name, followed by either the name of the headman or of the dominant kinship group.

that he might know who (between them) had killed his dog. And Shekaruru followed them; he went there with them. Among his two wives, Nyankuba was the preferred-one and Nyakwabo was the despised-one. As they arrived at the pool, he said to his wives that they should cross over on this vine, and that the one who would submerge with it was the one who had killed his dog. He said to the despised wife that she should proceed. The despised wife got hold of the *muntea*-vine; she passed on it singing:

> I did not kill together with the ones who have
>   killed Ringe,
> Ringe-of-the chief, Ringe.
> I did not kill together with the ones who have
>   killed Ringe,
> Ringe-of-the-chief, Ringe.

The despised wife crossed over to the other bank of the pool. The preferred wife also grasped the vine; and she also sang in the same manner as her co-wife had sung. As she was hanging from the vine, arriving at the middle of the vine, the water reached her chest. She was carrying her child on the back. As she was close to arriving on the other bank, the water reached her neck. Seeing that the young mother was close to submerging, Shekaruru said to Shakwece to go and fetch the child. Shakwece refused, saying: "Let her sink with her child, because she is the one to have killed my dog Ringe." After a while had passed, the beloved-one was swallowed by the water together with her child. Shakwece said: "Lo! She is the one who has killed my dog; she may die altogether."[100]

Having seen the wife of Shakwece die, Shekaruru went into the forest all by himself together with his dogs. Where Shekaruru had gone with his dogs, arriving in the hunting grounds, he let his dogs loose against baboons. The dogs killed twenty-five baboons; they died. And of this troop

---

100. The story about the burned hunting dog Ringe and the subsequent ordeal is unusual. Severe punishments were administered to those who mistreated or killed the hunting dogs, but in the story there is implicit criticism of those who are immoderate in their desire to retaliate. A tale I have collected describes the Ringe affair in more detail. A chief had a dog called Ringe. While the chief's wives were out in the forest, the beloved wife killed the dog and went back to the village to put the dead dog in the house of the despised wife. On his return home the chief decided to use an ordeal to find out who had killed the dog. A liana was strung across a fast-flowing river, and the chief ordered both wives to cross on it. The beloved wife was swallowed by the river. The chief refused to save her, but the woman's paternal aunt secretly delivered her from the water. After two days the paternal aunt showed the woman to her children; they built a house for her near the river and continued to feed her. One day an old man met her there and took the news to the chief. He went to reside with the woman and her son became a chief.

of baboons, three more remained on top of a tree. They sang, while weeping for their companions:

> We die a bad one.
> We die because of teeth.
> We die a bad one.
> We die because of teeth.

Having killed these animals, Shekaruru carried them off; he returned to the village where Mwindo had remained. Arriving there he gave Mwindo his dogs; he also gave him (portions) of the animals that he had killed. Seeing how his hunter had done him well, Mwindo took a maiden; he gave her to him, saying: "And you, my hunter, may you marry this woman."

When he saw the way in which his son performed all these wonderful things, Shemwindo called all his people; he assembled them together; he said to them: "You all who dwell here, counselors, noblemen, ritual experts, all of you and all you Pygmies, I enthrone my son in the chieftainship. And you all: he who brings tribute shall give it to Mwindo. And I, his father, I shall go eating behind my son Mwindo." Shemwindo took seven women; he gave them to his son so that he might marry them. He took the chief's bark cloth; he gave it to his son. He took five leopard teeth and a belt of wild pig's hide. He inserted the teeth into the belt; he gave them to his son saying that he should wear them. He took five red fruits; he gave them to his son: he also gave him an *utebe*-stool which was imbued with red color. He gave him a large *butenge*-spear. He also took a belt stitched with cowries, and he dressed him in it. He gave him a net of cowries. When he had given his son all these things, they beat the drum; all the people, the children and the old ones, finished hearing that Mwindo was the chief. This chief ruled in fame in his village Tubondo, together with all his people.[101]

---

101. The situation described here is unusual in that the chief himself decides to enthrone his son. The decision for enthronement belongs to the Chief-Counselor, and most of the proceedings are organized by a small number of ritual experts and counselors who are mentioned in epic III. The paraphernalia mentioned constitute the chief's insignia.

THE MWINDO EPIC III

SYNOPTIC TABLE OF CONTENTS

   I. *The setting*
     A. The events are set in remote times in an unspecified kingdom.
     B. The action extends into various places.
     C. The hero's father, Karisi, has many wives, among them the principal wife Kahindo, daughter of Hangi-of-Drum.
   II. *Rejection of the principal wife*
     A. The chief's principal wife Kahindo fails to have a child and is rejected by her husband.
     B. The chief wants the princes and the counselors to build a house for her on the garbage heap at the entrance to the village.
     C. The Chief-Counselor, Shebakungu, at first refuses, but since he cannot place Kahindo in his own kinship group he is forced to accept the chief's decision.
     D. The wife Kahindo settles by herself in a house on the outskirts of the village.
     E. The chief proclaims that no one may visit her or stay with her.
     F. Kahindo plants crops and banana trees; they quickly mature and ripen.
  III. *Conception and birth of Kabutwakenda (Little-one-just-born-he-walked)*
     A. When the beans she had planted begin to sprout, Kahindo is suddenly pregnant "without a male having given the pregnancy to her."

B. A year passes, and the woman is still pregnant.
C. The delivery is long and painful. The lonely Kahindo stretches out in the sun and sings in despair.
D. Hearing her lament, Shebakungu sends his wife Nyabakungu to check.
E. Nyabakungu consoles Kahindo and takes her back into the house.
F. Kahindo gives birth to a child that praises himself as Kabutwakenda (Little-one-just-born-he-walked), the Little-child-of-many-wonders.
G. Kabutwakenda informs his mother that he is leaving, but Nyabakungu convinces him to let her first take the news to the village.
H. People come to view Kabutwakenda; he removes himself from the house and scornfully praises himself.
I. The people encircle him, but he removes himself, "flying like a bird," and disappears forever.

IV. *Kabutwakenda and Bukumba*
A. Kabutwakenda arrives at the top of a high mountain, called Bukumba.
B. After many days Kabutwakenda is met there by a snake, also called Bukumba.
C. They remain together and till crops.
D. Kabutwakenda sends famine over the entire land, including his father's village.

V. *The birth of the hero, Mwindo*
A. Shebakungu advises the chief to bring Kahindo back to the village.
B. Instead, the chief goes to visit her and makes her pregnant.
C. With the help of Nyabakungu, Kahindo gives birth (without any complications) to a son.
D. The chief, informed about the birth, sends a goat as a gift to Kahindo.
E. After three days, Kahindo leaves the birth house.
F. The chief summons her back to the village.

VI. *Kahindo regains her status*
A. Back in the village, Kahindo receives servants from her husband.
B. Her child is named Mwindo.
C. The child grows up.

D. The chief decides to install his son.

VII. *Mwindo receives his own land and becomes chief*

    A. At the chief's request, a village is built for Mwindo.

    B. Mwindo establishes himself in that village with his mother and a crowd of people.

    C. Shebakungu goes to visit them once in a while.

    D. Mwindo grows up.

    E. The chief decides to leave his land to his son.

    F. He divides the people. He goes with half of them and Shebakungu, leaving half of the people and Shebakungu's son with Mwindo.

    G. Chief Karisi goes to settle in a land where he grows eleusine, leaving his son behind "in the land of downstream."

    H. Mwindo is enthroned. His mother's daughter's daughter becomes his ritual wife.

    I. Mwindo gains widespread fame.

    J. Mwindo has Pygmies, and he buys hunting dogs. The Pygmies hunt with the dogs, providing game meat for the people and wealth in the form of many women for Mwindo.

VIII. *Mwindo's hunt*

    A. Mwindo's wives encounter a huge wild boar near the river; they call Mwindo.

    B. Mwindo sends one of his Pygmies, urging him to locate the wild boar but not to kill it because he wants to see it.

    C. The Pygmy brings back the news that there is a very wild boar near the river.

    D. Mwindo sets out with spears, his Pygmies, and his two dogs, Bad-Luck and Fast-Eater.

    E. They arrive at the river and see the boar. But Mwindo does not allow his Pygmy, Meshemutwa, to spear it. Instead, he himself hurls a spear. The spear misses the target because of the boar's medicine.

    F. Mwindo and his dogs pursue the boar in vain.

    G. In despair, Mwindo calls for his paternal aunt.

    H. When night overtakes him, Mwindo calls again for his paternal aunt.

    I. The paternal aunt enters Mwindo and gives him sleep. When he awakens, the aunt brings a house for him.

    J. He also finds food that had been brought to him by Kahindo, the daughter of Nyamurairi.

K. This Kahindo is sent by her father to fool Mwindo, and it is she who transforms herself into the wild boar.

L. After he eats the food, Mwindo finds the wild boar behind the house again.

M. Mwindo and his dogs chase the wild boar and encounter the daughter of a blacksmith.

N. The woman drops her ax in a river, but Mwindo sees Otter and Water Duck bringing the ax back to her.

O. Mwindo arrives in a banana grove. He meets a woman who is cutting bananas. She gives bananas to the dogs, but they refuse, saying that "she is an enemy." (The woman is the same Kahindo who had previously transformed herself into a wild boar.)

P. Mwindo asks the woman to show him the way to the village.

IX. *The world of Nyamurairi*

A. Mwindo arrives at the outskirts of the village.

B. His paternal aunt helps him hide his dogs under the armpits.

C. Kahindo had already informed her father Nyamurairi about Mwindo's arrival.

D. A barricade of trees

Nyamurairi lowers trees so as to close the trail on which Mwindo travels. Mwindo, singing, removes the trees, identifying them as counselors. They return to Nyamurairi to tell him that Mwindo knows them.

E. A caravan of red ants

Nyamurairi lowers a caravan of red ants to stop Mwindo. Mwindo, singing, removes the ants, identifying them as brave-ones. They return to Nyamurairi to tell him that Mwindo knows them.

F. A wall of hides

Mwindo pursues the journey and has the village in sight. Nyamurairi lowers a wall of hides. Mwindo, singing, removes the hides, identifying them as the wives of his master. They return to Nyamurairi telling him that Mwindo knows them.

G. A wall of high grasses

Mwindo arrives in the middle of the village. Singing, he meets a wall of high grasses and removes them, identifying them as princes. They go to Nyamurairi to tell him that Mwindo knows them.

H. Encounter with Nyamurairi

Mwindo arrives in the men's house. Nyamurairi tells him not to stay there, but to take residence with his daughter Kahindo. Mwindo goes to stay with Kahindo.

I. Clearing of grasses

While Mwindo sleeps, grasses grow everywhere in the village. Nyamurairi orders Mwindo to cut the grasses. Mwindo requests large numbers of hoes and billhooks and gets them. Mwindo places the tools on the ground. (The spirit of) his paternal aunt comes to promise help. In return, Mwindo promises to dedicate cult objects to her. Mwindo offers an invocation. Quickly, the grasses cut themselves.

J. Cultivation of a banana grove

Nyamurairi is astonished because of Mwindo's toughness. He sends Mwindo out to cultivate a banana grove. Mwindo requests and receives many iron tools from Nyamurairi. Mwindo offers an invocation; suddenly all the agricultural work is done, and the bananas and crops are ripe. He harvests some and takes the food to Nyamurairi. Nyamurairi rejoices and blesses Mwindo.

K. Hunt of a buffalo

A buffalo is eating all the bananas and crops on the field. This buffalo is Kahindo's mother (Nyamurairi's wife) transformed. Nyamurairi sends Mwindo to guard the field. Mwindo sees the buffalo and sends his dogs, hidden in the armpits, against it. The buffalo reveals its identity; Mwindo lets it go and returns to Nyamurairi, criticizing him.

L. Mwindo's departure

Nyamurairi decides to abandon the tests. He gives his daughter as a wife to Mwindo and instructs him about social matters. He gives them gifts and instructs Mwindo never to hunt again. Mwindo and Kahindo leave.

X. *Encounter with the paternal aunt*

  A. Mwindo arrives at the place of his paternal aunt.

  B. She reminds him of his pledge to dedicate a shoulder bag, a double-edged knife, and a calabash to her.

  C. She shows him a shorter way home.

  D. He passes through the area of Black Ant and Baboon.

XI. *Mwindo's encounter with his mother Nyamwindo*

  A. Arriving in his mother's village, Mwindo finds her mourning his death.

B. The mother does not recognize him, but Mwindo reveals his identity. They greet warmly.

C. The village is overgrown with grasses; the people have left; Nyamwindo lives there alone with Mwindo's first wife.

D. Mwindo ponders the fate of his people.

E. His hoes clear the village.

XII. *Mwindo's reunion with his Pygmies*

A. Meeting with Nkango

"Where the Pygmies had fled," the Pygmy Nkango decides to go and visit Nyamwindo. The Pygmy arrives at the village entrance and sees that the village is again filled with houses. He meets Mwindo in the middle of the village and greets him warmly. Mwindo asks him why and where they have gone. The Pygmy tells him that they have settled in a village in the forest, but that he regularly comes back to look after Nyamwindo.

B. Return of the other Pygmies

Nkango goes to fetch the other Pygmies. They break up their village and return to Mwindo. Nyamwindo wants Mwindo to kill the Pygmies and the counselors because they have wronged him. Mwindo refuses, saying that he himself was the cause of the problems.

XIII. *Mwindo's offer to his paternal aunt*

A. Mwindo informs the assembly of people that he wants to offer a shoulder bag, a double-edged knife, and banana paste to his paternal aunt.

B. Nyamwindo prepares a huge banana paste which Elephant is unsuccessful in lifting, but Chameleon succeeds.

C. The people praise Chameleon and criticize Elephant.

D. Mwindo invites Muhima to make an invocation.

E. They build a shrine house.

F. Muhima invites Shebakungu to sacrifice a goat and to offer an invocation in the shrine house.

G. Muhima criticizes Shebakungu for offering the invocation in the name of Mwindo's father.

H. The shrine house collapses.

I. Muhima calls small children and builds a new shrine house.

J. Muhima offers the invocation, predicting new fighting and bad fate.

K. Right there the people start fighting.

XIV. *Mwindo is forged by his maternal uncles*

A. Mwindo asks Bat, his maternal uncle, to forge him.
B. Mwindo refuses to collect charcoal. Instead, he searches for the body hair of his paternal aunts and of the wives of his maternal uncles.
C. Mwindo collects their tears in a pot, in order to cool him when they forge him.
D. He requests that his cross-cousins be forged with him.
E. Mwindo gets on top of two cross-cousins on the fire to be forged.
F. They forge one side, pouring tears over him and consulting the oracle.
G. They lift him up and place two other cross-cousins on the fire, with Mwindo on top of them.
H. They forge the other side, consulting the oracle.
I. Mwindo is plain iron.

XV. *Mwindo's fight with Mutero Murimba*
A. In order to test himself, Mwindo goes to fight Mutero Murimba.
B. They challenge each other.
C. Mwindo cleaves Mutero into pieces and goes.

XVI. *Mwindo's ascent to Lightning*
A. Leaving Mutero, Mwindo encounters a wild banana tree obstructing the road. He removes it.
B. The fight and reconciliation
Mwindo climbs up to Lightning. Lightning blocks the road. They challenge each other. They fight; Mwindo seizes Lightning and throws him down. When Mwindo tries to cut Lightning with a knife, Lightning asks for mercy, promising to be Mwindo's servant. Mwindo lets him, taking Lightning's goods and people with him. Lightning asks Mwindo what he will give him in return for future help. Mwindo promises to consecrate a white chicken, a maiden, and sugarcane.

XVII. *Mwindo's return to Nyamwindo's village*
A. Mwindo returns home, asking Elephant to clear the trails for him so he can escape his enemies and invoking Kahombo's blessing.
B. Mwindo is greeted and praised by his mother.
C. Having rested for some time, Mwindo decides to fight Nyakatwakari.
D. He leaves his pregnant wife Kahindo behind with his mother.
E. Mwindo eats a paste of eleusine and leaves, together with Lightning.

XVIII. *Mwindo's encounter with Nyakatwakari*

    A. On the road to Nyakatwakari, Mwindo and Lightning devise a plan to attack her.

    B. The fight with Nyakatwakari

    On their arrival they are challenged by her. They fight her; Mwindo sweats blood; Lightning flattens Nyakatwakari's people. They seize Nyakatwakari and her daughter. Nyakatwakari promises her daughter to Mwindo if he will harvest honey for her which she has been unable to collect.

    C. The honey harvest

    Lightning advises Mwindo to accept the offer. Mwindo sends Meshe, the Pygmy, to harvest the honey. Meshe builds a platform and climbs the tree, taking his ax with him. He lights a piece of bark cloth with his fire drill. Mwindo orders him to climb down. Mwindo gives his knife to Nyakatwakari. Meshe climbs the tree; he opens the hole with his ax, but the hole seizes him. Meshe invokes Mwindo's help; Mwindo orders his knife to bend Nyakatwakari. Nyakatwakari is smashed against the ground; the hole releases Meshe. But Nyakatwakari refuses to give her daughter, and Meshe remains in the tree. His kinsman Nkango goes to consult the oracles of the animals and returns to help his kinsman who is still in the tree. Mwindo, considering that he will not get Nyakatwakari's daughter because of his Pygmy, leaves them and goes to forge. Nkango, seeing that Mwindo has gone, complains bitterly. He climbs the tree to help his kinsman. They fill two calabashes with honey and climb down. They give a calabash of honey to their kinsmen. The Pygmies leave for another chief, because Mwindo abandons and accuses them.

XIX. *Mwindo's Pygmies arrive in the village of Chief Mutero Murimba; encounter with the headman Kasiwa*

    A. The Pygmies arrive near the village of Chief Mutero Murimba.

    B. They are intercepted by Mutero's people under the leadership of the headman Kasiwa.

    C. Kasiwa promises that he will take them to the chief and gives them goats and banana beer.

    D. The Pygmies ask the women to collect firewood.

    E. The headman asks them what they want to do with the firewood (for Mutero's people live in a cave without fire).

    F. When the woman returns, a Pygmy carrying a fire drill goes to make a fire and brings it to the headman.

G. The headman in that cold place enjoys the fire and promises to take the Pygmies to the chief.

XX. *Mwindo's return to Nyakatwakari's village; Nyakatwakari's departure*

A. Mwindo returns with new spears.

B. He meets Nyakatwakari and tells her to join her sons (the Pygmies), that he does not want to kill her.

C. Messengers sent by the Pygmies meet Nyakatwakari on the road and take her to her sons.

XXI. *The Pygmies and Chief Mutero Murimba*

A. Arrival of Nyakatwakari

Nyakatwakari arrives. The headman Kasiwa gives the Pygmies a section of the village.

B. The hunt

The Pygmies go to hunt and fail to find animals. They find a big elephant which is all rotten. They remove the tusks and return to the village. The headman Kasiwa gives them beer and chickens and praises them.

C. Encounter with the chief

A messenger and the Pygmy Meshe are sent to the chief by the headman. The chief is astonished to meet a Pygmy. The messenger explains to him that they have brought fire and elephant tusks. The chief sends the messenger back to fetch the headman, his people, and the Pygmies and to bring many goods. The Pygmies and the people arrive. The chief asks them where they have come from. The Pygmies tell their story; they are invited to settle with the chief. They go to fetch their wives and their belongings. They settle with their mother Nyakatwakari on a hill given them by the chief. The people cultivate; they have children and grandchildren.

D. The Pygmies acquire ritual duties

Chief Mutero now gives the Pygmies the right to enthrone the chief and to provide some of the ritual necessities. The chief decrees that Pygmies must be given food and banana beer, and that they have the right to cut bananas in the banana groves.

XXII. *The chief is enthroned*

A. Since Mwamitwa (Chief-Pygmy) has now arrived, the people want to enthrone the chief.

B. They prepare various paraphernalia.

C. They call upon Shebakungu (Chief-Counselor) to provide the teachings.

D. They select various wives of special status for the chief.

E. They call upon the various ritual experts.

F. They go to the sacred ground for the enthronement procedures.

G. The chief receives the precepts of his office.

H. They return to the village.

XXIII. *Death and last will of Chief Mutero Murimba*

A. The chief does not observe the precepts.

B. Therefore he suffers from ancylostomiasis.

C. On the point of dying, he prescribes the sacred tasks for Shebakungu and Shemumbo.

D. After the chief has died, the ritual expert Musimba removes select parts of his body and dries them.

E. When the chief is buried, the counselors utter an imprecation, saying that he will become a leopard.

F. Gifts are given to the counselors by the princes.

G. They divide the belongings of the chief: some of the material possessions go to Muembwa and to Salt-of-the-land; some of the wives go to Shemumbo and others to the ritual wife (*mumbo*). A hill and a woman are given to Muembwa.

H. The Pygmies remain there with their offspring.

XXIV. *Mwindo's children*

A. Mwindo is also a chief.

B. He has ten children (sons and daughters) with his seven wives whom he has acquired as the result of his bravery (reconciliations and blood pacts). All the wives and children are enumerated.

C. When the children are big, Mwindo assigns political and ritual duties to them. These duties are enumerated for each of the ten children.

D. He predicts that there will be competition, noting that chieftainship is not pursued by one house alone.

XXV. *Mwindo's death*

A. He leaves his last oral will, urging his children to love one another and not to abandon one another.

B. Mwindo dies.

C. His children remove select parts of his body.

D. Mwindo's children follow his words and live in harmony.

THE MWINDO EPIC III: TRANSLATION

Long ago there was in a place a chief called Karisi.[1] He married many wives. His principal wife was called Kahindo, the daughter of Hangi-of-Drum.[2] After he had finished marrying those his wives, all of them bore children. Kahindo failed to give birth. When she failed to give birth, Kahindo was rejected by her husband; she failed to be loved by him.[3] Chief Karisi made a proclamation, saying: "You, my counselors and nobles, I do not want Kahindo to remain in this my village; I want to chase her from it; I want you to go and build (a house) for her, on the garbage heap, at the entrance to the village."[4]

Among those his counselors, there was a counselor senior to his colleagues called Shebakungu.[5] This Shebakungu did not agree with the chief, saying that his principal wife was not the sole cause of her failure to give birth, that it came from God.[6] The chief said to Shebakungu: "Since you

---

1. *Karisi*: the term *karisi* designates the epic genre. Combined with the morpheme *shé-* (father of, master of), the term refers to the expert narrator of an epic. The son of such a narrator may be called Karisi. In this epic the hero's father, who is usually known by the teknonymic name Shemwindo, is simply called Karisi. In one heroic tale the hero himself is named Karisi. The word is related to *murisi*, one who oppresses, crushes, or overpowers in action, and to the verb *irise*, to press, oppress, crush, force, but also to sit on top of, e.g., to sit on one's lap.

2. *His principal wife*: the term *nyabana* used in the text refers to a man's senior wife. In a chief's family this wife has top social authority and is treated with deep respect. Yet she must not be confused with the ritual wife (*mumbo*), whose son normally succeeds to the chieftainship. *Kahindo*: a frequently used personal name for women of Hunde origin and most often applied to a woman who stands in a special cult relationship with the divinity Kahindo. Here the wife Kahindo is referred to as the daughter of Hangi-of-Drum. Hangi is a divinity worshiped by the Nyanga and the Hunde. In other texts Kahindo is identified as the daughter of either Nyamurairi or Muisa, two major divinities among the Nyanga and the Hunde. Because of the confusion of the names of divinities and the names of their devotees, it is unclear whether the narrator means that Chief Karisi's wife is of divine origin or is simply a human devotee of Kahindo whose father is also a devotee of Hangi.

3. The theme of the mother of heroes who is rejected by her husband because she initially fails to have children, or because she bears male children contrary to her husband's decrees, is frequent in both epics and heroic tales.

4. *build . . . on the garbage heap*: here, as the further context indicates, the chief's order is to be taken literally. The wife is physically removed from her husband's homestead, even though in Nyanga practice the loss of preferred status does not commonly entail physical removal. The garbage heap, usually found behind the houses and outside the village fence, symbolizes a state of abjection.

5. *Shebakungu*: the Chief-Counselor, who is found in all Nyanga kingdoms. He fulfills important political and ritual functions related to the institution of divine kingship.

6. *God*: the term Ongo, which designates the creator god, is used. In Nyanga

refuse to chase this my first wife, go then to build (a house) for her in your kinship group." Hearing this, Shebakungu said to the chief: "The wife of a chief is not placed in a kinship group without having given birth to children. For if I place her in my kinship group and my people cause her trouble, commit adultery with her, then what will you think of me, you, chief? Will you not have bad feelings toward me?"[7] The chief said to Shebakungu: "So it is better that you go and build (a house) for her at the entrance to the village." Shebakungu agreed, saying: "Lo! A chief certainly makes resolutions."[8] He told the people to go to build (a house) for her at the entrance to the village. When the house was finished, they chased the principal wife over there. She went to move there by herself on the garbage heap. All by herself she dwelt there; no other person built there. The chief launched an interdiction, saying: "You understand, you, all my people: the one who will pass over there where the principal wife resides in order to go to see her, or in order to stay there with her, he/she is the same as her. I shall tear out a bone from his/her back."[9]

Where the first wife remained all by herself at the entrance to the village, she planted crops. One (crop) was eleusine; it was ripe already! She planted banana trees, and they were mature already![10] She planted beans;

---

thinking, Ongo is the ultimate source of life: i.e., *ongo ngi kibumbabumba*, God is the modeler, and *ongo ngi buingo*, God is life. He is the final reason "that some women have children and others do not, and that some children are male and others are female." The active agent behind life and death, however, is Nyamurairi, the chief of the divinities of the subterranean world, who is both a servant and a manifestation of the creator god.

7. A certain confusion exists between procedures involving the ritual wife (*mumbo*) and those involving the principal wife. The chief's ritual wife is removed from the chief's homestead after the enthronement rites and is placed under the guardianship of such officeholders as Shebakungu (Chief-Counselor), Shemumbo (Father-of-the-ritual-wife), and Shemwami (Father-of-the-chief). Kahindo, however, is the chief's principal wife, although later on she implicitly acquires the status of ritual wife when her heroic son Mwindo becomes chief. Because she is not a ritual wife, but just a chief's wife (*mowe*), Shebakungu refuses to place her under the protection of his kinship group.

8. *A chief . . . makes resolutions*: the verb *isisinya* has a complex set of meanings, such as to resolve, to be successful, to have good fortune.

9. *he/she is the same as her*: i.e., will undergo the same fate. *I shall tear out*: a formula to say "I shall kill." The severity of the interdiction is designed to emphasize the solitude of Kahindo and to introduce the exceptional sequence of events to follow. This passage also stresses the eminence of the Chief-Counselor and the necessity for a chief to heed his advice.

10. Nyanga agriculture is traditionally centered in banana growing. Subsidiary crops, such as beans and corn, are interspersed in the banana groves. Eleusine (*buhi*) is grown by Hunde inhabiting the highland grasslands and by Nyanga who live in areas bordering on the rain forest–highland grassland divide.

and when these beans began to sprout she carried a pregnancy without a male having given the pregnancy to her. As she was now heavy (with pregnancy), she always remained by herself with this pregnancy. "One year of the banana trees" passed, and she was still plagued by this pregnancy.[11] After "the year of the banana trees" had gone by, one day the pregnancy began to hurt. She was plagued by it, all by herself, without a person coming to visit her to look after her. When three days had passed after she was plagued by this pregnancy without giving birth, she left the house; she stretched out outside, saying: "This is rough! I have forgotten what dwells here in my belly. What shall I do here, all by myself? Lo! I will not pull through. Lo! My death has come to me." After she had spread a hide outside, and while she was basking in the sun and the pregnancy was still hurting her, she sang in the hope that somebody might hear her calling and would come to the place where she was troubled. She threw a sound in the mouth, saying:

> Support of the spirit is far away;
> Otherwise, I would have called my mother that she
>   may come.
> But lo! I am going to die without seeing my mother.
> What father has done to me was not perpetrated
>   gratuitously;
> It does bring bad luck.
> My father did to me a thing of tears;
> He went fooling me, saying that
> I was going to get chieftaincy as the honored wife.
> Lo! I went to turn into the state of despised wife,
> To settle down in a place of excrement;
> I, without being seen by other people.[12]

She uttered a cry, low and high, saying: "You, my mother, I am dying like this without seeing other people who come for me at the entrance to the village. The thing that my father has done to me, saying that I should marry, that I should be married to the chieftainship, that there was joy in it! And lo! He threw me away into a little house of red ants. Now then, the

---

11. The theme of parthenogenesis is absent from the other epics. The hero is usually conceived by normal intercourse between the chief and one of his wives. In some of the heroic tales, however, the hero is born from the union of a woman and a serpent or he is a child of undetermined origin who throws himself into a woman's womb and is then reborn. *One year of the banana trees*: lit., translation of *mwaka mpoko*, a standard time indication of the period between the clearing of a new banana grove and the maturing of the first crop.

12. In this bitter complaint the narrator mixes both direct and indirect discourse. The woman criticizes her father who had married her to a chief assuming that she would enjoy high status. Instead, she was abandoned and dishonored.

spirit who will come to remove me from here, be it Ruendo, be it another one, I will give worship to him."[13]

When those who were seated in the village heard her calling and the way in which she was weeping at the entrance to the village, the chief told Shebakungu to go and have a look. Shebakungu said to his wife: "You, my wife, rush first to where the principal wife remains; go to see, because a call like a lament comes from there." This wife of Shebakungu made no delays; she rushed over there. Arriving there and throwing a glance at her (the principal wife), she grasped her chin.[14] As the principal wife was lying on the ground, on the back with the legs open, she looked at the wife of Shebakungu; and tears welled up in her eyes. She sang:

> No, no, my mother Nyabakungu,
> Do not look at me; I am being pressed hard.
> The maiden, who is far, cultivates on a day of rest;
> She goes on just cultivating.
> Lo! Her mother has died without hearing the news.[15]

She said: "My mother, just let me alone; I am weeping for myself; there is no one who will weep for me." Nyabakungu said to her: "Hold on tightly; put your heart on the knee so that you may give birth quickly; do not indulge in self-pity. Now you are my girl; I have taken you on the side of chieftainship."[16]

After a while had passed, Nyabakungu helped the principal wife into

---

13. *She uttered a cry, low and high*: a formula indicating that one has exhausted all one's means. The Nyanga terms *mwihi* and *more* used in this expression literally mean "nearby" and "far," "short" and "long". *red ants*: a symbol of fierceness. *Ruendo*: a Nyanga divinity worshiped by women.

14. *those who were seated*: the verb *irika* is abundantly used as a formula referring to place and location. I have variably translated it as to dwell, to be seated, to remain, to reside, to perch, to live. *she grasped her chin*: a gesture of disbelief and profound astonishment.

15. *mother Nyabakungu*: the wife of Shebakungu is known as Nyabakungu; "mother" is an honorific title used for her by the chief's wife. *cultivates on a day of rest*: important events, such as an enthronement or the death of an important person or the beginning of the circumcision cycle, were celebrated by a day of rest when no one would go into the forest. To emphasize her desperate situation, the chief's wife compares herself with a woman who is far away from her kinsfolk and is compelled to work on a day of rest.

16. *put your heart on the knee*: a formula used to describe intense, but contained, suffering. A Nyanga who is suffering, in order to restrain himself from crying, holds his mouth firmly against his knee or arm as if biting it. *Now you are my girl*: with these soothing words the wife of Shebakungu seems to predict the future greatness of the chief's wife. The special protection of the Chief-Counselor and his wife is a warrant of high status.

the house. Arriving in it, she gave birth; and the afterbirth came out there. As the child emerged, he praised himself saying that he was the Little-one-just-born-he-walked, the Little-child-of-many-wonders, I-have-no-father, I-have-no-mother.[17] Little-one-just-born-he-walked, having praised himself in this manner, said to his mother that she was the mother who had brought him forth, but that she would not see him, that he was going away: "Thereafter, I will be as if I have made you pregnant, because you have carried a pregnancy without a male having mounted you."[18] He said to his mother that he was going away and (he said to Nyabakungu) : "You, midwife, Nyabakungu, get out of my way; I am going." Hearing this (what he said), Nyabakungu was greatly astonished; she said to him: "You, child, this is rough. What has never been seen is now being witnessed; this is the first time. Though I have toiled many times helping (women) to give birth, I have never yet seen a child come out of the womb and speak." The child stood up in the birth house.[19] As Little-one-just-born-he-walked was about to leave the house, saying that he was on his way, Nyabakungu said to him: "Wait first so that I may go to tell the village the news of this wonder, in the place where the chief is in the village. Go when I have returned." Little-one-just-born-he-walked said to her: "So go! Who is troubled by this? What will they do to me?"[20] Nyabakungu dashed quicly to the village. She arrived there; in the middle of the village place she gave the news about the marvelous happening, saying: "What is over there is as it is over there; it cannot be communicated. There is born a child who is walking and talking." Hearing this news, they (the villagers) said to her that she was telling lies: "Your lies and lies!" She said to them: "Not at all; go first to see for yourself." They rushed over there to see him. Arriving

---

17. Although this epic does not mention a miraculous birth, the conception was of course miraculous. There is emphasis, however, on a prolonged and painful delivery. The newborn hero assigns his own name to himself. He is Kabutwakenda, Little-one-just-born-he-walked. Kabutwakenda is also the personal name of one of the heroes in epic IV, and some protagonists in the heroic tales bear the same name. In epic I, Little-one-just-born-he-walked is the main epithet of the hero. The epithet Little-child-of-many-wonders (*kana ka mishinga mere*, lit., Little-child-of-long-wonders) is also used in other texts. *I-have-no-father, I-have-no-mother*: quasi epithets by which the newborn hero shows his boastfulness.

18. Little-one-just-born-he-walked boasts that he has no mother simply because he will not be raised by a woman. He decides to go into a kind of self-imposed exile as though he had conceived himself in an incestuous relationship with his mother.

19. The newborn hero treats the midwife rudely, giving new proof of his boisterous arrogance.

20. The hero scornfully agrees to wait for the people to view him. Although he knows in advance that they will cause trouble, he is unafraid.

there (they cried): "Look, it is true!" Little-one-just-born-he-walked, seeing the crowd of people coming to view him, removed himself from the house. He removed himself to the middle of the village, saying scornfully: "Here I am! Little-one-just-born-he-walked, Father-of-many-wonders." Having met with the people in this manner, he said to his mother: "You, my mother, I am leaving you; I am going away to Bukumba, to a mountain in Kishari, where there is no speaking, where there is no hunting, where there is no whistling." When he had finished speaking like this, the crowd of people encircled him. He removed himself from them, and he was flying like a bird. He disappeared; they did not see him again.[21]

Where he went, he arrived on top of the mountain Bukumba, (which was) a high mountain. On top of it, near its summit, there was a little lake.[22] He arrived there saying that this was his mountain. After many days had passed, there arrived a snake; he met him there. His (the snake's) name was Bukumba, and he came from Hot-Springs in the land of Bunyungu.[23] He was together with his one child; he came down with the Mbisi River. Arriving in Kihica, he left his child there in the Rwashi River. This snake Bukumba went down with the Rwashi River. Arriving at the point where the Rwama River flows into the Rwashi River, he climbed up with the Rwama River. Arriving at the point where the Rwama River encounters the Bukumba River, he went down with the Bukumba River. He went to climb the mountain of Bukumba.[24] As he arrived there, he met there (to his surprise) Little-one-just-born-he-walked. Both of them were there. Little-one-just-born-he-walked said to his companion Bukumba: "Because you met me here, I am the master of this place, because I am the first one to arrive here. And you, Bukumba, this mountain has your name. However, let us reside on it together; let us till it as we like." They tilled (the soil); they produced many foods.[25]

---

21. *Bukumba*: as is evident later on, the name stands simultaneously for a high mountain, a personified snake, and a river. The symbolic connotation of the term is with the verb *ikumba*, to join together, to share, to join forces, i.e., a place where a human and a serpent join to live together. *Kishari*: a vast region located east of the Nyanga and inhabited by subgroups of the Hunde. The narrator of this epic has roots in that region. *he was flying*: not an unusual characteristic of the hero, but generally he flies by means of his scepter or by means of wings he has manufactured.

22. *a little lake*: the region of Kishari (commonly known as Gishari) is famous for the beautiful lakes that formed in the craters of extinct volcanoes.

23. *Bunyungu*: another major region located east of Nyanga country and inhabited by subgroups of the Hunde.

24. The rivers mentioned here flow in Hundeland.

25. In this passage the right of first occupation of the land is emphasized, together with the Nyanga custom of sharing such land with latecomers.

When many days had passed after both of them were established there, Little-one-just-born-he-walked said to his companion Bukumba: "Let us send down much famine over the entire land, also down there, where father and mother have remained." They sent down much famine; the people of the land failed (to know) what to do. Little-one-just-born-he-walked said to himself: "Truly from there came a man who is getting to be known."[26]

Where the mother of Little-one-just-born-he-walked had remained, she was still staying in her hamlet.[27] Shebakungu went to tell Chief Karisi that it was befitting that he should remove his principal wife from the entrance to the village and take her back into the village. The chief answered Shebakungu, saying: "It is befitting that she remain there, but I will go to the place where she is to see her." After many days had passed, her husband arrived to sleep with her in the place where she was. The mother of Little-one-just-born-he-walked carried a pregnancy. After a countable number of days had passed, the pregnancy hurt. They sent a messenger to the village to call Nyabakungu.[28] The messenger arrived at Nyabakungu's place; he said to her that she should go again to help the principal wife give birth, that she was again being hurt by the pregnancy. Hearing this, she (Nyabakungu) said: "Will there again result something complicated? She does not give birth easily, this principal wife."[29] Nyabakungu went over there. She arrived there; some time passed, and the first wife gave birth. Nyabakungu helped her give birth. After the child was born, they sent a messenger to the chief to fetch a goat that would be killed for the young mother. The chief gave a goat "of the kind that does not defecate, that does not urinate"; it was very fat.[30] When it arrived there, they killed it; it was the young mother's ritual meal.[31] After three days had passed since the child was born, the young mother came out; she

---

26. With this famine, the story of Kabutwakenda's feats ends abruptly in epic III. In epic IV, however, there is a further elaboration of the theme, for it is precisely famine that brings the chief back to his abandoned wife.

27. *hamlet*: the term *kantsare*, hamlet, is used for the place on the outskirts of the village where the abandoned wife lives in a lonely house. The term usually refers to a small cluster of houses at some distance from the main village.

28. *a messenger*: as if in the meantime servants had settled with the principal wife.

29. *something complicated*: the Nyanga term *casuma* means something that climbs up, that is difficult to climb, that is rough.

30. *of the kind that does not defecate*: a formula to designate a very fat goat.

31. *ritual meal*: the term *miruo* refers to the complex purification rituals, accompanied by gift giving and eating, which follow the birth of a child. A chief does not engage in such rituals.

left the birth house. After the principal wife had finished leaving the birth house, the chief said to Shebakungu that he no longer rejected his advice: "So, go to fetch my principal wife and her child; remove her from the hamlet; bring her here into the village." When Shebakungu heard this word of the chief, he went to fetch the principal wife in the hamlet. He made her arrive in the village. The chief took two servants, saying that they should take care of the child and that its mother should eat food that was prepared for her.[32] When that child was born, they gave it the name of Mwindo. Chief Karisi said to his principal wife that he would give her good things.[33]

Mwindo could walk now. When Mwindo was big, Karisi said to Shebakungu: "I am very pleased with the way you have brought up the child." He also told Shebakungu that they should go and build (a village) for Mwindo together with his mother and the other servants on his own mountain; he mentioned one mountain. They went to build (a village) for Mwindo. When the houses were finished, Mwindo climbed up there together with a crowd of people and with his mother. They lived there.[34] And Shebakungu came to see him once in a while, coming from the big village where their master was, where their master dwelt. When Mwindo had finished growing up, Shebakungu said to the chief: "The child has grown up; what shall we do now?" When he heard the words of Shebakungu, Chief Karisi said: "I am planning to leave this land to my son; I myself shall go to Ihundi and Biomfu and Matembe." After the chief had spoken in this manner, he divided the people into two groups. He went with one group, and his son Mwindo remained with one group. He also said to Shebakungu that he wanted him to go with him (Karisi). Shebakungu agreed, saying that he was going with him, but that Bakungu, his son, would remain to take care of Mwindo. In this way they made the

32. *servants*: the chief, the unmarried sisters of the chief, and some of his important wives have servants.

33. *Mwindo*: the principal hero of the epic. There is no indication of an abnormally long pregnancy or of a prolonged delivery followed by a miraculous birth. Neither is it mentioned that Mwindo was precociously mature. A time lapse occurred between Mwindo's birth and the reintegration of his mother into the chief's village. The epic suddenly transposes us into a later period when Mwindo was grown up.

34. The status of Mwindo is unclear at this point. As the son of a chief hs is placed by Nyanga custom in the status position of prince (*murusi*). Moreover, as the son of the chief's principal wife, he has among princes the special status of First-born-of-the-land (*ntangi ya cuo*), but not of chief designate. In this and the following passage, however, Mwindo and his mother receive treatment reminiscent of that given to the ritual wife and her son. Differently from epics I and II, epic III does not describe Mwindo at this point as possessing any extraordinary gifts or capabilities.

division: Shebakungu went with Chief Karisi and a crowd of people while Bakungu remained with Mwindo and a crowd of people.[35]

Upstream where Karisi went, arriving there, he grew eleusine; it ripened. He remained there always, together with his people, having left to his son the land of downstream.[36] Where Mwindo remained in the land of downstream, they (the people) enthroned him; and his sister, daughter of Mwindo's mother, gave birth to a girl. She became the ritual wife of Mwindo. Musanduri came from Mwindo's maternal uncles.[37]

Having established widespread fame in his land, together with his people and his Pygmies, Mwindo bought two dogs. These two dogs became expert hunting dogs; they hunted much game. (Therefore) the people of Mwindo no longer ate plain banana paste. Mwindo bought for his expert hunting dogs other untrained dogs. Mwindo dwelled with his "two times seven" Pygmies who hunted with these dogs. These dogs brought for Mwindo wealth (in the form) of many wives.[38]

---

35. In deciding to leave the land to his son and to settle elsewhere, Mwindo's father follows an unusual procedure. In this instance the epic does not depict current political custom, but probably incorporates references to traditions about early migrations and subsequent political divisions. *Ihundi . . . Biomfu . . . Matembe*: three mountains that have symbolic connotations. Ihundi is a place covered with many trees producing a fruit from which oil, used as a cosmetic and also rubbed on hides and cloth, is extracted. Biomfu is a place covered with a thick layer of fallen bark. Matembe is a place where many wild banana trees grow.

36. *Upstream*: the Nyanga weave a complex system of symbols around the upstream-downstream dichotomy. In one set of meanings, upstream is synonymous with the east and downstream with the west, since several dominant rivers flow from east to west through Nyangaland. Volcanoes and the subterranean dwelling place of divinities and ancestors are located upstream, or in the east. Upstream is associated with life, strength, and good fortune. The decision of Mwindo's father to settle in a land upstream may be construed as a return of the father to the original homeland of the Nyanga. (Nyanga tradition places their origins in the east, beginning in Bunyoro, Uganda, and subsequently in various intermediate places between the great lakes and the rain forest.) It is also a symbolic way of indicating that the father goes where he can live prosperously and undisturbed, in contrast with his son who faces many hardships.

37. *they . . . enthroned him*: the Nyanga term *bamusimika* leaves no doubt that Mwindo was enthroned and received the sacred attributes of divine kingship. *the ritual wife*: it is indeed customary to select the ritual wife from among the very close kinsfolk of the chief. *Musanduri*: a wife with special status who is usually provided by the maternal uncles; she is married to the chief without the transfer of bridewealth.

38. *expert hunting dogs*: the Nyanga call these extremely well-trained hunting dogs *ntoso*; untrained dogs are called *myuntso*. The chief is closely linked with the hunting dogs, as he is also specially associated with Nyamurairi, the god of fire, who frequently presents himself in the form of a dog. Pygmies, who are closely attached to the person of the chief as hunters, singers, and ritual experts, have the

As Mwindo lived together with "these his two times seven" Pygmies, one day Mwindo's wives went to draw water at the wading place.[39] Arriving at the river, those women saw a huge wild boar sitting beside the wading place. They were greatly astounded to see this huge wild boar. They said to one another: "Truly Mwindo can kill this wild boar and marry (other) wives, many more than we are, surpassing us (in number)." Seeing it (the boar) in that manner, they called in the direction where their husband Mwindo was, saying: "Over here, near the river, there is a huge wild boar. You, Mwindo, have already killed wild boars; you have killed many animals, but you have not killed a wild boar like this one here." Mwindo, hearing the call of his wives saying that there was a wild boar near the river, sent one Pygmy there. He said to him: "When you encounter it, do not hurl a spear at it, but come rapidly back to give me the news; after I have seen it you will be able to hurl a spear at it." Having seen it, he (the Pygmy) returned quickly to the village to give his master the news about the wild boar. Arriving at the village entrance, he called into the village, saying: "You, Mwindo, it is not (just) a wild boar that is over there; it is a very big one. Let us take the spears and the dogs."

Hearing this news, Mwindo said to his "two times seven" Pygmies to take the spears and the dogs so that they could go to hunt the wild boar. They took the dogs—one was called Bad-Luck and the other one was called Fast-Eater.[40] Arriving at the river and seeing it (the boar), they were very much astonished. There emerged one Pygmy who said that he wanted to precede his master in throwing a spear at the wild boar. His master, Mwindo, took the spear and scornfully said to him: "You, my Pygmy Meshemutwa, young man of Nyakabotyo, do not yet spear this wild boar without my having preceded you in striking it. Do you surpass me, by any chance? I have finished killing and killing many, many animals; shall this

---

privilege of hunting with the chief's dogs. Expert hunters can, of course, sell and exchange game and thereby accumulate wealth, but it is astonishing that Mwindo's dogs brought him wealth in the form of wives. Chiefs do make blood pacts with other Nyanga; possibly the allusion here is to expert hunters who concluded pacts with Mwindo to provide a sister or a daughter as wife to their blood friend.

39. *"these his two times seven" Pygmies*: seven and two times seven are frequently used symbolic numbers that also have ritual significance. *wading place*: the Nyanga term *hitukuriro* means the place where women draw water; it is slightly upstream from the wading and bathing places.

40. These are unusual names for dogs. The term Kifunga is related to the verb *ihunga*, to eat very fast or to do something very fast. The term Muhanya, one who has bad luck, is also the name of a human character in the tales.

wild boar outdo me?"[41] When Meshemutwa heard the manner in which he was being scolded by his master, he upended the spear, planting the shaft of the spear in the ground and saying: "You are not a chief; you are a nothing. You are the reason that I do not spear the wild boar; you are stupid!"[42]

Mwindo, having prohibited his Pygmy from hurling the spear at the wild boar, pulled out the spear that had been planted in the ground; he himself seized it in order to throw it at the wild boar. When the wild boar saw the spear that was going to be thrown at him by Mwindo, he shouted, saying that he had (received) a medicine "which goes and kills, returns and kills," from the grandfathers of his mother: "May this spear pass over me; may it not fall on me."[43] When Mwindo heard these words, he threw the spear. It passed the wild boar without falling on him; it missed him. Having missed him (the wild boar) in this manner, he (Mwindo) cried out in astonishment; he went to fetch the spear where it had gone. He clapped the hands so that the dogs would follow him in the search for the place where the wild boar had gone.[44] He said: "You, my dogs, Fast-Eater and Bad-Luck, chase the animal; hunt it." As these dogs were now hunting, Mwindo put sweet words in his mouth; he shouted, imploring his mother Nyaruwe, calling: "My mother, I am dying; I am dying for the sake of my large country, the one (that belongs to) Mwindo, son of Nyaruwe."[45] Having spoken like this, he gave blows to his belly, saying: "My mother, I am dying. You were my Hunger-Belt. You are the belt that restrains the belly, not (the belt that) protects against sickness."[46]

---

41. *Meshemutwa*: also the name of an important divinity of Pygmy origin. The Pygmy is referred to by a patronymic name. Here Mwindo is boisterous and irascible, qualities that do not become a chief.

42. The Pygmy uses rough language to criticize his chief. Such insults would normally be treated in a severe manner, but Mwindo does not react. Pygmies who are considered as noisy, quarrelsome, rough talkers have many privileges; they enjoy a certain immunity.

43. Usually the personified animal actors in the tales do not have magical devices at their disposal, but the wild boar here is a metamorphosis of Nyamurairi's daughter.

44. The unsuccessful hunt sets the stage for many adventures that will lead Mwindo to the realm of Nyamurairi. Implicitly, the chief is being criticized for hunting, which is the work of the chief's Pygmies. The entire episode of the hunt contains a richly varied hunters' vocabulary for hurling a spear, striking, and missing the target.

45. *his mother Nyaruwe*: Mwindo addresses himself to the spirit of his paternal aunt Nyaruwe. The paternal aunt may be respectfully spoken of as a mother.

46. *Hunger-Belt*: the term *nyamurungo* is a praise name for the paternal aunt who is a provider of food. Along the same lines, the paternal aunt is frequently referred

Mwindo was now pursuing his dogs, and his Pygmies remained behind and even returned to the village. Night overtook him while he was at the place "coming from where and going where"; he called out, saying: "Our paternal aunt, protect me today; help me. If I were helped, I would be saved. I carry a child without the cradling rope. We call for Ntsiru and Bitembe mountains. Yes, a plate cannot be licked. The child that does not listen to its mother will experience it (death) in a land that is far away."[47] While Mwindo was calling for his paternal aunt in this manner, saying that he was dying, dying because of the wild boar, the wild boar of the uninhabited forest was destroying the roots of the banana trees; and it was grunting. His paternal aunt entered him.[48] She gave him a portion of sleep; he went into it.

When he awakened, his paternal aunt had built a house for him by the Ntsiru and Matembe mountains. As he looked on, Kahindo, daughter of Nyamurairi, had placed there for him banana paste and a goat's leg. This Kahindo had changed herself into the wild boar that he had been hunting. Nyamurairi had sent his daughter to go and fool Mwindo because he had killed masses and masses of animals. He had exterminated them.[49] When Mwindo awakened seeing the banana paste and the goat meat, he exclaimed, saying that lo! the one who had given him this food was his kinsman, that he/she was his salvation.[50] When he, together with his two dogs, had finished eating this food, it took him by surprise (to see) that in the early morning the wild boar was still behind the little house. He loosed his dogs again; they went chasing it (the animal) while he was singing:

---

to as "Mother-of-the-ladle-with-four-sides" to emphasize that one gets food rapidly when one visits her or as "Mother-of-the-package-that-contains-another-one" to stress the fact that one leaves her place loaded with packages of food. Here reference is made to a vine that people tighten around the belly to diminish stomach pains. Mwindo depicts his aunt as the provider of a belt against hunger, not a belt against disease.

47. *coming from where and going where*: a formula to indicate that Mwindo was now far away in the middle of the forest. *Our paternal aunt*: mashenge, the Hunde term for paternal aunt, is used. "Our" (*wetu*) means a member of our kinship group. *If I were helped*: the text literally says "if I were bathed." *the cradling rope*: young children are carried on the back by means of this rope; Mwindo is implying that he is helpless and overburdened. *The child*: this entire text is in the Hunde language.

48. *His paternal aunt entered him*: a frequently used image to say that the paternal aunt is bringing help or advice. In dreams the paternal aunt is said to enter the body to give warnings, desires, or counsel.

49. *Kahindo*: apparently not the Kahindo whom Mwindo's father had married. *Nyamurairi*: chief of the divinities living in the subterranean world.

50. *salvation*: the term *karamo* means strength, life, recovery from sickness. The Nyanga text says literally that "he/she was his salvation that healed (saved) him."

I have a helper;
I have a helper.
You, my mother, I am dying.
I have a helper;
I have a helper.
I am calling for Otter,
Son of the One-who-brings-death.
The ax of my mother,
Of the daughter of the good blacksmith,
It fell into the river.
Because of the size of the pool,
Because of it, it (the river) failed to have a
   shoal.[51]

While he was hunting and singing in this manner he met with the
daughter of a blacksmith; she was cutting firewood on the side of the pool.
Her ax fell into the river. The woman called imploring Otter and Water
Duck, saying that they should take her ax out of the pool, that if they
would remove it they could eat of the banana paste that her mother had
stirred. These expert swimmers entered the river; they remained for a long
time before emerging from the water; they came out with the ax; they gave
it to its owner, the daugher of a blacksmith.[52]

Mwindo left there; he threw himself into a banana grove; he arrived in
it; he met in it a woman who was cutting bananas. The dogs circled around
this woman. Fear gripped this woman; she was very frightened; she told
Mwindo to take the dogs so that they would not bite her. The woman
removed two ripe banana (stems); she gave one to the dog Fast-Eater. This
dog refused to eat the ripe bananas; she gave ripe bananas to the other
dog; he also refused them. The dogs looked at the woman, saying that she
was the enemy whom they had been hunting, "you, our master."[53]
Mwindo said to the woman to show him the trail to the village; the woman
showed him the trail to the village. Mwindo passed.

Arriving at the entrance to the village, he met his paternal aunt. His
paternal aunt said to him: "You are dead; you arrive here, but this is not

---

51. This difficult song is a bilingual mixture of Nyanga and Hunde, some of the
verse being entirely Hunde. The song is a summary of the event that follows. *Otter*:
referred to with a patronymic name which suggests that Otter is considered the son
of the killer, of the One-who-brings-death, i.e., the son of the divinity Nyamurairi or
Muisa.

52. This wonderful event adds to the mystery of the world in which Mwindo is now
moving. *the daughter of a blacksmith*: apparently Kahindo who has the power of
metamorphosis.

53. In many of the Nyanga tales the dogs often play the role of divulgers of
secrets.

the place to arrive. If you climb up with these dogs to this village, then you are dead." Mwindo said: "You, my paternal aunt, what shall I do with these dogs here?" His paternal aunt said to him that she would show him a place to hide his dogs. His paternal aunt slapped the armpit on one side of Mwindo; she inserted there one dog. She slapped the armpit on the other side of Mwindo; she inserted there the other dog. She hid those two dogs in the two armpits of Mwindo.[54] Mwindo climbed the hill to the village, walking cautiously like a chameleon, going slowly. As he was now climbing up to the village, Kahindo, daughter of Nyamurairi—she who had been cutting the bananas in the banana grove—passed Mwindo in the middle of the hill climbing up to the village, but Mwindo did not see her.[55] Kahindo arrived at her father's, saying: "It is Mwindo who is climbing up there to the village; go to trap him." When Nyamurairi heard the word of his daughter Kahindo, he lowered twenty *mibimbiro*-trees onto the trail; he set them as a trap for Mwindo. When Mwindo saw the *mibimbiro*-trees, he roared. He began a song in order that they might stand up. He sang:

> Counselors of my father;
> Counselors of my father.
> These are counselors of my father.
> These are counselors of father, Mwindo.[56]

When the *mibimbiro*-trees heard this (song), they rose up; they climbed up to their master Nyamurairi; they arrived there; they gave him the news, saying: "The one who is over there knows our names. What shall we do about him now?"

Nyamurairi, looking over there, lowered a caravan of red ants.[57] When Mwindo saw them, he sang for them a song:

> Brave-ones of the burning firewood.
> Brave-ones of the burning firewood.

---

54. In no other text have I found the theme of hiding dogs or anything else under or in the armpits. The creative imagination and the inventiveness of the narrators are apparently endless.

55. *cautiously like a chameleon*: similar examples of direct, self-evident comparisons are rare in the Nyanga literature. *Mwindo did not see her*: nothing in this passage indicates that Kahindo can make herself invisible. One may assume that she has this power, but it is not directly said.

56. *go to trap him*: Kahindo has no apparent reason to cherish a spirit of revenge against Mwindo, except that Mwindo wanted to kill her when she was metamorphosed into a wild boar. The theme of trials and ordeals through which a person must pass in order to conquer a woman found in many Nyanga tales, is also implied here. After enduring many hardships Mwindo receives Kahindo as his wife.

57. *a caravan of red ants*: the Nyanga term indicates that the red ants were wildly dispersed, as when they encounter an obstacle.

Brave-ones of the burning firewood.
Mwindo, you![58]

When the red ants heard the song, they fled; they dispersed; they climbed up to the village place; they arrived there, they said to their master: "The one who is over there knows our names." Where Mwindo remained, he climbed up slowly; he went on.

When he (Mwindo) saw the village "about there," Nyamurairi lowered hides against him.[59] When Mwindo saw these hides, he sang:

> Wives of father, Mwindo,
> We call Nyakatwakari,
> The daughter of Marumbu.
> She cuts bananas and cannot tie them together.
> Our (kinsman) Snake was the son of One-Beat.
> When he goes, he just goes.
> The trail on which he went, he did not go on it twice.
> Bee, son of Needle.
> Kihwira Mountain of Shenyangurube from Butuma,
> The day that we shall walk on the flat crest of
>   the mountain,
> It will become the mountain of Nyamukoba.
> Double thanks from the mother of the girl;
> The son-in-law is always giving her large gifts.
> Spider was the son of Bridge.
> Our (kinsman) Lightning was the son of Flashes.
> Our (kinsman) Quiver was the son of Dancer.
> Our (kinsman) Hawk was the son of Thief.
> When sky becomes day—
> The clouds lift from the mountains—
> Rooster does not crow; it gives news.[60]

When he had finished singing, the hides returned to the village, to

---

58. *burning firewood*: fire and smoke are the enemies of ants, which can be chased by them. *Mwindo, you*: an exclamation by the bard who expresses astonishment concerning Mwindo's skills.

59. *about there*: *buriha* is accompanied by a gesture to indicate that Mwindo is now very close to the village. *hides*: the Hunde term for the Nyanga *byoero*, dried hides, is used. Dried hides are placed underneath stones on which Nyanga women pound and grind dried plantain bananas.

60. This very difficult song is sung entirely in the Hunde language. It is a concatenation of various ideas, reflections, and reminiscences by the bard. After identifying the hides as "wives of father," the bard alludes to a coming struggle between Mwindo and the woman Nyakatwakari. He then refers to the departure of Kabutwakenda, described in the earlier stages of the epic. Next the bard alludes to a story in which Bee, formerly called Munindi (Needle), came to be known as *munamuntsuntsu* because of its humming. He then goes on to a historical event in which ownership of a mountain changed hands. He suggests the joy of a mother whose daughter is married and whose son-in-law brings her many gifts which she

Nyamurairi; they said to their master that Mwindo knew their names,
(saying) that they were the wives of their master.

When Mwindo arrived in the middle of the village place, he met there
bibatama-grasses constricting the road; they closed the road. Mwindo sang
again:

> You, princes of my father,
> Get out of my way!
> You, princes of my father,
> This very day,
> Get out of my way!
> Do not confound me.
> You are the princes of this place.
> The day that Mwindo will arrive,
> He will take a maiden and a mountain
> And the copper bracelet of headmanship.
> The spirit world is not a village:
> There goes a big man;
> There goes a little man.
> The spirit world is far;
> No sound arrives there.
> I am calling Leopard,
> Master-of-the-forest;
> Buffalo our kinsman, son of Toughness.
> Now, sky begins to turn dark.
> Kitute, (child) of Ripe-Banana
> (And of) Bad-Luck, does not ripen.
> Rumbici, mountain of Forks-of-the-road, where we
>   have killed antelopes;
> The belts (of hide) covered all the limbs.
> A man, yes, a true man
> Resides here;
> He does not wish that I put it on the ground.[61]

---

gratefully receives with both hands. In the next four lines the bard praises Spider
and Lightning, two faithful allies of Mwindo, and makes brief references to two
tales. Finally he talks of the impressive lifting of the clouds near the mountaintops
in the moist forest and praises the rooster as herald of a new day.

61. This song, sung entirely in the Nyanga language, also consists of various sets
of ideas and reflections. The identification of the grasses as "princes of my father"
is followed by Mwindo's prediction that at the end of his labors he will receive gifts
from Nyamurairi. Since Mwindo is on his way to the chief of the subterranean
world, there is a beautiful evocation of the remoteness of this world and of the
indiscriminate character of death. Mwindo then calls on Leopard and Buffalo, two
symbols of power, as though he wanted to absorb their toughness in order to cope
with the coming hardships. Next the bard makes a personal reflection about the late
evening. He is hungry; he thinks about food, bad food that is served, and about the
abundance of meat they had when they hunted in Rumbici. The song ends with
Mwindo's praise of himself. Yes, Mwindo is a true man, but Nyamurairi does not
want to hear Mwindo's self-praise.

After Mwindo had sung for the *bibatama*-grasses, they returned to Nyamurairi and told him that Mwindo knew them, saying they were the princes from here. When the *bibatama*-grasses had finished removing themselves, Mwindo drew close to the men's house; he threw himself into it. Nyamurairi said to Mwindo: "You, my child, do not stay here in the men's house; go to stay with my daughter, Kahindo."[62] Mwindo stood up; he went to stay with Kahindo.

When sky changed to dawn, grasses had planted themselves everywhere in the village in order that his (Nyamurairi's) young son, Mwindo, would cut them. Nyamurairi said to Mwindo: "You, my young son, cut for me these grasses that are here, because in the village grasses have grown a second time." He took a billhook and a hoe; and as he started to give them to Mwindo, Mwindo said to him: "You, my father, give me twenty hoes and ten billhooks so that I may cut with these iron tools."[63] Nyamurairi gave Mwindo these iron tools. When Mwindo saw these (tools), he laid them down "like there." His paternal aunt entered into him; she said to him: "You, my son, will you be able to do the clearing here where it is impossible (to do it)? But I shall help you again, as I have helped you (before), so that you may be saved." Mwindo said to his paternal aunt: "If you help me, if you remove me from here, I will offer as a cult emblem to you a shoulder bag and a sharp double-edged knife."[64] Mwindo shouted; he called loudly to Nyakatwakari, the daughter of Marumbu, saying that the masters of a work are the ones to do it.[65] As they looked up, all the grasses had cut themselves; the village place "was white."[66] Because of the word that he had said, because of it, he escaped this danger. When Nyamurairi saw this amazing deed, he was very much

---

62. *the men's house*: in tales and epics the encounter with Nyamurairi usually takes place in the men's house, which is his preferred residence. *You, my child*: this friendly appellation anticipates the future marriage of Mwindo to Nyamurairi's daughter.

63. In other texts Mwindo possesses his own billhook, which has magical powers, and in addition carries a massive supply of billhooks and axes in his shoulder bag which perform all tasks for him. *twenty hoes*: the hoe, a part of Hunde technology more recently introduced among the Nyanga, is almost never mentioned in Nyanga texts.

64. The objects mentioned are important emblems in various Nyanga cults, including the cult for the spirit of the paternal aunt. The text provides an etiological explanation for the origin of this cult.

65. This invocation turns out to be a warning against Nyakatwakari, the woman who imposes severe hardships on Mwindo in the later passages of the epic.

66. *was white*: i.e., the village place was completely cleared.

astonished; he said to himself: "Lo! This man is safe again; well, he is still here;[67] lo! he is also tough."

Nyamurairi said again to Mwindo that he should go to cultivate a new banana grove for him. Mwindo said to him: "Give me thirty axes and twenty billhooks and banana stipites and seeds." Nyamurairi got all these things for Mwindo; he went to show him the plot of land that he should cultivate. When they arrived in the forest, he showed him (Mwindo) the plot of land that he should cultivate. Afterward, Nyamurairi returned to the village. Mwindo exclaimed: "Now today I am going to die." He called loudly Fly-of-odor and Bee, the son of Marumbu, and Nyakatwakari, the daughter of Marumbu.[68] He said: "The masters of a work are the ones to do it; help me quickly; I am once again between the teeth of a leopard, where the sweetness of food is experienced."[69] When it was midday—the sun was now fulgent—it took him by surprise that the place that had been cultivated had planted itself: the trees had felled themselves; the banana trees had planted themselves; the seeds had planted themselves. All these were ripe that same day; the banana trees produced fully mature and ripe bananas, and the crops had reached maturity. He cut from the bananas; he tied up three baskets of bananas. He harvested from the vegetables: leaves of the bean plants, beans, pumpkins, corn; each (type) of crop filled a basket.[70] He carried this food to the village where his father was. When he arrived there, he put them (the baskets) down before his father, saying: "These are the crops that I have made ripen." When Nyamurairi saw the crops, he was very pleased; he was pleased because of his son Mwindo, saying: "Yes, my father of the body, may you be blessed."[71]

He (Mwindo) was astonished (to find) in the morning that in the

---

67. *he is still here*: this expression also means that he is still alive. The opposition between *to be here* and *to be there* marks the difference between to be alive (i.e., to be here in the world, in the village) and to be dead (i.e., to be there in the subterranean world). Such a distinction places the emphasis, not on the dichotomy between life and death, but on the concept of "being," which is a shift from one world to another.

68. It seems that Mwindo took care of the work with a magical formula. There is, however, an allusion to Nyakatwakari who later confronts Mwindo.

69. *between the teeth*: this entire, beautifully stated expression, saying that Mwindo is in grave danger, is an example of the bard's poetic skill.

70. The miraculous clearing of the field and growth of the crops are tersely suggested in this passage.

71. *my father of the body*: this expression indicates a certain tenderness. It is primarily applied to the paternal aunt, particularly if she is a uterine sister of one's father.

banana grove there was now a buffalo eating the bananas and all the crops.
Lo! It was his mother-in-law, the mother of Kahindo, the wife of
Nyamurairi. She had changed herself into a buffalo; her husband
Nyamurairi had sent her.[72] Nyamurairi said to his son Mwindo: "You, my
child, go to guard the banana grove and to chase the animals that destroy
the crops in the field." Hearing the word of his father, Mwindo took the
spear; he went fast to the banana grove. Arriving there, he saw the buffalo
cleaving the banana trees. He took hold of the spear; he shouted: "My
dogs, Fast-Eater and Bad-Luck, help me again." When they heard the call
of their master, they emerged from the armpits; they threw themselves
where the buffalo was; they bit it and bit it. As Mwindo was going to hurl
the spear at it, his mother-in-law howled; she asked for pity, saying: "No,
no! Now you, my child, you beat the drum; if you kill me it is bad, my
son."[73] This mother-in-law of his asked again and again for pity, then and
there. Mwindo looked up and left her. He arrived at his father's; he
(Mwindo) said to him: "Lo! You, my father, this is the way you act! You
have said to my mother-in-law to go and change herself into a buffalo, the
child of Toughness."

In the morning, after he (Mwindo) had escaped from this danger and
after his dogs had finished inserting themselves in the armpits, Nyamurairi
said to Mwindo: "You, my son, I do not want to test you anymore because
you have destroyed masses and masses of people. So then, you will now go
with this one, my daughter Kahindo."[74] After he had given Mwindo
permission to (have) his daughter Kahindo, he gave him counsel, saying:
"You here, you are going with Kahindo. The day that she will give birth,
Kahindo cannot wrap for me the banana paste of the grandchild, for me
her father; that day Mwindo is dead, he comes here where I am."[75] Having

---

72. The temporary metamorphosis of a human into an animal (Kahindo changes
into a wild boar, and her mother into a buffalo) is not found in the other epics and is
exceedingly rare in the Nyanga tales. When there is metamorphosis, it centers
mostly on Specter Mpaca, who changes into a beautiful woman or takes the
appearance of one's bride.

73. Mwindo is successful against Nyamurairi's ultimate trickery because of the
dogs which his paternal aunt had advised him to hide under his armpits.

74. *to test you*: the Nyanga verb means to make one tired, to exhaust. Mwindo
was lured into this series of hardships because, as a chief, he was too keen on
hunting and killing. After Mwindo has successfully undergone the tests, Nyamurairi
presents him with his daughter.

75. *the banana paste of the grandchild*: when a child is born, both the parents and
grandparents must pass through a series of purification ceremonies including ablutions
in a river, sexual intercourse, and ritual eating. As a god who is the source of life and
death, Nyamurairi cannot participate in such a ritual.

spoken to them like this, he (Nyamurairi) gave them a gift of goats, cattle, chickens, and crops, such as beans, bananas, corn, and peas.[76] He also said that the day he would again hear the news that a chief had gone to trap animals in the forest, all by himself, without being with any other men such as three or four servants, he would kill this chief. From there originates (the custom of) chiefs remaining in the village without going into the forest; he (the chief) invites people to kill animals for him, that is all.[77]

After his father Nyamurairi had launched this prohibition and finished giving him advice, Mwindo went to the entrance to the village together with his wife Kahindo. They went to arrive at the place of Mwindo's paternal aunt. His paternal aunt said to Mwindo that he should pay her a shoulder bag and should place in it a sharp double-edged knife and a calabash. His paternal aunt said to him: "You, my son, do not pass on the road where you have passed (before). I shall show you another road that is close by." Mwindo departed from his paternal aunt's place. He followed the crossroads (leading) to Black Ant "where there is not one place (to stay)" and to Baboon "who does not have a beer trough."[78]

He appeared at a wading place, together with his wife; he crossed the wading place. He arrived in the village of his mother, Nyamwindo. And his mother's mop of hair was like (that of) Specter because of grief for her son Mwindo, the one fruit she had borne.[79] When she saw him, his mother first did not remember him. She was hesitant and hesitant (in recognizing) him, saying that this young man appearing at the entrance to the village resembled her son who had died. When Mwindo saw his mother, he said to her that he was the one who had recovered, who had (a) risen again. When his mother heard this, she threw herself against the chest of her son; she

---

76. *a gift*: the term *mukosoro* suggests the distinctive category of gifts, including cattle, which are given to departing guests. The Nyanga have no cattle, but their Hunde neighbors, with whom they have numerous intimate relationships, have pastoral traditions.

77. While accepting Mwindo as a son-in-law, Nyamurairi also warns him not to transgress the hunting taboos. Nyanga chiefs have their own hunters, including Pygmies.

78. It is unclear where the encounters with Nyamurairi take place. Nyamurairi lives in the subterranean world, and in other epics Mwindo enters this world through a *kikoka*-fern. No reference is here made to such a mode of entry. Mwindo goes deeper and deeper into the forest until he meets with Kahindo, (the spirit of) his paternal aunt, and Nyamurairi.

79. *Nyamwindo*: Mwindo's mother, whose name is also Kahindo, is now called by a teknonymic name. *Specter*: the specter of the forest, called Mpaca, is said to have very long hair.

looked at him; she let her eyes go down over him; she let her eyes go up over him (to scan him). She looked at him seven and seven times.[80] She went with him into her sacred house.[81] Her son, seeing that the village was rusty and that grasses had encircled the village, asked his mother: "My mother, all the people who were here have gone where?" His mother answered her son, saying: "You, child, you are mocking me. You are asking about the people who lived here; I do not know where they have gone. I have remained here with your one wife, your principal wife." He said to his mother: "You, my mother, do not falter and falter: I am the one here, the one fruit that Nyamwindo has brought forth." When he saw that the grasses had encircled the village, he sang; he pondered, saying: "Sherubungo goes with one thousand people. He does not know that to go with people is hard. Lo! When a man has gone with his breed to the land of (other) people, he is amazed that he left his place, but it was the heart that was burning him. The night speaks fast and rapidly when a man is in the midst of the *isinga*-room. Lo! When a man is at home together with his wife, he is brave; there is not another man who can throw himself into his house to make him fight for nothing; he, together with his wife, will join forces to beat him."[82] Mwindo was pondering in this fashion because of the sorrows for his people: he does not know where they have gone. He said to his mother: "You, my mother, I have asked you, saying where the people from here have gone. You have answered me saying that I am mocking you. Am I not your son, then? I shall ask again for an answer when I have finished clearing the village place." Mwindo seized the hoes; he tried again the wonderful deeds that he had performed at Nyamurairi's. He said that the master of the work is the one to do it. When he looked around, the village place had cleared itself; it had finished being level. He called his mother Nyamwindo, saying: "I am the one, my mother! I have finished (the work) where I have gone. I have killed masses and masses of people and animals, where I have gone."

And where the Pygmies and the counselors had fled, in the village in

---

80. Surprise of the mother who thought her son was dead and tenderness between mother and son are beautifully suggested in a rich manipulation of verbs.

81. *sacred house*: *iremeso*, an oval-shaped dwelling dedicated as a shrine to the spirit of Kahombo.

82. *he pondered*: Mwindo's reflections are partly formulated in the Hunde language. Mwindo expresses his sorrows for the people who went to a foreign place and praises the values of the home. *isinga-room*: the Nyanga house is not partitioned but consists of four conceptual spaces. The space mentioned is in the left back part of the house, where wood, baskets, and other things are stored on a hanging rack.

which they were established in the forest, one Pygmy said to his companions that he was going to have a look where Nyamwindo had remained because Nyamwindo had been told by an oracle that the day Mwindo would return, eighteen years would have passed; that then he would know to arrive.[83] This Pygmy Nkango threw himself at the entrance to the village; he went. When he appeared where Nyamwindo had remained, he was very much astounded; he had food and honey with him.[84] He asked himself in his heart, saying: "What is that now? Here it is filled again with these things. Here it is filled again with houses; it is a big village now." Appearing at the entrance to the village, throwing the eyes toward the middle of the village place, he saw Mwindo. This Pygmy said to himself in his heart that this one was like their chief, Mr. Rejoicer-of-people, who does not foster hatred—the conciliator, the good speaker who does not rest.[85] He could not rest. He drew close to where he was; he threw himself against the chest. He abounded with joys because of him, saying: "You here, our master?" And he said to him: "Yes, this is I here." Mwindo asked the Pygmy, saying: "You have broken up the village because of what? You have left Nyamwindo behind alone in the abandoned village." He also asked him, saying: "Where are your kinsmen?" He (the Pygmy) answered him, saying: "We are in the village in the forest; that is where we dwell." The Pygmy said to Mwindo: "But I arrive here to look after Nyamwindo once in a while."

When Nkango had seen Mwindo, he returned where his companions were. When he arrived in the place where his companions were, he gave them the news saying that Mwindo had arrived. The Pygmies and the counselors, having received the news about their master, broke up their village; they went to Mwindo. When Nyamwindo saw the Pygmies

---

83. *eighteen years*: a rare reference to a specific time period between two sets of events. Temporal indications, such as the formulas "in the early morning" and "when sky had become day," which abound in other epics, are almost entirely absent from epic III.

84. *This Pygmy Nkango*: Nkango is the name of a person and of a divinity of Pygmy origin to whom hunting dogs are consecrated. *food and honey*: the Pygmies are providers of game meat and of honey in return for various commodities and as part of their political and ritual obligations. Their association with honey is particularly stressed by the Nyanga.

85. *Mr. Rejoicer-of-people . . .* : a beautiful set of praise names that reflect some of the basic values attached to the chief. The chief gladdens and diverts people; he brings conciliation and harbors neither resentment nor hatred. The strength of his oratory and argument is an important element in making decisions acceptable and in scrutinizing matters. There is a vast range of terms that emphasize the chief's qualities as a "Father-of-people" and a "Father-of-goods."

together with the counselors arriving, she said to her son: "You, Mwindo, let us kill the Pygmies together with these counselors here, because they have wronged you by failing to go with you and by breaking up this village." When he heard the word of his mother, Mwindo refused, saying that he could not kill the counselors and his Pygmies because it was as if he himself had brought these problems on himself, because his Pygmies wanted to hurl the spears at the wild pig and he refused (to let) them (do so). Therefore, it was not because of the Pygmies that he had suffered all these rigors and hardships.[86]

Having brought together all his people, he said to them that he wanted to present an offering of banana paste to his father and that afterward he wanted to dedicate to his paternal aunt the things she had mentioned: the shoulder bag and the sharp double-edged knife. After Mwindo had spoken to his people like this, Nyamwindo put water on the fire (to prepare) banana paste.[87] As she began to stir the paste, he (Mwindo) sang:

> We are stirring banana paste, Kahindo.
> We are stirring banana paste, Kahindo.
> Ndorera, kinsman of Moon.
> We are stirring banana paste, Kahindo.
> Ndorera, kinsman of Moon.
> Nyamirindi, may you be blessed.
> Nyamirindi, may you be blessed.
> We are mixing banana paste, Kahindo.
> And the hatred of Kanyama!
> We are stirring banana paste, Kahindo.
> And the hatred of Kanyama!
> We are mixing banana paste, Kahindo.
> Mberere was the son of Hope.
> We are stirring banana paste, Kahindo.
> Little-Bat cuts the back;
> It is broken because of it.
> We are stirring banana paste, Kahindo.

---

86. Nyamwindo makes an unusually fierce appeal for revenge. Her request gives Mwindo an opportunity to show the humility and fairness that are expected of a true chief.

87. *an offering . . . to his father*: an implication that Mwindo's father had died in the meantime and that Mwindo wanted to make an offering to his spirit. It is possible that the much earlier passage concerning the father's decision to go to the land upstream implied the father's death, for upstream, i.e., eastward, is where the dead reside in the subterranean world. *to dedicate to his paternal aunt*: Mwindo acts in conformity with an earlier request made by his paternal aunt and with his promise to fulfill the request.

> Our (kinsman) Nkurongo was
> The son of Korokoro.
> We are mixing banana paste, Kahindo.
> Our (kinsman) Nkurongo was
> The son of Korokoro.
> And our (kinsman) Pigeon was
> The son of Ritual-Drummer.
> We are stirring banana paste, Kahindo.
> Chameleon called Elephant,
> The son of Expert-Singer:
> —We are stirring banana paste, Kahindo—
> Our (kinsman) Elephant, carry the banana paste;
> You are the Strong-One.
> We are mixing banana paste, Kahindo.
> Let us carry it to the council
> Where the men are.
> We are stirring banana paste, Kahindo.[88]

The banana paste that had been placed on the dishes bulged underneath; it was large. Elephant arrived to lift it to carry it to where the men were; he was overcome by it. Chameleon jeered at Elephant, saying that he was unable to lift the banana paste. He said to Nyamwindo to give it to him, so that he might carry it to where the men were, to the place of offering.[89] Those who were standing on the side said to Chameleon: "Will you be capable of (carrying) this big banana paste by which Elephant was overcome, he the master of strength who surpasses all animals in strength?" Chameleon said: "Let me first try." He tried to lift it up; he sang:

> What is big is light.
> We are stirring banana paste, Kahindo.
> What is small is heavy.
> We are mixing banana paste, Kahindo.
> Quiver, son of Dancer,

---

88. The entire song is sung in the Hunde language, except for the refrains *We are stirring banana paste, Kahindo,* and *We are mixing banana paste, Kahindo.* The song is a sonorous concatenation of various ideas: reference to Ndorera (lit., a bunch of raffia worn around the arms; symbol of the dance); reminiscences about certain real persons (Nyamirindi; Kanyama; Mberere); allusion to Little-Bat who is a diviner among Mwindo's maternal uncles; references to symbolic personages (Nkurongo, the *bulikoko*-bird, a symbol of beauty and speed; Korokoro, another species of *bulikoko*-bird; Pigeon, symbol of ritual drumming); and finally a succinct evocation of the next episode (the quarrel between Chameleon and Elephant).

89. As in numerous tales, Chameleon is depicted here as a very active person who can carry heavy things. One of Chameleon's epithets is The-one-who-is-not-overcome-by-a-burden.

His work: merely to dance;
He has no other work.
We are stirring banana paste, Kahindo.[90]

Chameleon took and took the banana paste; he carried it to the place of offering where the men were. When those who were seated there saw Chameleon arriving with the banana paste, they were very much astounded; they said: "This one who has lifted up the banana paste, (his fame) will be dispersed over all the mountains." All the men gave him a hand, saying: "You are a man surpassing Elephant." They viewed Elephant as a nothing, without force. When they saw him, they decamped, saying: "Lo! What is swollen with excrement has no strength!"[91] When all the men were seated at the gathering at the place of offering and the banana paste was there, Mwindo said to Muhima to make an invocation over the banana paste.[92]

They were now erecting the house poles, and the men's house was now finished. Muhima said to his companions who were seated there: "You will know to respond to the song that I begin." Muhima gave a goat to Shebakungu, saying that he should offer an invocation over it in the men's house. Shebakungu took the goat; he offered an invocation, saying: "My father, may you be blessed; this is the goat. My father, may you be blessed; give us salvation; give us strength and many blessings." Muhima said to Shebakungu: "You act badly. Why are you offering an invocation over the goat while mentioning the name of Mwindo's father?" After Shebakungu had been criticized like that, the men's house collapsed. Muhima called small children saying that they should go and respond to him; the small children arrived. Muhima went together with the male children to erect another men's house in another place. When the men's house was finished, Muhima called the small children, saying to come and respond to him. Muhima offered the invocation over the goat, and the children there responded to him. He said: "You, small children, will you respond to me?" They responded, saying yes.[93] He began:

---

90. The song, in the Hunde language except for the refrain, is conceived as a magical formula used by Chameleon to lift a heavy weight.

91. Elephant is usually depicted without mercy in the tales. He is fooled by smaller creatures, like turtle, hedgehog, monkey, kingfisher, chameleon, squirrel, and duiker antelope. In an eating contest he is even beaten by chicken.

92. *Muhima*: one of Mwindo's elders who is in charge of the solemn offerings which draw large groups of dignitaries. Such rituals include prayers, praises, the offering of food, and the construction of shrines of various kinds. Muhima is also the term for a Nyanga divinity (provider of fertility) after whom many men are named.

93. *men's house*: a sacred place. The men of the local kinship unit spend a great deal of time here eating, smoking, drinking, discussing work, and settling problems.

In the village there is bad fate only,
Bad fate only.
In the village there is bad fate only,
In the village there is bad fate only,
Bad fate only.
In the village there is bad fate only,
Bad fate only.
A child and its father: only but bad fate,
Only but bad fate.

In saying this invocation during the offering Muhima set forth a taboo for the village; there had been no taboo in the village before this. He said that the people would go and fight one another. From then on, the people of the village began to quarrel with one another.[94]

When he had finished saying the invocation during the offering, Muhima sang:

I shall fight with Kiomfu Kiramba;
I shall take away from him the dice
That look upward and that look downward.
The day that it rains all day,
That day in the whole forest
There is no woman.
Then, it is good there.
When a junior wife throws down
A senior wife,
She throws her down
On a pile of eleusine.
My mother, I remain
A young woman
Who rejoices at home.
She mentions her mother, saying
That she is an inquirer, a vagrant.
Sky does not become day;
It becomes day because of the clouds.
The clouds break up;
When they have finished (breaking up), they say

Certain rituals, including offerings to the ancestors and blessings of the hunting dogs, also take place in the men's house. *Shebakungu*: the Chief-Counselor, who discharges numerous functions, including ritual ones. His invocation is in the Hunde language.

94. This passage describes the origin of the first quarrel, which arose from a misunderstanding. When Shebakungu begins the invocation with "My father," Muhima thinks that he is praying on behalf of Mwindo's father rather than of Mwindo himself. The seriousness of this initial criticism is enhanced by a quasi-cosmic event, the collapse of the sacred men's house, and the subsequent reliance of Muhima on small children who do not know what they are saying when they agree with Muhima, who wishes a bad fate for the village.

That sky became day.
Warthog, young son of Cutter,
Cuts young shoots,
Cuts young shoots;
He has no food to eat.[95]

When Muhima had finished singing, Mwindo also sang:

The sun comes from Kahanga,
From Musao who was overpowered.
Take up the sufferings for me;
Let the sufferings fuse together.
I see many things on the trip.
Katee is with blessing;
He has married Nyamiomba.
My mother, I am in search of Nanga (to marry her).
Turtle, my maternal uncle,
Mr. Cloth that is cut.
Sky changes to dawn, and we are speaking
Like the sound of the *mukuki*-initiation.
I am sitting, humming
Like a bee
That passes on the *itondo*-plant.
A girl could not reject her mother;
Whatever may be said she is mother:
Kampuku and Kabukeru!
Nanga overpowers the great ones;
You, small child, you are not capable against Nanga.
The father of a son bathes in aphorisms:
If you give him a girl, do not boast;
Tomorrow he exposes you in the middle of the
        village.
I am telling the story
That was told by Mutia and Irumbo,
Mutia, child of twins.
I have sung (with) the drum;
I am tired.
I am imploring Turtle, my maternal uncle,
Mr. Cloth that is cut.
Rooster crows, and Sparrow points him out,
Sparrow, child of Dancer.
I am imploring what dries up the river;
We descended with this little river;
We returned with Little Stone River,
Carrying them (the stones).

---

95. In contrast with the preceding song, this one is sung entirely in the Hunde language. It is rare for anyone but Mwindo to lead the song. In it Muhima announces the coming contests of Mwindo with Mutero Murimba and Lightning. The rest of the song is made up of joyful jests, personal recollections, and meditations by the bard.

Sky is changing to dawn in a while;
The bachelor is cooking tough beans.
I am squeezed, my father;
I am in pursuit of Mwindo Mboru;
I am in pursuit of Nanga.
Far is the spirit world.
Katee is with blessing;
He has married Nyamiomba;
He is searching for Nanga,
And he is being subdued by it.
Let the goats that are in Tubondo,
Nyakisa's (goats), join me.
Who will carry me to Biruri and Mikeme mountains?
Who will forge Little-Bat?
My maternal uncle, forge me, Mwindo Mboru;
Munkonde is the smith of large spears;
My maternal uncle, forge me.
If you do not forge me,
Then you were not born of my mother.
What is in the fireplace
Is Little Mwindo, the Smart-One.[96]

When Mwindo had finished singing, he said to Bat, his maternal uncle, and to Little-Bat to go and forge him.[97] Bat and Little-Bat answered Mwindo, saying: "You are our sororal nephew; go to cut wood to make charcoal." Mwindo refused, saying that he did not want to cut wood for making charcoal. He searched for body hair and hair of his paternal aunts and of the wives of his maternal uncles. He took a pot and put their tears in it in order to extinguish him when the forging began.[98] His maternal

---

96. The song contains a few words in the Hunde language. Only the last nine lines bear directly on Mwindo's story, for in the next episode he is going to be forged by his maternal uncles. The rest of the song is a masterful concatenation of personal recollections, reflections, meditations, proverbs, and references to tales and songs. Such an interlude gives the bard an opportunity to relax and to reflect. A few of the statements are formulas which also occur in the songs of epic I. *I am telling the story*: the bard refers to the people who knew the epic and from whom he indirectly learned it. In this song an unusually large number of statements refer directly to the bard and his psychological condition: *I am sitting, humming; I have sung . . . I am tired; I am in pursuit of Mwindo Mboru*. The bard is proud of his song, but he is tired and has difficulty in finding the right sequence.

97. Two different types of bats, a larger one and a smaller one, are mentioned under the names of Munkonde and Kikwe.

98. The forging of Mwindo is described in detail in this epic and in several heroic tales. The extraordinary character of the event is enhanced by the use of hair as charcoal and of tears instead of water. Both hair and tears have magical connotations; their usage is meant to heighten the quality of the forging. In other texts the tears are sometimes provided by animals.

uncles took the bellows and charcoal in order to forge him. Mwindo said to his maternal uncles that they should first go and take his cross-cousins so that they could be forged together with him. They took two; they placed them on top of the charcoal in the fire; and Mwindo went above them.[99] As they (the maternal uncles) were forging him, they sang:

> What is in the fireplace
> Is Little Mwindo, the Smart-One.

And Mwindo replied, saying: "My maternal uncle, my mother, forge me, you Closer-of-bellies, you who were brought forth by my mother. If you do not forge me, then you have not been brought forth by my mother, you Bat, forger of large spears."[100] They are now pouring the tears over him! As they were now pouring tears over him, Bat was forging him; and Little-Bat was the diviner giving the oracle. After they had finished forging one side of Mwindo, they lifted him up; they placed there two other cross-cousins of his; they placed him again on top of them. Mwindo sang:

> My maternal uncle, forge me,
> You, Closer-of-bellies;
> If you do not forge me,
> You, Closer-of-bellies,
> Then you have not been born of my mother.

Bat is the forger of large spears; Little-Bat is the diviner who is possessed (by the spirits) in order to divine. Little-Bat shouted, saying: "Let the goats that are in Tubondo join me, so that I may climb the Biruri and Mikeme

---

99. *his cross-cousins*: children of the maternal uncles. There is no indication whether the cross-cousins selected are male or female, or whether they are welded together with Mwindo or used as a cushion or an anvil. I have found no similar procedure alluded to in the rest of Nyanga oral literature. The symbolic content of this passage seems quite obvious. Until now, Mwindo had derived his power from the paternal side: he became a chief thanks to his father, and he was successful in the realm of Nyamurairi thanks to the advice received from the spirit of his father's sister. Now he makes his power complete by receiving the additional strength provided by the maternal uncles. For the Nyanga, who adhere to a patrilineal ideology, the social relationships with the relatives of the nonconnecting parent (i.e., mother and her kinsmen) are intense. The chief, who in Nyanga practice is conceived from a union between his father and a woman who is his father's close agnatic relative, achieves the ideal social status by merging the agnatic relatives with the maternal uncles. In Nyanga kinship terminology the chief's father is at the same time his maternal uncle.

100. *my mother*: the respect for mother is transferred to her brothers. The Nyanga term *mantire* for maternal uncle may be replaced by the term *koyo*, my mother, when one desires to show great respect. *Closer-of-bellies*: Mwindo means to say that his mother is senior to her brothers; the last-born child is frequently called Closer-of-bellies.

mountains." When they were finished forging him (Mwindo), they removed him. His body was now plain iron.[101]

Mwindo went to test himself; he went to fight with Mutero Murimba because Mutero Murimba subdues and subdues (people).[102] As they were now clashing with each other in order to fight each other, they sang:

> *Kirungo*-vine is strong for trapping.
> He who goes to Munongo
> Wakes up (to go early).
> When he arrives there,
> Shebukura is given supper.
> He is eating supper;
> He is given supper,
> (Supper) of warthog meat.[103]

Mutero said to Mwindo: "You, Mwindo, you are very, very difficult; your mouth is like a heavy stone." As they were now close to fighting each other, they spoke to each other. Mwindo said: "Surely, Mutero, you are not capable (of fighting) against me; I can cleave you into two parts." Mutero answered him, saying: "Well, then, am I your wife to be beaten by you? I also am able to fight with you. We can clash with each other, we two." When Mwindo heard this, he descended on him; he cleaved Mutero into pieces and pieces. Mutero was crushed to bits. Mwindo took all the spoils of Mutero's kinship group. Mwindo went, and he was singing to praise himself:

> Yes, Bat,
> My maternal uncle, I rejoice;
> I have overcome the enemy
> Where I have gone.
> He who wants to die rapidly,
> Let him climb up on me.
> Rufunda Mountain, where lived

---

101. Melting of iron and forging are complicated ritual affairs, involving many observances of prescriptions, the consultation of oracles, purifications, and ritual formulas.

102. *Mutero Murimba*: a double name covering two personages who appear elsewhere in the epics and in the heroic tales. In the short *karisi*-story published in Biebuyck and Mateene (1970, pp. 24–47), Specter Mpaca consecutively plays dice contests with Lightning, Murimba (Rock), Rundurundu (Fog), and Mutero (White Stone; sometimes Hail). In another heroic tale Mutero is a chief who rejects his son Mpa, is forced to reconcile with him because of a famine, and is finally chased by his son because he had plotted the son's death.

103. This playful song refers to the full day's trip to the village of Munongo where the bard went to trap. Leaving in the early morning, he arrived there when the men had already left the men's house for their own houses. *supper*: the term *utote* suggests the intimate late-evening meal that a man eats privately with his wife.

Kubuya of the Baanga,
Became the place of Shekabwe of Buremera.
Shekiruu and Muhu mountains of Elephant.
And, what is in the reeds
Is the little mother of (the Pygmy) Kabiho;
What is abandoned
Is not good.
Mutero has long ago entered
The shoulder bag of Mwindo;
Boldness has finished him off.[104]

When Mwindo was now on his return home, he met Wild-Banana-Tree in the middle of the road, obstructing it. He sang:

Wild-Banana-Tree, get out of the way for me;
To be big is not to be great.
I have fought with the chief of Specter.
Kibukuru-bird, (when) very old,
Has no force left to fly.
Let us go in pursuit of Nanga my father.
Kombi-bird called Turtle, saying:
Turtle, my maternal uncle,
Mr. Cloth that is cut,
We shall beat the neck on the nails.[105]

As Mwindo arrived in the middle of the road, he climbed up to Lightning, son of Striker. When Lightning saw Mwindo, he blocked the road for him, saying: "Now today you will not pass here; you, Mwindo, we shall know each other today, you and I, because they praise you much saying that you are not being smeared with a sign of vexation, but neither am I smeared with a sign of vexation."[106] When Mwindo heard this, he said to Lightning: "Surely, Lightning, if you climb onto me, I shall make you see what you want to (see). I am a master of strength; I also am (made of) iron; I am not thrown down twice; if you look for me, I shall meet face-to-face with you; I cannot let you go; you cannot do with me whatever you want." When Lightning heard these insults, he came down, saying that he was going to pulverize Mwindo. When Mwindo saw that his adversary was coming down, he climbed up; they met each other in the middle. Mwindo swelled; he seized Lightning. Lightning defecated out of fear, because

---

104. This song begins and ends with Mwindo's praises of himself. Interspersed are the bard's recollections and meditations.

105. Mwindo pursues his self-praise, interspersing it with reference to tales. *To be big is not to be great*: the verb *irungumana* concerns volume and distribution in space; *bukwakare* is greatness in the sense of seniority in kinship or in political position.

106. *Striker*: Rusasa is one of Lightning's praise names.

Mwindo had thrown Lightning down; he (Mwindo) wanted to cut him with a double-edged knife which he held. Where Lightning remained on his back on the ground, he acted submissively, saying: "No, no! Our senior, Mwindo, I shall not persist further. Leave me; do not stab me with the knife. My pride is finished; now I am your servant; I can no longer dominate you." When Lightning had finished acting submissively in this manner, Mwindo let him go. He took all his goods together with all his people away from him.[107]

When the war was finished, Mwindo went together with his crowd of people—the spoils of those whom he had overpowered. Lightning said to Mwindo: "You, my friend, what will you give me? What will you consecrate for me, when I give you help in war?" Mwindo said to him: "I shall consecrate a white chicken, a maiden, and sugarcane for you." He said that he who would eat from this sugarcane before harvest would pay five measures of money, that it would be as if he had bought it, that it would therefore not be as if he had stolen it.[108]

After Mwindo had finished overpowering Lightning in this manner, he returned to where his mother was, and he was singing:

> My mother, I am not talked about.
> My father has blessed me.
> I am carrying very many servants.
> My mother, sky becomes evening.
> The bananas of an ill-fated man do not ripen.
> I have a helper.
> Potto was the young son of Hopeful-One;
> Hoping for himself was the reason he failed
>   (to have) a tail;
> He said that he would take a tail,
> A nice one from among his maternal uncles;

---

107. As in other similar situations, the actual fight is preceded by a verbal challenge which includes self-praises and invectives. *adversary*: the Nyanga term *mine* literally means a companion. The term is used whenever two individuals are involved in a common event, action, or situation, either as friends or as antagonists. *defecated*: part of an often-used formula to indicate severe physical and/or emotional strain. *Our senior*: Lightning uses the honorific term *baba witu*, which is given to a senior brother or sister out of deep respect. *servant*: the term *muombe* refers to a politically dependent person who has no special status as counselor, prince, or ritual expert.

108. The victory of Mwindo over Lightning and the promise of Lightning's alliance provide a rationale for the cult of Lightning, which is intensively practiced by the Nyanga. Devotees of Lightning consecrate in his name a white chicken (which must die a natural death) and patches of sugarcane. They dedicate to Lightning a sister or a daughter as his ritual wife. Women who are ritually married to a divinity bear children on behalf of their own agnatic group by men to whom they are not married. *five measures of money*: meaning the *butea*-rings made from the inner fibers of the raffia palm.

He said that arriving there they would provide
    him one;
And when he arrived there,
Other animals had finished wearing them,
(Animals) such as squirrels and *bisindi.*
And the girl Ndorera
Is kinsman of Moon;
They wear raffia bunches (made) of flashes.
My mother, the sign of astonishment for a woman
    is life;
It has removed me from a big house.
My mother, I was staying behind.
The wild pigeon (is) a bird that flies in the
    hundreds.[109]

Mwindo called Elephant in a loud voice, saying: "You, Elephant, you are the great one, the master of all the forest; you cut for me the trails so that I may remove myself here from the midst of these my enemies. You are the one of whom they may be afraid. The little tree that is cut does not fail to get sunlight; it does not take long for it to dry up when it has been cut. Kahombo, bless me! The hatred of the animals! I shall fight with Chief Specter."[110]

When Mwindo had arrived where his mother was, together with the crowd of people whom he had taken by force, and when his mother saw him, she greeted him throwing herself against his chest, saying: "My father, Mwindo, good luck from where you come? May you and our servants be safe. You are iron that was forged by a hammer; he who will vex you will go first in death on the big road."[111]

---

109. In this song, which contains a few lines in the Hunde language, Mwindo tells his mother that he is returning victorious. The bard then synthesizes in unusual detail a tale that explains why the potto has no tail. Mwindo proceeds, announcing joyful dances. The song ends with two highly symbolic statements. First, the lines *My mother, the sign of astonishment for a woman is life* and *It has removed me from a big house* means that the mouth (i.e., the talk of a woman) is rough and that it causes trouble and brings many difficulties in which a man does not want to get involved. Second, in the final two lines Mwindo alludes to difficulties he apparently encountered on the way home which are more circumstantially suggested in the following passage. He was surrounded by a crowd of enemies who wanted to kill him. He called for help from his mother and his paternal aunt, who freed him from the enemies by making him fly.

110. Elephant, who was ridiculed by Chameleon in an earlier episode, is not mentioned in the most flattering terms. The text does not actually describe Mwindo's encounter with the enemies, but it suggests the hardships by means of Mwindo's implorations. *Kahombo*: divinity of Good Fortune. *Chief Specter*: the specter of the forest, Mpaca, is the symbol of the inimical forces that haunt the forest. The text suggests that Specter was among the unspecified enemies who tried to kill Mwindo.

111. *You are iron*: of course Mwindo is forged, but his mother really means to say that he is strong and is a daredevil. *on the big road*: when Nyamurairi wants

When Mwindo had finished resting for a countable number of days in his mother's place, one day he informed his mother, saying that he was going again to fight, but that he was leaving behind with her his wife Kahindo who was pregnant and with children: "Do not refer to my wife, saying that she is the daughter of a spirit or that her children are. I am going to fight with Nyakatwakari, the daughter of Marumbu."[112] After he had spoken like this, his mother gave him for his morning meal a small portion of eleusine paste surpassing in size a portion of banana paste, because he loved to eat it excessively.

When he had finished eating this morning food, he went together with Lightning; he went to fight with Nyakatwakari, the daughter of Marumbu.[113] As they were marching together, Mwindo and Lightning questioned each other: "Where we are going, we shall wage a fierce war. Who will be the first to desert his companion?" Lightning said to Mwindo: "You, my friend, neither of us will desert his companion. But I, Lightning, shall precede you in fighting Nyakatwakari. When I am overpowering her, then you may help me." He also said to Mwindo: "I shall fight on one flank, and you will fight on another flank." When they arrived at Nyakatwakari's, when they faced her, Nyakatwakari said to them: "These fools here! What will they be able to do? Do they perhaps not know that I reside here? I am a gorilla; I am not smeared with a mark of vexation."[114]

---

somebody to die, he sends two ancestor spirits to fetch the victim. They appear as in a dream before the dying person and invite him to walk a large, well-cleared road that suddenly lies before him and leads to the subterranean world of Nyamurairi.

112. *a countable number of days*: a formula referring to a certain period of fixed, but unspecified, time. Few time formulas are used in this text. *Nyakatwakari*: a term sometimes used to mean Little-Woman, but in fact, as is suggested in the long episode concerning Nyakatwakari, the name has a more complex meaning. As a teknonym, it can be read as mother of *katwakari*, which literally means little Pygmy female. Katwakari is the title of one of the chief's wives who is provided without bridewealth by the Pygmies on the occasion of the enthronement. It may also be read as a praise name or as a title meaning Mrs. Pygmy-Woman; it is in this sense that the name must be understood, for the Nyakatwakari who appears in this text is the mother of the Pygmies.

113. After his defeat Lightning became Mwindo's ally. Usually Lightning does not accompany Mwindo; instead, he renders his destructive services whenever Mwindo, in trouble, calls upon him.

114. Nyakatwakari engages in the usual verbal challenge, coupled with invectives, before the actual fight begins. *I am a gorilla*: a considerable number of gorillas inhabit the less accessible portions of the northern Nyanga rain forest. The gorilla (*muhumba*) is a symbol of extraordinary power and pride. The Nyanga fear the animal, yet the better hunters do not hesitate to attack it with spears. Several protective medicines (used in wartime or against sorcerers and killer spirits) are made from parts of the gorilla's body. Select exuviae also go into the chief's *ukenye*-bundle. It is interesting to note that the Nyanga, in their ethnoclassification of animals, assign the position of Chief-Pygmy (*mwamitwa*) to the gorilla.

When Mwindo and Lightning heard this, they were astounded, saying:
"This one here, with whom will she fight? She will perhaps fight with her
female companions, because she is incapable of fighting with male ad-
versaries." When Nyakatwakari heard these insults, she said to them as if
they were rubbing her with *keni*-leaves: "You sufferers of venereal
diseases! Are you then not in the count of males, you fools?"[115] Mwindo
said to Nyakatwakari: "I will show you what you are looking for. If you
are a woman, have you not heard that I cleave the heads of many strong
and courageous people who fight against me? For seven days and more, we
are involved in fighting; and I overcome them." After he had spoken like
that, they began to fight; Lightning fought on his side, and Mwindo con-
centrated on his side. As they now began to fight, Mwindo threw sweet
words in his mouth; he sang:

> Flashes, kinsman of Lightning,
> Cook large lumps (of paste) for them.
> I shall not eat them (the lumps).
> Cook large lumps (of paste) for them;
> I, Flashes, I am cooking
> Paste that I shall not eat;
> Nyamikora is the one who will eat it.[116]

Where Mwindo had gone, he had the worst of it: blood is the sweat
with which he wets the arm. And where Lightning had gone, he flattened
them all on the ground. Nyakatwakari, because of the grief for her people
who had died, wanted to flee. They seized her, together with her daughter.
Having seized her, they said: "Let us kill her." Nyakatwakari said to
Mwindo and to Lightning: "Do not kill me; it is befitting that you marry
my daughter, you, Mwindo. In order to carry away my daughter, you will
remove honey for me which is over there, which I have been unable (to collect)."[117] When Lightning heard this and saw that Mwindo had taken
away all the belongings of Nyakatwakari, he said to Mwindo: "My friend,
marry this woman; she is like the rays of the sun." Mwindo agreed; he said
to Meshe the Pygmy to go and harvest the honey of Nyakatwakari; Meshe

---

115. *as if they were rubbing her with keni-leaves*: since *keni*-leaves burn like
stinging nettles, the statement means that Nyakatwakari was becoming very angry.
sufferers of venereal diseases: the term *shekashu* is a frequently used insult.

116. The song is sung partly in the Hunde language. *Flashes*: a praise name for
Lightning. *Nyamikora*: lit., Mrs. Large-lumps-of-paste; it refers to Nyakatwakari
who is being beaten.

117. *he flattened them all*: Nyakatwakari's people also took part in the fight. *it is
befitting that you marry my daughter*: the promise of a daughter as prize for a
successful enterprise is a recurring motif in the tales.

the Pygmy went. When he (Meshe) arrived at the honey, he made a platform around the tree.[118] He climbed onto it (holding) his ax. When he was about to cut the honey, he lit a piece of twisted bark cloth with a fire drill. Mwindo said to Meshe the Pygmy: "Now come down since you have put the piece of twisted bark cloth with a fire drill up there." Meshe the Pygmy climbed down. Mwindo removed the sheath from his knife; he gave it to Nyakatwakari, saying to wear it (slung) across the shoulders. Nyaka-twakari wore it.[119]

Meshe the Pygmy climbed up on the platform. He chopped; he opened the hole containing the honey. He inserted his arm into the hole; the hole seized him. After the hole had seized him, he called loudly for Mwindo, saying: "Mwindo, my senior, I am dying; I, Meshe the Pygmy, child of Nyakabotyo, I am dying; I do not know what I have said; I die for nothing. I was used to speaking thus: that I would die in the middle of two brave ones who were clashing with each other in order to better each other. I have been placed up here; I have no strength to remove myself from here. My fathers, my mothers, and my paternal aunts who have died, give me your blessing. I am now in the spot where the sweetness of food is tasted; I am giving the last message (before death)."[120] When Mwindo saw that the Pygmy Meshe was dried up, up there, and that he had no way to remove himself from there, he called out, saying: "You, my knife, may you also bend Nyakatwakari; may you plant her mouth on the ground." The knife said: "I know this, my master." It planted her mouth and lips on the ground. Nyakatwakari's tongue burrowed into the soil. Nyakatwakari sang:

> I am cutting honey, I,
> Good honey.

---

118. *she is like the rays of the sun*: a formula suggesting great beauty. *Meshe the Pygmy*: it is not made clear whether this Pygmy and the others mentioned in the text had come with Mwindo or whether they lived in Nyakatwakari's village. The further context suggests that politically they were Mwindo's men, but that their kinship was with Nyakatwakari. *a platform*: a structure (*baka*) built around trees with massive buttresses and aerial roots to facilitate cutting the tree or climbing it.

119. *his ax*: a tool used to widen the hole so as to reach the honey more easily, though an adze is preferable for this purpose. *a fire drill*: carried on the back from a strap that is fixed over the forehead, the fire drill is a precious possession of all those who spend a lot of time in the forest. During a honey harvest the bees are chased with smoke. *Mwindo removed the sheath*: larger knives are placed in a protective sheath. The exchange of objects with magical powers frequently precedes a test of this sort and forewarns that trouble is ahead. In similar circumstances Mwindo exchanges his billhook or scepter for Nyamurairi's belt.

120. *in the spot where the sweetness of food is tasted*: a formula also used earlier to say that the speaker feels as though he is between the teeth of a predator.

> I am cutting honey,
> Good honey;
> It is in a very difficult place.

She also sang:

> My senior, I am dying;
> I am dying because of my good honey.
> My mother, I am dying;
> I am dying because of my good honey.
> My honey, let him loose now;
> I will die here on the ground.

After she had finished speaking like this, the honey let the Pygmy Meshe loose where he was being squeezed. He remained there in the tree without coming down.[121] Nyakatwakari called out saying that she had seen wonderful things, (but) that her child would not go to the Barea because a young woman of the Barea when cutting bananas needs banana bark strips; and this is why the banana trees fall down.[122] Nkango, the kinsman of Meshe the Pygmy, shouted, saying that the bell that hunts for the chief does not hunt for a common man, making him worthy of it.[123] Nkango called out, saying that the senior should not die and the juniors re-

---

121. *may you also bend; may you plant her mouth*: formulas revealing that the antagonist undergoes a number of hardships that make him powerless and compel him to abandon his magical tricks. The situation is unusual because the Pygmy, although released by the hole, is apparently unable to climb down from the tree. Thus the stage is set for the coming conflict between Mwindo and the Pygmies.

122. *Barea*: in their system of ethnic classification the Nyanga frequently make a symbolic distinction between Barea, the people from downstream, and Bira, the people from upstream. The concept is rooted in historical and cultural fact. The Hunde as a whole are referred to as Bira, as opposed to the Nyanga who are Barea in the sense that they are downstream from and west of the Hunde. The Nyanga, who have common origins with the Hunde, migrated westward into the deep rain forest and culturally differentiated from them partly because of exposure to Lega and Komo-Pere cultural influences. Since the Hunde do not practice circumcision rites, which are very elaborate among the Nyanga, the distinction between Bira and Barea marks the difference between uncircumcised and circumcised people. *a young woman . . . when cutting bananas*: in an interlude, the bard explained this point. When a menstruating woman cuts bananas of the *ibu*-variety, she ties a *kirere*, i.e., a strip of dried bark from the tree whose fruit she is harvesting, tightly around her waist. Afterward, she is surprised to find the banana tree falls down and decays. She thinks the destruction is caused by heavy winds, but it is the bad luck coming from the *kirere*-belt she tightened around the waist during menstruation which caused the banana tree to fall.

123. *the bell*: a small iron bell that is part of the chief's paraphernalia. Nkango is trying to say that the magical device, that helps Mwindo is not necessarily effective for the common man. Mwindo's knife has been only partly successful.

main troubled by weeping. Nkango shouted out, saying: "My mother, I have killed civet cat; it still goes to kill the master of my children. (The word) that was said in Burindu: whistling is more appropriate than a greeting! Lo! If a man fails to receive a dish of food to welcome him where he has gone, then a man reciprocates by whistling as a sign of astonishment."[124]

While Meshe the Pygmy was still up there, his kinsman Nkango went to consult the oracle. Where Nkango went to consult the oracle, when he arrived there, he questioned the animals. He asked Elephant, saying: "You, Elephant, you are the blazer-of-trails." He shouted to Buffalo, saying: "You Buffalo, child of Strength; and Baboon, child of Scraper; Wild Pig, child of What-has-been-said, whose grandfather is Teaser." Nkango consulted the oracle on behalf of his kinsman: "Nkurongo our (kinsman), young son of Korokoro who roars; and Wild Pigeon, young son of Drummer; and Ntanga, young son of Slender; and Small-Bat, young son of Mishero-Dancer, who broke while dancing; and Spider, young son of Cobweb, Spinner of Bridges."[125] After Nkango had left the place where he had received the oracles, he circled around the tree on which his kinsman was. He called Nyamurairi; he sang:

> The day that we shall go
> We shall kill a big (animal);
> Let us also kill a small (animal)
> And a bearer of animals.
> Let no one remain in the forest.
> They were thinking, saying that
> My kinsman would die
> Where he was squeezed on the tree.
> Lo! They do not know that
> He will be helped by the animals
> That are in the forest.[126]

When Mwindo saw that Meshe the Pygmy did not rapidly gather the

---

124. *the master of my children*: an honorific term given by Nkango to his senior brother Meshe. *Burindu*: land of the Bashi, an ethnic group established south of the Nyanga but territorially separated from them by other ethnic units such as Kanu, Hunde, Havu, and Tembo. The term *burindu* usually means a land that is far away.

125. In this passage the dialogue that marks an oracle and the verdict of the oracle are replaced by the suggestion that Nkango consulted many animals whom he addressed with choice praise formulas. Nkango's appeal gives rise to an astounding accumulation of sonorous epithets, many of which are not to be found in any of the texts I collected.

126. *He called Nyamurairi*: a direct appeal to the god of fire is extremely rare. Implicit in Nkango's song is the promise of many offerings for Nyamurairi and the prediction that his brother Meshe will be saved.

honey, he said: "What now! This Pygmy of mine is the reason I shall not marry this maiden quickly." He left them there at the foot of the tree; he went to forge.[127] When Meshe the Pygmy saw that Mwindo had gone to forge, he said: "What now! Here on earth there is no longer a brave-one, for that (brave-) one has gone." Meshe the Pygmy called his kinsman Nkango. When Nkango heard the call of his kinsman, he was close to the tree. He said, manifesting himself: "You, my kinsman, do not be troubled by fear. I here, I come from Potto, child of Healer." When Meshe the Pygmy saw Nkango below, he dropped down for him two pieces of honey-comb in which there was honey, saying: "We are dying, we here. The hatred of the maiden! See! The brave Mwindo has gone to forge." Nkango climbed up; he gave his kinsman a rope. He met his kinsman up there in order to take him away from there. He held two calabashes: one had a long neck, and the other had a short neck; they filled both of them with honey. They climbed down with the calabashes filled with honey.[128] When they arrived on the ground, they gave their kinsmen the long-necked calabash with honey; they said to them: "Now eat the honey fast. Let us go to reside with another chief; his name is Difficulties-do-not-come-together-with-others. Look! our chief here has gone. He hates us, saying that we are the reason he failed to marry a maiden." When they had finished eating the honey, the Pygmies went, saying: "We leave you and we go. And there, perhaps at Murimba's, where we shall meet with you, there we shall fight with you; and if we do not meet you there, we shall meet you at Chief Kihoro's; and we shall fight Mwindo there." The Pygmies went all together.[129]

Having arrived in the place of Mutero Murimba, they sang holding the bows, Nkango wearing the *isara*-billhook. When Murimba heard their

---

127. Mwindo had remained with Meshe while Nkango, distrustful of the efficacy of Mwindo's magic, had taken the initiative in consulting the oracle. While Nkango was away, Mwindo decided to leave also in order to forge more weapons. This passage is the only place where Mwindo himself is presented as a blacksmith.

128. The reasons that Nkango can climb the tree and descend from it are not explicitly stated. Apparently Nkango had received the simple advice that he should climb the tree himself in order to liberate his brother by means of a rope.

129. *Difficulties-do-not-come-together-with-others*: a purely symbolic name. The bard explained that the name meant that difficulties do not come in pairs like the quarrels of co-wives. The Pygmies are saying that their chief Mwindo hates them because he accuses them falsely, and that another chief would be better. *the Pygmies went*: the proverbs state that a subject, when wronged by his chief, will leave him. A chief must therefore practice verbal restraint.

clamor, he said to his people to go and intercept them at the fence opening at the village entrance.[130] They arrived at this village of Murimba in which there was no fire, in which there was nothing but darkness. There they dwell in a large cave; and when the sun shines, they open the cave and go to bask in the sun.[131] When they (the Pygmies) arrived there, they met with the people of that place. They (the Pygmies) asked them (the people) to open for them. The people of that place at first refused, but afterward the people of that place said to Kasiwa to open for them (the Pygmies). The Pygmies said to the master of that place: "Now we come to meet a big chief. But you, headman, you must lead us to a big chieftainship."[132] He said to them that he would lead them to the big chief. He gave them three goats and four jars of banana beer. They (the Pygmies) asked the women to go and collect firewood. The master of that place said: "Why shall they go and collect firewood?" They said to the master of that place, the chief: "You people of this place, you eat raw foods; but you will see." When the women arrived with the firewood, Nkango said to his kinsman to find a man carrying a pouch (for a fire drill) and to take it to the village entrance to make fire with the fire drill. This Pygmy went. Arriving at the village entrance, he made fire with the fire drill. After he had lit the fire, he went to show it to the village. They arrived there; they lit it. When it was blazing, they said to the master of that village to go and sit near the fire. When the

---

130. *Mutero Murimba*: a chief who in an earlier episode was crushed and apparently killed by Mwindo. The Pygmies settle with him (or his successor), who is the archenemy of Mwindo. The name may be translated as Heavy-white-stone-rock-that-cannot-be-lifted. *isara-billhook*: ownership of this iron tool, which is the center of many taboos and other ritual concepts, is indicative of headmanship. *fence opening*: the Nyanga village was traditionally protected by a fence which had two openings, one at each end of the village; each opening was closed off with a door.

131. A rare evocation of the physical aspect of a place. In the following episode the Pygmies are presented as culture heroes who bring the knowledge of fire to people who did not have it. I have translated into Dutch (Biebuyck, 1956a, pp. 15–17) the text that explains the advent of fire to the Pygmies and to their chief Iterere. The Pygmy Nkango lost his way in the forest and arrived at the place of Nyamurairi, the god of fire. He met the dog Rukuba, who was lying near the fire in the men's house. The Pygmy enjoyed the warmth of the fire, unknown to Rukuba. He made a blood pact with the dog and received from him a burning log which he took back to his chief Iterere. Because he had stolen the fire, the dog Rukuba was chased by Nyamurairi and went to settle with his friend, Nkango.

132. The Pygmies meet with the chief's subjects and their headman Kasiwa, who were sent by the chief to intercept them. *big chief*: instead of the usual word for big (*mukiri*), the unusual term *kinyantsita* is used. The Pygmies are saying that they offer their services and allegiance to a big chief, but that they expect something big in return for it.

master of that village saw this (the fire), he said: "You, Pygmy, you have saved us. We were very cold. Now I will take you to the chief."[133]

Where Mwindo had gone to forge, he returned carrying new spears to the place where Nyakatwakari had remained. He arrived; he questioned Nyakatwakari; he said: "Go, follow your sons where they have gone; I do not want to kill you."[134]

Where Nkango and the Pygmy Meshe had gone, they sent messengers to where their mother resided. When the messengers arrived in the middle of the road, they met Nyakatwakari on the road. They gave her the news. They returned with her to her sons. They were singing:

> Father, may you be blessed.
> We leave Mwindo behind;
> We leave him a place
> In his own state.
> We follow (our) children;
> We go in pursuit
> To the place where (our) children have gone to
>   the chief.
> He who receives political allegiance
> Cannot chase people.
> I am no longer a woman consecrated to spirits.
> Going elsewhere is a salvation;
> It helps me obtain headmanship.[135]

When Nyakatwakari arrived there, the master of that village gave them a section of the village, saying to look after it. They rejoiced. In the early morning they went to hunt. Where they had gone into the forest, they searched for wild pigs, (but) failed to find them. They searched for other animals; they failed to find them. They (finally) went to find a big elephant which was rotten. They found the elephant tusks; they went to the village

---

133. *he gave them three goats . . .*: the headman extends to these important guests all the courtesies of warm hospitality, thus giving the Pygmies the opportunity to reciprocate by providing fire without divulging the art of making it (the Pygmy went to light the fire in secrecy).

134. The story abruptly returns to Mwindo and Nyakatwakari. It is as though Mwindo finally realized that a kinship bond existed between Nyakatwakari and the Pygmies. The entire passage dealing with Mwindo, Nyakatwakari, and the Pygmies may be understood as a strong, but latently stated, critique of Chief Mwindo. Mwindo, boisterous and impetuous, had decided to fight Nyakatwakari without knowing who she was. He was driven by infatuation and blindness, which are not the hallmarks of a true chief. He paid for it with the loss of his Pygmies, who were the sons of Nyakatwakari. Mwindo belatedly shows generosity and humility by not killing her, the implication being that in this way he saved his chieftainship.

135. In this song Nyakatwakari thanks Mwindo, leaving him behind as chief in his own land. She predicts the coming honors to be bestowed upon her children.

with them. When the master of the village saw them arriving at the village entrance, he went to welcome them with a calabash of beer and a chicken. He said to them: "You have done well. You have done a great job which, I, master of the village, like." He also said to Mwamitwa: "You have arrived with the elephant; do not place it in my *kahombo*-guesthouse, but go to place it in your house; tomorrow I will send a messenger to the place where the chief is."[136] He provided one of his men; and Nkango provided his kinsman, Meshe the Pygmy. These two messengers went to the chief. When they arrived there and when the chief saw the Pygmy together with the messenger who was sent by his headman, he was very astonished. He questioned them; he said: "This man does not reside here; never has he been seen. Whence come these types of men?" The chief questioned his man; he said: "Come here; show me this man. I do not know him." This man said to the chief: "These men have killed an elephant for us; they have made fire for us. We have enjoyed it (the fire) because we were not used to sitting near a fire." The chief said to them: "I greatly rejoice. Lo! Now we see the manner in which sky turns to dawn. If trouble grows out of it, then it is my responsibility, I the chief." He gave a message to the messenger, saying: "I want my headman to come with those people and also with his own people, to bring the elephant tusks, and to take a maiden, ten goats, and a copper bracelet of headmanship." When they arrived in the village, they gave them (the people) the news that the chief had given them. In the morning the Pygmies and the people of that village went to the chief to meet with him; they were singing:

> The Pygmies do not work in the fields;
> They spend their time (to the sound of) the
>   drums.
> We are going to where it dawns,
> To Rejoicer-of-people.[137]

When they arrived at the chief's, the chief asked them, saying: "Is this the elephant?" He also asked them, saying: "You, Pygmies, from where have all of you come?" They said to him: "We were gathering honey, and

---

136. By bringing from the hunt a tribute of elephant tusks, the Pygmies show themselves to be fully worthy of the chief's protection. *Mwamitwa*: a title meaning Chief-Pygmy. The headman addresses himself to the leader of the Pygmies. The *mwamitwa* is one of several ritual experts attached to a Nyanga chief.

137. *If trouble grows out of it* . . . : the text literally says: if trampling (caused by war) comes out of it, then I perform it (i.e., I shall fight). *The Pygmies do not work*: besides being hunters, providers of honey, and ritual experts, the Pygmies are singers and dancers par excellence. *Rejoicer-of-people*: a praise name for the chief.

our master chased us because of a quarrel over honey gathering, saying that he might fail to marry the maiden. Since we were chased away like that, we said (among ourselves) : we no longer want to stay with him; we will go to settle with another chief. This, then, is the reason we have arrived at the place where you are, to reside with you."[138] After they (the Pygmies) had given this news to the chief, he said to them: "Now return to fetch your things, together with your wives, and come with them to build where I am, so that you may no longer be accused of a big thing that you have not done, of which I know nothing. And, if you stay close to me, I will know the one who would vex you, the one who would kill you for no reason." When they had heard the word of the chief, they returned (home) ; they went to fetch their wives. When they arrived at their wives' places, they bound together all their goods; they returned to the chief's place. The chief gave them a hill; they built on it, together with their mother Nyakatwakari, daughter of Marumbu.[139]

Where this chief remained, he gave them seeds and shoots; they went to plant banana trees, eleusine, peas, and corn. When they had brought their first crops to maturity, they took them to the chief; they went to give them to him as tribute. When the chief saw these (crops), he rejoiced greatly.[140]

---

138. *We were gathering honey . . .* : a typical example of caustic wit and elliptical speech which aptly summarizes the situation and reveals the bitterness of the Pygmies.

139. *they returned (home)*: earlier passages do not indicate where the Pygmies lived. Although they were dependent on Mwindo, they did not actually live in his village, for it is not customary for Pygmies to live in the chief's village. It will be recalled that in an earlier episode Mwindo's mother had been abandoned by the Pygmies, the counselors, and all the people. After Mwindo's return, they all broke up their village and went to Mwindo. For the Nyanga, this expression evidently means that they went to stay close to Mwindo, the counselors reintegrating his village and the Pygmies renewing their allegiance without actually going to live with him. *The chief gave them a hill*: when people establish themselves with a chief as "followers" (i.e., as dependents who give allegiance), it is customary for the chief to provide them with land on which they can settle, farm, gather food, fish, trap, and hunt.

140. *he gave them seeds and shoots*: a passage difficult to interpret. On the one hand, nothing in the Nyanga text indicates who is meant by "them": the Pygmies, other people who depend on the chief, or both. In the fifties, those who, like the Baremba, followed the true Pygmy ways among the Nyanga did not cultivate, but they exercised many special privileges, such as the free harvesting of bananas for immediate consumption. On the other hand, many descendants of Pygmies were incorporated among, and assimilated with, the Nyanga. Some individuals and groups who followed the Nyanga way continued to be identified as being of Pygmy origin. If in this passage the Pygmies are included among "them," it seems to be a reference to the Nyangaization of certain groups of Pygmies. The voluntary passage of the Pygmies from Mwindo to Mutero Murimba would then be the symbolic expression of the Nyangaization process.

Where they were settled, they brought forth (children); and their children brought forth (children); and their grandchildren brought forth (children). Chief Murimba called out, saying: "You my people, you my Pygmies, because you have come to settle with me, I now give you the (following) right: If the chief is enthroned, you go to search for honey and for the hide of a flying squirrel, which is for the ritual wife to wear."[141] The chief said to his people who lived with him: "(Beware) him who refuses a Pygmy the food (he has) or the banana beer (he has). And if he (a Pygmy) went to hunt and if, where he (a Pygmy) went, he cut ripe bananas or plantain bananas, he cannot pay for them. The owner of the banana grove must not accuse him or make charges to me (against him), for it is because of these Pygmies that we have seen fire in this land."[142]

The people of the land said they wanted to enthrone the chief because Mwamitwa had arrived. They looked for a wrist protector; they went to search for the claws of an eagle; they looked for leopard teeth; they looked for a *kembo*-hat. They said: "Call now Mwamihesi; let him look for a hammer." They took a dog that was living there. They went to search for red powder and for *rubuo*-bark cloth; they looked for the hide of a genet from which to make the *ukenye*-bundle. They said that on the genet's hide would be (placed) a belt made of the hide of a wild pig. They fastened to it the belt of the wild pig's hide, together with the animal teeth.[143] They called Shebakungu to give the teachings. Shebakungu arrived; he said to them: "Now look for a *nyabana*-wife." They looked for a *nyabana*-wife. They also made available a *musanduri*-wife, who follows the *nyabana*-wife

---

141. This etiological detail points to the acual ritual functions exercised by Pygmies in the enthronement rites. During the most secret parts of those rites, the bodies of the chief and his ritual wife are completely cleansed with honey brought by the Chief-Pygmy.

142. The chief's decrees serve as etiological explanations for the outstanding food privileges the Pygmies enjoy among the Nyanga.

143. This unique passage provides unusual detail about the royal insignia presented by Shebakungu to the chief and his ritual wife during the highly secret enthronement ceremonies, although some of the principal insignia are not mentioned here. Among the chief's insignia are a copper and an ivory bracelet; a small iron bell without clapper; a belt; a stool; an iron staff; a scepter; a billhook; a drum; a loin cloth made of two varieties of bark cloth, dyed red and imbued with oil; and, most important, the *ukenye*-bundle which contains, as is later indicated, a number of powerful exuviae. Among the insignia of the ritual wife are a hat made from the hide of a flying squirrel; a belt made from the hide of a wild pig onto which leopard teeth and the claw of an eagle are fastened; a wrist protector; a quiver containing poisoned arrows; and a double-edged knife. *They took a dog*: all chiefs possess hunting dogs as an expression of their linkage with Nyamurairi, who manifests himself in the form of a dog.

"in the back." They produced a *mumbo*-wife.[144] They looked for Minerusi, the one who kills fish for the chief when he is being enthroned. They called Mushumbia; they called Musao; they called Mwamihesi, the one who forges when the chief is being enthroned. They called Mwamitwa; they called Mubei, the one who shaves the chief, the one who looks for a copper razor. They looked for Muhakabi, the one who annoints the chief with oil.[145] They said to Shebakungu that he (Shebakungu) should go to fetch the *ukenye*-bundle of the chief at Musimba's. They (Shebakungu's people) fetched it; it arrived at Shebakungu's.[146] They said that the *ukenye*-bundle had arrived here: "All of you, let there be no man who sleeps with his wife; he (who does) will suffer from the hookworm disease. For the chief is going to be enthroned." They went to Ngusha, the place of enthronement. They climbed up Ngusha in Muremeri; they arrived there. They called Mwesi, and Mwamitwa, and the *mumbo*-wife. The chief called out, saying: "The honors are unending. I die. I do not know what I might

---

144. *Shebakungu*: the Chief-Counselor. He plays an eminent political and ritual role in the life of the chief. For example, he places the sacred grains in the hands of the newly born son (chief-to-be) of the ritual wife; he transmits the insignia to both the chief and his ritual wife; he provides the *mahano*-teachings during the enthronement ceremonies. Some of the teachings run as follows: "May you fear the chief. Let him who kills an elephant give the chief from it. Let him who brings crops to maturity give the chief from them, and also from the beer. You, chief, may you continue giving to the people; may you fear the people who arrive at the village entrance. Do not discriminate among people, saying that some are yours and others are not yours." *nyabana-wife*: one of several wives with special status who is generally provided by the chief's counselors without bridewealth; her son has the title of First-born-of-the-land. *musanduri-wife*: this woman, who is eventually provided by the chief's maternal uncles, is really a servant of the ritual wife; her son may be designated as chief if the ritual wife fails to have sons. *mumbo-wife*: the chief's ritual wife; she is a close agnatic relative of the chief (a consanguineal sister or the daughter of a junior consanguineal brother); her son is, in principle, the chief's successor. For further explanations, see Biebuyck (1956*b*).

145. Under these names several of the principal ritual experts are enumerated, some with a brief indication of their main functions during the enthronement rites. *Mushumbia*: the ritual drummer. *Musao*: a man of very special status who during the enthronement rites performs several typically female duties (preparing the bed; cooking food; cleaning the chief). With his wife he replaces the chief and his wife in certain prescribed rituals of the life cycle through which the chief is not allowed to pass. *Mwamihesi*: lit., Chief-Blacksmith, who gives some teachings to the chief while using two hammers as percussion instruments. *Mwamitwa*: the Chief-Pygmy, who brings honey, a wrist protector, and the hide of a flying squirrel to the enthronement.

146. *ukenye-bundle*: the most important of all the royal insignia, this bundle contains small durable parts removed from the body of the dead chief together with some other powerful exuviae, such as gorilla hair. *Musimba*: a dignitary who buries the chief, he inherits certain objects and temporarily guards others.

have said!"[147] When they enthroned him, they said to him: "When a chief arrives in his house, he does not look (for things) on the drying rack or remove food that lies on top of the drying rack."

After they had finished enthroning him, they returned to the village. After they had arrived in the village, the chief did not observe the prescriptions that had been set forth by the preceptors; he got the hookworm disease. After he had contracted hookworm disease, this disease brought him death; he died. As he was dying, he left his last oral will to his people, saying: "I am troubled here before dying. You, Shebakungu, together with Shemumbo, your work is to care for this my *mumbo*-wife."[148] After he had expired, when he was dead, they cut (select) portions (of his body). They fetched Musimba; he arrived there. Musimba removed two molars; he removed two eyelashes; he removed the tip of the tongue; he removed a little finger. They dried all these things.[149] As they buried him, they uttered an imprecation, saying that he would turn into a leopard. Thereupon, Musimba sang a song:

> *Tunga*-shrew dies;
> We look for it behind the houses.

For this reason a chief and Musimba do not get along, because Musimba does many very bad things to him.[150]

---

147. *Ngusha*: the most secret parts of the enthronement rites take place on a sacred mountain. Each autonomous state has its own sacred mountain. The chief and some dignitaries may live there for as long as two months in relative seclusion. *They called*: a rather cryptic statement, for only a few of the participating dignitaries are mentioned. *Mwesi*: the same as the above-mentioned Mwamihesi.

148. *last oral will*: the desires expressed by the dying have a compulsory force. *Shemumbo*: lit., Father-of-the-ritual-wife, the real brother or father of the ritual wife or a replacement. The concern of the chief for his surviving ritual wife is a real one. If she is well cared for, the continuity of the state is ensured. With the help of such dignitaries as those mentioned here, she may exercise real authority and wield great power during the interregnum.

149. The special functions of *musimba* are briefly and incompletely described. Various parts of the dead chief's body, mostly durable parts, are mixed together in the *ukenye*-bundle.

150. The belief that dead chiefs turn into leopards is widespread. *Tunga-shrew*: both the *tunga*-shrew and the leopard have an unpleasant smell. *We look for it*: refers to a song sung by women in the evening dances. Leopards came close to the villages to prey on goats or dogs which are running behind the houses near the garbage heaps in search of food. The leopard, as master of the forest (*minebusara*), inspires fear and awe. When a leopard is killed he is "exhibited" in the village and seated on a stool, holding in the left paw a wrist protector and in the right paw a bow. Elaborate dances are held in his honor, during which the songs normally sung for twins are performed. The dances are followed by ablution ceremonies near the river and purification rites in the village. The chief receives the hide and fangs of the leopard. The Nyanga worship the leopard divinity Kibira.

After they had buried the chief, the princes and Shemumbo produced goats; they gave them to the counselors to eat. After they had
finished eating this food, the counselors shaved the orphans whom the chief
had left behind. They took out all the belongings left by the chief; they
divided them. Muembwa arrived; he carried away the *utebe*-stool and the
copper spear. They called Mukwacuo; they gave him a bell without clapper and the leopard teeth. They also gave to Muembwa the hill of Buembwa; they also gave him a maiden. They gave Shemumbo four widows as
inheritance from the chief. They gave the widows who remained to the
mumbo-wife, saying that they would perform all labor for her.[151] After
the chief's death, the Pygmies remained there; they did not leave. They
secured food in the manner they wanted. They brought forth and brought
forth (children). They remained there, saying that there was no other place
where they could go.

Where Mwindo had gone, he also enjoyed the chieftainship.[152] As
Mwindo now resided in his village, his wife Kahindo, daughter of
Nyamurairi, brought forth. Ndurumo was the first child. Kahindo also
brought forth Kanyironge, the grandchild of Stone. Mwindo's second wife
Ufamba brought forth Ncongera; she also brought forth Ntindi, the
diviner of many ways. Nyakirimarimari, Mwindo's third wife, brought
forth Musukuiyera, whose mother had destroyed the Bahunga with
shrewdness. His fourth wife, Ntsukiwamunindi, brought forth Muntsuntsu.
Mwindo married Ntanga, his fifth wife, and she brought forth Kanyampanda. Mwindo married Mweri, his sixth wife; she brought forth
Bisheria. He also married Buriru, his seventh wife, and she brought
forth Utundo; she also brought forth Mwishi, daughter of Kandobefu.[153]

---

151. This passage is a brief synopsis of certain procedures connected with the
inheritance and distribution of the chief's belongings. Most of the royal insignia are
guarded by Muembwa, a person who is recruited from among the junior sons of the
dead chief or the descendants of ancient servants of the chief. Muembwa is also
charged with the first *mpero*-sacrifice for the dead chief. Musimba, who was
mentioned previously, keeps the *ukenye*-bundle and receives the garments of the
dead chief. Each of these two dignitaries receives a wife from the legacy of the chief.
They also receive their own landed estate on which they build their hamlet since they
must avoid physical contact with the new ruler. *Mukwacuo*: lit., Salt-of-the-land
(another name for First-born-of-the-land), he receives an iron bell without clapper.
Most of the goats left in the legacy are killed and distributed during the mourning
ceremonies. Some of the chief's widows (without special status) are inherited by
Shemumbo, but the widowed ritual wife herself receives several of these widows (and
their lovers) as servants. The chief's drum is buried with him.

152. *enjoyed the chieftainship*: the Nyanga text lit. says: "he ate the chieftainship."

153. This text is the only one that gives a full list of Mwindo's wives and children
by name. The names of all seven wives and ten children have symbolic connotations.

He acquired these seven wives because of his bravery. When he fought a war and overcame his opponents, they gave him a maiden (as a sign of) reconciliation. He also made blood pacts with them (his opponents).

After Mwindo had begotten these children and they had grown big, he said to them: "You, Ndurumo, you will become chief over your kinsmen; and you, Kanyironge, you will produce the hide that Ndurumo will wear when he is enthroned." He said to Ncongera: "And you will become the First-born-of-the-land; you will be Shemumbo." He said to Ntindi: "And you will become Musimba." Musukuiyera received the status of Shenyabana. Muntsuntsu received the status of Pygmyship (enabling him) to kill flying squirrels. Kanyampanda received the status of Buembwa. Bisheria received the status of princehood; Utundo received the status of princehood; Mwishi received the status of princehood.[154] All these were great princes who would bring forth still more chiefs, because all of them together had received chieftainship. They would fight one another and harbor hatred. Mwindo said to his children: "I have now divided the offices among you, but listen: chieftainship ascends; it does not descend; nor is it pursued by one house alone."[155] After Mwindo had finished dividing

---

Following are the interpretations given by the bard himself. *Ndurumo*: a child born while it was thundering (*iruruma*: to thunder). *Kanyironge*: a child born while they were packing to leave the village and settle elsewhere (*ironge*: to pack one's belongings). *Ncongera*: a child born while they noiselessly tried to escape danger (*ishongokara*: to go noiselessly like a thief). *Ntindi*: a child born during a halt in a journey (*itindira*: to stop for a rest while traveling, e.g., to bathe or to smoke). *Musukuiyera*: a child born while its father was being teased (*iyereka*: to tender somebody something and then pull it back when he tries to take it). *Muntsuntsu*: a child born with a wrinkled forehead (*isusa*: to wrinkle the forehead in anger). *Kanyampanda*: a child born of parents who are expert dancers (*ibandaura*: to disperse the seeds in many spots). *Bisheria*: a child born while there was lightning. *Utundo*: a child born while the sky was very cloudy. *Mwishi*: a child born while the sun was hot, in the middle of the day. Several of these names have broader symbolic connotations than is indicated in the bard's explanations. Some are animal names: Kanyironge is a genet; Ncongera is the tail of a snake; Ntindi is the civet cat; Muntsuntsu is a bee. Some are the names of natural elements: Ndurumo is thunder; Bisheria is flashes of lightning; Utundo is the clouds; Mwishi is the hot sun. Some of the names of Mwindo's wives are terms for animals. *Ufamba*: Monitor Lizard. *Ntsukiwamunindi*: Bee; child of Needle. *Ntanga*: Wasp. The exact significance of the names of Mwindo's other wives escapes me, except for *Mweri*, which designates the moon.

154. In this passage several of the status positions occupied by a chief's sons are outlined. *Shemumbo*: father of the ritual wife and one of her guardians. *Shenyabana*: provider of the *nyabana*-wife (lit., mother of the children) to the chief. She is the senior wife of the chief and her son becomes First-born-of-the-land. *the status of Pygmyship*: since Mwindo has lost his Pygmies, he is now fictively creating the position of Mwamitwa, Chief-Pygmy.

155. Mwindo predicts that, because of internal competition, chiefdoms will split into new entities.

these offices among his young sons, he left them with his last oral will, saying: "You, my children, all of you love one another; do not abandon one another, not even for one day. Be yourself among yourselves!" After he had finished giving this last oral will to his children, he died.[156] As they went to bury him, they removed from him (select) portions (of the body), as they usually do when chiefs die.

Where the children of Mwindo remained, they remained with their land in this manner; they lived well; they followed the words that their father had left them, his last oral will; they lived in harmony with one another.

He who is not advised among the people of the world is (like) a dead person.

Dispersal of the people of one and the same kinship group is bad fate and (a cause) of vilification of the land.

If you hear that the land of a particular chief is famous, (it means) that he (the chief) is in harmony with his people. Lo! The land that has no chief, has no people, it dies out; it is finished without hope of salvation.

To wrong the people of the earth is (as much as) to close the path of salvation.

Beauty on earth is (long) life and begetting children. Lo! He/she who does not beget children is already dead; he/she is finished without hope of salvation.[157]

---

156. The last oral will of the dying chief is a powerful appeal for love and mutual understanding.

157. The bard's conclusions are formulated in terse and incisive statements like those found at the end of epic I. Unity in the kinship group, harmony between chief and subjects, a long healthy life, and a large progeniture rank among the supreme values. To achieve these values, one must constantly seek advice.

THE MWINDO EPIC IV

SYNOPTIC TABLE OF CONTENTS

I. *The setting*
   A. Temporal and spatial
      The action is placed in an unidentified chiefdom. At the beginning of the epic there is not the usual indication that the events narrated occurred long ago. The action initially centers in the chief's village.
   B. Social
      A chief marries six wives. His principal wife Nyabana has no children and is despised by her husband. The chief commands his Chief-Counselor to build a house for her on the garbage heap.
II. *Nyabana saves the chief from famine*
   A. Nyabana, rejected by the chief and living in a house on the outskirts of the village, cultivates a large field of eleusine.
   B. Her co-wives neglect to cultivate, because they thrive on the crops brought as tribute to the chief.
   C. When the eleusine is ripe, Nyabana stores it carefully in her house.
   D. Famine strikes the country.
   E. In order to forget their hunger, the chief and his people play the *wiki*-game day and night.
   F. As the result of a dream in which her mother's spirit appears, Nyabana grinds eleusine on a grinding stone.

233

G. She prepares a meal of beans and eleusine and calls Shebakungu, the Chief-Counselor.

H. Shebakungu enjoys the meal and returns to the *wiki*-game to call the chief.

I. Shebakungu persuades the chief to leave the game and to accompany him. They enjoy Nyabana's meal and return to the game.

J. The next day Shebakungu and the chief secretly return to Nyabana's place to eat more of the food; and so it continues for many days.

III. *The birth of Little-one-just-born-he-walked and of his brother Mwindo*

A. One day, while the people are in the forest, the chief secretly goes to sleep with Nyabana.

B. Nyabana is pregnant.

C. She cooks food for the other men of the village.

D. Soon Nyabakungu, the wife of the Chief-Counselor, is called in because Nyabana is in labor.

E. Nyabana gives birth to a son, called Little-one-just-born-he-walked (Kabutwakenda).

F. The news that the chief's ritual wife has given birth to a son, called Mwindo, is also heard.

G. The chief's wives show their discontent and fling invectives against Nyabana.

H. The Chief-Counselor warns them.

I. The chief gives a cow to Nyabana and only two goats to his ritual wife.

J. The ritual wife grudgingly refuses the two goats.

IV. *Little-one-just-born-he-walked acquires objects and Pygmies from Mukiti (Water Serpent)*

A. Soon after his birth, Little-one-just-born-he-walked and his mother travel to the pool where Mukiti lives.

B. Mukiti gives him a copper zanza and a stool.

C. After his return home (his mother is still living on the garbage heap), Little-one-just-born-he-walked plays the zanza and sings a magical song.

D. The people inform the chief about this astonishing event.

E. Little-one-just-born-he-walked and his mother return to Mukiti.

F. They receive a spear and a scepter.

G. They return home and spend their time singing.

H. Little-one-just-born-he-walked returns to Mukiti to ask for singers.

I. Mukiti tells him to sit on a tree and to sing.

J. While he sings, the Pygmies appear.

V. *Nyabana threatened by the ritual wife*

A. While Little-one-just-born-he-walked is away, his mother is visited by the chief and informs him about her son's absence.

B. The ritual wife conceives a plan to burn Nyabana's house, but the Chief-Counselor prohibits her from doing so.

VI. *Little-one-just-born-he-walked and his Pygmies*

A. Little-one-just-born-he-walked and his Pygmies return home, singing.

B. Nyabana dances while her son and the Pygmies sing.

C. The son hears about the threat against his mother; in turn, he threatens the ritual wife.

D. The chief is informed about the arrival of his son and of the Pygmies.

E. He gives his son three goats for the Pygmies.

F. The son asks his father to remove his mother from the garbage heap.

G. Nyabana is established in a house in the middle of the village.

H. Jealous, the ritual wife asks for an explanation: "Were two chiefs born here?"

I. The Chief-Counselor retorts, saying that "a chief is not brought forth, that he to whom he likes to give it (i.e., the chieftainship) is chief."

J. Little-one-just-born-he-walked goes to Bat to ask for twelve spears.

K. He returns with the spears and asks the Pygmies to weave hunting nets.

L. He sends the Pygmies hunting with the nets and the spears.

M. The Pygmies kill many wild pigs and return with the animals.

N. Little-one-just-born-he-walked sends the game to his brother Mwindo.

O. Mwindo refuses to accept the game; Little-one-just-born-he-walked concludes that Mwindo is affected by his mother's hatred.

VII. *Competition between Little-one-just-born-he-walked and Mwindo over Mukiti's daughter*

A. Mwindo asks his father for bridewealth to marry Mukiti's daughter.

B. Little-one-just-born-he-walked hears the rumor that Mwindo made this request; at night he goes to Mukiti.

C. He informs Mukiti about Mwindo's pending arrival and claims Mukiti's daughter for himself.

D. Mukiti promises his daughter.

E. Little-one-just-born-he-walked returns home, while his brother Mwindo is still asleep.

F. Mwindo leaves for Mukiti's place; when he arrives there, Mukiti makes the river overflow.

G. Mwindo is forced to return home.

H. He informs his father about Mukiti's unwillingness to marry his daughter to him.

I. The chief declares that "the one who will marry the child of Mukiti will be chief."

J. Little-one-just-born-he-walked asks his father for bridewealth.

K. He arrives at Mukiti's; Mukiti informs him about Mwindo's mishap and takes the bridewealth.

L. Mukiti shows his beautiful daughter to Little-one-just-born-he-walked; there is instant love between the two of them.

M. On his return home, Little-one-just-born-he-walked informs the chief about Mukiti's agreement to accept the bridewealth.

N. Mwindo expresses his bitterness and foments war, saying that he will ask all the animals to help him.

VIII. *Little-one-just-born-he-walked receives his own village*

A. The chief proclaims Little-one-just-born-he-walked as master of the Biomfu and Ihuri mountains, while Mwindo becomes the master of the mountain Wingi.

B. Little-one-just-born-he-walked, his Pygmies, and his servants go to build their village and settle.

C. He sends the Pygmies out to hunt with nets.

D. All the animals of the forest throw themselves into the nets.

E. When the Pygmies return home, Little-one-just-born-he-walked sends the Chief Pygmy to call the chief.

F. The chief and his people come to eat; the people predict that Mwindo cannot measure up against his adversary.

G. The chief and his people return home.

IX. *Mwindo's hatred*

A. Mwindo asks the returning chief to tell him who his true son is.

B. The chief tells Mwindo that he is chief designate.

C. Mwindo scornfully refuses to be called in the same manner as his brother.

D. The chief replies that the one to "surpass his companion in intelligence" will become chief.

X. *The honey harvest*

A. Little-one-just-born-he-walked calls upon Bee to help him in the coming battle against Mwindo.

B. The Pygmies collect two jars of honey.

C. One jar is taken to Mukiti.

D. Little-one-just-born-he-walked refuses to take his wife (Mukiti's daughter) with him, because of the coming battle with Mwindo.

E. Mukiti promises help.

F. Little-one-just-born-he-walked takes honey to the chief.

G. The chief invites his sons to get married.

XI. *Renewed competition between Mwindo and Little-one-just-born-he-walked over Mukiti's and Muisa's daughters*

A. Mwindo returns to Mukiti's place.

B. Mukiti fills the river to chase him.

C. Mwindo beats the river with his staff to separate the waters, but Mukiti seizes the staff.

D. Mwindo returns home and tells the chief that Mukiti gave no answer.

E. In the morning, Mwindo and Pygmy leave for Muisa's place to ask for a wife.

F. Muisa shows his daughters.

G. Mwindo returns home to ask his father for bridewealth.

H. Informed about Mwindo's request, Little-one-just-born-he-walked goes to Muisa's place to solicit a wife.

I. Muisa shows his daughters; they prefer Little-one-just-born he-walked over Mwindo.

J. Little-one-just-born-he-walked returns home and learns about the chief's sickness.

K. The chief dies. Little-one-just-born-he-walked is loved by the people because he gives them much game.

L. He goes to take Mukiti's daughter as his wife. There are celebrations.

M. Mwindo, jealous, returns to Muisa to take his wife, but no woman wants to be married to him.

XII. *The battle between Mwindo and Little-one-just-born-he-walked*

    A. Mwindo meditates revenge; he returns to Muisa and receives a copper bracelet to protect him in battle.

    B. Mwindo calls his people together for the attack.

    C. Little-one-just-born-he-walked, informed about the coming attack, calls for the help of Wasp, Bee, Ant, Hawk, and Spider.

    D. He goes to inform Mukiti, who promises help.

    E. He arrives in his mother's place; she consults the oracle of Centipede.

    F. He is placed under the protection of Kahombo (Good Fortune).

    G. Mwindo and his people set out for the attack; Little-one-just-born-he-walked encounters them.

    H. The mothers of the two heroes appear at the scene of battle: Mwindo's mother shouts invectives; the mother of Little-one-just-born-he-walked, more reserved, asks for her son's victory.

    I. The fight begins; a heavy rain pours down. Wasps, Bees, Black Ant, and Fly decimate Mwindo's people.

    J. Mwindo and his mother return to a desolate village.

XIII. *Mwindo dies and is revivified by his brother*

    A. A month after the battle, Mwindo falls sick.

    B. His mother refuses to inform Little-one-just-born-he-walked.

    C. Mwindo expires, and now his mother decides to inform his brother.

    D. At first, Little-one-just-born-he-walked shows indifference; then he decides to go to see his dead brother.

    E. On his arrival he consults the oracle of Centipede.

    F. Centipede tells him how to proceed in order to revivify his brother.

    G. He kills a cow near the bed on which the dead Mwindo is resting; Mwindo resuscitates.

    H. Mwindo and his mother return with Little-one-just-born-he-walked to his village.

    I. Mwindo is given land, but then he starts saying again that he is also a chief. Little-one-just-born-he-walked tells Mwindo that he is not a chief.

    J. Later, Mwindo repents on the advice of the headmen; he receives the title of First-born-of-the-land.

XIV. *Mwindo's marriage*

    A. Since Mwindo knows of no place where he can get married,

Little-one-just-born-he-walked secretly goes to Muisa to take a wife.

B. On his return he is greeted by Mwindo and the other headmen and discloses that he has gone to take Muisa's daughter on behalf of Mwindo.

C. There are exchanges of gifts; Muisa's daughter is very happy with Mwindo "who was shining now."

XV. *The birth of Destiny and the death of his father*

A. Soon Mwindo's wife is pregnant; she bears a daughter called Protector-of-the-things-that-will-not-be-understood.

B. The wife of Little-one-just-born-he-walked is still without children; the men of the village ascribe her barrenness to the fact that Little-one-just-born-he-walked married a wife before his senior Mwindo.

C. His wife is therefore taken to Mwindo to be blessed by him.

D. Shortly thereafter, the wife is pregnant.

E. She visits her father Mukiti, and soon afterward she bears a son.

F. When the son is able to walk, he receives from his mother the name Destiny.

G. After many days, Little-one-just-born-he-walked dies.

H. His son Destiny, who is the chief, is cared for by Mwindo.

XVI. *Death, subterranean journey, and return of Mwindo*

A. After a long lapse of time, Mwindo says that he is "near death."

B. He spends his time dancing; he consults Mukiti and Centipede to learn how to act when he dies, but in vain.

C. All the animals come to dance for him and return to the forest.

D. Mwindo faints but recovers.

E. His wife tries to feed him vegetables and goat meat, but he refuses.

F. Mwindo calls on Lightning to cleave his house into two parts; he remains unhurt in the house.

G. Mwindo asks a blacksmith for twenty adzes.

H. He places his regalia on the ground and asks that they be buried with him.

I. Having declared that he is now ready to fight with Nyamurairi, he expires. The people bury him.

J. He arrives in the subterranean world of Nyamurairi's village; Nyarusumba, aide to Nyamurairi, chases him.

K. Mwindo decides not to return to his village; he stays near the wading place.

    L. He decides to return to Nyamurairi to fight with him.

    M. He is met by the spirit of his paternal aunt and on her advice returns to the world.

XVII. *Mwindo usurps the chieftainship*

    A. Mwindo returns to his village; he enters the men's house.

    B. He tells the people that he has lost the fight with Nyamurairi. Furthermore, during his subterranean journey, Little-one-just-born-he-walked has told him that henceforth he is to be the chief instead of Destiny.

    C. Mwindo is enthroned; against the advice of his counselors, he leaves Destiny without land.

    D. Destiny has a dream in which his father's spirit reveals Mwindo's lies.

    E. Soon afterward, Mwindo's child falls sick.

    F. Mwindo consults the oracle of Centipede.

    G. Centipede advises him that the chieftainship must be returned to Destiny.

    H. Mwindo refuses; his child dies.

XVIII. *Mwindo's death and the glory of Chief Destiny*

    A. Mwindo's child arrives in the subterranean world, accusing his father of his death.

    B. Mwindo's child "kills" his father and mother.

    C. Little-one-just-born-he-walked is informed by his counselors of the reason for Mwindo's death.

    D. Destiny is chief again "of all the land as he had been before."

THE MWINDO EPIC IV: TRANSLATION

One chief married six wives. After he had married them he remained with them for many days. Nyabana was the despised wife because she did not bear a child. After Nyabana had become the despised wife, tribute arrived in the houses of the co-wives. She said: "Lo! My husband does no longer fix his heart on me; all the tribute that used to come to my house now goes to other houses. Lo! I am now the wife who is not loved by her husband."[1]

---

1. *One chief*: later called by his teknonymic name, Shemwindo, father of Mwindo. *Nyabana*: the chief's principal wife who is usually kept in high esteem, particularly because she may have been provided by the counselors. Here she has lost her status because of apparent sterility. In the translation I use the term as a personal name because no other name is given here. *tribute*: Nyanga chiefs receive tribute of crops, game meat, and exuviae from their subjects. The principal wife normally plays an important role in the process of sharing the tribute.

One day the chief said to Shebakungu that he no longer wanted Nyabana to stay there with him. Shebakungu, not accepting the chief's (words), said: "Since you were enthroned together with Nyabana, let her stay here." Hearing this (advice), Shebakungu said that a house should be built in a place where the chief would not pass. Nyabana went, and a house was built for her on the garbage heap.[2] As Nyabana now dwelt there, she cultivated a field that was very large; she planted eleusine on it. Her co-wives (wives of the chief) refused to cultivate, saying that they would eat from that food (that was given as) tribute. Nyabana began to clear the field; those who loved her were helping her to clear it. They finished clearing the field. Nyabana waited. The eleusine was growing; and she watched over the field, because they (the people) eat eleusine. When the eleusine was ripe, she cut it, and those who loved her helped her. When the eleusine had been cut, she stored it in two *ntanda*-baskets. She placed them on top of the drying rack in order to dry them (their contents), and the rest she ate. When these two *ntanda*-baskets (their contents) had dried, she winnowed them (their contents). She placed the eleusine in *birearea*-leaves, and she hid the *birearea*-leaves on the drying rack; she covered them with wood. After she had acted in this manner, she dwelt there eating from her eleusine.[3]

Thereupon, hunger came. People ate the roots of banana trees and the fruits of the trees. As they were now tormented by hunger, the chief said: "The players of the *wiki*-game do not die of hunger when they are playing their *wiki*-game. So, you people of this village, let us play the *wiki*-game."[4] His people agreed.

During the night the despised woman dreamed (about) her mother,

---

2. *Shebakungu*: Chief-Counselor, one of the chief's main advisers and interlocutors. *Since you were enthroned*: the ritual of enthronement requires the prior acquisition by the chief of wives of high status, such as the *nyabana* and the *mumbo*. No bridewealth is provided for these women, although substantial donations are made to various officeholders. *the garbage heap*: this expression not to be taken too literally, symbolizes the loss of status. Here the wife is physically removed to a place at the outskirts of the village.

3. Throughout this passage the emphasis is on eleusine growing; thus, the action is transposed to areas of secondary savanna that border the Nyanga rain forest to the north and the east. These savanna regions are inhabited by Hunde and Nande subgroups, as well as by other ethnic units that have close cultural affinities with the forest-dwelling Nyanga.

4. *hunger came*: the theme of hunger and famine occasionally appears in the tales and is also mentioned in epic III, where it is deliberately caused by the rejected hero Little-one-just-born-he-walked. It is difficult to understand how real famine could occur in the abundant rain forest of the Nyanga, unless severe crop damage, as

who was telling her to fetch a stone from the river and a pebble: "You will grind the eleusine on it (the stone), and so there will be flour. This (flour) you will mix into a paste."[5] In the morning the despised wife went to search for a stone and a pebble. She climbed onto the drying rack; she took a small basket of eleusine; she began grinding it. She placed a *munaa*-pot with beans on the hearth. She ground the eleusine! She ground the eleusine! After she had finished grinding a small basketful of eleusine, she put the water (to make paste) on the fire. The paste was ready; she put animal fat in the beans.

When the paste was ready, the despised woman stood up outdoors; looking to the place where they were playing the *wiki*-game, she saw the men falling and falling down from their chairs because of hunger. The despised wife pondered, saying that perhaps the chief might refuse to eat her food. The despised wife called Shebakungu, saying: "Shebakungu, come here." Shebakungu arrived in the house of the despised wife. The despised wife took a little piece of paste and a plate with beans and gave them to Shebakungu. When Shebakungu saw these (foods) he asked: "What is this?" (He asked) because they (the people) were not used to eating paste (made) of eleusine. They boiled eleusine together with beans.[6] Shebakungu tasted the paste and the beans, in which there was animal fat, and they were very tasty. When Shebakungu had finished eating a handful of paste, the despised wife said to him: "Perhaps the chief may refuse to come here if you tell him." Shebakungu said: "Let me first tell him." Shebakungu arrived in the place where they were playing the *wiki*-game; he laughed and laughed because he had gained strength. He said to the chief: "When a chief plays (games) for a long time, then he must first

suggested here, compels people to eat replacement foods. Suggestions of famine in the Nyanga stories may also be linked with reminiscences of their ancestors, who lived in the savanna lands east of Nyanga country. *wiki-game*: a popular game, played according to complex rules, in which men often wagered large amounts of their possessions. The game basically consists in guessing the number of little black seeds held in each hand, but dice throwing is also part of it.

5. *dreamed (about) her mother*: i.e., had a dream in which her mother's spirit appeared to give her advice. Most commonly, it is the spirit of the paternal aunt who appears in dreams as an adviser. *a stone . . . and a pebble*: parts of an essential domestic implement: the flat grinding stone and the flat pebble that is rubbed over it. In fact, every Nyanga woman has two stones near the hearth in her house: one on which she pounds the dried bananas and one on which she grinds them.

6. The woman cooks a pot of beans while she grinds the eleusine; then she prepares a paste from the eleusine. The preparation is presented here as a new recipe.

stand up and go to defecate or urinate." When the chief heard this, he collected the *wiki*-dice; he poured them down saying that they should count them, that he was killing the *wiki*-game.[7] Thereupon he stood up; he said to those who were sitting there that they should remove the *wiki*-game, that he had killed it, that he was now going to urinate. He went with Shebakungu. Shebakungu said to him: "Let us go to the side of the despised wife." The chief said that he would not go to the side of the despised wife, that he would not go to encounter the enemy who was there. Shebakungu said: "Lo! If she has seen you and vexed you, you will nevertheless remain with your chieftainship." The chief said that he who scorns (the words of) the counselor breaks the rules, because he is master of the land.[8]

They went; they arrived at the place of the despised wife. The despised wife placed chairs outside, saying that the chief could not enter the house. The chief sat on the chair together with Shebakungu. The despised wife brought paste and a dish of beans. When the chief saw these (foods), he was astounded; he said: "Where has this woman gotten this food?" Shebakungu pulled off a handful (of paste); he dipped it in the beans; he ate it. When the chief saw this, he cleaned the hands; he began to eat the paste and the beans.[9] When he tasted that it was very sweet, he asked: "Is this vomit?" She said: "No, it is eleusine paste. I have ground eleusine and have made the flour into paste. Lo! Even though you have thrown me

---

7. Shebakungu's cryptic way of speaking to the chief is well known to the Nyanga. There are many ways, both verbal and kinetic, in which to symbolically call one's attention to something, to warn, or to advise.

8. *the enemy*: *enongo* is a rarely used term which strongly emphasizes the chief's resentment of his wife. *master of the land*: the term *mwisa ecuo* has a complex meaning; *cuo* is the political entity, the state; *mwisa* means, depending on the context, inhabitant of, master of, member of, or owner of. The political and ritual authority of the Chief-Counselor, who is referred to here, is considerable. From certain points of view he and his peers make the chief, in that important decisions concerning the ultimate choice of the chief and his ritual wife and the timing of the enthronement rites rest with them. If the ritual wife is childless, the counselors decide whose child shall be "placed against her chest" to become successor to the throne.

9. Despite the abject state in which she finds herself, Nyabana is a woman of high status, as reflected in her commanding tone. *Shebakungu pulled off . . .*: the rules of precedence in eating and of etiquette are strict. The Nyanga chief eats alone, differently from other men who eat together in the men's house; only high officeholders, like Shebakungu, may eat with him. Since the situation is unusual and the chief has expressed skepticism, Shebakungu eats first to allay the fear of sorcery or poisoning. *he cleaned the hands*: a wooden dish filled with fresh water is always available for the men to clean their hands before eating.

away, I cannot give you vomit."[10] The chief ate the paste; he finished it. When he had finished eating it, he cleaned both hands. Together with Shebakungu he went again to the place where they were playing the *wiki*-game. As they arrived there, they were laughing and laughing. Those who were there said: "You are laughing and laughing, for what reason?" They said that they were laughing because of hunger. They began to play again. The sky became dark. The chief went to his wives, and he was full. In the morning they again played the *wiki*-game and continued (to play) it without stopping. In the middle of the day the despised wife stirred paste again and (cooked) beans. Shebakungu said to the chief: "Let us first go to the toilet." Shebakungu took a stick for the chief to wipe himself with because this was the way it was done in olden times: Musao or another man takes (a stick) for the chief to use when he goes to the toilet.[11] Shebakungu went with the chief. They arrived at the house of the despised wife; they ate paste. They left there; they again went back to the place of the *wiki*-game.

This despised wife brought salvation to the chief every day. One day, when all the people had gone into the forest, the chief told the servants to stay at both entrances to the village to guard it. The servants remained at both entrances to the village. The chief went into the house of the despised wife; he slept with her because he no longer referred to her as the despised wife; now she was again a *nyabana*.[12] Having slept with her, he left the house. He again played the *wiki*-game. The chief and Shebakungu continued to eat paste without calling in the others. When one month was finished, the despised wife had grown very thick. Lo! She was now with

---

10. *"Is this vomit?"*: the chief is unfriendly, even hostile, toward his principal wife.

11. *Musao*: title of one of the male ritual experts (*bandirabitambo*) attached to the chief's person. Musao, helped by his wife, often performs normally female duties for the chief. This practice is particularly manifest during the enthronement rites, when Musao prepares the bed on which the chief sleeps with his ritual wife and afterward cleanses him. Human feces, urine, blood, nails, and hair are subject to special taboos, which are even more stringent for chiefs. As revealed here, Musao assumes very special functions in this regard.

12. *now she was again a nyabana*: not to be taken too literally, for the chief's *nyabana*-wife cannot lose her status; she is under the special protection of the chief's counselors. The narrator is implying that at this point normal social relationships were reestablished. Yet there is a seeming contradiction, because Nyabana continues to live alone outside the village until, much later, she is brought back into the village at her son's request. It must be remembered that the bard Sherungu holds the office of Musao and that he is extremely well versed in secret procedures connected with Nyanga chieftainship. The fact that Nyabana lives separately from the main village thus implies that, in the chief's opinion and in that of the counselors, she is being assimilated with the ritual wife.

child. The woman said: "My husband slept with me only one time, and he has produced this pregnancy." They remained like that. The despised wife said to the chief: "You are eating food, but you do not call the servants and the princes!" When all the women had gone into the forest, the despised wife stirred many pastes. When they were ready, Shebakungu and the chief went to her house. The despised wife said to them: "Call the princes and the servants so that they also may eat the food." They called them. They arrived; they ate the pastes and the beans. After they had finished eating, banana beer was brought in from the chief's side. They drank it. The men spent the day in the village; they were bloated. They were calling out loud, saying: "May the chief be saved; because of him people are cheerful again."[13] When the wives returned to the village they said: "Why are the men so cheerful with all this hunger?" The men kept silent.

When the despised wife was close to giving birth, the chief said to her: "Go fetch Nyabakungu to come here, because you might give birth here all by yourself." Thereupon Shebakungu said to his wife: "Go to where the wife of the chief is so that she may give birth without being alone." Nyabakungu arrived there. The despised wife said to her: "Take some little flour that is there and prepare some paste for yourself because the pregnancy begins to hurt now." Nyabakungu said: "I do not know of some little flour because there is no flour." The despised wife took hold of herself; she stirred paste for Nyabakungu. After she had finished eating the paste, Nyabakungu said: "Here there is salvation." They stayed there. In the morning the despised wife gave birth to a boy, (called) Little-one-just-born-he-walked.[14] They heard (the news) that the ritual wife had also given birth.[15] They arrived at the chief's, saying: "Your wife has also

---

13. *My husband slept with me only one time*: underscoring the unusual circumstances surrounding the hero's conception. Unusual circumstances also prevail in epic I when the chief's wives simultaneously become pregnant and in epic III when one of the heroes is conceived by parthenogenesis. *because of him people are cheerful again*: a principal attribute of the chief, also emphasized in other epics, is that he is a Rejoicer-of-people, one who gives things.

14. *Nyabakungu*: title given to the wife of the Chief-Counselor (Shebakungu). Because of the high status of Nyabana, it is not unusual for the wife of the Chief-Counselor to perform the duties of principal midwife. *Little-one-just-born-he-walked*: literal translation of Kabutwakaenda or Kabutwakenda. In epic I this name is the principal epithet for the hero Mwindo, but here it stands for the principal hero who is separate from his half brother Mwindo.

15. *the ritual wife had also given birth*: this ritual wife (*mumbo*) has not been previously mentioned. Since the epic concerns a full-fledged chief, however, it is fully clear to the Nyanga listeners that such a ritual wife exists. The fact that Nyabana and the ritual wife give birth simultaneously is an implicit reference to an extraordinary event.

given birth." The other wives (of the chief), when they heard this, said: "She is not one (a chief's wife). It cannot be said about her: the chief's wife has given birth. (She is) a fool eating excrement! May you not say that the ritual wife has brought forth. She is not (a chief's wife)! It is a fool who is there on the garbage heap."[16] Shebakungu said: "Do not laugh at your companion. Another while and you will become as she now is, and she will be with all the joy!" When the chief heard that the ritual wife had brought forth and that his wife for whom a house had been built on the garbage heap had also brought forth, he gave a cow, saying: "Shebakungu, go to kill this cow in the birth house of my wife. You will eat it there." He gave two goats, saying that they should be killed in the house of the ritual wife. When the goats arrived there, the ritual wife refused them, saying that she did not want them. How could a despised wife be given a cow and she, the ritual wife, be given these two useless goats?[17]

When the rooster crowed, the child of the chief's wife said to its mother: "Let us go to the river because I am Little-one-just-born-he-walked."[18] He preceded his mother (in going). They arrived at a pool. Mukiti came out. He gave this child a zanza in copper and an *utebe*-stool.[19] They returned; they arrived home on the garbage heap; they

---

16. The passage is difficult to translate because the Nyanga have different terms for "wife". When the chief is informed that his wife had given birth, the term *mowe*—a special generic designation for the chief's wives—is used. For the other wives of the chief (*mowe*), it is an insult to identify the rejected Nyabana as a "chief's wife"; they consider her merely as a despised wife (*nyakashombe*) and as a person of no importance (a fool: *mushire*). Ironically, their outrage is more intense because they do not know that the chief's ritual wife (*mumbo*) has also given birth; they think that the despised Nyabana has been designated as ritual wife.

17. By giving a cow to Nyabana and two goats to the ritual wife, the chief suddenly shows a preference for the formerly despised woman. It is really a preference for her son which, though never openly expressed by the chief, guides many of his future decisions. *a cow and . . . these two useless goats*: an opposition suggesting two different worlds in which some Nyanga and the bard Sherungu himself participate. The Nyanga are not pastoralists, but their friendly neighbors, the Hunde, with whom the Nyanga have numerous cultural affinities, possess cattle. Some Nyanga chiefs own cattle which are tended by Hunde herdsmen in Hundeland. The bard Sherungu has numerous personal connections with individuals in Hundeland; he has hunted and lived there. In strict Nyanga custom, the giving of goats is a perfectly normal practice on this occasion.

18. The hero Mwindo in epics I and II and the hero Little-one-just-born-he-walked in epic III are ready for action from the moment of birth, partly because they immediately have the ability to walk and to speak.

19. *Mukiti*: the extraordinary water serpent lives in a deep pool. The special connections between Mukiti and the hero, which lead the hero to make this visit, are not revealed in this epic. In epics I and II Mukiti is the husband of the hero's paternal

closed the door. The child took the zanza; he made it sing *ndiri! ndiri! ndiri!* He sang:

> I shall fight with Mrs. Pointed-Mouth;
> I shall fight with Nyakimarimari
> Who has overcome the Bahunga in shrewdness.[20]

When the people heard this (song), they went to the chief, saying: "You, chief, what is born over there is what is born over there! The child together with its mother are singing a song, and the child is holding the copper zanza and sitting on the *utebe*-stool."[21] The chief remained silent.

In the morning mother and child went again to the pool. Mukiti gave the child a spear and a scepter, saying: "This spear will fight for you."[22] They returned to the village. Little-one-just-born-he-walked and his mother did nothing but sing.

One day Little-one-just-born-he-walked, (child) of Mutobi of Nyantsinde, said that he was going to look for singers, that his mother should not say that he had disappeared.[23] Little-one-just-born-he-walked went; he arrived at the pool; he entered it; he encountered Mukiti. Mukiti

---

aunt. In this epic Mukiti seems to occupy the unstated position of a maternal uncle because he is apparently unable to refuse anything the hero asks, suggesting the ideal relationship the Nyanga perceive between a maternal uncle and his sororal nephew. *a zanza in copper: kantsambi* is the name of a musical instrument consisting of tongues in reed (Pygmies) or iron (Nyanga) which are placed on and resonated by a gourd. Since the Nyanga have no such instrument in copper, the extraordinary character of the gift is here emphasized. In this instance and later, when the hero acquires spears for his Pygmies, there seems to be a remote reference to acquisition of the knowledge of metal. The same knowledge is suggested in epic II when the hero's sister acquires from her husband Lightning certain knives to kill Big-Bird. *utebe-stool*: a low wooden stool made from a solid block of wood. Its slightly hollowed, spherical seat and its base are connected by a massive supporting pole. The *utebe*-stool, linked with political power and authority, may be possessed only by chiefs and "men of weight." The acquisition of the zanza and the stool establishes the hero as a great singer and as an important man.

20. This recurring song, which is the identification chant of Little-one-just-born-he-walked, has magical meaning. Indirectly, it alludes to the outspoken mother of his half brother Mwindo and to Mwindo himself, who is deceitful and rash with words.

21. *what is born over there is what is born over there*: an extension of the formula, "what is there is what is there," frequently used to express astonishment about an extraordinary event.

22. *a spear and a scepter*: the spear (*itumo*) is not part of the regalia; it is replaced by an iron staff (*nkoma*). The word used for scepter (*conga*) is the term identifying Mwindo's incredible magical object in epics I and II. The scepter does not play a special role in this epic, although at one point Little-one-just-born-he-walked threatens to kill Mwindo's mother with it.

23. *Mutobi of Nyantsinde*: possibly the name and the patronym of the hero's father, who up to this point is simply called "chief."

asked him, saying: "What are you coming to fetch here?"[24] Little-one just-born-he-walked said that he was coming to fetch singers. Mukiti said: "Go! When you arrive at the bank of the pool, be seated on top of a tree. Sing, and singers will meet you there." Little-one-just-born-he-walked came out of the pool; he was on the bank of the pool; he sat down in a tree; he played the zanza; he sang:

> I, Little-one-just-born-he-walked,
> (Child) of Mutobi of Nyantsinde,
> I shall fight with Mrs. Pointed-Mouth,
> Nyakimarimari,
> Who has overcome the Bahunga in shrewdness.
> I am calling for singers;
> I am calling the Pygmies in the forest, *rere!*

After he had sung twice, the Pygmies appeared. They asked: "Who has taught you to sing in this manner?" He said that no one had taught him, that he was born with his zanza and spear and scepter, that he was Little-one-just-born-he-walked.[25]

Where his (the child's) mother had remained in the village, the chief arrived there; he asked the mother, saying: "Where did the child go?" The mother said: "You ask about the child, but he is Little-one-just-born-he-walked, (child) of Mutobi of Nyantsinde. He is not here; he went to look for singers." The chief left; he went home. When the ritual wife saw this, she said that she was going to burn the house of the mother of Little-one-just-born-he-walked, because she was again being esteemed by the chief. As the ritual wife planned to go to the mother of Little-one-just-born-he-walked, saying that she would burn her house, Shebakungu forbade her. The ritual wife returned home.[26]

Little-one-just-born-he-walked said to the Pygmies: "As we are going, you will respond when I sing." Little-one-just-born-he-walked went singing and playing the zanza, saying:

> I shall fight with Mrs. Pointed-Mouth,
> Nyakimarimari,
> Who has overcome the Bahunga in shrewdness.
> I am with the Pygmies of the forest.

---

24. *he entered it*: the hero has many connections with water. In epic I he travels in a drum in the water to find his paternal aunt. In a heroic tale Mwindo travels in the water like a giant crab, luring his sister away from her husband.

25. The Pygmies are presented here as also in epic III, as singers par excellence, not merely as great hunters. For the Nyanga, the Pygmies are indeed great singers and dancers. Whenever I saw the Baremba Pygmies perform in the villages of Maniema and Mutongo, the atmosphere of festivity reached a peak. On each occasion the Pygmies were given large quantities of banana beer as an expression of appreciation.

26. The authority of the Chief-Counselor is emphasized in this epic.

They arrived in the village. The mother of Little-one-just-born-he-walked danced, and the Pygmies responded to her son as he was singing. His mother gave him the news that the ritual wife had intended to burn her house, (but) Shebakungu had forbidden her. Little-one-just-born-he-walked said: "If she had burned you with the house, then I would have killed her with my scepter."

They went to take the news to the chief, saying that Little-one-just-born-he-walked had arrived with the Pygmies, that they produced wonderful things from their mouths while singing. When the chief heard this (news), he took three goats; he gave them to Little-one-just-born-he-walked, saying that he should give them to the Pygmies.[27] Thereupon Little-one-just-born-he-walked said to his father: "Lo! Will my mother always remain on the garbage heap?" The chief said: "No! Let them go and build her a house in the very middle of the village place." They built a house. It was finished in one day; it was surrounded by a fence. The mother of Little-one-just-born-he-walked entered this house. When the ritual wife saw this, she called the chief and Shebakungu. They arrived; she asked them: "Lo! Were two chiefs born here?" Shebakungu said that a chief is not brought forth, that he to whom he likes to give it (the chieftainship) is chief designate. The ritual wife kept silence; she did not speak another word. That was all.[28]

Little-one-just-born-he-walked said that he was going to Bat, forger of large spears. Little-one-just-born-he-walked went to Bat. Arriving there,

---

27. The text implies that the chief has no Pygmies. Little-one-just-born-he-walked is depicted as a culture hero who brings new culture elements (symbolically represented as a copper zanza, a stool, a spear, a scepter, and Pygmies) to the Nyanga. The chief gives the Pygmies the kind of welcome gifts usually presented to people who pay political allegiance.

28. *a chief is not brought forth*: a highly succinct and overly simplified statement of a fundamental principle of Nyanga chieftainship. Very secret procedures, in which the Chief-Counselor plays a significant role, surround the birth and the selection of the candidate for chieftainship. The stated principle is that the future chief must be a son of the ritual wife and that he must be born with the sacred grains in his hand. The latter requirement immediately suggests a number of options, particularly when the ritual wife has no son (a child selected from among the children of other women, including her female servants, is then "placed against her chest") or when there is strong competition between dissident factions of counselors (in this instance, the chief may have two ritual wives or the son of a *nyabana* may be selected, as in this epic). The entire selection process is shrouded in mystery in order to enhance the concept of uniqueness of the chief. *chief designate*: in various places the text differentiates between the terms *mubake* and *mwami*. Both are sometimes used as synonymous with "chief," but they really mark a difference in status. *Mubake* is the candidate for chieftainship who is born of the ritual wife with the sacred grains in his hand and who is recognized as such by the counselors. *Mwami* is a full-fledged chief who has completed the enthronement ritual. In all four epics the introductory sentence uses the term *mwami* to emphasize the fact that the hero's father is a full-fledged chief.

he told Bat to forge for him twelve spears. Bat forged for him twelve spears. When the twelve spears had been forged, Little-one-just-born-he-walked returned with them to the village, singing:

> I shall fight with Mrs. Pointed-Mouth,
> Nyakimarimari,
> Who has overcome the Bahunga in shrewdness.

He arrived in the village; he placed the spears in the house. He said to the Pygmies to weave nets; the Pygmies wove nets. The nets were finished. When they were completely finished, Little-one-just-born-he-walked asked the Pygmies to go and hunt. They went with the nets into the forest.[29] Arriving there, they set up the nets. Having set them up, the Pygmies said: "If it is (true) that Little-one-just-born-he-walked was brought forth by the woman who is not loved by her husband, then let the wild pigs throw themselves into the nets." The Pygmies made a battue.[30] All the wild pigs threw themselves into the nets; they (the Pygmies) hurled spears at them, because they now had the spears that had come from Bat. The whole herd of wild pigs died, but one wild pig escaped. Little-one-just-born-he-walked said: "Let us return with the animals to the village." They returned with the animals. Arriving in the village, Little-one-just-born-he-walked said that the animals should go to the house where his kinsman was, the child of the ritual wife: "Even though the ritual wife hates my mother, I am not with it (hatred)."[31] When the animals arrived at the house of the ritual wife, her son came out and heard that the animals came from Little-one-just-born-he-walked. Hearing this, Mwindo said: "Return his animals! We

---

29. *Bat*: the large *munkonde*-bat appearing as a blacksmith in the other epics. Usually, Bat is also presented as the hero's maternal uncle. *to weave nets*: large hunting nets used by the Pygmies, the Nyanga, and many other forest-dwelling ethnic groups are *makira*. The Pygmies in Nyangaland are masters of hunting with nets. —

30. There are many prescriptions about hunting with nets. For example, the hunters must have the right mental attitude. Many formulas—invocations, imprecations, wishes—are spoken to make the nets strong and the hunting successful. *a battue*: the term *bihimbo* emphasizes the noises made (by beating the undergrowth with sticks and by shouting) to flush out and drive the game toward the nets.

31. The half brother of Little-one-just-born-he-walked, whose birth was briefly mentioned in an earlier passage, is suddenly brought into the action. The epic does not suggest that this half brother was born with any special capabilities, such as premature adulthood. There are time lapses in the epic, but they do not deter the course of events. Little-one-just-born-he-walked exhibits the characteristics of a great leader: he does not act callously; he is generous in words and deeds; and he respects the seniority principle (for his brother is automatically his senior as child of the ritual wife).

do not want the animals from the child of a despised wife." The animals returned again to Little-one-just-born-he-walked. Little-one-just-born-he-walked said: "It is all right. Lo! Mwindo is also with the hatred of his mother."[32]

Mwindo left his place; he said to his father: "You, my father, give me bridewealth that I may go to marry the daughter of Mukiti."[33] Little-one-just-born-he-walked heard through rumors that Mwindo was going to marry the daughter of Mukiti, that his father had given him goats and cattle to marry.[34] Little-one-just-born-he-walked told Mwamitwa and one of his servants to accompany him. They went at night. They arrived at the cave in the pool.[35] Little-one-just-born-he-walked fingered the zanza, saying:

> Little-one-just-born-he-walked is here.
> I shall fight with Nyakimarimari,
> Mrs. Sharp-Mouth,
> Who overcomes the Bahunga in shrewdness.
> My father Mukiti, open up for me.

When Mukiti heard this (song) in the river, he came out. Little-one-just-born-he-walked said to him that Mwindo would come tomorrow to give him bridewealth (consisting) of goats and cattle, but that he had chosen long ago Mukiti's daughter for himself. Mukiti said: "I cannot give Mwindo my daughter. If Mwindo arrives here, the entire river will overflow. He will not find a place to pass; you will not see him anymore. You, Little-one-just-born-he-walked, return to the village; you will marry my

---

32. *Mwindo*: first mention of the name of the son of the ritual wife. Mwindo shows signs of impetuosity, rashness, and thoughtlessness which are not indicative of true leadership and seniority.

33. It is unusual for a youth like Mwindo to take the initiative in marriage affairs; furthermore, the text does not identify the special bond he has with Mukiti which allows him to claim Mukiti's daughter. Such bonds, of course, do not have to be explained to the Nyanga public. They are suggested in numerous stories, and the general epic atmosphere reveals that the major personages are in constant interaction with divinities, personified animals, and extraordinary beings such as Mukiti. *bridewealth*: the general term *behe* (goods, valuables) is used.

34. *cattle*: not commonly part of the bridewealth, which consists mainly of goats, *butea*-raffia rings, and iron tools.

35. *Mwamitwa*: title of one of the chief's ritual experts who plays a major role in the enthronement rituals. Elsewhere I have translated the term literally as Chief-Pygmy, but in this passage it signifies the senior elder among the Pygmies whom the hero had obtained through Mukiti's help. *at the cave*: Mukiti dwells in a cave in a pool.

daughter because you are the one who will bring her salvation."[36] Little-one-just-born-he-walked returned during the night. He arrived in the village; he went to sleep.

Sky became daylight, and Mwindo was still asleep. The sun came out, and Mwindo said to his servants: "Let us go to Mukiti." They went with the goats and the cattle. They arrived at the cave; they beat the drum; they called Mukiti. Thereupon the river overflowed. They called Mukiti, saying: "Mwindo arrives to marry your daughter, and we bring you offerings." Mukiti remained silent. When Mwindo and his people were exhausted, they said: "Let us return to the village." Mwindo returned with his servants and the goats and the cattle. They arrived in the village. His father said to him: "Mwindo, you do not arrive here with the daughter of Mukiti!" Mwindo said that Mukiti had refused (to give) his daughter. When his father heard this, he said: "You, my children, the one who will marry the child of Mukiti will be chief."[37]

Little-one-just-born-he-walked also asked for cattle and goats, saying that he also wanted to go to Mukiti. His father gave them to him. Little-one-just-born-he-walked went with his Pygmies and his servants together with the bridewealth. As they arrived at the cave, Little-one-just-born-he-walked planted his spear in the ground; he played the zanza, saying:

> I shall fight with Nyakimarimari,
> Mrs. Pointed-Mouth,
> Who has overcome the Bahunga in shrewdness.
> Mukiti, open up for me;
> I am here with the bridewealth.

Hearing this, Mukiti came out. He gave the news to Little-one-just-born-he-walked that Mwindo had arrived there the day before, that he was exhausted from beating his drum thinking that he (Mukiti) would emerge: "I have filled the river for him. Having seen this, he returned with

---

36. The otherwise diligent and respectful Little-one-just-born-he-walked offends the rules of seniority in this instance, for normally the senior brother, Mwindo, would marry before his junior. The offense has mystical consequences. As explained later in the text, the wife of Little-one-just-born-he-walked remains childless because her husband had disobeyed the rules of seniority. *you . . . will bring her salvation*: Mukiti's reasons for preferring Little-one-just-born-he-walked are unstated, but implied, in this passage. Like the chief, Mukiti knows in advance that the hero is destined to be chief, and so is his son (Mukiti's grandchild).

37. *Mwindo was still asleep*: in contrast with the alert and astute Little-one-just-born-he-walked, Mwindo is humorously depicted as sluggish and scatterbrained. *the one who will marry the child of Mukiti will be chief*: the father's prediction, cryptically presented as a competition in which the stakes are the acquisition of a wife, will later be realized.

the cattle. You, Little-one-just-born-he-walked, I have said that you will marry my daughter; bring the bridewealth here." The cattle and the goats: Mukiti carried them all off! Thereafter, Mukiti brought his daughter out. When the servants and the Pygmies saw her, they said: "She is plain ivory!" Little-one-just-born-he-walked said: "Let me die, right here, on account of this woman." And the girl said that there was no one else whom she would marry, only Little-one-just-born-he-walked![38]

After they had spoken in this manner, Little-one-just-born-he-walked returned with his Pygmies and his servants. They arrived in the village. The father of Little-one-just-born-he-walked called the people who had gone with Little-one-just-born-he-walked, and they said that Mukiti had agreed upon the bridewealth of Little-one-just-born-he-walked and that his daughter loved Little-one-just-born-he-walked. After the chief had heard these things, he said that the next day he would say the words he wanted to, (the words he had) in his heart. When Mwindo heard this, he said: "If I do not fight with Mukiti and Little-one-just-born-he-walked, then there is no salvation for me. What! The child of a despised wife is to marry the daughter of Mukiti! I shall go to fetch all the animals; they shall fight together with me."

In the morning the chief called both his sons and the ritual experts; all of them arrived. The chief said: "You, Little-one-just-born-he-walked, you are the master of the Biomfu and Ihuri mountains; and you, Mwindo, remain here on the mountain Wingi; you are the master of this place. I shall spend a month here, and then I shall go and spend a month there in the place of Little-one-just-born-he-walked."[39] When Little-one-just-born-he-walked heard this, he said to the Pygmies and his servants: "Let us go; we shall build, and the necessities for building are already in the village place."[40] All moved out; they built houses there.

After they had finished building houses, Little-one-just-born-he-walked said: "Go to set up the hunting nets. Whatever kinds of animals you

---

38. *She is plain ivory*: a rarely used symbol for beauty among the Nyanga, where ivory is part of the tribute given to chiefs. *Let me die*: the hero expresses his deep emotion at the sight of the woman.

39. It is customary for a chief to place specific tracts of land under the control of the chief designate and of some of his other, status-holding sons. It is not customary for the ruling chief to reside alternately in two different places. The allocation of Biomfu and Ihuri mountains to Little-one-just-born-he-walked has a symbolic meaning. The two terms refer, respectively, to places with a rich ground cover of bark and with many oil-producing trees, thus expressing the idea of abundance.

40. *and the necessities for building are already in the village place*: there will be no problem in bringing together all the materials necessary for building; they will be ready when Little-one-just-born-he-walked and his people arrive in their new place.

see, bring them because Mwindo has referred to them as if they were his braves. But if you see snakes, do not beat them because they are my braves."[41] The Pygmies went to set up the nets, saying: "Doubtless, Little-one-just-born-he-walked will become chief. Let each animal of the forest throw itself into the nets." They made a battue. Each animal that dwelt in the forest threw itself into the nets, and the Pygmies hurled and hurled spears at them. They finished killing the animals; they arrived with the animals at the place of Little-one-just-born-he-walked.

When Little-one-just-born-he-walked saw this, he took the pouch with the fire drill; he handed it to Mwamitwa, saying: "Give the news to my father that Little-one-just-born-he-walked is calling him." Mwamitwa went; he arrived at the chief's, saying: "Little-one-just-born-he-walked says to come to his place." When the chief heard this, he said to his servants and to Shebakungu: "Let us go to Little-one-just-born-he-walked." They went. As they arrived there, the animals were piled up with banana pastes! They began to eat the pastes and the animals; and the women who had gone into the forest arrived there and ate from the banana pastes and the animals. The men joined in one murmur, saying: "This Little-one-just-born-he-walked will become chief even though Mwindo is saying that he is going to fight with him. This Mwindo will be incapable against him. Your companion, the one who was born and who was walking, is not a weak person."[42]

When the chief had finished eating the banana pastes, he returned home. After he had returned home, his son Mwindo asked him, saying: "Who is the (true) son of the chief between both of us, I or Little-one-just-born-he-walked?" The chief said: "You are chief designate." Mwindo said: "No, my father, you are calling me in the same manner as a child that was born on the path (leading) to the toilets." The chief said: "However, he who will surpass his companion in intelligence, he is the one who will become chief."[43]

---

41. In an earlier passage Mwindo said that he would call all the animals to fight for him against Little-one-just-born-he-walked. By catching all the animals, the Pygmies eliminate this source of support for Mwindo. *if you see snakes, do not beat them*: throughout most of the epic there is a special relationship between Little-one-just-born-he-walked and Mukiti, the water serpent, who is the chief of the water and of the other snakes.

42. *Your companion*: the term *mine* has many shades of meaning, such as companion, peer, age-mate, and possibly, in this context, antagonist or adversary.

43. Mwindo continues to manifest jealousy and impatience. The father gives a subtle answer to Mwindo who thinks that he is necessarily more eligible than his brother to become chief. The father says that Mwindo, as the son of the ritual wife, is a possible successor (chief designate, *mubake*, in a position to succeed as chief), but that the full-fledged, enthroned chief (*mwami*) will be the more intelligent (*mine wenge*) of the two.

After the father of Little-one-just-born-he-walked had left Little-one-just-born-he-walked, Little-one-just-born-he-walked sang:

> I shall fight with Mrs. Pointed-Mouth,
> Nyakimarimari,
> Who has overcome the Bahunga in shrewdness.
> Bee, son of Needle,
> Fight for me
> That you may eat from the banana paste
> That my mother will cook.[44]

Hearing this song, Bee told the Pygmies to go and look where her children were. The Pygmies climbed up the tree; they began to remove the honey. They removed the honey; it filled two jars. They brought the honey to Little-one-just-born-he-walked. Little-one-just-born-he-walked said: "Let one jar go into my house, and let one jar go to Mukiti." Little-one-just-born-he-walked began to play the zanza and to sing:

> My mother-in-law is eating.
> I shall fight with Nyakimarimari,
> Mrs. Pointed-Mouth,
> Who has overcome the Bahunga in shrewdness.

The Pygmies were responding, and Sparrow was dancing because he was his dancer. Little-one-just-born-he-walked and the Pygmies went to Mukiti with the honey. When they arrived at the cave, he called Mukiti, saying: "Mukiti, open up for me." Mukiti emerged with his daughter and with Big-Crab, Mukiti's daughter's servant. Little-one-just-born-he-walked gave Mukiti the jar of honey. Mukiti said: "Go now with your wife." Little-one-just-born-he-walked said: "Not yet. Mwindo insults us, saying that he will fight with me and that afterward he will fight with you." Mukiti shook his bristles. Little-one-just-born-he-walked hurled his spear into the river. Some of the water went downstream and the other went upstream.[45] Mukiti said that Little-one-just-born-he-walked should not be

---

44. *Bee, son of Needle*: Ntsuki musiki waMunindi or Ntsuki waMunindi, honorific and patronymic title used to designate the personified bee. The Nyanga have several terms for Bee, and sometimes designate her simply as Needle (i.e., sting). *Fight for me*: the hero is making an advance appeal for help in the upcoming struggle against Mwindo. *That you may eat*: for the battle against Mwindo, the hero secures the help of Wasp, Bee, Fly, and Ant by promising them food that will be cooked by his mother.

45. *Sparrow . . . was his dancer*: Sparrow (Kantori) seems to be included among the Pygmies. In epic I Sparrow and Hawk show Mwindo the place to which his father had fled. In epic III Sparrow is called "child of Dancer." In Nyanga tales Sparrow appears as a symbol of elegance and cleanliness. *Big-Crab* (Ikukuhi): as in epic I, the servant of Mukiti. *hurled his spear*: the hero is momentarily seized with panic, thinking that Mwindo is already there for battle. *Some of the water went downstream*: suggesting the power of the spear thrust.

afraid, that he would give him braves who would fight with Mwindo, that Mwindo was incapable (against him). Little-one-just-born-he-walked and the Pygmies returned home.

When they arrived home, he gave his father a calabash of honey. Their father told them, saying: "You, my children, look for maidens." Little-one-just-born-he-walked said that he had a maiden, the daughter of Mukiti. He said: "Now, you Mwindo, where is your maiden?" Mwindo said that he had no maiden. His father said: "You, my child, shall it be that I die without your being married?" Mwindo pondered, saying that he would first return to Mukiti.

Mwindo and his servants arrived at the cave; they beat the drum. Mukiti heard the drums. He said that it was not Little-one-just-born-he-walked, the one who was there; for he would have heard his song. Mukiti said: "Now, you Mwindo, where is your maiden?" Mwindo said that he the cave. He saw Mwindo. He went back into the cave; he gave Mukiti the news that Mwindo was there. When Mukiti heard this, he filled the river. When Mwindo saw this, he beat the river with his iron staff, saying: "You, river, break into two parts." River seized the staff; the staff arrived at Mukiti's. When Mukiti saw the staff, he said that it was the staff of the Fool, the one who always says that he will fight with Little-one-just-born-he-walked. Mwindo and his people returned to the village.[46]

Mwindo's father asked him, saying: "What did Mukiti give you as answer? Mwindo said: "He did not give me an answer at all." In the early morning Mwindo took leave of his father, saying that he was going to look for a maiden. Mwindo went with one Pygmy. They went; they arrived at the place of Muisa of Bibandi.[47] Muisa said: "Eh! Mwindo, what do you come to fetch?" Mwindo said: "I come to ask you for a maiden to marry." Muisa showed him all his girls, saying: "Now, Mwindo, look at all my girls." After Mwindo had seen them, he said to the Pygmy: "Let us return

---

46. *iron staff*: in this passage the narrator uses both the Hunde term *bubasi* and the Nyanga term *nkoma* to designate one of the insignia of chieftainship possessed by Mwindo. *River seized the staff*: River and Pool are alternate praise names for Mukiti.

47. *Muisa of Bibandi*: Muisa, one of the principal divinities living in the subterranean world, is servant to Nyamurairi, but his attributes are so similar to those ascribed to Nyamurairi that the two are easily confused. Bibandi occurs as the name of a primordial ancestor among some Nyanga groups. The Barenga Pygmies considered Bibandi to be the great chief in the remote past who was the father of all Pygmies. In this text, however, there is no explicit indication that Mwindo travels to the subterranean world to meet Muisa.

home." They arrived in the village. He gave his father the news that Muisa had shown him his maidens and that therefore he was now looking for bridewealth. His father said that there was no lack of valuables.

When Little-one-just-born-he-walked heard this, he also went with his Pygmies to Muisa. As Little-one-just-born he-walked arrived at Muisa's, he played his zanza, saying:

> Muisa of Bibandi,
> I shall fight with Mrs. Pointed-Mouth,
> Who has outdone the Bahunga in shrewdness.

Little-one-just-born-he-walked arrived at Muisa's, saying that he arrived there in the hope that he (Muisa) might give him a woman to marry. When Muisa heard this, he called all the girls, saying: "Stand in a row there." When the maidens heard this, they came, all of them, to see Little-one-just-born-he-walked. They said: "What a young man! There is nobody who surpasses him." As he passed, they said: "I shall be married to this one; I shall not be married to anybody else." When Little-one-just-born-he-walked saw that the maidens liked him, he returned to the village. In returning to the village, (he found) his father Shemwindo sick. As he was sick, he (Shemwindo) called the counselors, the princes, and the followers saying that he was going to die without leaving a chief, that the child who would be loved (by the people) would become chief. On the second day (of his sickness), Shemwindo died.[48]

After Shemwindo died, they lived (like that). Little-one-just-born-he-walked said to the Pygmies to go and set up the hunting nets. The Pygmies went to set up the hunting nets; they killed a large number of animals. Since (many) animals had died, Little-one-just-born-he-walked called the princes and the counselors and the followers. All (of them) had arrived there. Little-one-just-born-he-walked distributed the animals among them. They were very satisfied, saying: "You are the chief, surely! Your father has said that he who is loved (by his people) will become chief. He did not deny that you would be chief, (but) he refused to give you the

---

48. The sudden sickness of Shemwindo, father of both Little-one-just-born-he-walked and Mwindo, immediately follows the visit of his sons to Muisa. Since Muisa is a bringer-of-death, the sickness and death of the father may be construed as a form of punishment inflicted by Muisa because of the illicit visits to the subterranean world by his sons. *that the child who would be loved*: the powerful oral will (*irai*) of the dying chief. The Nyanga text literally states that "this child which will be *murongu* will also be full-fledged chief." *Murongu* is a special honorific term which qualifies the chief as the beloved-one.

permission, fearing that you might kill each other."[49] All the people remained, having placed their hearts with Little-one-just-born-he-walked, saying that he would be chief.

As Little-one-just-born-he-walked remained like that, he said to the Chief-Counselor that he wanted to go and fetch a wife. The Chief-Counselor agreed. Little-one-just-born-he-walked tied up two goats and one cow. He said to his Pygmies: "Let us go to Mukiti." As they arrived at the cave, Little-one-just-born-he-walked sang as he was accustomed to sing for Mukiti. When Mukiti heard this (singing), he emerged. Little-one-just-born-he-walked said that he had come to fetch a wife with these two goats and one cow. Mukiti said: "Stay here. I am going to fetch your wife." Mukiti cleaved the river into two parts; it was dry in the middle. He said to Little-one-just-born-he-walked to stay there, that he was going to dress his wife. Mukiti arrived at his place; he dressed his daughter. When he had finished dressing her, he took her to Little-one-just-born-he-walked. Little-one-just-born-he-walked returned (home) with his wife.[50] He arrived home. He took a cow; he gave it to the ritual experts. All ate from it. He took another cow, saying that it should be killed in the house of his wife. The drums resounded. Two days passed, and the drums were still speaking.[51]

When Mwindo heard the way in which the drums were resounding, he asked (his people): "Why do the drums speak over there, in the place of Little-one-just-born-he-walked?" They said that Little-one-just-born-he-walked had just married a maiden who was like a drop of rain, the daughter of Mukiti. When Mwindo heard this, he said: "Lo! This man will surely become chief, because my father has said that the one to marry first will be chief."[52] Mwindo went again to Muisa. When he arrived there, all

---

49. Little-one-just-born-he-walked continues to excel in generosity; he proves himself as *shebehe,* a father and dispenser of goods, and as *mubanyie iyana,* a distributor of hundreds (of things). Therefore he is, in the opinion of the people, the real chief. *he refused to give you the permission*: i.e., he did not want you to be proclaimed as the sole chief or to be enthroned.

50. The context indicates that, in the hero's conception, Mukiti's daughter is to be his ritual wife.

51. *the ritual experts*: with minor regional differences and adaptations, there are seven *bandirabitambo* who play an essential role in enthronement rites. The bard Sherungu occupies the position of *musao.* As a member of the college of ritual experts, he likes to stress their importance.

52. There is ambiguity in Mwindo's words. The father never said that "the one to marry first will be chief," but rather that he who would marry Mukiti's daughter would become chief. Engrossed in his own thoughts and his own course of action, Mwindo is still saying that he himself will become chief, because from his point of view custom prescribes that the senior be married before the junior.

the maidens refused Mwindo. Mwindo returned (home). They (the people) asked the person who had gone with Mwindo: "What is the news where you have gone?" The servant gave them the news that the maidens had refused Mwindo.

Mwindo continued to meditate about his fight with Little-one-just-born-he-walked and Mukiti. Mwindo returned to Muisa. When he arrived there he said: "You, Muisa, give me objects with which to fight." Muisa took a copper bracelet. He put it on Mwindo's (arm), saying: "Go to fight with Little-one-just-born-he-walked. I will make you fight, even though my daughters refuse you."[53]

Mwindo returned home. When he arrived home, he said to his people: "Today I am going to attack Little-one-just-born-he-walked! This very day!" They sounded the drums. A man came to give Little-one-just-born-he-walked the news that Mwindo was coming to attack him. Little-one-just-born-he-walked placed a song on it (the zanza) to call the braves:

> Mrs. Pointed-Mouth defeats the Bahunga with
>   shrewdness.
> Wasp, our kinsman, you will fight for me.
> Bee, son of Needle,
> You will fight for me.
> You, Ant, you will fight for me
> That you may eat from the banana paste
> Which my mother is stirring,
> You Digger.
> You, Hawk, son of Nyeshumya,
> You will fight for me.
> You, Spider, son of Cobweb,
> You make a bridge.
> Hangi-of-Drum!
> I call the Pygmies in the forest.[54]

Little-one-just-born-he-walked arrived at Mukiti's place. He called, singing:

> Mukiti, son of Pool,
> I shall fight with Mwindo.

---

53. Muisa, who is the bringer-of-death, is also depicted here as one who is intent on battle. *a copper bracelet*: usually a symbol of headmanship and a cult emblem, here it is intended to be a talisman that protects in war. This talisman, however, becomes useless. There is a tendency to depict Mwindo as a fool (*mushire*, as he is qualified by Mukiti), i.e., as one who is easily deceived because of his thoughtlessness and rashness.

54. This song is sung in the Hunde language, interspersed with some Nyanga words. The hero addresses Wasp, Bee, Ant, Hawk, and Spider with choice praise names and patronyms in order to secure their help.

Mukiti appeared. He said: "Mwindo will attack me today." Mukiti said: "Go! I will fight for you. Go to fight!"

Little-one-just-born-he-walked arrived at his mother's place. He said that he was going to fight with Mwindo. His mother said: "You will fight with Mwindo who has provoked you." The mother of Little-one-just-born-he-walked went to consult the oracle of Centipede. Centipede said: "Let Little-one-just-born-he-walked make an offering of a necklace and a bag for Kahombo."[55] His mother arrived; she said to her son: "You will fight with Mwindo, after you have made an offering of a necklace and a bag for Kahombo. You will wear the necklace on the chest." When Little-one-just-born-he-walked heard this, he went to Mukiti's place. He sang; Mukiti emerged. Little-one-just-born-he-walked said to him that he must make an offering of a necklace and a bag for Kahombo; Mukiti provided him with a necklace and a bag for Kahombo. Little-one-just-born-he-walked arrived home; he made an offering for a necklace and a bag for Kahombo. After he had made the offering, he wore the necklace on his chest.[56]

Thereupon Mwindo and his people climbed up; they went to attack Little-one-just-born-he-walked. When the people of Little-one-just-born-he-walked saw this, they told Little-one-just-born-he-walked that Mwindo was coming. Little-one-just-born-he-walked said: "And you, take up the arms! Let us go to meet him on the road!" And they took up the arms. They went; they met him in the middle of the road. The mother of Little-one-just-born-he-walked appeared, and the mother of Mwindo appeared. The mother of Mwindo said: "Little-one-just-born-he-walked, why do you compare yourself with Mwindo, whereas you are but the child of the despised wife? You were born on the trail (that leads) to the toilets. But your companion Mwindo is the child of a ritual wife. You are but a mushroom to be plucked." The mother of Little-one-just-born-he-walked also spoke, saying: "Even though you say that Little-one-just-born-he-walked was born on the toilet, it is true that Shemwindo has given me my pregnancy. May Little-one-just-born-he-walked be victorious in the war!"[57]

---

55. *Centipede*: *kiringeshe*, once again the supreme diviner. *Kahombo*: female divinity of good fortune. Nyanga men offer a necklace and a bag to her and build a large, oval-shaped shrine house in which they regularly spend the night alone.

56. Mukiti is once again placed in the role of a maternal uncle as a provider of the things the hero needs.

57. The sudden appearance of the two mothers at the scene of battle is interesting. Mwindo's mother continues to utter invectives, while the mother of Little-one-just-born-he-walked is shown as poised and dignified. The bard implicitly recalls the hatred of Mwindo's mother to show how deeply it affects her son. The proverbs stress the fact that tensions between half brothers often result directly from competition between their mothers.

After she had finished speaking, they (the half brothers) began to fight. As they were fighting, a huge rain poured down. The wasps fell down; they were continually stinging Mwindo's people. And the bees were now fighting for Little-one-just-born-he-walked because Little-one-just-born-he walked had called them, saying that those who would fight for him would surely eat from the banana paste that his mother would stir. Black Ant also scratched the soil; and Fly also flew around, buzzing and saying *busa! busa!* Then they (the people) saw that all the people of Mwindo had been exterminated; Mwindo was the only one to remain there. He went home with his mother; Mwindo and his mother remained there in an abandoned village.[58]

When a month had passed since they were in the abandoned village, Mwindo became sick. When he was close to dying, he told his mother to go to the place of Little-one-just-born-he-walked to tell him that he (Mwindo) was ailing. His mother said: "No!" Mwindo put a song in it (the mouth):

> Shemwindo did not bring forth a brave-one;
> I am dying.
> Shemwindo did not bring forth a brave-one.

When his mother heard the song, she said to Mwindo: "You, child, in what manner do you sing?" He said he was singing that Shemwindo had not left a brave-one, because his father used to say that he was the child of a ritual wife, that he would be chief, and lo! he had fooled him; it was another one of his children who would be chief. In the evening Mwindo was still singing:

> Shemwindo did not bring forth a brave-one;
> I am dying.
> Shemwindo did not bring forth a brave-one.

In the early morning Mwindo expired. When his mother saw this, she failed (to know) what to do. Then and there she left (the village). She went to the place of Little-one-just-born-he-walked.

When Little-one-just-born-he-walked saw her, he said: "Where are you going?" Mwindo's mother said: "Mwindo is dead." Little-one-just-born-he-walked said: "Let him be dead over there!" Thereafter Little-one-just-born-he-walked asked: "You, his mother, why did you not bring us the message that Mwindo was ailing?" Little-one-just-born-he-walked

---

58. *a huge rain poured down*: the cosmic impact of the hero is emphasized. In epic I it rained for seven days when the hero was thrown into the river in a drum. The actual role of the two antogonists in the battle is not described.

called the Chief-Counselor and the Chief-Pygmy, saying: "Let us go to the place where Mwindo has died." They went. They arrived in the place where Mwindo had died; Little-one-just-born-he-walked saw that Mwindo was cold.[59] Little-one-just-born-he-walked went to Centipede's place. He said: "You, Centipede, Mwindo is dead; I want to revivify him." Centipede said: "Look there!" Little-one-just-born-he-walked spit some phlegm. Centipede ate it. Then Centipede pronounced the oracle: "You, Little-one-just-born-he-walked, go to find a cow; kill the cow near the end of the bed on which Mwindo rests. You must lock the house; in the house there must not remain a single person." Little-one-just-born-he-walked brought a cow; it was killed near the end of the bed on which Mwindo was resting. He locked the door; all the people remained in the village place. The blood dripped down where Mwindo was. In the twinkling of an eye they (the people) heard sneezing coming from the house in which Mwindo was. They said that the cow had (a) risen.[60] When they had heard two sneezes, Little-one-just-born-he-walked said: "Open that house here!" They opened it up. When they entered it, they saw Mwindo sitting up. Little-one-just-born-he-walked asked him: "From where do you come?" Mwindo said: "I have been in a state of death." Thereupon Little-one-just-born-he-walked said to Mwindo's mother: "Let us proceed to my village." They went. The Chief-Counselor gave Little-one-just-born-he-walked a hand, saying: "Lo! You are a true man, indeed!"[61]

After they arrived there, Little-one-just-born-he-walked gave land to Mwindo, saying: "And you, my kinsman, settle in that land." Mwindo said: "All right; you are a chief and I am a chief!" Little-one-just-born-he-walked said: "You, my kinsman, you start again! Look once: my land is filled with people. I shall not give you my people. You will remain like that,

---

59. *Mwindo became sick*: no reason is given for Mwindo's illness, nor is his death attributed to wounds received in battle. The choice of verbs (*ihuhuka*: to expire; *isusa*: to be cold) leaves no doubt that Mwindo is really dead. The terminology used by Mwindo's mother, *Mwindo wakukwa* ("Mwindo is dead"), might make Little-one-just-born-he-walked uncertain whether his brother was really dead or just severely ill. Hence his rash reply, "Let him be dead over there" (*wakweko*), and his question, "why did you not bring us the message that Mwindo was ailing?" (*Mwindo ukire usambange*).

60. *spit some phlegm*: in the Nyanga tales, phlegm is also the price to be paid to Centipede before he gives the oracle. *kill the cow near the end of the bed*: a similar procedure for revivification is prescribed in epic II.

61. *The Chief-Counselor gave ... a hand*: the clapping of hands (*ikaso*) would be a more customary procedure, but under Western influence handshaking became a regular way of greeting.

like that! Not a person will do work for you because you say that you also are a chief." Mwindo settled there in that way, without a person to work for him, but Little-one-just-born-he-walked had a house built for him.[62]

After Mwindo had remained like that (for some time), the headmen made Mwindo go to a secret council, saying: "You, Mwindo, tell your kinsman that he is the big chief and that you are behind him." Mwindo arrived at the place of Little-one-just-born-he-walked. He said: "You, Little-one-just-born-he-walked, you are the big chief, and I am behind you."[63] When Little-one-just-born-he-walked heard this, he was very satisfied, saying: "Is this not the manner in which I want it?" Thereupon the headmen said that Mwindo was First-born-of-the-land. Mwindo became First-born-of-the-land; they gave him people to work for him.[64]

As Mwindo was now First-born-of-the-land, the Chief-Counselor said to Little-one-just-born-he-walked: "Will your kinsman then remain in (the state of) bachelorship? Have him marry!" Little-one-just-born-he-walked agreed. He asked Mwindo to search for a maiden and promised that, if he (Mwindo) found one, he himself would provide the bridewealth. Mwindo said that he knew no place where he could get married. Little-one-just-born-he-walked remained silent; he meditated, saying that he had asked for a maiden from Muisa, that all the maidens had marked their agreement with him. Little-one-just-born-he-walked brought together his cows and his goats. He went to Muisa's. He arrived there; he said to Muisa that he came to give him bridewealth. Muisa said: "Give me the bridewealth." Little-one-just-born-he-walked gave him three cows and four goats. Muisa took them. He dressed his daughter with beaded necklaces. Then Little-one-just-born-he-walked returned with his wife, because Muisa did not know that Little-one-just-born-he-walked was marrying this girl on Mwi-

---

62. *you are a chief and I am a chief*: the hero shows extreme generosity toward his half brother, but the latter stubbornly pursues the controversy over the chieftainship. Little-one-just-born-he-walked, however, promptly makes Mwindo understand that without people there is no chieftainship. As stated in epic I, "Kingship is the stamping (of feet) ; it is the tremor of people."

63. *the headmen*: the heads of villages and/or kinship groups. The fact that Mwindo is advised by them instead of by the counselors is another indication of Mwindo's removal from the chieftainship.

64. *First-born-of-the-land*: a prominent title usually conferred upon the son of the *nyabana*-wife. In other words, this epic makes a complete reversal of the theoretical rules of succession. Under normal circumstances Mwindo would become chief as the son of the ritual wife, whereas Little-one-just-born-he-walked would be the First-born-of-the-land as son of the *nyabana*-wife. But, as the Chief-Counselor points out much earlier in the epic, "a chief is not brought forth"; nobody is automatically a chief. Mwindo, obsessed by his mother's hate, could not become a chief.

ndo's behalf. Little-one-just-born-he-walked arrived home without show-
ing the woman.

When Mwindo heard that Little-one-just-born-he-walked had arrived,
he said that he was going to greet Little-one-just-born-he-walked. He did
not know that Little-one-just-born-he-walked had gone to marry a woman
for him, because Little-one-just-born-he-walked had not told him
(Mwindo) that he would fetch him a woman. Mwindo arrived; he greeted
Little-one-just-born-he-walked. After he had greeted him, the Chief-
Counselor and the other headmen arrived. They greeted Little-one-just-
born-he-walked. When Little-one-just-born-he-walked saw that all were
present, he gave the news saying: "You, Chief-Counselor, I have arrived
with the wife of Mwindo. Here she is! You, headmen, go to introduce her
into the homestead of Mwindo." He took a young steer, saying: "You,
Mwindo, you will kill this steer for the headmen, for those who will introduce for you your wife into your homestead." Mwindo said: "May you
be blessed, you chief!" The Chief-Counselor said: "Lo! You are an accomplished chief." Mwindo went home with the steer, and the headmen
came behind with the maiden. Mwindo introduced the wife into his
homestead. The headmen ate the steer. The young woman appreciated
Mwindo very much, because Mwindo was shining now; he was no longer
as he (previously) had been.[65]

After Mwindo had finished marrying, his wife carried a pregnancy.
The men said that Mwindo's wife was now the first to carry a pregnancy
although she came later than the wife of Little-one-just-born-he-walked.
She had not carried a pregnancy; she had turned out to be barren. Shortly
thereafter, Mwindo's wife brought forth a girl. They said: "What is its
name?" Mwindo said: "She is Protector-of-the-things-that-will-not-be-
understood." When the men heard it, they said: "A difficult name, this
one!"[66]

The men were seated (together), saying that the wife of Little-one-
just-born-he-walked would not bring forth; (she would have borne a child)
perhaps if Little-one-just-born-he-walked had not preceded in marrying,
when his senior brother Mwindo was not yet married. The men said that

---

65. *Mwindo was shining now*: in some heroic tales Mwindo appears initially as
Scurvy Mwindo, who undergoes a transformation that changes him into a beautiful
youth. This passage suggests a similar physical transformation (paired with a moral
one), although there is no earlier reference to any change.

66. *Protector-of-the-things-that-will-not-be-understood*: indeed a difficult name. It
is probably an allusion to the fact that Mwindo had died before and that his ghost had
been to the world of the spirits, whose secrets cannot be revealed.

this was the reason why the wife of Little-one-just-born-he-walked did not bear children.[67] They went to tell Little-one-just-born-he-walked to take his wife to Mwindo so that he might bless her and his wife might carry a pregnancy. Little-one-just-born-he-walked took goats. He told the Chief-Counselor to take his wife and these goats to Mwindo so that he might bless her. The Chief-Counselor went with the wife of Little-one-just-born-he-walked to Mwindo. When they arrived there, the Chief-Counselor gave the goats to Mwindo's wife, saying: "Mwindo, these goats here (are for you). May you bless the wife of Little-one-just-born-he-walked." They said that they had been informed through an oracle that Little-one-just-born-he-walked should not have preceded in marrying without the senior brother being married. When Mwindo heard this, he said that it was good. He killed all the goats; they were cooked. When they were ready, Mwindo gave the blessing to the wife of Little-one-just-born-he-walked, saying: "When you bring forth, you bring forth for me. I am the senior." The Chief-Counselor and the other men who had arrived with the wife of Little-one-just-born-he-walked ate the goats. They returned with the wife of Little-one-just-born-he-walked. They gave him the news that Mwindo had given his wife the blessing "on the goats." Little-one-just-born-he-walked rejoiced.[68]

He remained with his wife. After a month had passed, the wife of Little-one-just-born-he-walked was pregnant. The men said: "Lo! Mwindo was the reason she could not bear children." When the wife of Little-one-just-born-he-walked was close to childbirth, she said that she could not give birth without first arriving at the place of her father Mukiti.

The wife of Little-one-just-born-he-walked went to her father Mukiti. When Mukiti saw her, he said (he had thought that) his child would not bring forth, that he knew that she would not bring forth because the days had passed. His daughter said that she carried this pregnancy because Mwindo had given her his blessing, that the reason she had not brought forth was that he (Mwindo) had not preceded in marrying, since he was the senior. Hearing this, Mukiti said: "Your husband excelled in obstructing the road of his colleague. Each one could have married you; (but) his colleague blocked him." His daughter said: "The name of the child of Mwindo is Protector-of-the-things-that-will-not-be-understood."

---

67. In Nyanga conception, the nonobservance of certain matrimonial prescriptions may result in barrenness.

68. In Nyanga culture, ceremonial blessing of people and objects is of fundamental significance in order to clear away taboos and offenses. *you bring forth for me*: the ambiguity here stems from Mwindo's insistence on his seniority.

Mukiti gave his daughter two goats; his daughter returned with the two goats. She arrived at her husband's place. Her husband took one goat; he gave it to Mwindo and the other one to the headmen; they ate them.

When two weeks had passed, the wife of Little-one-just-born-he-walk-ed gave birth to a boy. The men said that it was Mwindo's child. "You, Lit-tle-one-just-born-he-walked, you are bringing forth for Mwindo." Little-one-just-born-he-walked said: "When a man brings forth, he brings forth for his kinsman." This child did not receive a name, because its mother had said that she alone would give it a name when it was grown up. When the child was able to walk, its mother gave it the name Destiny, because Destiny was the reason that the father of this child was born and Destiny was the reason that his child was born.[69]

Mwindo and his kinsman were established; they were established there, each one in his own state. After they had been established for many days, Little-one-just-born-he-walked died. After he died, Mwindo said that his kinsman had died leaving a child and that his task was to take care of it. This child was to be a chief (and nothing less) because his father had saved him and he could not put aside Destiny, the sororal nephew of Mukiti. Destiny went to his maternal uncle. He gave him the news that his father was dead: "What shall I do now?" Mukiti said: "You are a chief, but you must honor Mwindo because he is your father. When tribute for you arrives, you may not refuse (to give) Mwindo from it."[70]

Destiny returned; he was chief. Mwindo continued to take care of Destiny. When Little-one-just-born-he-walked died, he left to Mwindo his

---

69. *Destiny*: the Nyanga word *buingo* is not easy to understand. A close Swahili translation of the term is *maisha*, which means life in respect to duration and content and, according to Ch. Sacleux (*Dictionnaire Français-Swahili* [Paris: Institut d'Eth-nologie, 1949]), also means destiny in the sense of life. In *Mwindo Epic from the Banyanga* (1969, p. 53 n. 51) I have translated *buingo* as destiny (Lat., *fortuna*). Buingo is not commonly included among the Nyanga divinities, but in a discussion of hierarchical linkages among the divinities of the subterranean world, I was told that Buingo was Chief-Counselor to Nyamurairi. Nyamurairi, as chief of the divinities, brings life and death, and Buingo counsels him regarding the duration of life. I have rarely encountered Buingo as an actor in the tales. One heroic tale, recited by Sherungu, narrator of this epic, centers on Buingo, son of Drum (Ngoma), and his friendship with Chameleon, who found a way to transport a heavy stone that was needed as an anvil to forge an iron staff and a spear for Buingo.

70. The death of Little-one-just-born-he-walked might have caused a successoral crisis between his son, Destiny, and his senior half brother, Mwindo. Mwindo, however, is in a conciliatory mood, recalling that he owes his life to his dead half brother. *you must honor Mwindo*: the verb *isubaha* entails the idea of awe and fear. The chief must respect certain rules of kinship, particularly those relating to seniority.

conga-scepter, his stool, and his spear. They were established there. Destiny was chief, and Mwindo was taking care of him. Destiny was also a true man.[71]

Little-one-just-born-he-walked died having brought forth four sons and one daughter. Mwindo also brought forth three sons and three girls.[72]

When they had been established (like that) for many days, Mwindo said that he was now near death. When Mwindo experienced this (forewarning), he spent his time dancing (to the sound of) the drums. Afterward he went saying: "Who will give me the oracle?" He went. He arrived at Mukiti's place: "You, Mukiti, I am going to die. Teach me how to act." Mukiti said: "I do not know what I would tell you. You die; you die; and that is all." Mwindo departed (from) there. He threw himself into Centipede's place: "Give me the oracle!" Centipede said: "My throat is dried up. Look at me." Mwindo coughed; he spit some phlegm. Centipede ate the phlegm. Centipede wrinkled his face. He said: "You die; you die; and that is all, you, Mwindo." Mwindo returned home.[73]

When he (Mwindo) was back in the village, he called all the animals in the forest asking them to come to dance. All the animals arrived. They danced; they danced! After they had finished dancing, they returned again into the forest.

And Mwindo fainted. He was there; he was there![74] He went to sneeze. His wife said that her husband had recovered. Mwindo asked his wife for food. His wife gave him an *isusa*-vegetable, saying that an ailing person was accustomed to eating *isusa*-vegetables. Mwindo refused it. His wife gave him bean soup. He refused it. His wife said: "You, my husband,

---

71. Here the bard is somewhat confused and disorganized. It is unclear why the precious possessions (scepter, stool, and spear) of Little-one-just-born-he-walked were passed on to Mwindo, because certain dignitaries (*muembwa* and *musimba*) guard such objects at the death of the chief.

72. This passage is also somewhat out of context. The names of these children are not provided, and it is unclear whether or not Destiny and Protector-of-the-things-that-will-not-be-understood are included in the count.

73. *that he was now near death*: we can only speculate as to whether Mwindo's impending death is caused by age or sickness or whether Mwindo is going to die of his own will. The latter interpretation seems plausible because, according to a later passage, Mwindo is sent back from the subterranean world by Nyamurairi. Nyanga ideology holds that Nyamurairi makes the decision when someone must die and that the ghosts of persons who take their own lives cannot enter the subterranean world, but must ramble on earth.

74. *he was there* (*urinko*): i.e., it looked as though he was already in the subterranean world. The opposition between "to be here" and "to be there" marks for the Nyanga the distinction between life (to be here in the village, the world) and death (to be there in the subterranean world).

which foods are you looking for?" He said that he wanted to eat the urine of a goat. His wife went to tell the Chief-Counselor that Mwindo wanted to eat a goat. The Chief-Counselor killed a goat; they cooked it. When the goat was ready (to eat), they removed the liver and the intestines, saying: "Mwindo, this is the meat." Mwindo said: "I do not want it." The Chief-Counselor said to him: "The boy died without knowing which word to speak." After Mwindo had refused this meat, he asked Lightning to come down. Lightning came down; he cleaved the house—the one in which Mwindo was—into two parts; one part went on one side, and the (other) part (went) on the other side. When they looked inside the house, Mwindo was still there (alive). They said: "He is with salvation, this one!"[75]

When Mwindo emerged, he went to the blacksmith, telling him to forge twenty adzes for him (Mwindo). The blacksmith forged these adzes. Mwindo returned home. Upon arriving home he said that he now wanted to die, that the children of Little-one-just-born-he-walked were chiefs, because he could not deprive them of it (the chieftainship) because Little-one-just-born-he-walked had made him arise (from the dead): "My children are Fathers-of-the-chief. You, my children, honor Destiny." Mwindo placed on the ground the conga-scepter, the butenge-spear, the stool, the bow, the bag of Good Fortune, the fire drill sheath, and the adzes. He said: "When I am buried, then you will place all these things on my grave."[76] He said that he was going to fight with Nyamurairi and to search for the place where his kinsman, Little-one-just-born-he-walked, had gone. Mwindo expired. They went to place him in the grave with all the objects that he had mentioned.

Mwindo climbed up into the subterranean world. When he arrived at the entrance to Nyamurairi's (village), he said that he had come to fight with Nyamurairi. When Nyamurairi heard this, he said: "Who is the fool who says over there at the entrance that he is going to fight with me?" He said to Nyarusumba: "Go tell that person over there to return there (to the world).'"[77] Mwindo returned to another place; he settled there. When he

---

75. In this curious passage Mwindo hopes to give belated proof of his heroic stature. It also foreshadows Mwindo's aggressive intentions.

76. *Fathers-of-the-chief* (*bashemwami*): their special task is to take care of the chief's ritual wife and her child. The mind of Mwindo is still muddled with the problem of succession. *When I am buried, then you will place all these things on my grave*: an unusual procedure, since the chief is buried only with his drum. The objects mentioned are normally placed under the protection of *musimba*, a special officeholder. In the light of subsequent events, all these decisions seem to constitute trickery on the part of Mwindo; he does not confer upon Destiny the material objects that are the symbols of chieftainship.

77. *Nyarusumba*: a servant to Nyamurairi, usually identified as the sacrificer of goats and cattle.

was established there, he said that Nyamurairi had made him retrace his steps, but that he—the one here—was not going to return anymore to the village. He said that he was now going to settle at the wading place of their village.[78] He arrived there; he said that he would cut *ncangu* there, that the people would be very astonished.[79] Mwindo cut *ncangu* at the wading place. When the people saw this, they said: "Another problem over there." When Mwindo had finished hearing how astounded the people were, he left that place. He said that he was going back to Nyamurairi, that he had not yet seen his kinsman and his father. And he left that place, saying that he was going to fight with Nyamurairi.

Mwindo followed again the road (leading) to Nyamurairi. When he arrived in the middle of the road, he met (as in an apparition) with his paternal aunt. His paternal aunt said: "You, Mwindo, where is it close?" He said: "To Nyamurairi, to go and fight with him, because he killed my kinsman and my father. And I am going to find out why he has carried them off." His paternal aunt said: "Return quickly now to the world; and when you arrive in the world, do not give the news of what you have seen here." Mwindo went.[80]

He arrived at his *ncangu*; he bathed; he climbed up to the village. He entered his house, he left it; he went to the men's house. He smoked tobacco, saying that he, Mwindo, had arisen. He said that he had been overcome in the fight with Nyamurairi and he said to the son of Little-one-just-born-he-walked: "You, Destiny, your father has said that I am the chief, that you are no longer (chief)." Destiny said: "All that is well and good, but even though you become chief, you cannot chase me because you are my father." Mwindo said: "A man can chase his son, even though he is a chief." Mwindo became chief; he was enthroned. The counselors said to Mwindo: "You have become a chief, but you cannot hate the child of Little-one-just-born-he-walked. Give him a state, for he also is a chief."[81]

They were established there in the land. When the crops were ripe

---

78. *Mwindo returned to another place*: the stubborn Mwindo does not want to return to his own village, but there is no other place between the subterranean world and his village (i.e., the world). Thus he settles near the wading place of his village, which is the only "other place" that he can find.

79. *ncangu*: I do not know the exact meaning of this term.

80. The spirit of the paternal aunt acts as an adviser whose words cannot be ignored. *where is it close*: a standard expression meaning "where are you going?"

81. Mwindo assumes the chieftainship through deception. In the event of insoluble conflict between two contestants for the throne, the Nyanga would divide a kingdom into two parts, each having its own chief. That does not seem to have happened here. This passage indirectly points to the power of the oral will left by a dying father or a chief.

enough to harvest, Destiny had a dream in which his father Little-one-just-born-he-walked told him that Mwindo had said out of his own (invention) that he was chief and that the day he would harm him he (Mwindo) would be looking out toward the subterranean world.[82] Mwindo and Destiny were established in the land, both of them. When many days had passed, Mwindo's child became sick. When it was close to death, Mwindo went to consult the oracle in the place of Centipede. Centipede gave him the oracle, saying: "You, Mwindo, you have fooled Destiny, saying that his father had told you that you are chief. Thereupon you became chief. That is the reason your child is ailing. If you want it to heal, return to Destiny his land so that he may become chief again." When Mwindo heard this, he said: "For me to abandon again the joy that I have! It is better for the child to die."[83]

There remained two days, and the child died. When the child arrived in the subterranean world, it said that its father was the cause of its death, that he had refused to leave his land to him (Destiny). The child killed its father Mwindo and its mother; they also died.[84] Little-one-just-born-he-walked asked the counselors, saying: "What then? Is it I then who has killed these people?"[85] The counselors said: "No! They have killed themselves, because Mwindo received an oracle saying that he should return the chieftainship to you. He refused, saying that it was better for his

---

82. *that the day he would harm him*: i.e., Destiny's father predicts the coming death of Mwindo in a dream.

83. *Mwindo's child became sick*: the sickness is obviously attributed to Mwindo's deceit and to the transgression of the taboos. Implicitly, it is Destiny's anger and dissatisfaction which cause the sickness. *For me to abandon again the joy that I have*: Mwindo is never depicted with any sympathy in this epic; here his egoism and arrogance are at their worst.

84. *The child killed its father Mwindo and its mother*: it is rather bizarre that the mother was also killed, because she was not even mentioned in connection with the incidents that led to the disaster. Implicitly, the mother is guilty because she let her husband act arbitrarily after the oracle had been given, instead of seeking help against him. It will be recalled that Mwindo had a daughter, called Protector-of-the-things-that-will-not-be-understood, by his wife who was a daughter of Muisa, and that six unnamed children are attributed to Mwindo; the child that killed its father and its mother is not identified, but it is reasonable to think that it was Protector-of-the-things-that-will-not-be-understood. As the nephew of Muisa, the bringer-of-death, she was in a special position to demand the death of her parents. Also her name seems to cast her in the role of protector of justice; her action is guided by the hidden principles that also guide chieftainship.

85. *Is it I then who has killed these people*: the conversation between Little-one-just-born-he-walked and the counselors takes place in the subterranean world. The human and physical surroundings in which people live in the subterranean world are very similar to those in the terrestrial world.

child to die than for him to give up the chieftainship. Lo! Mwindo himself is the one who has given himself counsel, saying that Little-one-just-born-he-walked had told him that he would be chief. Lo! It was deception!"[86] Destiny was now chief again of all the land as he had been before.

Here originiated (the custom) for the counselors always to enthrone the junior child. And the firstborn child becomes Father-of-the-chief.

---

86. This simplified statement—the sole conclusion the bard Sherungu added at the end of his story—conveys a deep and secret truth. The selection of the successor to chieftainship is secret and complex; the overt rules specify that the chief-elect must be the son of a ritual *mumbo*-wife. This epic has helped to show that this concept is not necessarily correct. The procedures at work in the process of choosing the successor are particularly secret when the *mumbo*-wife has no children, has no sons, or dies childless. In the strict Nyanga custom, the child of the *mumbo*-wife selected for the position of chief must not be her firstborn son (according to some sources, if the first child of the *mumbo*-wife was male, it was killed); ideally, he must be a son following a daughter (i.e., a junior).

PPENDIX I

I. *The setting: Mwindo's village*

A man Shemwindo has a child called Mwindo. Shemwindo sets many types of traps. He goes to inspect the traps and finds all kinds of animals caught in them. He returns to the village to enlist the people's help in carrying the animals home. They skin the animals and take them home. The same events happen on other occasions. Shemwindo falls sick "without a single limb of his body aching." Near death, he calls his child Mwindo to give him his last will. The will specifies that during the mortuary rites Mwindo must be shaved, not with water, but with meat sauce and that the mortuary food must also be meat. Shemwindo dies. The men (hunters) want to shave Mwindo, but he reminds them about his father's will. Mwindo goes to inspect the traps his father had left. For two months he does not find a single animal in them.

II. *Mwindo's journey*

Mwindo, taking his stool, his spear, his bag of Good Fortune, his fire drill, his tobacco pouch, and fourteen potatoes, goes to inspect the traps. He sets up camp and repeatedly inspects the traps without finding animals. He meditates for three days; then he examines the traps again. Since there are no animals, he decides "to follow his father where he had gone to Nyamurairi." Mwindo arrives on the mountain Tubondo, in the land of Kikomo. He lights a fire, smokes tobacco, and expires. His heart encounters Good Fortune (Kahombo); she tells him to return to his village and to consecrate various cult objects to her. Mwindo receives back his life; he refuses to return home and continues the trip. He arrives on the mountain Wingi, in the land of Kikomo. He lights a fire, smokes tobacco, and expires. He encounters the divinity Nkango, who tells him to return to his village and to consecrate various cult objects to him (Nkango). Mwindo "awakens"; he refuses to return home and continues the journey. He arrives on the mountain Bukumba. He lights a fire, smokes tobacco, and expires. He encounters the divinity Hangi-of-Drum, who tells him that his father is on the top of a mountain in the village of Nyamurairi; he urges Mwindo to return home and to consecrate cult objects to him. Mwindo awakens; he decides to continue the journey.

III. *Mwindo's village*

Mwindo's wife and kinsfolk decide to search for him. They cannot find him near the traps and conclude that he is dead.

IV. *Mwindo in Nyamurairi's village*

Mwindo climbs Mount Bukumba. He arrives at a junction of roads and hides. He hears Nyamurairi give instructions to his servant Nyarusumba to call all the guardians of animals. Nyarusumba arrives at the crossroads and calls the people together; they thatch Nyamurairi's house. Shemwindo is also called, but he is late in arriving. Nyarusumba calls all the guardians of animals; they arrive. Shemwindo reaches the crossroads when all the others have already gone to the village. Mwindo appears; he explains the purpose of his visit. Shemwindo hides him in the bundle of leaves he is carrying and takes him to the village. There Mwindo hears Nyamurairi, Nyarusumba, and the guardians make the account of the animals. All go to sleep; Shemwindo reminds Mwindo of how the guardians gave the account and concludes that "animals have their owners." He informs Mwindo that he should have made offerings to one of the divinities in order to catch animals in the traps. Shemwindo goes to sleep in the house of Kahindo, his sister, while Mwindo remains outside. Kahindo "smells a human" and finds Mwindo. As Mwindo's paternal aunt, Kahindo orders him to return home; she provides him with a list of "injunctions about the ways in which to act when arriving home": he must make offerings to the divinities Hangi, Nkango, Muhima, and Kahombo; he is not to tell the people that he was at Nyamurairi's; he must enter into his house of Good Fortune and sneeze; he must borrow a goat and be shaved; he must inspect the traps. Kahindo takes Mwindo and makes him fly back to his village.

V. *Mwindo's homecoming, glory, and dream*

Mwindo arrives in his house of Good Fortune; he coughs and sneezes (to indicate his arrival). His wife and mother hear the noise, but they are scared because of the night and because of grief over Mwindo's death. Good Fortune enters Mwindo and teaches him a song. In the morning the wife and the mother find Mwindo in his house; he informs them that he is back from inspecting his father's traps. Mwindo reveals himself to the people; he asks to be shaved. They refuse because there is no meat. Mwindo obtains a goat from his blood friend Hangi. The goat is distributed; Mwindo is shaved. The paraphernalia of chieftainship, left by the father, are kept in the custody of two officials, Muembwa and Musimba. The decision is made to confer a chief's name upon Mwindo. With the help of the officials Musao and Chief-Pygmy, Mwindo passes through the ablution ceremonies with his wife. Back in the village there is ritual beer drinking to complete the "teachings" connected with the mourning rites. Mwindo makes the prescribed offerings to the divinities Nkango, Kahombo, and Hangi-of-Drum, asking them for force, long life, and success in hunting. Mwindo and the Chief-Pygmy arrange the traps left by Mwindo's father. Mwindo's wife is pregnant; she gives birth to a son. Mwindo and the Chief-Pygmy find many animals in the traps; successful trapping continues. When his child begins to walk, Mwindo goes alone to the traps; he does not find any animals; he sleeps in the hunting camp. In a dream he receives a zanza that will enable him to go to the subterranean world; he is forewarned by spirits of his coming death. Awakening, Mwindo finds himself with a zanza; he returns to the village, to his house of Good Fortune.

VI. *Mwindo's death*

Mwindo's wife tells her child to stay with his father while she and the child's grandmother collect firewood. The child must cry until the father reveals "the news of where he has gone." The child stays with Mwindo; it cries and cries, saying to its father: "Give me the news from where you have come." Mwindo tells the child that he "went only to inspect the traps"; the child continues to cry, refusing meat, honey brought by the Pygmies, and banana paste. The mother returns. Mwindo gives her the child; the child refuses to be breast-fed or to eat. The grandmother cannot pacify it. The next morning the child is still crying. Mwindo assembles the Pygmies and all the people. Seated among them on his stool, with his other paraphernalia displayed around him, Mwindo announces his coming death, because his wife has asked the child to cry until Mwindo reveals the secret. He asks them whether they want him to divulge the secret. The people do not want Mwindo to die; the mother and the child should die. The wife is persistent in asking that Mwindo reveal the secret. The people refuse, saying that the land needs a chief. Mwindo decides to fulfill his wife's wishes; he sings and plays the zanza, pinpointing his wife's curse and promising his dogs to the Pygmies. In secret council, however, Mwindo had already told the Pygmies about his real intentions: he is going to look for a ritual wife, Kahindo, the daughter of Mukiti; they must place the mother and the child in a pit and tell them to search for him; one Pygmy must keep watch every evening and every morning in a tree near the wading place, singing and playing the zanza; he (Mwindo) will return one year after his wife's death. Seated on his stool in the middle of his people, Mwindo sings; he sinks slowly into the ground, predicting his return; he divulges his secret and leaves his zanza and his dogs with the Pygmies. The people disperse.

VII. *Mwindo consults the oracle*

"Where Mwindo went," he arrives in the place of the diviner Centipede. He offers gifts to Centipede and receives his oracle: in order to get Mukiti's daughter, Mwindo must take his Pygmy Lulema along and bring a calabash of honey.

VIII. *Live burial of Mwindo's wife and child*

The wife is led to the river to complete the "teachings" connected with her husband's death. In the meantime, people in the village dig a deep pit in the place where Mwindo was swallowed by the earth. Back in the village, the woman is shaved; she is placed with her child in the pit; the pit is covered with soil; the wife and child die. The Pygmy Lulema goes to the river, hides inside a tree, and sings as he was instructed. He does the same every evening and every morning.

IX. *The Pygmy Lulema joins Mwindo in the river*

In the river Mwindo hears the praises by Lulema. Mwindo receives a drum filled with cowries from his paternal aunt. One night Mwindo calls Lulema, beating his drum. The Pygmy tells Mwindo to fetch him if he is indeed Mwindo. Mwindo instructs Lulema to join him in the water. The Pygmy descends into the river carrying the zanza and a calabash of honey; he informs Mwindo about the death of his wife and child.

X. *Mwindo's aquatic journey to Mukiti*

Mwindo and Lulema travel downstream to Mukiti's place. They arrive at the location where Mukiti's people draw water, beating the
drum, playing the zanza, and singing. Star, who is also in pursuit of
the girl Kahindo, has been refused several times by Mukiti and his
son Bintsibu. Aware of Mwindo's quest, Star descends and makes
Lightning strike. The power of Mwindo's words keeps Star at a
distance. The Pygmy Lulema is sent to fight with Star; Lulema
keeps Lightning at a distance and stabs Star. In the meantime
Mwindo is playing music and singing; he asks his paternal aunt for
an engraved calabash. Mukiti, hearing the song, sends his son
Bintsibu to see the man who is singing. Bintsibu meets Mwindo and
receives honey from him; Mwindo explains his intentions and asks
Bintsibu to be his spokesman. Bintsibu returns. Mwindo continues
playing and singing; he asks Spider for a bridge and his paternal
aunt for a copper staff. Lulema returns from his battle with Star.
Mwindo takes the calabash and the spear, then crosses the bridge to
Mukiti; Lulema continues to make music. Mwindo meets Mukiti in
his house; Mukiti knows his intentions thoroughly. Mukiti tastes
the honey; he takes the calabash and the spear to his daughter.
Kahindo agrees to marry Mwindo. Mukiti informs Mwindo and requests an *isia*-crest made of long pig's hair as bridewealth for his
daughter. Mwindo takes the good news to his Pygmy Lulema; he
asks his paternal aunt for help in finding the crest. The aunt hurriedly informs him that she has no crest and cannot get one.
Mwindo sends Lulema to his village to secure a crest.

XI. *Lulema's quest for an* isia-*crest*

Lulema arrives in Mwindo's village. Since no crest is available, he
sends the other Pygmies to hunt a *ngiri*-pig. The Pygmies hunt with
Mwindo's dogs.

XII. *Mukiti prepares his daughter's paraphernalia*

Viper must provide a wrist protector, a small bow, a quiver, and
leopard teeth. Monitor Lizard must bring the *rubuo*-bark cloth.

XIII. *Lulema obtains a crest*

The Pygmies hunt a *ngiri*-pig, offering invocations to Mwindo's
father and the ancient Chief-Pygmy. They slay the pig; they skin it
and return home. Lulema removes "the long hairs from around the
pig's neck" and departs, urging his people to preserve the pig's hide
and to make a crest of the remaining hair. Lulema arrives in the
place where he has left Mwindo; both rejoice.

XIV. *Mwindo receives Kahindo in marriage*

Mwindo's paternal aunt manufactures the *isia*-crest; she departs. Mwindo and Lulema arrive at Mukiti's. Mwindo is shown Kahindo; they embrace. Mukiti receives the crest and Mwindo's drum. Kahindo is ceremonially dressed by her mother. Kahindo is given to Mwindo; her brother Bintsibu reminds Mwindo of his duties; Mukiti advises Mwindo to make offerings.

XV. *Mwindo's homecoming and glory*

Mwindo, Kahindo, and Lulema return home. Mwindo sends Lulema ahead to prepare the village. Lulema arrives and gives instructions. Mwindo and Kahindo are joined at the wading place of Mukiti's village by his paternal aunt. The paternal aunt instructs them: Mwindo, the chief, must never again hunt or trap. Mwindo and Kahindo, pursuing the journey, are met by Lulema and two women to carry Kahindo. They arrive home; much food is provided; the drums resound. The celebrations last for two weeks; Mwindo is enthroned. Mwindo's wife becomes pregnant; she bears a daughter; later she becomes pregnant again and gives birth to a boy. They live prosperously and happily; Mwindo has great fame and much praise.

PPENDIX II

THE FRAGMENTARY VERSION
BY BITANDA ASANI

Chief Kaboru ka Mwindo marries a wife among his maternal uncles (the animals). He orders all his people to make a large chief's field for him and to designate a guardian of the field. Muntori (Sparrow) is selected; the people build a shed for him. The chief launches an interdiction that no one must harvest bananas in his field. When the bananas are ripe, heavy rains fall continuously; the guardian is starving and cuts bananas. The rains cease; the chief sends his wife with food for Muntori. When she arrives, Muntori hides the cut bananas. She sees them and informs the chief. Muntori flees to Muisa, whose daughter Kahindo the chief had wanted to marry for a long time. Muntori asks her to become Mwindo's wife. Since she is made of iron, she requests Muntori to inform Mwindo that she will accept him if his body is forged. Muntori returns home with a goat received from Kahindo and explains her wishes. Mwindo calls his maternal uncles (the animals) to be forged; Muntori is temporarily imprisoned. The animals deliberate who will be the blacksmith. Munkonde (Large Bat) refuses; Kakutu (Small Bat) is chosen. Kikwe is selected as helper and diviner to preside over the forging. The animals amass a large quantity of charcoal; Kikwe constructs the forge. Mwindo places his legs in the glowing charcoal; Kikwe invites the animals to bring their tears to be used as water to cool the iron. Elephant sheds his tears in a large trough near the forge. Kakutu hammers the chief's legs on the anvil; the sparks hit Elephant; he flees without ever mingling again with his peers. Wild Pig sheds tears in the trough; Kakutu hammers Mwindo's feet; the sparks hit Wild Pig; he flees cursing Muntori. The animals enjoin Kikwe to collect

279

their tears at a distance from the forge. Mwindo is completely forged. Mwindo calls his people and his maternal uncles, saying that he is leaving for Muisa's. He arrives at Muisa's with twenty goats and one cow as bridewealth. Toro (Sleep), the brother of Kahindo, hears in the place where he has gone that his father Muisa plans to keep all the bridewealth for himself. Toro hurries back, throws himself onto Mwindo, and makes him fall asleep. Kahindo tries in vain to awaken her husband Mwindo. Mwindo's maternal uncles ask Kahindo to tell her brother that they will provide additional bridewealth. Toro allows Mwindo to recover. Mwindo returns home with Kahindo as his ritual wife. Mwindo now decides to fight other chiefs in order to capture their lands. He departs with several blood friends (Iguana, Hedgehog, Turtle, Hawk, etc.) and with his maternal uncles. They arrive near a lake; Turtle separates the water with a whip; they pass. They encounter "a people of Trees" that bar the road; they beat the trees on the crowns; they disperse into a forest. They confront "a people of Wild-Banana-Trees" that block the road; they beat them on the crowns; the trees disperse. They meet Ukanga (Big-Rock) and scatter him with the whips. They encounter Muhumba (Gorilla); Mwindo challenges him in a game of dice and wins; he takes Gorilla's people with him. They arrive at the place of Kabaraka, Lightning's brother; he destroys Mwindo's wives and servants. Mwindo calls Turtle who is trailing behind, carrying the magical bag; Turtle arrives. With the help of the bag, Mwindo revivifies his people; he wins against Kabaraka in a game of dice. Mwindo engages Lightning in a game of dice; he wins with the assistance of his maternal uncles. Mwindo arrives in the middle of a group of trees where Nyamurairi is hiding; he urges Nyamurairi to leave the trees and go to the men's house. Arriving in the men's house, Mwindo refuses to sit on a stool under which Nyamurairi is hiding. He refuses to eat food in which Nyamurairi is hidden. Nyamurairi invites Mwindo to harvest honey; Mwindo gives his belt to Nyamurairi. He climbs the tree and starts working, but he is seized by the tree; he orders his belt to subdue Nyamurairi. The tree releases Mwindo and the belt relinquishes Nyamurairi. Nyamurairi informs Mwindo that he is Muisa and must be given all the maidens who previously were dedicated to Muisa. Mwindo returns home with his maternal uncles and all the booty collected in his struggles. Mwindo rules in glory.

A GLOSSARY OF PERSONAGES

The people who listen to the epics, as well as readers of the translated texts, are presented with hundreds of names, including generic as well as specific terms for humans, divinities, animals, rivers, mountains, villages, places, regions, and groups. Many of the names belong to the routine vocabulary of the Nyanga; others are less frequently used epithets, praise names, teknonyms, and patronyms; still others are titles. Some come from the creative imagination of the bards, who at times compose complicated names for reasons of sonority or symbolic connotation. Most of the names in all these categories can be translated or interpreted, and wherever it was feasible to do so I have provided translated names in the text. In certain instances, however, I have refrained from translation, preferring to restrict myself to explanations in the footnotes. In general, I have avoided translating teknonymic names and titles, such as Shemwindo (Father-of-Mwindo), Shemumbo (Father-of-the-ritual-wife), and Minerusi (Master-of-the-river). I have followed this policy partly to escape the danger of misunderstanding or misinterpreting names with ambiguous overtones.

Name-giving procedures and symbolisms among a Bantu-speaking people like the Nyanga are complex. Personal names, often inspired by social situations affecting the parents and kinsmen of newborn children, are open to ad hoc and euphemistic interpretations. For example, certain Nyanga children are called Tubi (Excrement), not because they are disliked or scorned, but euphemistically to typify a family in which many children have died. It is believed that the name will increase the life

281

chances of the newborn child by diverting the attention of evil-inspired forces.

Names also reflect physical situations that coincide with the birth of children. One of Mwindo's sons is called Utundo; another one, Mwishi. Utundo means cloud and Mwishi is the fulgent sun, but the name Utundo denotes a child born in one of the endless periods of overcast and rainy skies, whereas Mwishi signifies a child born in the hottest part of the day. Names are indicative of special skills and statuses of the parents or of special events coinciding with the birth. Mwindo's paternal aunt is called Iyangura, a name suggesting that her father was a famous arbitrator; the son of the Chief-Counselor is called Bakungu, which indicates the high status of his father; Musukuiyera, the name of one of Mwindo's sons, specifies that the child was born while people were dancing the *musuku*-dances in the village.

Finally, the etymological meaning of certain names in languages that, like Nyanga, have barely been studied is extremely difficult to identify. For example, the name of one of Mwindo's sons is Kanyironge; the term with the same tonal structure means genet (*Genetta tigrina*), but the bard himself associated the name with the verb *ironge*, meaning to break up the village in order to settle elsewhere. In other words, in the opinion of the bard, Kanyironge did not mean genet; rather, it reflected the fact that the child was born while the people were dismantling the village to move elsewhere. The problems of name giving are intensified through the consecration and dedication of persons to divinities and, in the tales, through personifications and symbolic references. In one of the epics the chief marries a woman called Kahindo, daughter of Hangi-of-Drum. Kahindo and Hangi are names of Nyanga divinities, but they also refer to individuals who are consecrated to those divinities. Unless the further context allows an explicit judgment, it is impossible to decide whether the chief married a female divinity or simply a woman named for that divinity.

In the glossary I list all major personages (human, divine, animal, and extraordinary) occurring in the four epics, with a brief identification and characterization of each. The numbers in parentheses after a name indicate the epics in which it appears. Sometimes an important personage in one epic is only briefly mentioned in a second or third epic. In addition to these major dramatis personae, a large number of personages are enumerated and suggested, mainly in songs and terse statements. Some are real persons (alive or dead) whom the narrator knows because of an event, an anecdote, a kinship link, or a political function, or because of the villages or mountains where they lived. A few personages are fictive characters directly taken from proverbs, riddles, and tales. Some unusual names are created by the bards because of their sonority of symbolic scope. There are also a number of names for groups (mostly kinship groups, but also ethnic units). Some of them exist in either Nyanga- or Hundeland; others pertain to the remote past; still others are fictive and symbolic (particularly in epic I, which mentions several groups whose names are derived from fish and crabs which symbolize evil).

Ants (I, II, III, IV) : Usually the migratory red ants (*mbari*) which symbolize fierceness. In the tales they overpower Leopard. In epic II they are chased by Mwindo's Pygmy while devouring Hawk. In epic III Nyamurairi lowers a bridge of red ants to obstruct Mwindo's passage. Occasional references, however, are made to black ants. In epic III Mwindo, on his return from the subterranean world, passes through their village on his homebound journey. In epic IV Little-one-just-born-he-walked asks for the help of Ant (called by the Hunde name *nyonso*) in his battle against Mwindo. The solitary ant *kinkete* is an ally of Little-one-just-born-he-walked in the battle against Mwindo (IV). In the tales the *kinkete* never sleeps, because it distrusts sleep as the bringer of dreams that are never realized.

Baboon (III) : Returning from the subterranean world, Mwindo passes through Baboon's place which "does not have the husk of a drum." Baboon is invoked in the oracle of the Pygmy Nkango as "child of Scraper."

Bakungu (III) : Son of the Chief-Counselor Shebakungu. When Mwindo's father leaves the chiefdom, Bakungu remains as Mwindo's counselor. Bakungu is also the general term for counselors.

Banamburu (II) : Lit., Members-of-the-*mburu*-group. *Mburu* is a species of monkeys much admired for their flat bellies and frugality. See *Mburu*.

Banamitandi (I) : Lit., Members-of-the-cobwebs-group. A praise name for the Spiders. See *Spider*.

Baniyana (I) : Lit., Members-of-the-hundreds-group. A praise name for the Bats, who are Mwindo's maternal uncles. Mwindo spends the night in their village; he is forged by them; they accompany him to his home village, where they are wiped out and revivified by Mwindo. See *Bat*.

Bat (I, II, III, IV) : Bats appear under different names—*kakutu, munkonde,* and *kikwe*—specifying three different categories according to size. In epic II the small bat *kakutu* provides Mwindo with nails enabling him to climb a tree in order to harvest honey.

In epic III the small bat *kikwe* acts as diviner; the large *munkonde*-bats forge Mwindo. In epic IV *munkonde*-bat forges spears for Little-one-just-born-he-walked. The bats are presented as eminent black-smiths and as the maternal uncles of Mwindo. In the tales they are in conflict with other animals over food and they bring discord to the animal world by giving a spotted hide to the leopard.

Beautiful-One (II) : Under the name Kongo, he is the last person to emerge from the heart of the dragonlike Big-bird-born-by-itself which was defeated by Mwindo's sister.

Bee (III, IV) : Bee is invoked by Mwindo as the "son of Marumbu" and the brother of Nyakatwakari, mother of the Pygmies (III). Bee, addressed as son of Needle (sting), fights for Little-one-just-born-he-walked against Mwindo (IV). Bees have no special role in epics I and II, but the harvesting of honey is important in all the texts.

Big-Crab (I, IV) : Known as Ikukuhi, Big-Crab is an ally of the Water Serpent Mukiti (I) and the servant of Mukiti's daughter (IV). The name is derived from the crab's blackness and slowness.

Big-bird-born-by-itself (II) : Hatched from an egg, found by Mwindo and his sister, a young bird develops into a dragon-ogre, called Kinkobongo. It is defeated by Mwindo's sister, who is aided by iron weapons obtained from Lightning.

Bisheria (I, III) : Lit., Flashes; the son of Mwindo's sixth wife Mweri who receives the status of prince (III). In epic I Bisheria is also an epithet for Lightning.

Blacksmith (IV) : An unidentified blacksmith (*mwesi*) provides the dying Mwindo with twenty adzes which he intends to use in a fight against Nyamurairi. See *Bat*.

Blacksmith's daughter (III) : Mwindo encounters her in the forest and sees Otter and Water Duck retrieve an ax that she had lost in the water. She is Kahindo, daughter of Nyamurairi. See *Kahindo*.

Buffaloes (II) : Mwindo and his people visit the chief of Buffaloes and the Buffaloes themselves to obtain their hairy tails, from which they make scepters. The scepter of Mwindo in epic I is made of a buffalo tail. In epic III Buffalo is invoked by Mwindo as "our kinsman, son of Toughness," and is mentioned in an oracle consultation as "child of strength."

Bukumba (III) : Name of a personified snake who travels through a river Bukumba and settles on a mountain Bukumba. Little-one-just-born-he-walked and the snake Bukumba live together in this area; hence the name *bukumba*, related to the verb "to mix, to join together."

Bukumba's child (III) : The unnamed child travels with its father, the snake Bukumba, from Hot-Springs, through various rivers, to the Rwashi River in Kihica, where it stays behind.

Buriru (III) : Seventh wife of Mwindo, daughter of Kandobefu, and mother of Utundo and Mwishi.

Centipede (IV) : The Nyanga vocabulary distinguishes at least seven kinds of centipedes. The general term is *ngongo*, but in both the tales and the epics *kiringeshe*, the name of one variety, is always used. Centipede is the diviner par excellence who, in return for phlegm, gives short and precise oracles to the mother of Little-one-just-born-he-walked, to the hero himself, and to Mwindo. People dream about Centipede as the master interpreter of hidden things.

Chameleon (III) : *Kou*, who carries for Mwindo a huge banana paste which Elephant was unable to lift, is rewarded with land and fame. He is also invoked in Mwindo's song as the symbol of caution. In the tales Chameleon is "the one who is not overcome by a burden," the very active and astute person who gains everyone's respect.

Chief (II) : An unidentified chief gives a wife to the Pygmy Shekaruru because he has revivified the chief's dead son. In return, the Pygmy leaves his son behind with the chief.

Chief-Counselor (III, IV) : Shebakungu is one of the foremost officeholders in the Nyanga political system. As senior among the chief's counselors, he acts in the epics as adviser and executive officer of the chief. He takes certain personal initiatives. His role in selecting a successor and in enthronement and death rituals is secret. During these rituals he acts as the preceptor of the chief; he consults the oracles on behalf of the chief.

Chief-Pygmy (III, IV) : The title of *mwamitwa* is held by a Pygmy or a descendant of the Pygmies. He is a member of the college of ritual experts who discharge many diverse, but complementary, functions during a chief's enthronement. In epic III the Chief-Pygmy is designated as provider of the honey and the hide of the flying squirrel which are essential for Murimba's enthronement. In epic III the name is used in a more general sense to designate the leader of the Pygmies.

Chief's son (II) : This unnamed son resuscitates from the dead because of a magical whistle and magical action by Mwindo's Pygmy, Shekaruru. Fully dressed with the insignia of chieftainship, the son is led from the house in which he died.

Children (I, II, III) : Unidentified small children appear on occasion. Mwindo feeds small children whom he encounters during his sub-

285

terranean journey to Sheburungu (I). He feeds two thousand children who are collecting eleusine on the road to Sheburungu (II). Muhima, in the course of a solemn offering to Mwindo's father, asks small children to respond to his song (III).

Cricket (I): *Kitundukutu* is present at Mwindo's birth and betrays his sex. In epic I he is referred to by the epithet "The-one-who-hears-secrets" as would-be maternal uncle of Mwindo.

Destiny (IV): Buingo is the son of Chief Little-one-just-born-he-walked and of the daughter of Mukiti. After his father's death he gains, loses, and regains his chieftainship from his father's half brother and archrival, Mwindo. In the same epic Destiny is also a divinity who dispenses life.

Difficulties-that-do-not-come-together-with-others (III): This unusual name is given to a chief, possibly Murimba, with whom Mwindo's Pygmies decide to settle after their defection from Mwindo.

Dogs (I, II, III): Closely linked with the hero-chief and his Pygmies, dogs are either individually named or referred to under a generic term (such as trained hunting dogs; untrained dogs). In epic I they accompany the Pygmies on the hunt that leads to an encounter with the Dragon-Ogre Kirimu. In epic II Mwindo buys his dogs Ndorobiro and Ngonde from the Buffaloes; they accompany the Pygmies on numerous hunts and help a young trapper destroy the Dragon-Ogre Kirimu. In epic III the dogs are called Bad-Luck and Fast-Eater; they are fine hunters and bring riches to Mwindo. On his trip to Nyamurairi, Mwindo hides his dogs under his armpits; they are instrumental in unmasking Nyamurairi's wife who has changed into a buffalo. Epic III relates the story of Shakwece's dog Ringe, whose death prompts Shakwece to organize an ordeal in which his preferred wife and her child perish.

Elephant (III): Elephant is outdone by Chameleon in trying to lift a huge banana paste prepared by Mwindo's mother, but in the same epic he is praised by Mwindo in his songs as "son of Expert-Singer" and as "the blazer of trails."

Father-of-the-chief (I, IV): Known as Shemwami, this officeholder is one of the special guardians of the ritual wife and her son; he is generally a close agnatic relative of the ruling chief. In epic IV the sons of Mwindo are in the position of Fathers-of-the-chief vis-à-vis the sons of Little-one-just-born-he-walked.

First-born-of-the-land (III, IV): The title *ntangi ya cuo* is usually reserved for the son of the chief's principal wife (*nyabana*). In epic IV the situation is reversed; it is Mwindo, son of the ritual wife, who becomes First-born-of-the-land. In epic III this officeholder is identified as Salt-of-the-land (*mukwacuo*).

Fly (III, IV) : Fly is invoked by Mwindo as "child of Odor" (III) ; he fights against Mwindo with Ant, Wasp, Bee, and Spider (IV).

God (III) : The creator god Ongo is characterized as the ultimate cause of both fertility and barrenness.

Hail (I) : Personified and quasi-divine Hail helps Rain, Lightning, Moon, Sun, and Star punish Mwindo.

Hangi-of-Drum (III, IV) : Hangi, an important divinity in the Nyanga pantheon, is the father of Chief Karisi's principal wife Kahindo (III) ; he is briefly evoked in a song in epic IV.

Hawk (I, II, IV) : In epic I Hawk (Kahungu) acts as a messenger who is both friendly and unfriendly to Mwindo. He tells Mwindo where his father has fled and where his paternal aunt has gone to be married; on the other hand, he informs Kasiyembe, one of Mwindo's antagonists, about Mwindo's meeting with his paternal aunt. In epic II the Pygmy Shekaruru finds Hawk being devoured in the forest by red ants. The Pygmy frees him, and Hawk promises aid in return. Later, Hawk liberates the Pygmy from a tree to which he had fled to escape the wrath of warthogs and receives chickens from Mwindo.

Itewa (II) : Lit., A small predator. Itewa is a chief who rebels against Mwindo because of jealousy.

Iyangura (I) : Sister to Chief Shemwindo and the paternal aunt of Mwindo, she is married to the Water Serpent Mukiti. Mwindo, rejected by his father, sets out to search for her; when he finds her, he transforms her into his concerned supporter and faithful adviser.

Iyangura (II) : Wife of Chief Shemwindo and mother of Mwindo and his sister Nyamitondo Mwindo.

Iyangura Katende (II) : Sister of Chief Shemwindo. She is married to the Water Serpent Mukiti, but she does not play a role in the epic.

Kahindo (I, II, III) : An important female divinity of Hunde origin. In epic I she is the daughter of Muisa, the bringer-of-death. On his subterranean journey Mwindo meets her at the wading place; Mwindo heals her yaws; she gives him advice to help him overcome her father's trickery. She becomes Mwindo's temporary lover, but when Muisa is revived and proposes her as wife to Mwindo, he rejects the offer by saying that he will marry later. In epic II she is the daughter of Nyamurairi, the god of fire. Mwindo meets her at the wading place during his subterranean journey; she is scurvy, but Mwindo heals her and receives her advice and love. In epic III she leads Mwindo deep into the forest by metamorphosing herself successively into a wild boar, the daughter of a blacksmith, and a woman harvesting bananas, and then she exposes him to tests prepared by her father Nyamurairi. She finally becomes Mwindo's wife and bears Ndurumo and Kanyironge.

Kahindo (III) : Daughter of Hangi-of-Drum and principal wife of Chief Karisi. Rejected by her husband because of barrenness, she conceives a son, Little-one-just-born-he-walked, through parthenogenesis; she later has another son, Mwindo, who is conceived normally.

Kahindo's mother (III) : In distress, Kahindo, the wife of Chief Karisi, addresses her mother's spirit.

Kahombo (I, III, IV) : Female Nyanga divinity; lit., the Spirit of Good Fortune. In epic I Mwindo is born carrying the bag of Good Fortune; in epic III he calls for her blessing; in epic IV Centipede prescribes that Little-one-just-born-he-walked must obtain a bag belonging to Kahombo before he fights with Mwindo.

Kantori (I) : See *Sparrow*.

Kanyampanda (III) : Child of Mwindo's fifth wife; his name indicates that his parents are fine dancers. After his father's death he obtains special status with reference to the burial and the distribution of the father's legacy.

Kanyironge (III) : Lit., Genet; son of Mwindo's first wife Kahindo and full brother to Ndurumo. He is called "the grandchild of Stone." The genet is the chief of the animals; its hide is part of the royal paraphernalia.

Karisi (III) : A chief who married many wives, he is the sociological father of the hero Little-one-just-born-he-walked (born of Karisi's wife through parthenogenesis) and the father of the hero Mwindo. At times he is called by his teknonymic name, Shemwindo.

Kasiwa (III) : Headman to Chief Murimba, he receives Mwindo's Pygmies and introduces them to his chief. The name denotes a person who is born after his father's death.

Kasiyembe (I) : Headman to Mukiti, he occupies the position of Father-of-the-chief and holds guardianship over Mwindo's aunt Iyangura. He is referred to as the "man of hatred."

Katee (I, III) : Hedgehog informs Mwindo about traps set for him by Kasiyembe and makes tunnels allowing Mwindo to travel underground to the house of his paternal aunt (I). In epic III Katee is recalled in song by Mwindo.

Katobororo (I) : Given as wife to Mwindo by his father Shemwindo after Mwindo's enthronement. The woman's name is a reflection of the tensions that existed in the chiefdom because of the conflict between Mwindo and his father. The name signifies a woman born in a kinship group later destroyed by the evil talk of its members.

Kihoro (*III*) : Chief mentioned by Mwindo's Pygmies.

Kirimu (I, II) : The dragon-ogre, an extraordinary being that lives in the deep forest. In epic I he is described as having "seven heads and seven horns and seven eyes"; he swallows all but one of Mwindo's Pygmies, but is defeated by Mwindo. Many people resuscitate from his body. Mwindo must suffer, however, because he is Lightning's friend and because he has killed Kirimu, who is also Lightning's friend. In epic II Kirimu "returned leveling all the trees with gusts and gusts." He and his daughter Ukano are visited by a lost trapper who must play the zanza and sing with it all night in order to obtain Ukano and to preserve his own life; but the trapper is defeated and killed. His brother, aided by Mwindo's dogs, destroys Kirimu and revivifies the young trapper, taking Kirimu's daughter home.

Kubikubi-star (I) : With Rain, Hail, Sun, Moon, and Lightning, Star imposes suffering on and gives teachings to Mwindo to purify him of his arrogance.

Lightning (I, II, III, IV) : Nkuba is a Nyanga divinity. Known under the epithets Flashes (*mirabyo*) and Opener-Cleaver (*iyobora*), Lightning is the master of destruction. In epic I Mwindo exercises so compelling an influence over Lightning that whatever destruction the hero desires is granted by Lightning. Also in epic I, Lightning is the source of and the reason for the purification of Mwindo, changing him from a boisterous hero to a generous and poised chief. In the other epics the role of Lightning is sharply reduced. In epic III Mwindo engages in a battle with Lightning, making him his servant in return for the dedication of cult objects. Together with Mwindo, Lightning engages in a fierce battle against Nyakatwakari, mother of the Pygmies. In epic IV the dying Mwindo requests Lightning to cleave the house in which he dwells as a last, somewhat desperate, show of force.

Little-one-just-born-he-walked (I, II, III, IV) : In epics I and II Kabutwakenda is the most important epithet of Mwindo, because he knew how to walk (and to speak) from birth on. In epics III and IV Kabutwakenda is the name of a different person. The role of Kabutwakenda is limited, but his heroic stature is evident in epic III:

he is born of parthenogenesis after a long pregnancy and after a painful and lonely delivery. He disappears, flying away from a hostile crowd, and settles in Bukumba with a snake. He sends famine to his homeland. In epic IV Little-one-just-born-he-walked is the glorious hero in contrast with his half brother Mwindo, who plays the role of the villain. He is born of the chief's principal wife; his mother, who had been barren for some time, has lost her status and lives on the outskirts of the village. He is married to Mukiti's daughter and becomes chief as the result of his generosity and intelligence. He has a son, Destiny, who succeeds him. See *Destiny; Mukiti; Mwindo; Nyabana.*

Maidens (I, II, III) : Unnamed maidens, in groups or alone, appear from time to time. They are in Iyangura's following; Mwindo is seen by maidens at the wading place; Shemwindo gives a maiden to Lightning after his son Mwindo returns from his celestial journey (I). Shemwindo gives two maidens to Lightning in return for his help in destroying Big-bird-born-by-itself; Mwindo obtains two maidens from the spoils of Sheburungu, giving one of them to his lover Kahindo; Mwindo's Pygmy Shekaruru receives a maiden from a chief whose son he revivifies; Mwindo offers a maiden to his Pygmy Shekaruru (II). A maiden is given to Muembwa, the dignitary who takes care of Chief Murimba's burial (III).

Maternal uncles (I, II, III) : Mwindo is forged by his maternal uncles. There is no indication that they are his mother's agnates. In epic IV the maternal uncles are absent, but Mukiti assumes the role of a maternal uncle to some extent. See *Baniyana; Bat.*

Maternal uncles' wives (III) : When Mwindo is forged by his maternal uncles, the hair of his paternal aunts and of the wives of his maternal uncles is used as charcoal and their tears are utilized to cool him.

Mburu (II) : Lit., *mburu*-monkey. He is one of the chiefs who rebel against Mwindo, but his role in the fight of the rebel leader Itewa is not explained. In a separate episode, however, Chief Mburu of the Banamburu group is caught in the snares of one of Mwindo's trappers. In the ensuing battle between Mwindo and the Banamburu, the latter are defeated by Mwindo's dogs and scepter. See *Banamburu.*

Meshe the Pygmy (III) : Meshemutwa is the son of Nyakabotyo and one of Mwindo's Pygmies. He is treated rudely by Mwindo during a wild boar hunt. The hunt leads Mwindo to a series of adventures. Meshe takes part in an unsuccessful honey harvest, the stakes being

Nyakatwakari's daughter, which causes a rupture between Mwindo and his Pygmies. Meshemutwa is also a Nyanga divinity.

Messengers (I, II, III) : Unidentified messengers are sent to call, to inform, and to warn people, or to fetch things.

Minerusi (III) : Lit., Master-of-the-river. He is a member of the college of ritual experts and as such is present at Chief Murimba's enthronement. He is described as "the one who kills fish for the chief when he is being enthroned." During the rites he brings water and fish from the sacred river. (Each autonomous kingdom has such a river.)

Moon (I, III) : The personified and semideified Moon contributes to the punishment of Mwindo which leads to his purification (I). In Mwindo's song, Ndorera (i.e., bunches of raffia fiber worn around the arms for dancing) is labeled the "kinsman of Moon."

Mubei (I, III) : Lit., Barber. He is a member of the college of ritual experts and as such is present at Mwindo's (I) and Murimba's (III) enthronement rites. He is described as "the one who shaves the chief, the one who looks for a copper razor."

Muembwa (III) : A ritual officeholder selected after Chief Murimba's death to dispose of the regalia.

Muhakabi (III) : Lit., Giver-of-the-*kabi*-ordeal. As a member of the college of ritual experts, he is present at Chief Murimba's enthronement. In that ceremony he is "the one who anoints the chief with oil."

Muheri (I) : Lit., Sacrificer, a ritual killer of goats who is made available by Shemwindo for Mwindo's enthronement.

Muhima (III) : A person of Mwindo's village charged by him to organize the offerings for Mwindo's father. A quarrel between Muhima and the Chief-Counselor leads to strife and battle in the village. Muhima is the name of a divinity.

Muisa (I, II) : A prominent divinity of the subterranean world, Muisa is the child and servant of Nyamurairi and is frequently confused with the latter. In epic I Muisa exposes the hero Mwindo to a number of tests which Nyamurairi imposes upon him in epic II. The world of Muisa is aptly described in epic I by his daughter Kahindo as "the place where no one ever clusters around the fire." She describes her father as "a very big man and tall, curled up in the ashes near the hearth," and as "the chief of all the people." Like Nyamurairi, Muisa has close connections with dogs; he presents himself in a dream as a black dog curled up in the ashes. In epic II Muisa is briefly designated as the husband of Nyamwanda. See *Kahindo*; *Nyamwanda*.

Muisa wa Bibandi (IV): An unidentified person (chief, divinity, or primordial ancestor?) whose daughters are courted by Mwindo and by Little-one-just-born-he-walked. One of his daughters marries Mwindo.

Mukiti (I, II, IV): A fabulous water serpent believed to live in a deep pool in the river. Mukiti is chief of the river. He is married to Mwindo's paternal aunt (I, II) and is unfriendly toward Mwindo (I). In epic IV he is a friend and ally (possibly a maternal uncle) of Little-one-just-born-he-walked and inimical toward Mwindo. He provides Little-one-just-born-he-walked with a copper zanza, a stool, a spear, a scepter, a necklace, a bag, and a wife. His epithet is Master-of-the-unfathomable (I); his praise names are Pool and River. See *Iyangura*.

Mukiti's daughter (IV): Beautiful as "plain ivory," she is courted by both Mwindo and Little-one-just-born-he-walked; she marries the latter. Childless for some time, she becomes pregnant after Mwindo has lifted a taboo weighing on her husband. She is the mother of Destiny, who succeeds his father as chief.

Mumbo-wife (III, IV): The chief's ritual wife, provided at his enthronement, is a close relative of the chief. In principle, one of her sons (real or secretly adopted) is chief designate. The ritual wife resides in a separate village; she has her own landed estate and her own servants. She and her children are placed under the protection and guardianship of several high-ranking officials. If she has no sons, secret arrangements presided over by the Chief-Counselor provide her with a son, such as the child of a common wife of the chief, her own junior brother, or the son of one of her female servants. If her own son is unacceptable as future chief, he may be replaced by the son of one of her possible substitutes (junior title-holding wives of the chief). In epic III Chief Murimba receives a ritual wife at his enthronement; after his death she is placed under the protection of Shemumbo and the Chief-Counselor; she inherits some of her husband's widows to work for her. In epic IV the *mumbo*-wife is the mother of Mwindo, who covets the chieftainship but does not get it.

Munkonde (II): Lit., a large bat. A chief and a blacksmith, he is allied with Chief Itewa against Mwindo. See *Bat*.

Muntsuntsu (III): Lit., Bee; one of Mwindo's sons by his fourth wife Ntsukiwamunindi. He receives the status of Pygmyship.

Murimba (III): Lit., Heavy-Stone. This chief lives in a place "in which there was no fire, in which there was nothing but darkness. There they (his people) dwell in a large cave." After their defection from Mwindo, the Pygmies join Murimba and teach him about fire.

Musanduri (III): Title of one of the chief's wives who is provided by Mwindo's maternal uncles. Chief Murimba also receives such a woman during the enthronement rites. The chief's successor may be selected from among her sons if the ritual wife has none.

Musao (III): As a member of the college of ritual experts, he assumes various female functions during the enthronement rites (making the bed; cleansing the chief). He is present at Murimba's enthronement.

Mushonga (I): The chief's cook, provided by Shemwindo at Mwindo's enthronement.

Mushumbia (I, III): Lit., Ritual-Drummer. As a member of the college of ritual experts, he participates in the enthronement rites for both Mwindo and Murimba.

Musimba (III): A "sacred" person, he presides over the chief's burial rites and guards part of the regalia. The position is inherited within certain kinship groups. Musimba lives in a separate village; he cannot be seen by the ruling chief. In epic III the Chief-Counselor receives from him the *ukenye*-bundle for Chief Murimba's enthronement; he is later requested to preside over the burial of Murimba and to remove select parts of his body to be kept in the *ukenye*-bundle.

Musoka (I): The junior sister of the Water Serpent Mukiti, Musoka is herself a long snake on whose back people cross rivers in the tales. She is unfriendly toward Mwindo and tries to obstruct the road to Iyangura. Musoka is a Nyanga divinity.

Musukuiyera (III): Son of Mwindo by his third wife Nyakirimarimari. The name suggests that he was born while the people were dancing *musuku*-dances on banana leaves spread out on the ground. He occupies the status of father of the *nyabana*-wife.

Mutero Murimba (III): Lit., Heavy-White-Stone. He is a chief whom Mwindo fights after being forged by his maternal uncles. Mwindo cleaves him into pieces.

Mutobi of Nyantsinde (IV): In epic IV the name of the chief who is the father of the two heroes, Mwindo and Little-one-just-born-he-walked, is not explicitly stated. A casual reference to Little-one-just-born-he-walked as "the son of Mutobi of Nyantsinde" apparently names the chief.

Mwamihesi (I, III): Lit., Chief-Blacksmith. As member of the college of ritual experts, he is present at Mwindo's (I) and Murimba's (III) enthronement rites. During the most secret phase of those rites he recites formulas, accompanying himself with two *ncengero*-hammers used as percussion instruments.

Mwamitwa (III, IV) : Lit., Chief-Pygmy. He is a member of the college of ritual experts. See *Chief-Pygmy*.

Mweri (III) : Lit., Moon, she is the sixth wife of Mwindo and the mother of Bisheria.

Mwindo (I, II, III, IV) : Lit., the name for a boy who follows a number of female children in the family. Some spokesmen see a relationship between the name and the verb *iindo* (to fell trees, to eradicate). In epics I, II, and III Mwindo is the principal hero who achieves widespread fame and supreme glory as an enthroned chief; in epic IV he is second to his half brother, Little-one-just-born-he-walked, and assumes the role of a villain. In epics I and II Mwindo is the miraculously born son of Chief Shemwindo and his preferred wife Nyamwindo (who temporarily lost her preferred status because she bore a son against her husband's will). In epic III he is the normally born second son of Chief Karisi and his principal *nyabana*-wife. In epic IV he is the normally born son secretly conceived by the chief and his *nyabana*-wife (who had been rejected because of barrenness). Mwindo is known, particularly in epic I, under numerous epithets and patronymics, such as Little-one-just-born-he-walked; Little-Castaway; Man-of-many-feats; Little-child-of-many-wonders; Master-of-strength; My father, eternal savior of people; child of Iyangura; the one fruit that Nyamwindo has brought forth.

Mwindo Mboru (II) : A double name for Mwindo, probably meaning Mwindo the Opener.

Mwindo's brothers (II, III, IV) : Mwindo has no brothers in epic I. In epic II he has an unnamed half brother who plays no role in the story. In epic III he has a quasi half brother, Little-one-just-born-he-walked (born of parthenogenesis), who disappears early in the action. Epic IV describes an intense competition between the two half brothers (different mothers, same father), Mwindo and Little-one-just-born-he-walked.

Mwindo's children (III, IV) : Children are not specified in epics I and II. In epic III Mwindo has ten named children (all sons) by seven wives, but none of them take part in the action. In epic IV Mwindo has three sons and three daughters, one of whom is called Protector-of-the-things-that-will-not-be-understood. Fascinated by his newly acquired chieftainship, Mwindo refuses to relinquish power when one of his children falls sick. The child subsequently dies and, as a spirit, kills its father and mother.

Mwindo's cross-cousins (III): When Mwindo is forged by his maternal uncles, two sets of two cross-cousins (mother's brother's children) are used as supports.

Mwindo's sisters (I, II, III): In epic I Mwindo has six half sisters (different mothers, same father), but they are inactive. In epic II Mwindo has a uterine sister, Nyamitondo Mwindo, who plays a prominent role in the earlier part of the epic, and a half sister (different mothers) who plays no role at all. In epic III Mwindo has an unnamed sister whose daughter is his ritual wife.

Mwindo's sister's daughter (III): Unnamed, she becomes the ritual wife of Mwindo.

Mwindo's wives (I, II, III, IV): In epic I Mwindo has no wives until his enthronement, at which time he receives four: one from his father, one from the Pygmies, one from his maternal uncles, and one from Father-of-the-chief. In epic II Mwindo initially has a senior wife, who is his beloved wife; he obtains nine wives from his father when they return home from the subterranean world and seven more at his enthronement. In this epic he takes the two wives and one maiden of the defeated Sheburungu and one maiden from his Pygmy Shekaruru (whom the latter had received because he had revivified a chief's son). In epic III Mwindo has seven wives, explicitly enumerated with their children, possibly in addition to his senior wife. In epic IV Mwindo is married to Muisa's daughter.

Mwishi (III): Lit., Sun. As a child of Mwindo's seventh wife Buriru, he achieves the status of prince.

Ncongera (III): Lit., Snake-Tail. A child of Mwindo's second wife, Ufamba, he receives the status of First-born-of-the-land and Shemumbo.

Ndurumo (III): Lit., Thunder. Child of Mwindo's first wife Kahindo, he has the status of chief designate.

Nkango (III): A Pygmy in Mwindo's following who is the first to meet with Mwindo after his long absence and to announce the news of Mwindo's return to the other Pygmies. Abandoned by Mwindo, he later liberates his brother Meshe the Pygmy from a tree in which he had remained captive and contributes to the defection of Mwindo's Pygmies to another chief.

Nkurongo (I, III): Lit., the *bulikoko*-bird. In epic I Nkurongo is one of Mwindo's Pygmies who manages to escape from the dragon-ogre and to alert Mwindo. In epic III he is recalled as the son of Korokoro (a variety of the *bulikoko*-bird) and as their kinsman by both Mwindo and the Pygmy Nkango.

Ntanga (III) : Lit., Wasp; the fifth wife of Mwindo.

Nteta (II) : Lit., duiker antelope; one of the chiefs who rebel against Mwindo.

Ntindi (III) : Lit., Civet Cat. Child of Mwindo by his second wife Ufamba, he is called "the diviner of many ways" and is awarded the status of *musimba* (organizer of the chief's burial ceremonies).

Ntsukiwamunindi (III) : Lit., Bee, child of Needle, she is Mwindo's fourth wife.

Ntumba (I) : Lit., Aardvark. A quasi-divine being, Aardvark lives in a huge lair in the subterranean world. Mwindo, in search of his father, defeats Ntumba .

Nyabakungu (III, IV) : Lit., Mother-of-the-counselors. The wife of the Chief-Counselor, in epics III and IV she acts, at her husband's request, as midwife for the abandoned *nyabana*-wife of the chief.

Nyabana (III, IV) : Lit., Mother-of-the-children; title of the senior or principal wife of any person. In epic III a *nyabana*-wife is provided for Chief Murimba. In epic IV Nyabana, the chief's wife, is barren and therefore is rejected by her husband. Because of her diligence in times of famine she regains his confidence and, after bearing the hero Little-one-just-born-he-walked, is restored to her former status.

Nyakabotyo (III) : Mother of the Pygmy Meshemutwa.

Nyakatwakari (III) : Lit., Mother-little-Pygmy-woman. She is the daughter of Marumbu and the mother of the Pygmies. She calls herself a gorilla and a person who is "not smeared with the mark of vexation." Mwindo and Lightning defeat her, but she causes the conflict between Mwindo and his Pygmies which results in their defection to another chief.

Nyakatwakari's daughter (III) : The girl, beautiful "like the rays of the sun," is promised as a wife to Mwindo if he manages to remove honey from a *mpaki*-tree, but Mwindo does not succeed. Instead of becoming Mwindo's wife, this girl causes Mwindo to accuse his Pygmies of laxness and to separate from them.

Nyakimarimari (IV) : A personage often recalled in the magical song of Little-one-just-born-he-walked. See *Mrs. Pointed-Mouth.*

Nyakirimarimari (III) : Mwindo's third wife and mother of Musukuiyera. She may be the same person as Mrs. Pointed-Mouth, because both are praised as she "who has overcome the Bahunga in shrewdness" or "she who had destroyed the Bahunga with shrewdness."

Nyakwabo (II) : Despised wife of Shakwece. Accused of having killed the dog Ringe, she survives the ordeal imposed by her husband.

Nyamitondo Mwindo (also, Nyamutondo Mwindo; II) : Daughter of Chief Shemwindo and his wife Iyangura and uterine sister of Mwindo. She is married to Lightning and lives with him in the celestial realm. She teaches her brother the art of cultivation, which she learned from her husband. Lightning provides her with iron weapons to destroy Big-Bird, a monster that decimated all the people and animals of Mwindo's village.

Nyamurairi (II, III, IV) : God of fire and chief of the subterranean world. In epics II and III he exposes Mwindo to various trickeries and tests in a fairly even contest. In epic III he marries his daughter to Mwindo. In epic IV Mwindo dies and then proceeds to fight with Nyamurairi; however, he is returned to earth by the latter's servant. In epic I Nyamurairi is only briefly evoked as Nyarire, but Muisa acts and speaks in a manner reminiscent of Nyamurairi in the other epics.

Nyamurairi's daughter (II, III) : See *Kahindo.*

Nyamurairi's wife (III) : Mother of Kahindo, she changes herself into a buffalo to trick Mwindo.

Nyamwanda (II) : Lit., Mrs. Ax; she is the wife of Muisa and dwells in an iron house. The Pygmy Shekaruru encounters her in the forest; she has a pregnancy the size of a house. When the Pygmy gives her a blow on the belly, a mass of stones emerge. Shekaruru receives from her a magic whistle and the knowledge of magical techniques to revivify people.

Nyamwindo (I, III) : Lit., Mother of Mwindo. Nyamwindo is a teknonymic name for Mwindo's mother; it corresponds to Shemwindo for Mwindo's father. The term is only occasionally employed in epics I and III. In all the texts its substitutes are the personal names of the chief's wives (such as Iyangura in II or Kahindo in III) or status terms (such as ritual, preferred, principal, or despised wife).

Nyankuba (II) : The preferred wife of Shakwece. Accused of killing the dog Ringe, she drowns together with her child.

Nyarusumba (IV) : A divinity of the subterranean world and servant to Nyamurairi. He sends Mwindo, who has died in order to fight Nyamurairi, back to earth.

Otter (*ntsibi*; I, III) : Otter is briefly evoked in songs in epics I and III. In epic III Mwindo calls him "son of the One-who-brings-death," establishing a connection between Otter and the divinities Muisa and Nyamurairi. In epic III Otter is an expert swimmer who, together with Water Duck, retrieves Nyamwanda's ax from the water.

Peternal aunt (I, II, III, IV) : In all the epics except II the role of Mwindo's paternal aunt is of great consequence. In epic II his paternal aunt is married to the Water Serpent Mukiti, but her role is reduced to nothing. Much of epic I concerns the marriage of Iyangura (i.e., Mwindo's paternal aunt) to Mukiti, Mwindo's quest for her, their encounter and return to the homeland, and their moral and spiritual attachment (including telecommunication), until Mwindo is enthroned as chief and she can return to her husband Mukiti, who dwells in the water. In epics III and IV it is the spirit of Mwindo's paternal aunt who enters the field of action. (Note that the term "spirit" is not used in the texts; the aunt is presented as a living person, the difference between living and dead being conceived of in terms of "living here," i.e., in the world, and "living there," i.e., in the subterranean world.) In epic III the paternal aunt brings sleep and a house to Mwindo who is lost faraway in the forest. In the same epic she advises Mwindo on his journey to Nyamurairi to hide his dogs under his armpits; she helps him perform the agricultural work prescribed by Nyamurairi. When finally he returns to her place, on his way home from a visit to Nyamurairi, she shows him a shorter route and asks him to dedicate to her, as part of a cult, a bag, a calabash, and a knife. In epic III Mwindo is forged in the village of his maternal uncles with hair and tears taken from his paternal aunts and from the wives of his maternal uncles. In epic IV Mwindo, on his second trip to the subterranean world to fight Nyamurairi, is advised by his paternal aunt to return to earth and not to reveal the things he has witnessed in the subterranean world.

Mrs. Pointed-Mouth (IV): This personage, called Nyabunu-mushuto, is mentioned in a magical song frequently sung by Little-one-just-born-he-walked. It is unclear who is designated by this formula. In epic I there is a certain Nyaruwi (a fish known for its long and pointed mouth), an ally of Mukiti against Mwindo. Mpaca, the Specter of the forest, is sometimes said to have a long, sharp snout. It is probable that the name applies to Nyakatwakari, the mother of the Pygmies, who describes herself as a gorilla.

Potto (III): The Pygmy Nkango consults his oracle to save his kinsman Meshe the Pygmy who gets stuck in a tree while he is harvesting honey for Mwindo. Nkango calls him "child of Healer."

Protector-of-the-things-that-will-not-be-understood (IV): Daughter of Mwindo and his wife who is Muisa's daughter. The name alludes to the background of the girl's mother (her father Muisa is the bringer-of-death) and possibly to the unsuccessful subterranean voyage of Mwindo.

Pygmies (I, II, III, IV) : The Pygmies (Batwa) are prominent in all the epics, either in a group or individually, as status holders, as hunters, and as singers. In epic I Mwindo receives them from his father at the enthronement rites. On their first hunt three Pygmies are swallowed by the dragon-ogre; Mwindo is alerted by Nkurongo, who escaped; he kills the dragon and frees the Pygmies. In epic II Mwindo is established with his Pygmies, one of whom, Shekaruru, occupies a central role as hunter and healer. In epic III Mwindo resides with his Pygmies in the land of downstream. They defect to Chief Murimba because of a quarrel with Mwindo concerning honey and their mother; they bring the knowledge of fire to Murimba's people and provide Murimba with the Chief-Pygmy at his enthronement. In epic IV the Pygmies are portrayed essentially as the singers of Little-one-just-born-he-walked. The hero requests singers from Mukiti and gets Pygmies who "produced wonderful things from their mouth while singing." The Chief-Pygmy also accompanies the hero on his quest for a wife. See *Chief-Pygmy*; *Meshe the Pygmy*; *Nkango*; *Nkurongo*; *Nyakatwakari*; *Shekaruru*.

Ringe (II) : Dog belonging to Shakwece and killed by one of his wives.

Ritual wife (IV) : In general, the ritual wife or *mumbo* is given to the chief at his enthronement; one of her sons (real or adopted) is destined to succeed as chief. In epic IV an intense conflict develops between the ritual wife (i.e., Mwindo's mother) and the *nyabana*-wife (i.e., the mother of Little-one-just-born-he-walked) because the latter's son achieves power and authority. See *Mumbo-wife*.

Ruendo (III) : Divinity of the subterranean world who is invoked by Kahindo, the chief's abandoned wife, and is promised worship in return for assistance.

Servants (I, II, III, IV) : Under the general term *baombe*, servants of Mwindo, of Shemwindo, of the ritual wife, and of the divinities function in various capacities. Mwindo is usually accompanied by servants when he travels (I, IV) : the chief gives two servants to his wife after the birth of his son Mwindo (III) ; the wives of the dead Chief Murimba are allocated as servants to his ritual wife (III) ; servants guard the entrances to the village while the chief sleeps with his rejected wife.

Shakwece (II) : Mwindo's Pygmy Shekaruru witnesses a strange event in Shakwece's village. Because one of his wives has killed his dog Ringe, Shakwece orders both wives to cross a pool on a liana to find out which one is guilty. His beloved wife, carrying her child, drowns, while Shakwece refuses to rescue her.

Shebakungu (III, IV) : See *Chief-Counselor*.

Sheburungu (I, II, III) : A name at times applied to the creator god Ongo, but in the epics Sheburungu is apparently a separate divinity living in the subterranean world. His separateness from the creator god and from Nyamurairi is not fully clear, because the creator god is the "heart of the earth" and Nyamurairi lives in a men's house, according to Nyanga cosmology; in epic II Sheburungu resides in a men's house inside a cave. In epic I Mwindo beats him in the game of dice and discovers his father hidden in Sheburungu's place. In epic II Mwindo is sent by Nyamurairi to play the dice against Sheburungu; Mwindo defeats him and claims his wives. In epic III Sheburungu is celebrated as the one "who is walking with one thousand people."

Shekaruru (II) : Lit., Master-of-the-*karuru*-call (in the cupped hand, to encourage the dogs). A Pygmy and a great hunter in Mwindo's service, Shekaruru is in many episodes the center of the action; he has a number of wonderful encounters with Hawk, warthogs, Nyamwanda, Specter, a chief's son, and Shakwece. Fascinated by the murmur of a river, he offers all his animals to the river.

Shekaruru's son (II) : He is left with a chief whose son Shekaruru had revivified, in return for the gift of a maiden.

Shemumbo (I, III) : Lit., Father-of-the-ritual-wife; a close agnatic relative of the chief. Shemumbo is the father, or provider, and guardian of the ritual wife. In epic I he is installed at Mwindo's enthronement. In epic III he and the Chief-Counselor must care for the ritual wife after Chief Murimba's death.

Shemwami (I, IV) : Lit., Father-of-the-chief. He is an officeholder who has a specific role in the guardianship of the ritual wife, like Kasiyembe's guardianship of Iyangura (I). In epic IV the children of Mwindo become First-born-of-the-land and Shemwami simultaneously; this fusion of offices is customary in some states.

Shemwindo (I, II, III, IV) : Lit., Father-of-Mwindo. Shemwindo is a teknonymic name by which Mwindo's father is known exclusively in epics I and II; the name is casually used for the father of both Mwindo and Little-one-just-born-he-walked in epics III and IV. In all the epics Shemwindo is a chief who has married several wives, one of whom (the mother of the hero to be born) loses her status. In epics I and II he is in disagreement with the hero because he had decreed that he wanted no sons; the conflict is protracted in epic I and short-lived in epic II. In each instance the hero reconciles with the father after finding him in the subterranean world where he had fled. In epics III and IV the discord is absent.

Sparrow (I, IV) : Kantori is a friend of Mwindo. In epic I he shows Mwindo the fern through which Mwindo's father fled to the subterranean world and, with Hawk's help, he designates the place where Mwindo's father is hiding at Sheburungu's. In epic IV he is the dancer of Little-one-just-born-he-walked.

Specter (II) : Mpaca, the aggressive long-haired specter (male or female), wants to get hold of Mwindo's Pygmy Shekaruru who, on a trapping expedition, spends the night in her house. But Mpaca gets stuck in resinous glue which Shekaruru had left on the drying rack.

Spider (I, I I, III, IV) : Spider, called (*mune*) *buebue*, is an actor in epics I and II. He builds bridges over pitfall traps which Kasiyembe has set up against Mwindo (I). In epic II he provides Mwindo with cobwebs to help him climb a tree, acting together with Bat who supplies the nails. In epics III and IV Spider is recalled in songs and oracles as "son of Bridge" and "young son of Cobweb, Spinner of Bridges."

Trapper (II) : One of Mwindo's men who goes to inspect his traps arrives in the village of Kirimu, and is defeated because he is unable to sing and play the zanza for the entire night. He is killed and later revivified by his brother. See *Kirimu*; *Ukano*.

Trapper's brother (II) : One of Mwindo's men who journeys with Mwindo's dogs in search of his brother. Arriving in Kirimu's village, he plays and sings all night and then, aided by Mwindo's dogs, kills Kirimu, leads him to the place where his brother's bones and skull have been discarded; he takes a grub, places it on a hot potsherd, and revivifies his brother.

Ufamba (III) : Lit., Monitor Lizard; the second wife of Mwindo and the mother of Ncongera (Snake-Tail) and Ntindi (Civet Cat).

Ukano (II) : Daughter and accomplice of Kirimu, she is promised as wife to a young trapper and subsequently to his brother, if they are able to sing and play the zanza for a whole night. She is forced to reveal the place where the bones of the first young trapper have been thrown away and is abducted by the trappers and taken home to Mwindo. See *Kirimu*; *Trapper*.

Utundo (III) : Lit., Cloud. Child of Mwindo's seventh wife Buriru, he achieves the status of prince.

Warthogs (II, III) : In epic II they are hunted by the Pygmy Shekaruru but they chase him into a tree where he is saved by Hawk. In epic III they are identified in Muhima's song as "young sons of Cutter (who) cuts young shoots."

Wasp (III, IV) : In epic IV Wasp helps Little-one-just-born-he-walked in his fight against Mwindo. In epic III he is mentioned in Nkango's oracle as "young son of Slender."

Water Duck (III) : An expert swimmer, he and Otter retrieve from a river the ax lost by a blacksmith's daughter.

Wild-Banana-Tree (III) : Known as Itembe, he obstructs the road when Mwindo returns home from fighting with Mutero Murimba; Mwindo removes him with the formula, "to be big is not to be great."

Wild Boar (III) : A large wild boar, into which Nyamurairi's daughter Kahindo has changed herself, is chased by Mwindo and his Pygmies. Mwindo tries to hit the boar with his spear, but the animal escapes, luring Mwindo farther and farther into the forest for a long journey that leads him to Nyamurairi. See *Kahindo*; *Nyamurairi*.

BIBLIOGRAPHY

Biebuyck, Daniel. "De mumbo-instelling bij de Banyanga (Kivu)," *Kongo-Overzee*, XXI, 5 (1955), 441–448.

———. *De hond bij de Nyanga: ritueel en sociologie*. Brussels: Académie Royale des Sciences d'Outre-Mer, 1956*a*.

———. "Mwéndo de Zwoeger: een heldendicht van de Banyanga," *Zuiderkruis*, I, 1 (1956*b*), 77–90.

———. "L'organisation politique des Nyanga: la chefferie Ihana (Part I)," *Kongo-Overzee*, XXII, 4–5 (1956*c*), 301–341.

———. "L'organisation politique des Nyanga: la chefferie Ihana (Part II)," *Kongo-Overzee*, XXIII, 1–2 (1957), 59–98.

———. "Les divisions du jour et de la nuit chez les Nyanga," *Aequatoria*, XXI, 4 (1958*a*), 134–138.

———. "Mwéndo de Zwoeger: een heldendicht van de Banyanga (Part II)," *Zuiderkruis*, III, 1 (1958*b*), 34–35.

———. "Six Nyanga Texts." In *A Selection of African Prose*, Vol. 1, ed. W. H. Whiteley. Pp. 55–61. Oxford: Clarendon Press, 1964.

———. "Prières des chasseurs Nyanga." In *Textes sacrés d'Afrique noire*, ed. G. Dieterlen. Pp. 135–143. Paris: Gallimard, 1965.

———. "On the Concept of Tribe," *Civilisations*, XVI, 4 (1966*a*), 500–515.

———. *Rights in Land and Its Resources among the Nyanga*. Brussels: Académie Royale des Sciences d'Outre-Mer, 1966*b*.

———. "The Epic as a Genre in Congo Oral Literature." In *African Folklore*, ed. Richard M. Dorson. Pp. 257–274. Bloomington: Indiana University Press; and New York: Doubleday and Company, 1972.

———. "Nyanga Circumcision Masks and Costumes," *African Arts*, VI, 2 (1973), 20–25, 86–92.

———. "Mumbira: Musical Instrument of a Nyanga Initiation," *African Arts*, VII, 4 (1974), 42–45, 63–65, 96.

303

————. "The Mwindo Epic (Nyanga)." In *A Treasury of African Folklore,* ed. Harold Courlander. Pp. 322–351. New York: Crown Publishers, 1975.

————. "The African Heroic Epic," *Journal of the Folklore Institute,* XIII, 1 (1976*a*), 5–36.

————. "Nyanga Cosmology and Space Categories," *Cultures et Développement,* VIII, 3 (1976*b*), 408–435.

Biebuyck, Daniel, and Brunhilde Biebuyck. "Zaïre (Nyanga Tales)." In *Folktales Told around the World,* ed. Richard M. Dorson. Pp. 380–387. Chicago: University of Chicago Press, 1975.

————. *The Nyanga Tale.* In preparation.

Biebuyck, Daniel, and Kahombo Mateene. "Un chant Hunde," *Afrika und Uebersee,* XLIX (1965), 157–169.

————. *The Mwindo Epic from the Banyanga.* Berkeley and Los Angeles: University of California Press, 1969. (Paperback, 1971.)

————. *Une anthologie de la littérature orale Nyanga.* Brussels: Académie Royale des Sciences d'Outre-Mer, 1970.

Bird, Charles, Mamadou Koita, and Bourama Soumaouro. *The Songs of Seydou Camara.* Bloomington: African Studies Center, Indiana University, 1974.

Boelaert, E. "Nsong'a Lianja, het groote epos der Nkundo-Mongo," *Congo,* I (1932), 43–70, 198–215.

————. *Nsong'a Lianja, l'épopée nationale des Nkundo.* Antwerp: De Sikkel, 1949.

————. *Lianja-Verhalen I: Ekofo-Versie.* Tervueren: Musée Royal du Congo Belge, 1957.

————. *Lianja-Verhalen II:De voorouders van Lianja.* Tervueren: Musée Royal du Congo Belge, 1958.

Bowra, C. M. *Heroic Poetry.* London: Macmillan, 1952.

Bryan, M. A. *The Bantu Languages of Africa.* London: Oxford University Press, 1959.

Burssens, Amaat. *Introduction à l'étude des langues bantoues du Congo Belge.* Antwerp: De Sikkel, 1954.

Chadwick, H. Munro, and N. Kershaw Chadwick. *The Growth of Literature.* 3 vols. New York: Macmillan, 1932, 1936, 1940.

Chadwick, Nora K., and Victor Zhirmunsky. *Oral Epics of Central Asia.* Cambridge: The University Press, 1969.

Courlander, Harold, ed. *A Treasury of African Folklore.* New York: Crown Publishers, 1975.

De Rop, A. *Lianja: l'épopée des Mongo.* Brussels: Académie Royale des Sciences d'Outre-Mer, 1964.

Dieterlen, Germaine, ed. *Textes sacrés d'Afrique noire.* Paris: Gallimard, 1965.

Dorson, Richard M. *African Folklore.* Bloomington: Indiana University Press, 1972.

————. *Folktales Told around the World.* Chicago: University of Chicago Press, 1975.

Dumézil, Georges. *The Destiny of the Warrior.* Chicago: University of Chicago Press, 1970.

Finnegan, Ruth. *Oral Literature in Africa*. Oxford: Clarendon Press, 1970.

Guthrie, Malcolm. *The Classification of the Bantu Languages*. London: Oxford University Press, 1948 (1967).

———. *Comparative Bantu: An Introduction to the Comparative Linguistics and Prehistory of the Bantu Languages*. Vol. I. Westmead: Gregg Press, 1967.

Hoffmann, A. T. "Croyances et coutumes des Bapere." Kingiri: AIMO, 1932. Manuscript.

Holman, C. Hugh. *A Handbook to Literature*. 3d ed. New York: Bobbs-Merrill, 1972.

Jacobs, John. "Le récit épique de Lofokefoke, le héros des Mbole (Bambuti)," *Aequatoria*, XXIV (1961), 81-92.

———. "Het epos van Kudukese: de Culture Hero van de Hamba," *Africa-Tervuren*, 9 (1963), 33–36.

Lord, Albert B. *The Singer of Tales*. Cambridge: Harvard University Press, 1960.

Lord, Albert B., and David E. Bynum. *Serbo-Croatian Heroic Songs. Collected by Milman Parry*. Vol. III. *The Wedding of Smailagic Meho. Avdo Mededovic*. Cambridge: Harvard University Press, 1974.

Meeussen, A. "De talen van Maniema," *Kongo Overzee*, XIX, 5 (1953), 385–391.

Moeller, A. *Les grandes lignes des migrations des Bantous de la Province Orientale du Congo Belge*. Brussels: Institut royal colonial belge, 1936.

Schebesta, Paul. *Les Pygmées du Congo Belge*. Brussels: Institut royal colonial belge, 1952.

Schumacher, Peter. *Die Physische und Soziale Umwelt der Kivu-Pygmäen*. Brussels: Institut royal colonial belge, 1949.

———. *Die Kivu-Pygmäen*. Brussels: Institut royal colonial belge, 1950.

Turnbull, Colin M. *The Forest People*. New York: Doubleday, 1962.

———. "The Mbuti Pygmies of the Congo." In *Peoples of Africa*, ed. J. L. Gibbs. Pp. 279–317. New York: Holt, Rinehart and Winston, 1965a.

———. *The Mbuti Pygmies: An Ethnographic Survey*. New York: American Museum of Natural History, 1965b.

———. *Wayward Servants: The Two Worlds of the African Pygmies*. Garden City, N.Y.: Natural History Press, 1965c.

Viaene, L. "Uit den Kunstschat der Bahunde," *Congo*, VII, 2 (1926), 28–35, 226–237.

———. "Uit het leven der Bahunde," *Congo*, X, 2 (1929), 48–53, 267–281.

———. "La vie domestique des Bahunde," *Kongo Overzee*, XVII, 2 (1951), 111–156.

———. "L'organisation politique des Bahunde," *Kongo Overzee*, XVIII (1952a), 8–33, 111–121.

———. "La religion des Bahunde," *Kongo Overzee*, XVIII, 5 (1952b), 388–425.

———. "Coup d'oeil sur la littérature orale des Bahunde," *Kongo Overzee*, XXI, 3–4 (1955), 212–240.

Whiteley, W. H., ed. *A Selection of African Prose*. 2 vols. Oxford: Clarendon Press, 1964.

INDEX

Aardvark, 31, 117. *See also* Ntumba
Ablution, 34, 37, 45
Administrative centers. *See* Masisi
Adze, 32, 100, 268
Agriculture, 45, 49, 137, 156, 185 n *10*, 201, 241
Ancestors, 16, 46, 65, 67; primordial, 42
Animals, 3, 7, 14, 16, 17, 26, 36, 37, 39, 48, 49, 64, 95, 98-99, 111, 112, 117, 194 n *43*, 195, 216, 221, 250-251, 253, 254 and n *41*, 267. *See also* Aardvark; Antelope; Ant; Baboon; Bat; Bird; Boar, wild; Buffalo; Bush-Baby; Cattle; Chameleon; Chimpanzee; Civet cat; Cows; Crabs; Dog; Dramatis personae; Elephant; Fish; Genet; Goat; Gorilla; Hedgehog; Insects; Leopard; Lion; Monkey; Otter; Pangolin; Pig, wild; Potto; Rodent; Serval; Snake; Squirrel; Turtle; Warthog
Ant, 27, 31, 98, 255 n *44*, 259; black, 203, 261; red, 28, 32, 146 and n *35*, 186, 187 n *13*, 197 and n *57* and n *58*, 198
Antelope, 26, 64; bongo, 47; duiker, 27
Aphorisms, 25, 34, 87, 91. *See also* Proverbs
Archaisms, 6, 75
Arrows, 11, 19, 44, 59, 110, 121, 166
Asa, 40
Associations, 27, 112; *mbuntsu*, 14; Mpandi, 16
Aunt, paternal, 4, 7-9 *passim*, 22, 27, 28, 37, 50, 53, 120, 122, 137 n *12*, 194-195 *passim*, 201 n *71*, 219, 246 n *19*; husband

of, 8, 50; spirit of, 30, 51, 53, 54, 122, 200 n *64*, 242, n *5*, 269 and n *80*. *See also* Hero; Kabutwakenda; Mwindo
Autobiography, 12-17 *passim*, 36, 48
Avdo Mededovic, 91
Axes, 20, 32, 88, 100, 119, 142, 156, 196, 200 n *63*, 201, 219 and n *119*

Baanga, 55
Baasi, 13
Babies, newborn, 159. *See also* Children, small
Baboon, 32, 172, 203; child of Scraper, 76, 221
Babuya, 19, 25
Bad-Luck, 193, 194, 199, 202; Mr., 27
Bafuna, 40, 42, 43, 141 n *26*
Bag, 32, 47, 49, 260 and n *55*, 268; magical, 33; shoulder, 88, 100, 116, 135 and n *5*, 141, 156, 159, 165, 200, 203, 207, 214
Bahimbi, 43, 55, 56, 63
Bahunga, 247-249 *passim*
Bakumbure, 10, 40, 42. *See also* Kumbure
Bakumbure-Basimba, 42, 49
Bakungu, 191, 192
Bakusu-Bashwahili, 15
Baleke, 63
Banaa, 10
Banabirurumba, 55
Banakindi, 56
Banamaka, 55
Banamburu. *See* Monkey
Banamitandi. *See* Spider
Banampamba, 45

Banamukiti, 76

Banana, 20, 48, 99, 103, 137 n *13*, 138, 157, 197, 198, 202, 203, 215, 220 and n *122*, 227; of the *bakoro*-variety, 156; beer, 16, 44, 49, 60, 67, 112, 119, 153, 154, 223, 225, 227, 245; groves, 38, 39, 45, 63, 137 and n *15*, 156 and n *66*, 157, 185 n *10*, 196, 197, 201, 202, 227; growing, 5, 6, 49, 68-69; paste, 49, 143, 145, 152, 154, 156, 159, 162, 163, 192, 195, 196, 202 and n *75*, 206-208 *passim*, 217, 254, 261; stems, 196; stipites, 100, 135 n *5*, 201; trees, 32, 156, 167, 185, 195, 226, 241

Banankomo, 55

Banankuta, 10, 11

Banashemwindo, 76, 79

Baniyana. *See* Bat

Bantu, 6, 40

Banyungu, 42

Barber, 60. *See also* Mubei

Bard, x, xi, 4, 8, 35, 37, 40, 41, 56, 61, 68, 70, 71, 75, 79, 80-87, 90-92, 211 n *96*; identity of, 10-11, 23-25; portrait of a, 12-23. *See also* Bitanda, Asani; Irumbo; Mataki; Mutia; Nyakace; Rureke, Candi; Rwanowa; Shekarisi; Shekwabo; Sherungu

Barea, 220 and n *122*

Bareke, 62

Barengeke, 13, 15

Bark cloth, 49, 59, 61, 67, 168, 169, 173, 219; *rubuo*, 227

Baroba, 55

Barrenness, 51, 52, 69, 71, 86, 99, 240, 265 n *67*

Barungu, 42

Barungwana, 41

Bashari, 10, 40, 42, 141 n *26*

Bashi, 221 n *124*

Basimba, 42

Baskets, 201; *ntanda*, 241

Bat, 26-28 *passim*, 31, 32, 39, 54, 64, 76, 96, 98, 99, 103, 119, 155 and n *61*, 211-213 *passim*, 249, 250 n *29*; Little, 206, 211, 212; Small, 221. *See also* Munkonde

Batembo, 10, 55. *See also* Tembo

Batobo, 55

Batondo, 55, 152

Batwa ba Ncangu wa Shemakara, 10

Beads, 49

Beans, 49, 108, 183 and n *10*, 186, 201, 203, 242-245 *passim*

Beautiful-One, xi, 29, 142, 143 and n *28*

Beauty, 70, 80, 90, 101, 141, 153, 168, 219 n *118*, 253 and n *38*, 258, 264

Bee, 25, 31, 76, 93, 97, 98, 103, 198 and n *60*, 201, 210, 230-231 *passim*, 255 and n *44*, 259, 261

Beings: categories of, 4, 26; fabulous, 3, 31, 36, 39, 66. *See also* Kirimu; Mpaca; Mukiti

Bellows, 212

Bells, 110, 220 and n *123*, 230; dog, 11, 61, 145 and n *34*

Belt, 32, 47, 66, 102, 110, 155-160 *passim*, 173, 199; cowrie, 117; *karemba*, 79, 101; woven raffia, 169

Bembe, 54

Bese, 10

Biebuyck, Brunhilde, 114

Bieya (Sky), 122

Big-Bird, 55, 113, 247 n *19*

Big-bird-born-by-itself, 31, 76, 139 and n *19*, 140

Big-Crab, 31, 255 and n *45*, 256

Big-Rock, 33. *See also* Mutero Murimba

Billhook, 32, 88, 100, 117, 152 and n *56*, 155, 158-160 *passim*, 200 and n *63*, 201, 219 n *119*; *isara*, 222, 223 n *130*

Bira, 220 n *122*

Bird, 7, 26, 31, 39, 65, 117, 138, 142, 189; *bulikoko*, 143; *kibukuru*, 214; *kombi*, 214; *muntindi*, 151. *See also* Big-Bird; Chicken; Eagle; Hawk; Hornbill; Pigeon; Sparrow; Sunbird; Water Duck

Bisheria, 21, 97, 230, 231 n *153*

Bitanda, Asani, 23, 32-33, 279

Bitashimwa, 13

Blacksmith, 28, 37, 54, 87, 98, 149, 155, 196, 205 n *29*, 268; daughter of a, 196 and n *52*

Blessings, 5, 71, 72, 98, 102, 145, 146 and n *35*, 164, 265 and n *68*

Blood, 49, 218; bond, 13; pact, 14, 192-193 n *38*, 231

Boar, wild, 7, 31, 90, 193-195 *passim*. *See also* Pig, wild; Warthog

Boelaert, E., 23

Bow, 11, 19, 59, 110, 268

Bowra, C. M., ix, 3

Boy: Little, 115; lonely, 67; newborn, 7

Bracelet, 59, 63; copper, 23, 49, 101, 199, 225, 259

Bridewealth, 15, 33, 44, 50, 54, 55, 58, 66, 241 n *2*, 251-253 *passim*, 257, 263

Bridge, swinging, 171

Bubingo, 6

Buembwa, 231. *See also* Muembwa

Buffalo, 7, 18, 22, 32, 64, 76, 104, 144 and n *31*, 202, 221; son of Toughness, 76, 199 and n *61*

Bugingo, 7, 64, 65

Buhingo, 65
Buhini, 13-15 passim
Buingo, wa Ngoma, 115. See also Destiny
Bukore, 13
Bukumba, 189-190 passim
Bull-roarer, 112
Bunches, raffia, 216
Bundle, ukenye, 57, 110, 112, 217 n 114, 227-229 passim
Bunyoro (Uganda), 42, 135 n 5
Bunyungu, 13, 189 and n 23
Burial, 51, 60, 110, 112. See also Chief, burial of
Burindu, 221 and n 124
Burio, 115
Buriru, 97, 230
Burssens, A., 40
Bush-Baby, 117
Buuma, 139
Buuni, Amato, x
Bwito, 10, 42, 46, 49, 65
Byarenga, 13

Calabashes, 21, 203, 222
Calamitous, Mr., 64
Camp: fishing, 36; hunting, 4, 12, 17-19 passim, 22, 24, 36-38 passim, 48, 56; trapping, 36
Catalogues, 34, 47
Cattle, 35, 45, 49, 140-141 passim, 203 and n 76, 246 n 17, 251-253 passim
Cave, 39, 45, 159 and n 70, 160, 223, 251 and n 35, 252, 256, 258
Celestial bodies, divinized, 27. See also Moon; Star; Sun
Centipede, 28, 31, 64, 250 and n 55, 262 and n 60, 267, 270. See also Diviner
Chadwick, H. M., and Chadwick, N. K., 3
Chair, 169, 243
Chameleon, 26, 27, 31, 197, 207-208 passim, 266 n 69
Charcoal, 119, 211, 212
Charm, mwika, 117
Chicken, 48, 49, 121, 138, 147, 167, 203, 225; white, 215 and n 108
Chief, 3, 4, 6, 9, 12, 19-23 passim, 26, 35, 37, 39, 46, 106, 107, 109-112 passim, 121, 148 n 40, 150 n 45, 154 n 60, 249 and n 28, 254 and n 43, 263, 268 n 76, 269 and n 81; ancestors of, 42, 43; attributes of, 5, 104, 106-109, 205 and n 85, 223 n 129; brothers of, 50, 57, 59, 60; burial of, 61, 67, 112; children of, 107-108; conceptions about, 50, 70-71, 110-113; dogs of, 144 and n 31, 192 n 38, 227 and n 143; enthronement of, 6, 55, 58-61 passim,

67, 106, 109-110, 112, 135 n 3, 169 n 94, 185 n 7; father of, 27, 50, 54, 59, 60; and hunting, 48-49; maternal uncles of, 50, 54, 55; mother of, 50, 106; paraphernalia of, 27, 47, 57-61 passim, 110, 155 n 62, 173 and n 101, 227 and n 143, 229, 230; and Pygmies, 43-44, 60, 70, 109, 112, 144 n 31, 192 n 38, 194 n 42 and n 44, 203 n 77; ritual killing of, 59, 60; sisters of, 50, 53, 58, 86, 112; social identity of, 107-109, 144 n 30, 212 n 99; wives of, 27, 51, 55, 57, 58, 61, 86, 96, 99, 107-108, 161 n 74, 185 n 7; young son of a, 169. See also Bukumba; Destiny; Difficulties-that-do-not-come-together-with-others; Hero; Hero-Chief; Kabutwakenda; Karisi; Kihoro; Mutero Murimba; Mwindo; Nteta; Shemwindo
Chief-Counselor, 21, 29, 51, 52, 58, 59, 61, 62, 64, 70, 76, 85, 108-110 passim, 184-185 passim, 187 n 16, 243 n 8, 245 n 14, 248 n 26, 258, 262-265 passim, 268. See also Shebakungu
Chief-Pygmy, 7, 10, 11, 21-23 passim, 30, 43, 44, 59, 61, 62, 76, 110, 217 n 114, 262. See also Mwamitwa
Chiefdom, 46, 56, 57
Children, small, 208
Chimpanzee, 16, 27
Chunks-of-Meat, 150
Circumcision rites, 27, 34, 91, 107, 110
Civet cat, 221. See also Ntindi
Clothing, 58, 110
Cloud, 122. See also Utundo
Cobwebs, 55, 155
Color, red, 173
Congera, 62
Congo Free State, 41
Congo-Rwanda, 15
Corn, 49, 201, 203, 226
Cosmic turmoil, 93, 97, 103
Counselors, 7, 13, 23, 27, 29, 39, 53, 58, 59, 99, 108, 109, 121, 136, 167, 173, 184, 197, 204-206 passim, 240 n 1, 243, 249 n 28, 257, 269-271 passim
Cows, 64, 139, 246 and n 17, 258, 262
Cowries, 49, 155
Crabs, 20, 21, 26, 32, 55, 116. See also Big-Crab
Cricket, 28, 31
Crops, 38, 39, 45, 49, 71, 85, 167, 185, 201-203 passim, 269
Cult, 5, 34, 54, 67; emblems, 200, 203. See also Divinities; Paraphernalia
Culture hero, 45, 103, 117, 223 n 131, 249
Curse, 111, 162. See also Insults

Dance, 5, 7, 16, 65, 67, 68, 70, 101, 143, 145, 157, 162 n 77, 208, 249, 267

De Rop, A., 23

Dead, souls of the, 46

Death, 5, 62-64 *passim*, 67, 68, 77, 112

Descent groups, 55-57 *passim*. *See also* Baanga; Baasi; Babuya; Bahimbi; Banaa; Banabirurumba; Banakindi; Banamaka; Banamitandi; Banamukiti; Banankomo; Banankuta; Banashemwindo; Baniyana; Baroba; Batembo; Batobo; Batondo

Descriptions, 80, 87, 89, 91, 141 and n 26, 161

Destiny, 5-7 *passim*, 21, 62, 64, 65, 98, 104, 266-271 *passim*. *See also* Buingo, wa Ngoma

Dice, 33, 101, 116, 158-160 *passim*, 209; iron, 117

Difficult-Things-That-Exceed, 21

Difficulties-that-do-not-come-together-with-others, 30, 76, 222 and n 129

Dishes, wooden, 49

Divination, 35, 44, 60, 67. *See also* Centipede; Oracles

Diviner, 21, 28, 212, 229, 260 n 55. *See also* Centipede

Divinities, 3, 21, 30, 39, 45, 46, 48, 53, 61-66, 95, 96, 98, 102. *See also* Bisheria; Bubingo; Bugingo; Buingo, wa Ngoma; Congera; Destiny; God, creator; Hangi; Kahindo; Kahombo; Katondo ka Musao; Kentse; Kiana; Kibira; Lightning; Meshe; Meshemutwa; Muhima; Muisa; Muriro; Musoka; Nguba; Nkango; Nyamulagira; Nyamurairi; Nyangengu; Nyarusumba; Nyaruwe; Ongo; Ruendo; Sheburungu; Wind

Dog, 18, 20-22 *passim*, 36, 44, 49, 61, 63, 64, 67, 87, 88, 117, 121, 144-146 *passim*, 151, 152, 162-164 *passim*, 168-173 *passim*, 193-197 *passim*, 202 n 73, 227; hunting, 5, 11, 13, 16, 17, 27, 31, 35, 39, 45, 48, 59, 98, 103, 111, 145 n 32 and n 33, 153 n 58, 171, 172 n 100, 192 n 38, 205 n 84. *See also* Bad-Luck; Fast-Eater; Ndorobiro; Ngondo; Ringe

Dragon, 64, 141-143 *passim*

Dragon-Ogre, 19, 21, 22, 27, 45, 67, 104, 120, 141 n 25; daughter of, 67; wife of, 67. *See also* Kirimu; Ukano

Dramatis personae, 3, 4, 75; abstract characters as, 27; animals as, 26-28, 31-32; divinities as, 27, 30, 32; humans as, 26-30, 32, 49-54; minerals as, 32-33; objects as, 27, 32; plants as, 32. *See also* Animals; Divinities; Hero

Dreams, 12, 53, 63, 64, 104, 242

Drums, 25, 32, 47, 53, 58, 61, 101, 110, 116, 122, 145, 149, 154, 157, 161, 165, 167, 168, 173, 210, 252, 256, 258, 259, 267, 268 n 76

Eagle, 27, 67, 227

East Africa, 6

Edwards, Susan, x

Egg, 121, 137-138 *passim*

Egypt, 42

Elephant, 7, 17, 28, 31, 64, 65, 99, 117, 207-208 *passim*, 214, 216 and n 110, 221, 225

Eleusine, 49, 63, 107, 159, 185 and n 10, 192, 209, 226, 241-242 *passim*; paste, 217, 243-245 *passim*

Enthronement rites, 22, 35, 37, 41, 43, 44, 55, 97, 107, 108, 110, 113. *See also* Chief, enthronement of; Mutero Murimba, enthronement of; Mwindo, enthronement of

Epic: animals in, 26-28, 31-32; characteristics of, 3-9; differences of, 86-87; divinities in, 27-28, 30, 61-67; as ethnographic document, 34-35; etiological explanation in, 137 and n 13, 141, 147 and n 39, 200 n 64, 203, 209 n 94, 215 and n 108, 223, 227 n 141 and n 142; fabulous beings in, 27, 30-31, 67-68; and heroic tales, 114-124; as historical document, 41-46; human environment of, 27, 30, 39, 95-99; kinship patterns in, 49-56; language of, 40-41; and material culture, 47-49; physical environment of, 32, 36-39, 96; political organization in, 56-61; space plan of, 72-74, 77; style of, 40-41, 75-92; summaries of, 273-280; values expressed in, 35, 68-74

Epic I, mentioned, x, xi, 4, 7-10 *passim*, 19, 24, 37, 42, 43, 46-56 *passim*, 60, 64, 66-70 *passim*, 77, 80-88 *passim*, 90, 92-101 *passim*, 103-105 *passim*, 109, 111, 113, 136-137 *passim*, 159 n 69 and n 70, 162 n 78, 164 n 81, 188 n 17, 191 n 34, 211 n 96, 246-248 *passim*, 255 n 45

Epic II, mentioned, xi, 6-10 *passim*, 24, 41, 43, 45-48 *passim*, 50-53 *passim*, 55, 56, 63, 66, 67, 69, 71, 72, 80-88 *passim*, 92, 94, 96, 97, 99-101 *passim*, 103-105 *passim*, 109, 113, 137 n 12, 162 n 78, 191 n 34, 245-247 *passim*, 262 n 60; synoptic table of, 127-134

Epic III, mentioned, xi, 6, 8, 9, 19, 24, 41, 43, 45, 46, 50-52 *passim*, 54-61 *passim*, 63, 69, 71, 76, 80, 85, 86, 90, 91, 94, 96,

97, 99, 100-102 *passim*, 104, 105, 109-
111 *passim*, 113, 137 n *11*, 151 n *50*, 173
n *101*, 190 n *26*, 241 n *4*, 248 n *25*, 255
n *45;* synoptic table of, 174-183

Epic IV, mentioned, xi, 8, 9, 11, 12, 19, 24,
37, 41, 44, 46, 51, 52, 54, 56-61 *passim*,
63, 64, 66, 69, 71, 80, 85, 86, 94, 96, 97,
99, 102, 103, 107, 109, 112, 113, 137
n *12*, 188 n *17*, 190 n *26;* synoptic table of,
233-240

Ethnic units. *See* Asa: Bahimbi; Bakum-
bure-Basimba; Banampamba; Barung-
wana; Basimba; Bembe; Havu; Hunde;
Kanu; Komo; Lega; Mande; Pere-
Pakombe; Pygmies; Rwanda; Shi;
Tembo; Tiri

Europeans, 36, 93

Excrement, 71, 155-160 *passim*, 186, 208,
246

Fame, 4, 71, 72, 85, 94, 111, 113, 168, 173,
192, 208

Famine, 48, 85, 86, 116, 121, 190 and n *26*,
241 and n *4*

Fast-Eater, 193, 194, 196, 202

Fate, 71, 105, 140 n *22*, 209

Father-of-the-chief, 29, 57, 268 and n *76*,
271. *See also* Shemwami

Father-of-the-ritual-wife, 23, 57. *See also*
Shemumbo

Fern, *kikoka*, 66, 88, 152 and n *56*, 161

Fibers, 49, 67

Field, 241

Field research, ix, x, 12

Finnegan, Ruth, ix

Fire, 45, 48, 223 and n *131*, 225, 227

Fire drill, 47, 219 and n *119*, 223, 254, 268

Firewood, 52, 100, 197 and n *58*, 223

First-born-of-the-land, 29, 57, 58, 62, 191
n *34*, 231, 263 and n *64*

Fish, 26, 32, 49, 55, 60

Fishing, 47, 60

Flanigan, Beverly, x

Flashes, 121. *See also* Lightning

Fly, 31, 255 n *44*, 261

Fly-of-odor, 201

Food, 7, 8, 14, 16, 25, 44, 49, 69, 90, 91, 93,
112, 116, 121, 138, 140, 189, 191, 195,
201, 205 and n *84*, 219, 221, 227 n *142*, 230,
241-243 *passim*, 245, 255 n *44*, 268;
gathering, 6, 35, 49

Forest, 14, 15, 36, 38, 39, 45, 48, 53, 56, 67,
90, 156, 163-165 *passim*, 167, 170, 195
n *47*, 201, 205, 209, 221, 224, 244, 245,
248, 259; secondary, 146, 147 n *37*, virgin, 145 and n *34*, 162

Forging, 99, 119, 249

Formulas, xi, 6, 11, 12, 24, 38, 70, 75-92,
135-138 *passim*, 146 n *35*, 150 n *47*, 155
n *63*, and n *64*, 160 n *71*, 161 n *76*, 185 n *9*,
187 n *13* and n *16*, 190 n *30*, 195 n *47*, 201
n *68*, 205 n *83*, 211 n *96*, 217 n *112*, 219
n *118* and n *120*, 220 n *121*, 247 n *21*, 250
n *30*

Fowl, white, 121

French, 75; Nyangaized, 6, 41, 42, 162 n *78*

Friendship, 8, 14, 16, 17, 95 '

Frogs, 154

Fruits, red, 173

Gaffs, 32

Game, *wiki*, 241-244 *passim*. *See also* Dice

Garbage heap, 77, 85, 184 and n *4*, 185,
241 and n *2*, 246, 249

Genealogies, 42, 54

Generous, Mr., 27

Genet, 27, 227. *See also* Kanyironge

Gifts, 20-25 *passim*, 44, 54, 58, 60, 61, 64,
66, 71, 109, 121, 138 and n *16*, 140, 143,
147, 149, 161, 167-170 *passim*, 173, 190
and n *31*, 203 and n *76*, 223, 225, 226,
230, 231, 246 and n *17*, 248-249 *passim*,
258, 262, 266

Gishari, 11, 17

Glue, resinous, 67, 170, 171

Goat, 23, 26, 49, 58, 60, 63, 108, 121, 138,
140, 141, 149, 160, 161, 167, 190, 195,
203, 208, 211-223 *passim*, 230, 246 and
n *17*, 249, 251-253 *passim*, 258, 263, 265,
266, 268

Goatskin, white, 63

God, 16, 36, 111, 120, 152, 184-185 *passim;* creator, 5, 33, 62, 63, 65, 66, 123,
152 n *54*, 159 n *69*. *See also* Ongo

Gongo, 63

Good Fortune. *See* Kahombo

Gorilla, 33, 99, 117, 217 and n *114*

Grains, 7; sacred, 249 n *28*

Grasses, 167, 199 n *61; bibatama*, 32, 199,
200

Grave, 136, 268 and n *76*

Grentzenberg, Georgiana, x

Guesthouse, 140, 225

Guthrie, Malcolm, 40

Hail, 32, 103

Hailstones, 167

Hair, 111, 112, 211 and n *98*

Hamlet, 38, 56-58 *passim*, 106

Hammer, 216, 227; iron, 60

Hangi, 6, 7, 65

Hangi-of-Drum, 21, 30, 52, 54, 62, 184
and n *2*, 259; daughter of, 96

Hat, 110; *kembo*, 227
Havu, 43, 46, 221 n *124*
Hawk. 27, 28, 31, 98, 99, 101, 103, 122, 146-147 *passim*, 153, 198, 259; son of Nyeshumya, 76
Headman, 38, 56, 57, 77, 121, 171 n *99*, 263 and n *63*, 264
Healer, 63, 169
Healing, 68, 170
Hedgehog, 28, 31, 103
Hen, 138
Hero, 3, 4, 7, 9, 26, 38, 100, 113, 115-124 *passim;* allies of, 102-103; and animals, 98-99; attributes of, 4-5, 70-71, 93-94, 98, 101-105, 116-117; birth of, 99-101, 115-116; brothers of, 28, 50, 96; children of, 28, 50, 97-98; cross-cousins of, 29; father of, 28, 51-53 *passim*, 85, 96, 99, 100, 115-117 *passim;* maternal uncles of, 29, 54, 102, 116-119 *passim;* mother of, 27, 51-54 *passim*, 85, 96, 99, 100, 103, 115-117 *passim;* names of, 94-95, 135 n *6;* objects of, 100-101, 116-117; paternal aunt of, 27-28, 51, 53, 66, 67, 88, 96, 100, 103, 117, 119; physical appearance of, 116; and Pygmies, 29, 51, 102; sisters of, 28-29, 50-51, 96; social milieu of, 95-99; wives of, 29, 50, 52, 96. *See also* Hero-chief; Little-one-just-born-he-walked; Mwindo; Pygmies; Wives
Hero-chief, 9, 26-30 *passim*, 39, 48, 68, 113
Hide, animal, 22, 32, 44, 47, 59, 144 n *31*, 159, 160, 186, 198, 227, 231; black, 67; white, 117
Hill, 37, 38, 56
Hoe, 200 and n *63*, 204
Hoffman, A. T., 65
Honey, 22, 28, 36, 39, 44, 45, 49, 59, 68, 101, 144 n *31*, 154-156 *passim*, 205 and n *84*, 218-222 *passim*, 225-227 *passim*, 255
Honeycombs, 20
Hornbill, 27
Hot-Springs, 189
House, 38, 47, 66, 93; iron, 168 and n *92;* men's, 38, 39, 48, 153, 154, 159, 162, 200 and n *62*, 208 and n *93*, 269; sacred, 204 and n *81;* shrine, 260 n *55*
Huge-Rock, 117
Hunde, 5-8 *passim*, 11, 13, 15, 17, 23, 24, 35, 37, 39, 42-46 *passim*, 49, 54, 63, 65, 94, 95, 135 n *5*, 143 n *26*, 184-185 *passim*, 189 n *21*, 195-196 *passim*, 198 n *59*, 200 n *63*, 203 n *76*, 220 n *122*, 241 n *3*, 246 n *17*, 256 n *46;* language, 6, 11, 12, 16, 40-41, 75, 91, 162 n *78*, 195, 198 n *60*, 204 n *82*, 207-211 *passim*, 216 n *109*, 218 n *116*, 259 n *54;* Pygmies, 18. *See also* Bafuna; Banyungu; Bashari; Bwito
Hunter, 18, 28, 38, 39, 44, 45, 67. *See also* Pygmies; Shebahi; Shekaruru; Shemuhahi; Shendabu; Shenyancira
Hunting, 6, 14, 16, 18, 36-37 *passim*, 47, 48, 68, 98, 103, 123, 144-146 *passim*, 164-165 *passim*, 171, 193-194 *passim*, 224, 250 and n *29* and n *30*, 253-254; grounds, 166, 172

Ifako, 15
Iguana, 99
Ihana, 10
Ihimbi, 25, 43, 56, 77
Ikunga, 42
Incantations, 12
Initiation, 7, 25, 34, 67, 71, 72, 104, 106, 109-111 *passim; mukuki*, 210
Insects, 26, 31, 39, 48, 66, 117. *See also* Ant; Bee; Centipede; Cricket; Fly; Spider; Wasp
Institut pour la recherche scientifique en Afrique centrale, x, 12
Insults, 214, 217, 218, 260
Interdiction, 5, 86. *See also* Proclamation
Invocations, 5, 6, 102, 151 and n *51*, 200 n *65*, 208, 209
Iramba, 20
Irangira, 15
Iron, 99, 213 n *101*, 214, 216 and n *111*, 247 n *19*
Irumbo, 11, 19, 25, 210
Iryamba, 13
Ishebe, 171 and n *99*
Itewa, 31, 87, 147-150 *passim*, 157 n *67*, 166 n *84*
Ituri, 43
Ivory, 253 and n *38*
Iyangura, 28, 50, 53, 67, 70, 76, 85, 134-135; Katende, 28, 75, 137. *See also* Hero, paternal aunt of; Mwindo, paternal aunt of

Jacobs, John, 23
Jar, 100, 153, 154, 223, 255
Joking relationship, 44, 60

Kabaraka, 33
Kabasha, 115
Kabira, 154 and n *59*, 166
Kabiribiri, 115
Kabotyo, 23

Kabucarange, 115, 123
Kabutwakenda, 9, 43, 44, 52, 64, 76, 93-95 *passim*, 115, 136 n 6, 198 n 60; birth of, 85, 100; brother of Mwindo, 28, 98; as chief, 113; as epithet, 101; as hero, 28, 94; maternal uncle of, 66; as musician, 102; son of, 98, 113. *See also* Destiny; Little-one-just-born-he-walked; Mwindo
Kahindo, 7, 21, 22, 28, 30, 45, 63, 65, 70, 87-91 *passim*, 94-96 *passim*, 99, 101, 103, 117, 119, 120, 152-153 *passim*, 197 and n 55, 206-208 *passim*; brother of, 33; as lover of Mwindo, 153-160 *passim*; metamorphoses of, 194-196 *passim*; as wife of Karisi, 184-191 *passim*; as wife of Mwindo, 200, 202-203, 230
Kahombo, 27, 45, 62, 63, 65, 95, 204 n 81, 216 and n 110, 260 and n 55, 268
Kamiseke, 20
Kandobefu, 231
Kanu, 221 n 124
Kanyama, 206
Kanyampanda, 97, 230, 231
Kanyangara, x, 44
Kanyironge, 97; grandchild of Stone, 76, 230, 231
Karibiri, 13-17 *passim*
Karisi *(karisi)*, 4, 28, 96, 115, 121; dividing the land, 191-193 *passim*; interdiction by, 185 and n 9; meaning of name, 184 n 1; offerings to, 206-209; proclamation by, 184; and wife, 184-191
Karunga, 115, 151 and n 52
Kashari, 43
Kasiwa, 31, 223
Kasiyembe, 30, 101
Katawa, 76, 115, 136 n 6
Katee, 160 and n 71, 210, 211
Katembo ka Ntare, 43
Katondo ka Musao, 16
Katukamumpoko, 42
Katumbi, 58
Kentse, 21, 62
Kiana, 65
Kibira, 229 n 150
Kibumba, 42
Kihoro, 30, 222
Kikwe. *See* Bat
Kindi, 42
Kingwana, 16
Kinship, 5-9 *passim*, 20, 21, 37, 39, 46, 49-60 *passim*, 67, 69, 71, 72, 76, 94, 95, 98, 109, 121, 122, 142 n 27, 202, 211, 212 n 99, 260 n 57, 263 n 62, 265. *See also* Aunt, paternal; Hero; Uncle, maternal; Wives

Kinyungu, 43
Kiomfu Kiramba, 209
Kirimu, 7, 27, 30, 76, 114, 117, 121, 123, 138 n 17, 151 n 52, 157 n 67, 161-164 *passim*; daughter of, 22, 30, 161. *See also* Dragon-Ogre; Ukano
Kiruka-nyambura, 31
Kisa, 115
Kishwa, 20
Kisimba, 10, 42
Kitawala, 42
Kitute, 199
Knives, 32, 67, 119, 141 n 24, 219 and n 119; double-edged, 141, 200, 203, 206, 215; *mimbo*, 141 and n 24. *See also* Billhook
Komo, 40
Komo-Pere, 220 n 122
Konzo-Ndandi (Nande), 40
Korokoro, 207, 221
Kubuya, Amato, 12
Kumbure, 7, 39
Kyigana, 65

Ladle, 72
Lake, 189 and n 22; Edward, 42; Mokoto, 42
Languages. *See* Bantu; French; Hunde, language; Kingwana; Komo; Konzo-Ndandi; Lega; Nande; Nyanga, language; Rwanda; Swahili
Leaves: *birearea*, 241; *keni*, 218 and n 115; *phrynium*, 37
Lega, 6, 23, 40, 43, 54, 63, 137 n 13, 220 n 122
Leopard, 17, 18, 26, 27, 48, 64, 199 and n 61, 229, and n 150
Life: cycle, 59, 95, 112; force, 72, 111, 112; good, 4, 94; long, 98, 102, 156-157 *passim*, 164. *See also* Values
Lightning (Nkuba), 7, 22, 23, 27-30 *passim*, 45, 50, 52, 55, 62, 64, 65, 69, 75, 76, 96, 99, 100, 102, 103, 114, 117, 119-122 *passim*, 137 and n 11, 138, 140-141 *passim*, 144 n 29, 152 n 56, 155, 156, 158 and n 68, 160, 166 n 85, 198-199 *passim*, 210 n 95, 214-215 *passim*, 217-218 *passim*, 247 n 19, 268; wives of, 45, 143
Lion, 7, 36, 64
Little-one-just-born-he-walked: attributes of, 188-190, 241 n 4, 250 n 31, 252 n 36, 257, 258 n 49, 262, 264; birth of, 188 and n 17 and n 18, 245 and n 14; children of, 267-269 *passim*; competition with Mwindo, 250-253, 261; cosmic impact of, 261 and n 58; journey to

Bukumba, 189-190; and mother, 246-248, 260; and Pygmies, 248, 250, 253-255, 257; obtaining spears, 249-250; receiving objects from Mukiti, 246-247, 260; wife of, 253, 258, 264-267. *See also* Destiny; Kabutwakenda
Loanwords, 6, 41, 42
Lord, Albert, 24, 75; and Bynum, David, 91
Lugira. *See* God, creator
Lukweti, 17
Lulema. *See* God, creator

Mafura, 13, 15
Magene, 7, 8
Magic, 43; verbal, 68, 102
Maheshemutwa, 65
Maiden, 22, 29, 54, 91, 101, 143, 160, 169, 170, 173, 199, 215, 225, 226, 230, 231, 256, 258, 259, 263, 264
Maniema, 16, 248 n *25*
Marondi, 13
Marumbu, 198, 200, 201, 217, 226
Masisi, 15
Masokora, 13
Master-of-the-river, 62, 76. *See also* Minerusi
Mataki, 11
Mateene, Kahombo, xii, 19, 72, 87, 91, 171 n *98*
Meat, 48, 49, 138, 152, 159, 163, 167; warthog, 213
Medicine, 100, 135 and n *5*, 170 and n *97*, 194
Meditations, 5, 40, 91, 148-150 *passim*, 198-199 *passim*, 210-211 *passim*, 214 n *104*
Meeussen, A., 40
Memorats, 5
Mera, 10
Meshe, 21, 29, 76, 218-225 *passim*
Meshemutwa, 7, 27, 44, 62, 193-194 *passim*
Messengers, 29, 45, 190 and n *28*, 224, 225
Metamorphosis, 202 n *72*
Midwives, 29, 116, 188 n *19*
Mikema, 77, 166-167 *passim*
Minerusi *(minerusi)*, 60, 61, 228
Mirliton, 112
Misri, 42
Moeller, A., 43
Money, 215 and n *108; butea,* 49, 110, 169 and n *95*
Mongo, ix, 23
Monitor Lizard, 97
Monkey, 19, 26, 32, 55, 164, 166 and n *86*, 167; Mburu *(mburu),* 31, 147, 149 n *40*, 151 and n *49*, 166-167 *passim*

Moon, 32, 97, 119, 122, 206. *See also* Mweri
Mosses, 59
Mountain, 37, 38, 56, 63, 189, 199; Biomfu, 191, 192 n *35*, 253 and n *39;* Biruri, 211, 212; Bitembe, 196; Ihundi, 191, 192 n *35;* Ihuri, 253 and n *39;* Kihwira, 198; Kishibe Bukumbure, 42; Matembe, 191, 192 n *35;* Mikeme, 211, 212; Mincence, 10; Muhu, 214; Ntongi Birumdure, 42; Ntsiru, 196; Rufunda, 213; Rumbici, 199; Runandi, 162; Shekiruu, 214; Wingi, 253
Mpa, 115, 120
Mpaca, 27, 31, 67, 114, 117, 162 n *77*
Mubei, 61, 228
Mubuza, 7, 8
Muembwa *(muembwa),* 57, 58, 60, 61, 112, 230 and n *151,* 267 n *71*
Mueshera, 42
Mugisha. *See* God, creator
Muhakabi *(muhakabi),* 59-61 *passim*, 228
Muhima, 7, 16, 27, 55, 65; as a sacrificer, 29, 208-210
Muhimankiri, 62
Muhindo, 42, 94
Muisa, 15, 27, 28, 30, 39, 62, 64-66 *passim*, 76, 80, 87, 89, 90, 96, 99, 101, 114, 117, 159 n *69,* 168 n *92,* 184 n *2,* 196 n *51,* 257 n *48,* 259 n *53,* 263, 270 n *84;* daughter of, 88, 263; wife of, 168-170 *passim*
Muisa of Bibandi, 256 and n *47,* 257
Mukiti, 8, 15, 27, 29, 30, 50, 55, 67, 70, 76, 80, 96, 99, 101-103 *passim*, 114, 117, 137 and n *12,* 142 and n *27,* 160 n *71,* 246-248 *passim*, 250-256 *passim*, 258-260 *passim;* daughter of, 30, 64, 70, 98, 251, 253, 256, 259. *See also* Little-one-just-born-he-walked; Mwindo; Nyamitondo Mwindo
Mukobya, 13, 42
Mulamba, 63
Mumbara, 17
Munkonde, 31, 148 and n *40,* 149, 155 n *61,* 211 and n *97*
Munongo, 213 and n *103*
Munyanga, 42
Muremeri, 228
Muriro, 14
Mururiyana, 42
Musanduri, 192 and n *37*
Musao *(musao),* 12, 13, 15, 19, 20, 59-61 *passim*, 210, 228 and n *145,* 244 and n *11,* 285 n *51;* wife of, 59
Mushroom, 260
Mushumbia *(mushumbia),* 61, 228 and n *145*
Music, 5, 16, 66, 70, 91, 162 n *77*

Musician, 39, 44, 102, 116. *See also* Kari-biri; Mumbara; Pygmies

Musimba *(musimba)*, 57, 60, 61, 112, 229-231 *passim*, 267 n *71*, 268 n *76*

Musoka, 15, 30, 62, 66

Musukuiyera, 97, 230, 231

Mutero, 96

Mutero Murimba, 39, 43, 45, 55, 60, 61, 110, 151 n *50*, 210 n *95*, 213 and n *102*, 222, 223 n *130;* death and burial of, 229-230; enthronement of, 227-228; and Pygmies, 222-227

Mutia, 11, 19, 25, 210

Mutobi of Nyantsinde, 247 and n *23*, 248

Mutongo, 15, 248 n *25*

Muuma, 139

Mwamihesi *(mwamihesi)*, 59, 60, 227, 228

Mwamitwa, 61, 225 and n *136*, 227, 228 and n *145*, 232 and n *154*, 251 and n *35*, 254

Mwangi, 171 and n *99*

Mwanya, 146 and n *37*

Mweri, 230, 231

Mwico, 65

Mwindo, 12, 19-23 *passim*, 28, 33, 42, 43, 45-47 *passim*, 50, 61, 69, 75, 76; attributes of, 71, 102, 135 and n *5*, 139, 144 and n *30*, 148-152 *passim*, 155, 157, 158, 160, 163 n *79*, 164, 193 n *41*, 211-213, 224 n *134;* and Big-Bird, 138-143; birth of, 85, 135 and n *4*, 190; brothers of, 28, 98; burial of, 136; celestial journey of, 138-141; children of, 230-231 and n *153;* comitatus of, 93, 144, 155, 156, 158, 160, 215, 217; defeating the Banamburu, 165-167; defeating Lightning, 214-215; defeating Mutero Murimba, 213; defeating rebellious chiefs, 148-150; and dogs, 88, 119, 144-146, 151, 152 and n *55*, 163, 166, 167, 170, 171, 173, 192, 194-195, 196, 202; enthronement of, 54-55, 173, 192 and n *37;* fainting, 153; father of, 55, 87; gifts made by, 147, 167, 173; and Kahindo, 193-196 *passim*, 202-203; magic of the bill-hook of, 152 n *56*, 155-158 *passim;* magic of the scepter of, 150-152 *passim*, 155-158 *passim*, 160, 166-167; maternal uncles of, 55, 87, 96, 99, 192, 211-212; meaning of name, 94, 135 n 6; mother of, 69, 203-206, 216; names for, 22, 25, 76, 95, 99, 135 and n *6;* and Nyakatwakari, 217-225; and Nyamurairi, 154-160, 200-203, objects of, 135 and n *5*, 219, 221 n *123;* oral will of, 230-231; paternal aunt of, 69, 85, 87, 90, 93, 101, 142 n *27*, 211; proclamations by, 151, 166-167; and

Pygmies, 27, 55, 95, 144-147, 192-195, 205-206, 218-222; sisters of, 45, 50, 55, 69, 76, 135 and n *6*, 141-143, 192; and spirit of paternal aunt, 194-197 *passim*, 200, 203, 206; and wives, 97, 145, 161, 167, 170, 173, 192, 193, 204, 217, 230-231 and n *153*

Mwindo (as a villain): attributes of, 52, 251-252 *passim*, 254 n *43*, 258-259 *passim*, 266-268 *passim*, 270; birth of, 245, 250 n *31*, children of, 264, 267 and n *72*, 268, 270 n *84;* conflict with Little-one-just-born-he-walked, 250-251, 253, 254, 259-262; courts Mukiti's daughter, 252, 256; death of, 270; and Muisa's daughter, 256-259, 264; powers of, 261 and n *59*, 262, 267-268 *passim;* subterranean journey of, 267-269 *passim;* usurping the chieftainship, 271

Mwiria, 10, 11

Mwishi, 97, 230, 231

Nails, 60

Names, 75-77 *passim*, 86, 97, 98; for chief, 106; descriptive, 76; for dogs, 144; epithets, 6, 24, 53, 66, 75, 76, 87, 93-95 *passim*, 101, 115, 135-138 *passim*, 188 n *17*, 207 n *89;* of heroes, 115; honorific, 76, 154 n *60*, 215 and n *107*, 221, 257 n *48;* matronymics, 76, 95; nicknames, 14, 18; patronymics, 6, 76, 196 n *51*, 214, 247 n *23*, 259 n *54;* personal, 75, 76, 93, 188 n *17;* place, 75; praise, 6, 53, 75, 76, 95, 147 and n *38*, 188, 189, 194-195 n *46*, 205 and n *85*, 212, 218 n *116*, 221 n *125*, 256 n *46*, 259 n *54;* symbolic, 222 n *129;* teknonyms, 76, 96, 134 n *1*, 144-145 n *31*, 152 n *54*, 184 n *1*, 217 n *112*, 240 n *1*

Nande, 40, 135 n *5*, 241 n *3*

Nanga, 25, 210, 214

Narrator, x, 23, 119-120. *See also* Tales, heroic

Ncongera, 97, 230

Ndorera, 206, 216

Ndorobiro, 144-146 *passim*, 149, 161, 163, 165-167 *passim*

Ndura Katwa, 115, 120, 121

Ndurumo (Thunder), 97, 230-231 *passim*

Necklace, 260 and n *55;* beaded, 58, 263

Neckrings, 64

Net: of cowries, 173; hunting, 11, 250, 253, 257

Nfiri, 115, 120

Ngesi, 42

Ngonde, 144-146 *passim*, 149, 161, 163, 165-167 *passim*

Nguba, 7

Ngusha, 229 and n *147*
Ninanguba, 65
Nkango, 7, 16, 21, 27, 29, 44, 62, 95, 111, 205 and n *84*, 220-222 *passim*, 224, 225
Nkurongo, 29, 207, 221
Nkuku Nkumbirwa, 13, 15
Nkuta, 117
Nobles, 167, 173, 184
Ntabana, 11
Ntanga, 221, 231
Nteta, 31, 148 and n *40*
Ntindi, 97, 231
Ntsukiwamumindi, 230
Ntumba, 39
Nyabakungu, 187 and n *15*, 188, 190, 245
Nyabana: becomes despised wife, 240 and n *1*, 241; conflict with ritual wife, 246, 248; gives birth, 245; restored to status, 249; saves people from famine, 241, 242, 244, 245. *See also* Shemwindo, wives of; Wives, principal
Nyabirunga, 121
Nyakabotyo, 29, 193, 219
Nyakace, 23, 115
Nyakatwakari, 30, 198-201 *passim*, 217 n *112*; daughter of, 30, 76, 218; fights Mwindo, 217-219; joins her sons, 224; tricks Mwindo, 218-225. *See also* Meshe; Nkango; Pygmies
Nyakirimarimari, 97, 230, 247-252 *passim*, 255
Nyakwabo, 30, 172
Nyamasangwasangwa, 151 and n *49*, 166
Nyamirindi, 206
Nyamitondo (Nyamutondo) Mwindo, 28, 30, 45, 70, 80, 102; celestial ascent of, 137-138, 142; celestial encounter with Mwindo, 140-141; defeats Big-Bird, 141-142; meaning of name, 135 n *6*; sister of Mwindo, 137; teaches Mwindo to cultivate, 137-138
Nyamulagira, 7, 8, 46, 63, 65
Nyamunga. *See* God, creator
Nyamurairi, 7, 21, 27-30 *passim*, 38, 46-49 *passim*, 55, 58, 62-66 *passim*, 76, 87, 89-93 *passim*, 95, 98, 100, 102, 104, 114, 117, 119, 152-160 *passim*, 184-185 *passim*, 192 n *38*, 194-197 *passim*, 199-204 *passim*, 212 n *99*, 216 n *111*, 219 n *119*, 221 and n *126*, 230, 256 n *47*, 266-269 *passim*; daughter of, 88, 97, 119, 153 and n *57*, 156; people of, 157, 158; subjects of, 136 n *10*; wife of, 157, 202
Nyamwanda, 168
Nyamwindo, 28, 76, 96, 203-206 *passim*

Nyanga, language, xi, xii, 6, 16, 40-41, 72, 77, 78, 101. *See also* Bakumbure; Batembo; Ihana; Ihimbi; Iryamba; Mwiria; Robe
Nyangengu, 21, 62
Nyankuba, 30, 172
Nyantari, 162, 163
Nyarusumba, 30, 62, 268 and n *77*
Nyaruwe, 27, 194 n *45*
Nyiragongo, 63

Objects, 47, 49, 167; iron, 64; magical, 101
Offerings, 58, 122, 206 and n *87*, 260
Office holders, 57-61. *See also* Chief; Counselors; Ritual experts
Ogre, 37, 66. *See also* Dragon-ogre
Oil, 49, 59; palm, 169
Omens, 5, 12, 93
Ongo, 114, 117. *See also* God, creator
Ongomana, 111
Opener-of-dark-clouds, daughter of, 97. *See also* Kandobefu
Oracles, 22, 53, 64, 109, 212, 221, 222 n *127*, 260, 262, 265, 267, 270
Ordeals, 67, 71, 112, 120, 172 and n *100*
Ornaments, 47. *See also* Paraphernalia
Otter, 31, 196 and n *51*
Owl, 65

Pangolin, 27
Paraphernalia, 67, 101, 110, 112, 113, 144 n *30*, 173
Parry, Milman, 75
Parthenogenesis, 50, 100, 186 n *11*, 245 n *13*
Peas, 49, 203, 226
Percussion, 24, 40; stick, 91; talking, 112
Pere-Pakombe, 65
Pigeon, 207; wild, 216, 221
Pig, wild, 17, 18, 26, 36, 47, 99, 119, 146, 173, 206, 221, 224, 227, 250. *See also* Boar, wild; Warthog
Pipe, 63
Pirikii, 115, 123
Plant, 25, 36; *itondo*, 25, 210
Plate, 242
Pointed-Mouth, Mrs., 247, 248, 250, 252, 255, 257, 259
Pool, 37, 42, 76, 151, 171, 172, 196, 246, 247, 251, 256 and n *46*, 259; Mukingetua, 157, 158 n *68*
Pot, 49, 72; *munaa*, 242
Potatoes, 49, 138
Potter, 37
Potto, 31, 215, 216 and n *109*, 222

Powder, red, 59, 61, 169
Praises, 5, 12, 167, 204, 213, 214, 257-258
Prayers, 5, 12, 146 n *35*
Pregnancy, 97, 100, 136, 186, 190, 264, 265
Prescriptions, 61, 109, 112
Princes, 28, 39, 57, 65, 99, 107, 191 n *34*, 199, 200, 230, 245, 257
Proclamation, 91, 134, 144
Prohibition, 48, 203
Protector-of-the-things-that-will-not-be-understood, 264 and n *66*, 265, 267 n *72*, 270 n *84*
Proverbs, 5, 12, 26, 41
Pumpkin, 108, 201
Purifications, 34, 37, 45
Pygmies, 5-7 *passim*, 9-11 *passim*, 13-15 *passim*, 17, 19-22 *passim*, 24, 26-28 *passim*, 30, 33, 36, 39, 41, 43, 45 *passim*, 48, 49, 52, 55, 58, 60, 61, 63, 67, 70, 95, 96, 99, 102, 103, 109, 119, 121, 123, 144 n *31*, 173, 192-195 *passim*, 204-206 *passim*, 217-227 *passim*, 247-250 *passim*, 252-259 *passim*; daughter of, 123. *See also* Meshe; Nkango; Nyakatwakari; Shekaruru
Pygmy-Dog, 18

Quiver, 11, 44, 59, 110, 121, 198, 207

Rain, 32
Rattles, 122
Razors, 7, 141 and n *24*, 142; copper, 228
Recitations, 109
Reed, Deborah, x
Reminiscences, 12
Riddles, 5, 12
Rikesa, 42
Ringe, 90, 153 and n *58*, 171, 172 and n *100*
Ringesa, 42
Ritual-Drummer, 207. *See also* Mushumbia
Ritual experts, 27, 29, 39, 55, 57, 59, 61, 96, 107, 109, 110, 112, 167, 173 and n *101*, 225 n *136*, 228 n *145*, 253, 258 and n *51*. *See also* Minerusi; Muhakabi; Musao; Mushumbia; Mwamihesi; Mwamitwa
River, 21, 38, 51, 66, 76, 152, 153, 158, 164, 167, 168 n *91*, 171, 189 n *24*, 193, 196, 242, 251, 252, 256 and n *46*; Bukumba, 189; Little Stone, 210; Roba, 143 and n *28*, Rwama, 142, 189; Rwashi, 189; sacred, 59, 60
Roba-Land, 149 and n *44*
Robe, 13

Rock, 27, 64, 70. *See also* Mutero Murimba
Rodent, 26; Mukei, 98
Room, *isinga*, 204
Rooster, 198, 210, 246; red, 64
Rope, 32, 53, 100, 155, 222; cradling, 195 n *47;* magical, 88
Ruendo, 21, 27, 62, 187 and n *13*
Rukundura, 15
Rungoma, 10
Rureke, Candi, x, 10, 19
Rurema. *See* God, creator
Rwanda, 16, 42, 43, 46
Rwanowa (Wanowa), 12, 17, 19, 33, 48, 102, 273

Sacleux, Ch., 266 n *69*
Salt, 49
Salt-of-the-land *(Mukwacuo)*, 61, 230 and n *151*
Salvation, 195 and n *50*, 208, 224, 244, 245, 252 and n *36*
Sand, 108
Scabies, 153
Scepter, 32, 49, 66, 101, 103, 117, 135 and n *5*, 144 and n *30*, 145, 149, 150 and n *47*, 152 and n *56*, 156-158 *passim*, 160, 165-167 *passim*, 219 n *119*, 247-249 *passim;* conga, 88, 100, 135 n *5*, 267, 268
Schebesta, Paul, 6, 33, 43
Schumacher, Peter, 7, 42-44 *passim*, 46, 94
Secrecy, 109
Secrets, 37, 110
Seeds, 32, 201, 226; sacred, 107, 108
Serpent, 116, 123. *See also* Water Serpent
Serval, 7
Servants, 7, 29, 191 and n *32*, 215 and n *107*, 216, 244, 245, 249 n *28*, 251-253 *passim*, 259
Shabihango, 63
Shakwece, 30, 171
Sharp-Mouth, Mrs., 251. *See also* Pointed-Mouth, Mrs.
Shebahi, 18
Shebahinga, 152 n *54*
Shebakungu, 184, 185, 190-192 *passim,* 208, 242, 244, 254; as advisor and teacher, 190, 228-229, 241, 243, 245, 246, 248; wife of, 188, 245. *See also* Nyabakungu
Shebukura, 213
Sheburungu, 30, 66, 91, 158-160 *passim;* wives of, 160
Shekarisi, x, 10, 11, 19, 86
Shekaruru, 9, 29, 55, 67, 144, 154 n *59*, 169-170, 173; encounter with Hawk, 145-147; encounter with Muisa's wife, 168-

169; encounter with Shakwece, 171-172; encounter with Specter, 170-171; encounter with warthogs, 146-147; meaning of the name, 144 n *31;* and Mwindo's dogs, 144-147, 167, 172; revivifying a chief's son, 169-170; son of, 29, 170 and n *96*

Shekwabo, x, 10

Shells, polished, 49

Shemuhahi, 19

Shemumbo, 57, 58, 61, 229-231 *passim*

Shemwami, 55, 58, 60, 185 n 7

Shemwindo, 21, 22, 28, 70, 71, 76, 77, 80, 85, 87, 90, 93, 96, 134-137 *passim,* 142, 149, 150 n *45,* 157 and n *67,* 159-161 *passim,* 173 and n *101,* 184 n *1,* 240 n *1,* 241, 244 n *11,* 245 n *13,* 247 n *19,* 249 and n *28,* 252, 253 and n *39,* 256, 257 and n *48;* playing *wiki*-game, 241-244; proclamations by, 134, 143, 144; wives of, 85, 134 and n *2,* 240-244 *passim,* 246

Shendabu, 18

Shengano, 36

Shentsimia, x

Shenyabana, 231 and n *154*

Shenyancira, 18

Sherubungo, 204

Sherungu, x, 12-22, 24, 33, 36, 44, 48, 64, 86, 102, 115, 244, 246 n *17,* 258 n *51,* 266 n *69,* 271 n *86;* texts by, 14-23 *passim,* 36 44-45, 48, 64-65, 273-278

Shi, 43, 46

Shoneno, x

Shoots, 226

Shrew, 229

Shrines, 63, 64

Shrubs, 7

Singer, x, 39, 44, 102, 116

Singing, 70, 101, 139-142 *passim,* 145, 147-150 *passim,* 153, 154, 162, 163, 166, 168, 171-173 *passim,* 186, 187, 195, 197-199 *passim,* 206-208 *passim,* 214-216, 218-221 *passim,* 224, 225, 247-252 *passim,* 255, 257, 259, 261

Skullcap, 44, 47, 59

Sleep, 33

Snails, 150

Snake, 26, 198, 254. *See also* Serpent

Snares: *mpota,* 47, 164-165 and n *83; tumponda,* 15

Soldiers, 93

Songs, xi, 5-7 *passim,* 11-14 *passim,* 16, 24-26 *passim,* 32, 34, 40, 45, 47, 66-68 *passim,* 70, 75, 77, 79, 91, 94, 102, 121, 139-143 *passim,* 145, 147-151 *passim,* 153, 154, 162-164 *passim,* 166, 168, 171-173 *passim,* 186, 187, 196-199 *passim,* 206, 209-216 *passim,* 218-221 *passim,* 224, 225, 229, 247, 248, 250-252 *passim,* 255, 257, 259, 261

Sorcerer, 111, 170

Sorcery, 7, 68, 243 n *9*

Sorghum, 108

Sparrow, 27, 31, 88, 98, 99, 120, 160 n *71,* 210, 255 and n *45*

Spears, 18, 36, 49, 51, 52, 101, 116, 119, 148, 149, 153, 166, 193, 194, 202, 206, 211, 212, 247-250 *passim,* 255 and n *45,* 267; *butenge,* 173, 268; copper, 61, 230

Specter, 37, 97, 170, 171 and n *98,* 202-203 *passim,* 214, 216 and n *110. See also* Mpaca

Speeches, 5

Spider, 27, 31, 32, 55, 76, 98, 103, 117, 119, 122, 155 and n *61,* 198-199 *passim,* 221, 259

Spirit, 8, 9, 14, 16, 21, 28, 37, 104, 165, 186, 187, 212; ancestral, 27, 109; erring, 27; of father, 66; metamorphosed, 7; of mother, 242 n 5. *See also* Aunt, paternal

Squirrel, 216; flying, 22, 27, 44, 47, 59, 144 n *31,* 227, 231

Staff, iron, 247 n *22,* 256

Star, 32, 141

State, autonomous, 6, 106. *See also* Chiefdom

Steer, 264

Stimson, Grace, xi

Stone, 168, 213, 230, 242; flat, 167; *murimba,* 151 and n *50; mutero,* 151 and n *50. See also* Rock

Stool, 49, 58, 61, 63, 66, 110, 117, 120, 139, 267, 268; *utebe,* 173, 230, 246, 247 and n *19*

Strangers, 39

Style, x, xi, 4-6 *passim,* 8, 11, 12, 19, 24, 26, 40, 75-92, 138 n *17,* 143 n *28. See also* Formulas

Subjects, 39, 62, 99

Sugarcane, 215 and n *108*

Sun, 32, 64, 117. *See also* Mwishi

Sunbird, 27, 119

Swahili, 16, 75, 162 n *78;* Nyangaized, 6, 41, 42

Swimmers, 29

Taboos, 12, 27, 61, 63, 109, 112, 209, 244 n *11,* 270 n *83*

Tails, buffalo, 103, 144, 145, 147, 148. *See also* Scepter

Tales (mentioned), 4, 5, 12, 13, 16, 19, 20, 27, 28, 37, 44, 45, 48, 56, 62-67 *passim*, 69, 70, 114, 135 n *3*, 137 n *12*, 148 n *40*, 150 n *45*, 168 n *92*, 171-173 *passim*, 194 n *43*, 197 n *56*, 200 n *72*, 207-208 *passim*, 211 n *96*, 216 n *109*, 218 n *117*, 255 n *45*, 262 n *60*
Tales, heroic, 19, 21, 23, 109, 151 n *50* and n *52*, 184 n *1*, 211 n *98*, 213 n *102*, 264 n *65*, 266 n *69*; characters in, 115-117; kinds of, 114; moral code in, 123-124; narrators of, 114-115; patterns in, 117-123
Tattoo, 122
Teachings *(mahano)*, 4, 5, 72, 109, 227, 228 n *144*
Tears, 119, 211 and n *98*, 212
Teeth, 60; dog's, 67; leopard, 23, 61, 173, 227, 230
Tembo, 7, 43, 46, 221 n *124*
Termites, 153
Texts, x, 5, 11; quoted, v, 14, 16, 19, 22, 24, 25, 36, 37, 44, 48, 50, 52, 60, 62, 69-71 *passim*, 79-85, 87-90, 93, 101-104 *passim*, 107-112 *passim*, 119-120, 123-124, 228 n *144*; summarized, 17, 19-23 *passim*, 62, 65-67 *passim*, 70, 99, 100, 104-105, 109, 118-123, 172 n *100*, 213 n *102*, 223 n *131*, 266 n *69*
Thoughts, 12
Thunder, 62
Tiri, 40
Titimbe, 67
Tobacco, 269
Toilets, 244, 254, 260
Tolls, 135 n *5*; iron, 5, 49, 140-142 *passim*, 200
Toro (Uganda), 42
Trapper, 9, 38, 45; young, 29, 161-164
Trapping, 6, 18, 35-37 *passim*, 47, 68, 98, 103, 164-165 *passim*, 203
Traps, 66, 121, 170, 197 and n *56; byoo*, 47, 161, 163, 170. *See also* Snares
Trees, 157, 158, 162 and n *77*, 167; buttresses of the, 156; fallen, 158, 171; Ficus, 32, 138-141 *passim*; hollow, 122, 139 n *18; mibimbiro*, 32, 197; *mpaka*, 155; *murundu*, 169; *musone*, 167 and n *89; musuku*, 164; *ntsembe*, 79; raffia, 37, 56, 121, 169 n *95*; wild banana, 32, 117
Tribute, 49, 173, 226, 240 and n *1*, 241, 253 n *38*, 266
Trickery, 43, 63, 89, 101, 116
Trickster, 28, 64, 111, 148 n *40*; divine, 63
Tubi, Stephano, x, 12
Tubondo, 77, 90, 121, 149, 150 n *45*, 161, 173, 211, 212

Turnbull, Colin, 7, 43
Turtle, 27, 33, 99, 210, 214
Twins, 107, 111

Ubunge, 115, 116, 122
Ufamba, 230
Uganda, 46, 192 n *36*
Ukano, 30, 161-164 *passim. See also* Kirimu
Uncle, maternal, 8, 50, 54, 118, 122, 142 n *27*, 192, 212 n *100*, 215, 250 n *29*, 260 n *56*, 266; children of, 50; wives of, 50, 76
University of Delaware, xi
Urine, 155, 157, 159, 268
Utensils, 44
Utundo, 97, 230-231 *passim*

Valley, 166
Values, 4-7 *passim*, 14, 16, 20, 21, 24, 38, 43, 44, 62, 68-74, 90, 94, 105, 107, 111, 113, 117, 121, 123-124, 138 n *16*, 144 n *29*, 250-252 *passim*, 254 n *43*, 258, n*49*, 266 n *70*
Vegetables, 52, 100, 201; *isusa*, 49, 267
Viaene, L., 7, 65
Village, 4, 24, 36-39 *passim*, 47, 51, 52, 56, 57, 77, 106; abandoned, 37. *See also* Bese, Ifako; Irangira; Lukweti; Maniema; Mera; Mikema; Munongo; Mutongo; Rungoma; Tubondo
Vine, 49, 171, 172, 194-195 n *46; kirungo*, 213; *muntea*, 171; strangler, 164 and n *83*
Volcanoes, 7, 46, 61, 63, 192 n *36*

Wading place, 37, 139 and n *20*, 153, 193 and n *39*, 203, 269
War, 140, 148-150 *passim*, 165, 215, 231, 260; leader, 94; warfare, 6
Warriors, 39, 43, 65, 93
Warthog, 32, 64, 145-147 *passim*, 154 and n *59*, 163, 165, 167, 210, 213
Wasp, 31, 97, 98, 103, 255 n *44*, 261
Water Duck, 31, 197
Water Serpent, 37, 53, 62, 64, 66, 85, 86. *See also* Mukiti
Waterbuck, 154 and n *59*
Weapons, 139, 140, 166, 222 n *127*
Whistle, 49, 62, 63, 167 and n *90*, 168 n *93*, 170
Whistling, 221
Wild-Banana-Tree, 214
Will: last, 61, 94; oral, 229 and n *148*, 232, 257 and n *48*
Wind, 62
Witchcraft, 7, 67

Wives, 50, 54, 60, 69, 71, 246 and n *16;*
belove *(ngantsi),* 20, 44, 51, 69, 86, 135
n *3,* 171; co-wives, 20, 44, 51, 52, 69, 85,
240, 241; commoner, 55, 57, 58; despised *(nyakashombe),* 51, 69, 85, 96, 122,
135 n *3,* 171, 172, 186, 240, 242-245
passim, 251, 253; honored, 186; junior,
118, 209; *mpombwe,* 20; *musanduri,* 228
n *144;* preferred, 51, 69, 85, 96, 99, 167,
172; principal *(nyabana),* 8, 52, 53, 58,
69, 71, 76, 85, 86, 96, 99, 108, 109, 145,
184 and n *2,* 186 and n *7,* 187, 190,
191 and n *34,* 204, 227, 228 n *144,* 231
n *154,* 240 n *1,* 244 and n *12;* Pygmy, 44;
rejected, 69, 86; ritual *(mumbo),* 6, 20, 22,
44, 46, 51, 52, 53, 54, 57, 58, 59, 60, 86,
96, 106, 107, 108, 109-110, 122, 140
n *23,* 144 n *30,* 184 n *2,* 185 n *7,* 191 n *34,*
192 and n *37,* 215 n *108,* 227 and n *141,*
228 and n *144,* 229, 230, 243 n *8,* 245 and
n *15,* 246, 248-251 *passim,* 254 n *43,* 258
n *50,* 260, 271 n *86;* senior, 57, 58, 118,
209; spirit, 53, 55
Women, 39, 44, 49, 54, 63, 64, 66, 160
World: aquatic, 38, 72; celestial, 38, 62, 72,
73, 116; subterranean, 9, 38-39, 46, 53,
61, 66, 67, 72, 73, 77, 87, 88, 96, 100,
102, 103, 116, 152-160, 199 and n *61,*
203 n *78,* 206 n *87,* 216 n *111,* 256 n *47*
and n *48,* 266 n *69,* 267 n *73* and n *74,* 268,
270; terrestrial, 67, 72, 73, 77, 103
Wrist protectors, 47, 59, 227

Zaire, 42, 46; eastern, 40, 41, 46, 54, 64
Zanza, 47, 49, 101, 102, 116, 120, 162-164
passim
Zither, two-stringed, 12, 17